Modern Eclectic Therapy

A Functional Orientation to Counseling and Psychotherapy

Modern Eclectic Therapy

A Functional Orientation to Counseling and Psychotherapy

Including a Twelve-Month Manual for Therapists

Joseph Hart

California Polytechnic University, Pomona, California and
Hart and Associates, Los Angeles, California

With the Assistance of John Hart

PLENUM PRESS • NEW YORK AND LONDON

Library of Congress Cataloging in Publication Data

Hart, Joseph Truman, 1937–
  Modern eclectic therapy.

  Bibliography: p.
  Includes index.
  1. Psychology, Pathological—Eclectic treatment. 2. Functionalism (Psychology) 3.
Counseling. 4. Psychotherapy. I. Title. [DNLM: 1. Psychotherapy—Methods. 2.
Counseling—Methods. WM 420 H 325m]
RC480.5.H343 1983   616.89′14   83-11088
ISBN 0-306-41213-6

© 1983 Plenum Press, New York
A Division of Plenum Publishing Corporation
233 Spring Street, New York, N.Y. 10013

Printed in the United States of America

This book is
affectionately dedicated
to my wife, Regina

Foreword

This book is a hybrid; it contains theoretical sections and sections devoted to technique; it attempts to provide a historical perspective and to give a contemporary formulation of theory and practice; and it discusses both practical problems of day-by-day therapy sessions and philosophical issues related to the meaning of psychotherapy in modern society. In a way the book reflects, in its own style and contents, the subject it is about.

Eclectic therapy is certainly a hybrid of many strains of influence; it is more diverse in its structures, theories, and techniques than any other therapeutic orientation. Still, eclectic therapy does have a definite consistency and coherency that I hope will be clearly revealed in this book.

The plan of the book is as follows. In Part I, I will present the arguments and evidence that there is a modern trend toward eclecticism among therapists and then in Part II, tie this trend into the historical tradition of functionalism. Both the common features of clinical functionalism and the specific ideas and methods of James, Janet, Burrow, Taft, and Thorne are presented. I believe it will be a revelation to many readers to see the contemporary significance of the therapies practiced by these eclectic pioneers.

In Part III, I develop a general theory of clinical functionalism and in succeeding chapters apply this theory to an evaluation of a variety of therapeutic techniques from a wide variety of sources. Part III brings together the ideas of the early functionalists, which were covered in Part II, and ideas from other traditions such as psychoanalysis, humanistic therapy, existential therapy, and behavior therapy.

Part IV presents techniques and ideas in a different way, in the form of a day-by-day manual for conducting a series of eclectic therapy sessions. The chapters in the manual draw upon both historical sources of eclecticism (James, Janet, etc.) and upon eclectic selections of ideas and methods from other orientations.

The book concludes, in Chapter 17, with a broadened discussion of the part played by philosophy in therapy.

Students and professionals who read this book from cover to cover will be able to think about clinical problems from the functional orientation and will be able to design their own programs of eclectic therapy. The book can be read in different ways, depending on each reader's main interests. Those readers who are most curious about practical applications could begin with the manual in Part IV and then read Parts II, III, and I in that order. Readers who are most interested in theory and history should proceed through the book as it is ordered with a concentration on Parts I, II, and III.

There are limits to the range of eclecticism discussed in this book. For instance, I do not include psychiatric and other medical approaches to treatment. This exclusion influences every part of the book. The history sections of Part I give very little mention to Meyer and Sullivan because their contributions had more influence on psychiatry than on psychological therapies. Nor in the manual section do I discuss the use of drugs in therapy. Any truly eclectic therapy must be open to the use of drugs both in conjunction with psychological treatment and in place of psychotherapy. However, limits of time, space, and my own background preclude the coverage of medical therapies.

Also, I do not try to include special target treatment procedures (such as sex therapy, family therapy, or the treatment of special problems—alcoholism, weight control, drug addiction, juvenile delinquency, stuttering, and so forth) in this presentation of eclectic therapy. Eclectic therapists are certainly likely to see many types of clients, but this book is written from a general treatment approach rather than a special problem approach.

Similarly, I discuss the role of community psychology and preventive psychology only briefly (in Part II and Part IV) in relation to eclectic therapy. My reasons for excluding these relevant and fascinating fields from full consideration are the same as my exclusion of medical therapies—limitations of time, space, and my own scholarship. I hope some enterprising scholar in the future will put together a multivolume *Handbook of Eclectic Therapy* that will give a fuller picture of eclectic theories, research, fields, and methods. For now, this book will stay within the limited psychological framework I have indicated.

Despite these limitations, I hope many diverse therapists will find the ideas and methods of *Modern Eclectic Therapy* useful.

JOSEPH HART

Preface

It took a number of years for me to discover that my approach to therapy was eclectic. Not until the last five years did I come to understand that not only was I an eclectic, but I was applying a special brand of eclecticism called functionalism. In a way I felt like Molière's bourgeoise gentlemen who discovered he was "speaking prose." All along I thought I was just "doing therapy" but no, I had been "doing functional eclectic therapy." What a distinction!

My purpose in writing this book is, first, to address the many other therapists who may be practicing functional eclectic therapy without knowing, in detail, the history and theory behind their eclectic practice. I believe many therapists will be surprised and pleased, as I was, to find that the theory of functional eclecticism provides a well-developed, coherent, and creative framework for therapeutic work and thought.

My second purpose is to speak to the many students across a wide variety of disciplines who are studying to be counselors and psychotherapists. Most students are practical eclectics out of necessity—when enrolled in one course they take on that point of view (Professor A's), in another they take on another point of view (Professor B's), and so on throughout the academic alphabet. I believe students within the fields of counseling and psychotherapy will be pleased to learn that a meta-theory exists that can bring order and meaning to many of the competing theories and techniques that they are learning. (An added plus is that the theory of functional eclecticism provides a natural bridge between the sometimes contrasting and conflicting viewpoints of the clinician and the researcher.)

I have been very fortunate throughout my career in the opportunities I had to study with leading theorists, clinicians, and researchers. At the University of Wisconsin, where I took an M.S. in clinical psychology, I studied and worked closely with Drs. Carl Rogers, Eugene

Gendlin, and Charles Truax. At Stanford University, where I obtained a Ph.D. in experimental psychology, I studied with Drs. Albert Hastorf, Karl Pribram, Leon Festinger, and Ernest Hilgard. Earlier, in my undergraduate years at Lewis and Clark College, I had the good fortune to begin my study of psychology with two clinical psychologists who had strong interests in hypnosis and organizational psychology (Drs. Volney Faw and Norman Hickman). Later, in postgraduate studies, I traveled to the Jungian Institute in Zurich and the Esalen Institute, Kairos, and other growth centers throughout the United States where I worked with a great variety of therapists and workshop leaders (including Fritz Perls, Claudio Naranjo, and Arthur Deikman). I also learned from close associations with Stanley Keleman and Dr. Alexander Lowen in bioenergetic therapy and Dr. Arthur Janov in primal therapy. For a time (1966 to 1970) I participated in the development and growth of biofeedback research. (Drs. Joe Kamiya, Perry London, and Barbara Brown were particularly stimulating colleagues.) During the 1960s I was also influenced by contacts with Alan Watts, Dr. Timothy Leary, Dr. James Fadiman, Dr. Charles Tart, Dr. Robert Ornstein, and other proponents of meditation and psychedelics.

In the 1970s I was deeply involved in the creation of a therapy and therapeutic community called "Feeling Therapy," described in *Going Sane* (1975). My colleagues during that period (Drs. Stephen Gold, Werner Karle, Richard Corriere, Gerald Binder, Lee Woldenberg, and Mr. Dominic Cirincione) helped me to explore the benefits and limits of a community-based therapeutic structure.

More recently (1980–81) I was influenced by my colleagues (particularly Drs. Albert Marston and Milton Wolpin) and students at the University of Southern California, where I learned firsthand about the cognitive behavioral approach.

That brings me right up to the present, in which my main clinical activities are conducted with John Hart, my brother and professional associate, at Hart & Associates in Los Angeles. My major applied interest today is in management consulting, sports psychology, and sports counseling. (In Chapters 7 and 11, you will see how these new emphases contribute to my formulations of eclectic therapy.)

Out of this long list of associations and influences I hope the reader comes away with one strong impression: *variety* and *exploration*. Whatever else eclecticism is, it is most characterized by an open-minded willingness to try out almost anything and everything. The reason William James emerges so prominently in this book as a prototype for the eclectic is because he exemplifies a daring and open-ended risk-taking that must be associated with eclecticism if it is not to become merely a safe and cliché-ridden haven for intellectual retirement. This may sound too strong, but I want to caution at the beginning that eclecticism can take many forms, and not all of them, to my mind, are socially and intellectually valuable.

I am not eclectic about eclecticism. This book will present a very definite and selective point of view that will contrast not only with other general viewpoints, such as psychoanalysis and behavior therapy, but with other types of eclecticism. This point will become clear in Part I, which discusses types of eclecticism. Part II goes on to develop the history and theory of functional eclecticism in detail.

I should mention that very few of the colleagues and associates I have named would agree fully with the formulations that are presented in this book. Nor would I agree with their ideas and methods in the same fashion that I did in the past. My reason for taking the time, in introducing this book, to name many of the individuals who have influenced my thinking is because I want to be frank about the sources of my "creative borrowing."

I have been a member of the Association for Humanistic Psychology and the Association for the Advancement of Behavior Therapy. I have published articles in clinical journals such as *Psychotherapy* and the *Journal of Clinical Psychology* and research journals such as *Science* and the *Journal of Verbal Learning and Behavior*. I have attended conventions devoted to workshops and experiential presentations and conventions devoted to presentations of experimental findings. Amid this variety of experiences the main thing I have noticed is that the practitioners in one area know (and care) very little about what happens in other areas. Although lip service is paid to the "value of research" by clinicians and to the "necessity for clinical experience" by researchers, in fact most clinicians pay no attention to research and most experimenters do not care to learn about clinical theories and methods. The famous scientist–practitioner model of the Boulder Conference (Raimy, 1950) remains the dominant model for academic training of Ph.D.'s in clinical psychology, but it does not really produce many practitioners who are scientists or scientists who do clinical work.

There is no one reason for this isolationism in psychology. Politics, accidents of history, and temperamental differences all surely play a part. However, I suggest that one important reason for psychology's factionalism is that no general theory that comfortably covers both experimental concerns and clinical concerns has achieved prominence. Among the three major orientations that have dominated the field of therapy in the last 50 years, psychoanalysis has seemed "too subjective," behavior therapy "too objective," and humanistic therapy "too programmatic." I also suggest in this book that functional eclecticism is potentially such a metatheory.

I hope that students and professionals will come away from this book having learned at least three valuable things: (1) a theoretical perspective (functional eclecticism or clinical functionalism) that integrates many seemingly disparate techniques, (2) a practical framework for the systematic application of ideas and techniques, and (3) a refined appreciation for the interconnectedness of clinical and experimental contributions.

JOSEPH HART

Contents

IV TECHNIQUE: A FUNCTIONAL MANUAL

APPENDIXES

I

Introduction

1

Modern Eclecticism in Therapy

What is the evidence that contemporary therapists are becoming more eclectic in their approach? Are there different kinds of eclecticism? Are there certain emphases that most eclectic therapists have in common? These are the central questions considered in this introductory chapter.

What the Surveys Show

In 1961 Kelly reported on a survey of the attitudes of 1,024 clinical psychologists. His survey showed that a shift in emphasis had taken place among clinical psychologists during the 1950s from diagnostic testing to psychotherapy. His survey also strongly indicated the popularity of psychoanalytic and related theories among 41% of the clinical psychologists. In a similar survey reported by Garfield and Kurtz in 1976, only 19% of the sampled clinical psychologists identified themselves with analytic theories. In this later survey 55% of the practitioners identified themselves as eclectics, compared to 40% in the earlier survey.

Garfield and Kurtz commented, "A tendency does appear . . . for clinical psychologists to adopt a more eclectic orientation" (1976, p. 4). They found the psychoanalytic and learning theory adherents to be at two poles in their viewpoints, with eclectics and others in the majority middle: "The eclectics tend to be relatively less intuitive and less psychodynamic than most of the other groups . . . but they do not particularly favor behavioral modification views" (Garfield & Kurtz, 1976, p. 8).

Swan and MacDonald (1978) surveyed 353 behavior therapists; 42% of the respondents identified themselves as eclectic. In a follow-up study Swan (1979) applied cluster analytic statistical techniques to the respondents who identified themselves as eclectic. He found four types of eclectics. The largest clusters, Type 1 and Type 2, both tended to rely on relationship enhancement and attitude modification methods and tended not to use hypnosis. The main difference between these groups was that the second did not use operant, fear-reduction, and other non-relationship methods. Type 3 practitioners were similar to Types 1 and 2 but they also used hypnosis. Type 4 clinicians, the smallest group, described themselves as "eclectic" but tended not to use any methods other than operant ones. Swan concluded,

> These results suggested that eclectic therapists, as a whole, do indeed use a broader range of therapeutic techniques than do other groups that are bound closely to a specific theoretical orientation (e.g., operant, cognitive, etc.). These results indicate that eclectic therapeutic philosophy may translate into eclectic therapeutic behavior. (Swan, 1979, p. 733)

In a later survey, which reflects on shifts from his earlier results, Kelly (Kelly, Goldberg, Fiske, & Kokowski, 1978) did a 25-year follow-up of the clinical psychology graduate students who had participated in a Veterans Administration selection research project. He found that 58% of the professionals contacted did *not* adhere to a single orientation.

Larson's recent survey (1980) drew upon the work of a number of investigators who developed self-report measures of therapeutic beliefs and practices.[1] He sent a lengthy questionnaire to 879 therapists identified with one of four different methods. The response rates were very good; 398 (45%) completed questionnaires were returned within 10 weeks. The professional groups sampled were: trainers and members of the Gestalt Therapy Institute of Los Angeles and therapists listed in the 1976 Gestalt Directory; clinical fellows of the Behavior Therapy Research Society; clinical and teaching members of the International Transactional Analysis Association; members of the Los Angeles Society for Psychoanalytic Psychology; fellows in the psychoanalytic training program at the New York Post-Graduate Center for Mental Health and Research; and selected staff members of the Mount Zion Hospital and Medical Center Department of Psychiatry in San Francisco.

The final sample consisted of 115 gestaltists, 70 behaviorists, 87 transactionalists, and 67 psychoanalysts. There were 110 females and 229 males; the breakdown by discipline showed 159 psychologists, 53

---

[1] A number of investigators have developed self-report measures of therapeutic beliefs and practices. See Fey (1958), McNair & Lorr (1964), Rice, Gurman, & Razins (1974), Sundland (1976), Sundland & Barker (1962), Wallach & Strupp (1964), Weissman, Goldschmid, & Stein (1971).

psychiatrists, 63 social workers, and 64 counselors. (A total of 55 therapists were eliminated from the final sample because they did not identify themselves with the definite orientation category they had been chosen to represent. This group is significant for the argument that I shall make about the tendency of modern therapists to shift or broaden their therapeutic identifications. Unfortunately, they were not included in Larson's data analysis.)

However, even in the sample of therapists included in Larson's analysis, a majority (65%) indicated multiple school allegiances and a majority (62%) believed that a one-school approach is not most effective. In response to one questionnaire item, "An effective therapist adheres closely to one major school of thought in conducting his therapy sessions," only 13% of the gestaltists, 17% of the transactionalists, 39% of the behaviorists, and 45% of the analysts expressed agreement.

Larson concludes his article with these comments:

> Psychotherapists do need theories—the benefits of primary school allegiance include social and financial support as well as a therapeutic philosophy. The pull toward eclecticism is also strong. The varied needs of clients and the challenges of different stages in the helping process . . . require drawing upon what is best or most effective in all approaches. (1980, p. 18)

Larson compared his results with an earlier survey of 244 psychologists by Goldschmid, Stein, Weissman, and Sorrells (1969) and found that "only the psychoanalytically oriented therapists endorsed a therapy relationship similar to the traditional style described by Goldschmid and his colleagues" (1980, p. 13). This "traditional" style emphasized a patient–therapist relationship in which the therapist is not active, does not use conditioning techniques, and does not disclose personal feelings. Larson comments, "The therapy style profiles obtained here may reflect the widespread changes occurring in psychotherapeutic practice" (p. 13).

Larson did find clear differences in attitudes, ideas, and styles among the four different orientations. There is no doubt that schools of therapy do exist and that these schools do guide the therapeutic preferences and thinking of the members. There is, however, considerable controversy over the extent to which these different attitudes and affiliations are reflected in what the therapists actually do. Indeed, Fiedler (1950), in a well-known survey that is now more than 30 years old, found that greater similarity was to be found among experienced clinicians of different affiliations than among beginning therapists of varying orientations. With increased experience, clinicians apparently become less doctrinaire.

In a very different kind of survey, Goldfried (1980) asked a few of the leading representatives of different orientations to respond in depth to five clinical questions. He found a surprising commonality in their answers.

The questions were:

1. What is the role played by new experiences provided to the patient/client in facilitating change?
2. To what extent does offering patients/clients feedback on their thinking, emotions, and behavior facilitate therapeutic change?
3. In what way do you see the therapist–patient/client relationship as contributing to the change process?
4. How have you used language (cognition) awareness in facilitating change within the therapeutic setting?
5. What clinical strategies or principles of change do you believe to be common across all therapeutic orientations?

These questions are sufficiently general and jargon-free to be answered by almost any therapist. Indeed they offer a kind of paradigm for the level of discourse that can be said to characterize eclectic approaches.

Goldfried summarized the respondents' answers by pointing out three emphases that these therapists had in common:

1. One is struck by the very strong emphasis placed on the importance of new experiences in the therapeutic change process, which was referred to as "critical," "crucial," "essential," "basic," and the like . . . .
2. The therapeutic interaction was also referred to as being "crucial" or "central" to the change process . . .
3. Also emphasized was the importance of a caring, trustworthy and confident attitude by the therapist. (Goldfried, 1980, p. 305)

The one conclusion that can be confidently drawn from all of these surveys is that *modern therapists are becoming more eclectic in their approach.* Schools still exist, but therapists are less likely to have a lifelong membership in just one school, and even therapists who affiliate with a single school are likely to borrow ideas and techniques from other schools.

Textbooks and Movies

Another sign of the developing eclectic tendency is the appearance of two recent textbooks about eclectic therapy: Garfield's (1980) *Psychotherapy: An Eclectic Approach* and Palmer's (1979) *A Primer of Eclectic Psychotherapy.* These, of course, are not the first books to appear with the word *eclectic* in their titles. But books from earlier decades were directed mainly to professionals; they were casebooks or theoretical treatises.

When textbooks are issued by publishers it is because they believe there is a definite market for the subject covered by the text that warrants the book's adoption in a number of courses.

Garfield introduces his book by identifying eclecticism with the search for the "implicit theory" actually used by most therapists,

> Most books on psychotherapy . . . either adhere to a particular theoretical orientation or . . . present a brief survey of a variety of psychotherapeutic approaches. . . . I have tried to present a view of psychotherapy . . . that includes emphases and procedures drawn from a variety of approaches. This being essentially what most psychotherapists appear to do in practice. (Garfield, 1980, p. vii)

Palmer defines eclecticism in a way similar to Garfield and Goldfried:

> I call this selection of the essential features of the various theories about human behavior and their integration into a comprehensive theory *eclecticism*. (Palmer, 1979, p. 6)

Although I quite agree with Goldfried, Garfield, and Palmer in their efforts to achieve a theoretical integration, I believe much of the work of theoretical integration already has been done by pioneers of eclecticism. As will be seen in the chapters of Part II, this book differs very much from Goldfried's, Garfield's, and Palmer's approaches to eclecticism. They are all peculiarly ahistorical. To them eclecticism is a modern trend, a creation of the late 1970s. I hope to show convincingly that as far as the theory is concerned this is not true at all. The implicit theory behind modern eclecticism was developed in the late 1800s by Janet, James, and others. Only by appreciating this historical background is it possible to identify the most important features of eclectic therapy and to understand why eclecticism is the therapy and theory of choice for most modern therapists.

Media Therapists[2]

Another very different source of evidence about the trends toward eclecticism comes from depictions of the role of the therapist in novels, television, and movies. There is a very big difference between the psychoanalytic psychiatrists shown in Alfred Hitchcock's 1945 movie *Spellbound* and the modern eclectic therapist played by Judd Hirsch in the 1981 production of *Ordinary People*.

In the earliest films about psychological treatment, such as Charlie

---

[2] Interestingly, the pioneering psychological study of film was written by Hugo Munsterberg (1916/1970), who is also one of the leading figures in the development of the Harvard line of clinical functionalism (see Chap. 3). The next significant book on the psychological study of film was not published until 1950 (Wolfenstein & Leites, 1950/1970).

Chaplin's 1917 *The Cure,* the therapist is always a medical doctor who works in a sanatorium. Often the therapist is depicted as evil, with special powers of mind control through hypnosis (as in the famous 1919 German film *The Cabinet of Dr. Caligari*).

Writing in *Film Society* in 1963, Rosenblatt discussed the development of the analyst's image as conveyed in film. He likened this film development to the process of psychological maturation seen in therapy:

(1) Psychosis as gothic excitement: sex, violence, murder, suicide

(2) The psychiatrist as hero-villain (Negative transference, fear)

(3) The analyst as comic-relief (Negative transference, belittling)

(4) Psychoanalytic Romanticism (Positive Transference), and

(5) Finally we reach the current period of *Maturity.* Psychoanalysis is a technique which can be utilized in the treatment of the emotionally disturbed. The analyst is a kindly, "warm" human being who has solved almost all of his personal problems, although he has a few, lovable failings. (pp. 33–34)

In the thirties, forties, and fifties, the film therapist is most often an analyst, although it is frequently difficult to tell whether the therapist is a psychiatrist, a psychologist, or a social worker. The professional lines of identification are not clearly drawn.

Davidson (1964) examined cartoon depictions of therapists and found very clear differences between the pre-1940 cartoons and those of the 1950s and 1960s. In the earlier cartoons the images are slanted toward the European stereotype of the psychiatrist. But in 42 randomly selected cartoons from 1963 he remarks that "not a single cartoon portrayed a hospital psychiatrist" (1964, p. 329). Parallel findings on the changing image of the therapist can be found in studies of novels. (See Meehan, 1964, and Winick, 1963.)

In modern times the psychologist has become sufficiently recognizable by the public to be the main character in a weekly TV comedy program, "The Bob Newhart Show." Dr. Hartley, the psychologist, has an office suite in an all-purpose office building that he shares with a dentist, businessmen, and other professionals.

In the most comprehensive review of film therapists to date, Solow (1978) concludes that the modern film therapist most often is shown as

a positive personality and as compassionate, supportive, caring, and open with his emotions. The negative aspects of his personality include nervousness, anger and jealousy. . . . Psychotherapy consists of talking about the past, dreams, sex, and relationships. (Solow, 1978, Abstract)

Solow also remarks that "his approach to psychotherapy is from a Freudian-based perspective and he deals with his patients in an active or a passive manner, or both" (Solow, 1978, Abstract). The representations in the popular media always lag behind the actual developments in any field. Indeed, psychiatrists did not begin to appear in American novels until the 1920s, although they had appeared in European literature and films before 1910 (Winick, 1963). It is fair to expect that in the next decade the media representations of therapists will depart more often from analytic stereotypes and reflect more strongly the eclecticism of the field.

There is a persuasive reason for therapists to pay attention to the media depictions of therapy, therapists, and clients. No doubt more people have been influenced in their expectations of what therapy is and what therapists are like and what clients and therapists do in therapy by movies than by the books written by therapists.

It makes a good deal of difference whether clients go to see a therapist with expectations drawn from *The Snake Pit* and *A Clockwork Orange* or expectations drawn from *Ordinary People*. And it makes a more subtle difference whether prospective clients enter therapy expecting analysis or expecting a varied program of eclectic psychotherapy.

The Search for a Unified Theory

In addition to textbooks and surveys, there have been a great many journal articles and several books in the last decade that have stated the case for constructing a unified theory or metatheory of therapy. These articles have appeared in general professional journals such as the *American Psychologist* and in the journals of the various therapeutic camps (behavior therapy, psychoanalytic therapy, and humanistic therapy).[3]

What all of these efforts have in common is the conviction that a general theory of therapy is needed and possible, a theory that can go beyond particular schools and unify them. Goldfried, for example, actually tried to publish his paper anonymously in the *American Psychologist* (but editorial policy prevented this) because

> all of us interested in the field of psychotherapy seem to have a tendency either to read or ignore articles and books on the basis of our allegiance with the author's theoretical camp. We have all "taken up sides," and have placed far too much emphasis on *who* is correct, not *what* is correct. I want to circumvent this tendency, as I believe the message has relevance to therapists of all orientations. (Goldfried, 1980, p. 1)

---

[3] See Appelbaum (1975), Bergin & Strupp (1972), Birk & Brinkley-Birk (1974), Brady (1968), Burton (1976), Dewald (1976), Egon (1975), Feather & Rhoades (1972), Ferster (1974), Goldfried & Davison (1976), Haley (1963), Hart (1970), Karasu (1979), Lazarus (1977), Lewis (1972), London (1964, 1972), Marmor (1971), Marston (1979), Martin (1972), Meichenbaum (1977), Raimy (1975), Segraves & Smith (1976), Silverman (1974), Wachtel (1977), Wondersman, Poppen, & Ricks (1976).

Goldfried goes on to suggest that the search for commonalities is not likely to succeed by looking at either the highest level of abstraction (the philosophy of each therapy) or the lowest level (the techniques of the therapy) but rather at the level of strategies. Strategies or principles of change are said by Goldfried to function as "clinical heuristics that implicitly guide our efforts during the course of therapy" (Goldfried, 1980, p. 11). He gives as examples of two such strategies one that provides the client with new, corrective experiences and a second that offers the client direct feedback.

I do not wish to discuss the content of Goldfried's or other theorists' unifying principles. Instead, I want to focus on his argument that therapists of different persuasions and eclectic therapists are *implicitly* using a theory to guide and organize their clinical procedures and philosophical ideas. In other words, Goldfried is saying not only that the field needs a broader, more general theory but that in some way this theory already exists. Therapists are implicitly going beyond the confines of the schools within which they were trained. It is this possibility, that an implicit theory exists and is in use, that I will develop in the next chapter. My argument is that the implicit theory, which Goldfried and others are now trying to make explicit, is the theory of clinical functionalism, a theory that was explicitly formulated by Janet, James, and others a hundred years ago.

What does it mean that there is a tendency for modern therapists to be more eclectic? Could it be simply that schools are going out of fashion, that there perhaps is a more academic dominance in the training of therapists? Is the eclectic tendency a by-product of the scientist–professional model?

Or could it be that there is a growing skepticism about all general theories and metatheories? Perhaps more and more specialization is occuring; perhaps therapists no longer are much concerned with the big, general questions (What are the necessary and sufficient conditions of therapeutic change? What is repression?).

Or could it be that now that the major battles for the definition of psychology have been fought, and passed by, therapists, along with other psychologists, have arrived at an inherited accumulation of definitions:

- Psychology is the study of mental life.
- Psychology is the study of behavior.
- Psychology is the clinical and experimental study of behavior and consciousness.

- Psychology is the clinical, experimental, and applied study of behavior, consciousness, and paraconscious phenomena.

Out of this amalgam definition of general psychology there arises a basis for a new eclectic attitude toward clinical psychology.

Types of Eclecticism

From this chapter's survey of the surveys, I believe we can define several types of eclecticism:

1. *Grab Bag Eclecticism* is the kind of eclecticism that simply lumps all kinds of theories and techniques together with the simple rationale "let's use everything and everyone."
2. *Hyphenated Eclecticism* is the kind of eclecticism practiced by behavior therapists who want to use Gestalt therapy or rational-emotive therapists who want to apply systematic desensitization. A core theory is broadened to include ideas and methods from other core theories. If the hyphenation is carried on indiscriminately, then Type 2 eclecticism becomes Type 1 eclecticism.
3. *Metatheory Eclecticism* is the kind exemplified by Goldfried (1980) and Strupp (1973), who attempt to define underlying strategies and ideas that cut across many particular therapies and therapists.
4. *Textbook Eclecticism* is similar to Type 3 but is designed to give academic coverage to many diverse points of view for students. Textbooks on eclectic therapy such as Garfield's (1980) and Palmer's (1979) are similar to books such as C. Hall and Lindzey's classic textbook *Theories of Personality* (1978). They do not attempt to formulate a single theory underlying the variety of theories but instead evaluatively cover each separate theory.
5. *Medical Model Eclecticism* is a special kind of Type 2 and Type 3 eclecticism that argues that each clinical technique and theory best can be applied to particular kinds of clinical problems. The medical model of diagnosis and selective treatment is applied to psychotherapy. Some behavior therapy eclectics (such as Lazarus, 1976, 1977) argue for this type of eclecticism.
6. *Functional Eclecticism* is the kind of eclectic viewpoint presented in this book. The functional approach to therapy is a definite historical tradition that provides a set of ideas and methods that compete with and influence other major therapeutic traditions,

such as psychoanalysis and behavior therapy. The functional approach also provides a framework for Type 3 eclecticism.

There are, of course, some convincing arguments for all of these kinds of eclecticism. If we put them in the form of shibboleths we get:

1. "All ideas and methods are worth considering, let's be open-minded."
2. "Theories should be broadened to include contributions from other relevant viewpoints."
3. "The most generally useful theories are the metatheories that cut across particular emphases and biases."
4. "Students should be fairly exposed to all points of view."
5. "Patients deserve the best treatment that can be applied for their specific illness."
6. "The historical tradition of functionalism provides an already tested general framework for clinical work."

I feel sympathetic to all of these emphases. However, to my mind, eclecticism becomes most interesting when it is revealed as a historical and general theory of therapy. It is not so interesting if it means merely a broadening or connecting of approaches and definitions that were too narrow from the beginning. If behavior therapists decide to pay attention to mental contents, that is certainly an advantage for them and their clients, but who but the narrowest of behavior therapists ever doubted that cognitions and willful choices were of importance? If humanistic psychologists start to admit to the influences of habit patterns and social conditioning, that is all to the good, but who but the most ardent believer in a disembodied self ever doubted that feelings and intentions must be related to actions? If psychoanalysts begin to give equal weighting to consciousness and programs of change for carrying out insights, that is laudable, but, after all, very few practioners ever really believed that unconscious determinisms were the be-all and end-all of therapy.

What I am saying is that too much back patting has gone on in professional circles when a narrow straw man is outfitted with a newer, larger, flashier wardrobe. A truly eclectic therapy and theory must *start* from a broad-based perspective of human behavior and experience and then proceed to generate ideas and programs for therapeutic change. In the next chapter I will sketch the basic ideas of the pioneers of eclectic therapy who did create such a theory and practice.

II

History

2

A Historical Overview of Eclectic Therapy

The first chapter dealt with trends toward eclecticism that have been occurring over the last 20 to 30 years. In this chapter I will expand the time frame to look at developments in eclectic therapy from the late 1800s up to the eclectic therapy of Frederick Thorne which was formulated in the 1940s and 1950s.

No self-respecting graduate student who is studying to be a therapist would be content to remain ignorant of techniques such as systematic desensitization, free association, directed daydreaming, or the reflection-of-feelings method. Nor would modern students be unfamiliar with concepts such as modeling, repression, and congruence. All students, however, recognize that these methods and concepts come from very different theoretical domains. Questions about *how* to put them together or *if* they can be coherently related are seldom considered. These questions and concerns are at the core of this book. It is my conviction that most modern therapists not only are eclectics but are using an implicit metatheory to interrelate the many different techniques and concepts that they apply to therapy. *Clinical functionalism, eclectic functionalism,* and *functionalism* are interchangeable labels I use to describe this metatheory. It is the central task of this book to make that metatheory explicit and clear. (The task of making the theory complete will require work over the next several decades.)

My reasons for choosing the five theorists (James, Janet, Burrow,

Portions of this chapter were reported in an earlier chapter (Hart, Corriere, Karle, & Woldenberg, 1980) and article (Hart, 1981).

Taft, and Thorne) covered in this historical overview as signal contributors to the development of eclecticism are these:

1. All of these theorists made an effort to cut across professional
   and theoretical boundaries in their work.
2. Each of them made a valuable contribution to the general theory
   of functional eclecticism.
3. Each theorist tried to construct a comprehensive system rather
   than merely borrow pieces from other theories. Each was a the-
   ory-minded eclectic, not merely a grab-bag eclectic.
4. All of them stayed apart from the main camps of psychology that
   flourished in their times (structuralism, analysis, and behaviorism).

The Significance of Functional Psychology for Eclecticism[1]

In his book *A History of Clinical Psychology* the historian John Reisman
makes this statement about the general importance of the functional
orientation: "Many psychologists found the functional position conge-
nial since they had been functioning as functionalists in everything but
name" (1976, p. 86).

George Miller, in his book *Psychology: The Science of Mental Life* says
of William James and the other functionalists:

> By broadening the definition of psychology, the American functionalists were able
> to incorporate studies of animals, of children, of the mentally retarded and the insane,
> and of primitive, preliterate peoples. And they were able to supplement introspection
> by other methods of collecting data; physiological experiments, mental tests, ques-
> tionnaires, and descriptions of behavior all became legitimate sources of information
> in the study of psychological processes. . . . In the U.S. today functional psychology
> *is* psychology. (1962, p. 66)

Although William James was not primarily a clinician and is not usually
cited for his contributions to psychotherapy, I will argue that his "functional psychology" is the greatest single unrecognized influence on the
attitudes of the majority of today's psychotherapists and counselors.
The definition of psychology used by the functionalists (the study of
mental processes and the behaviors resulting from them) and the inclu-
sive methods they applied to general psychology are exactly applicable

---

[1] This discussion of functionalism is short and selective; consult Schellenberg (1978), Schutz
(1960), and Wolman (1968) for detailed appraisals of functionalism and for discussions
of other functional contributors such as Francis Galton, Charles Darwin, G. S. Hall, James
Cattell, James Angell, Harvey Carr, and Robert Woodworth.

and widely used today by therapists of many different theoretical persuasions. Indeed, I believe, in the United States today the functional orientation to psychotherapy *is* psychotherapy.

The tradition of emphasizing conscious determinants of personality change comes directly from the functional definition of psychology as the study of mental processes and the behaviors resulting from them. Most eclectic therapists (whether they are hyphenated eclectics or purely humanistic or behavioral eclectics) are actually operating within the functional conception of psychology. The eclectic emphasis on doing what works is the same emphasis as James's pragmatic test for the truth of ideas—the truth of a concept lies in its practical consequences when applied to a real human situation.

It is no accident that William James is claimed as a forerunner by *both* behaviorists and humanists. As Rychlak (1977) cogently points out, William James's functionalism was a mixed model functionalism which gave equal weight to the search for physiological, psychological, social, and phenomenological causes and explanations. It was quite different from the reductive functionalism of Angell (1896) which led directly to Watson's behaviorism.

A recent compendium of psychotherapy approaches edited by Herink (1980) listed 250 different therapies in use today; it was appropriately subtitled "The A to Z Guide." A report of the Research Task Force (1975) issued by the National Institute of Mental Health referred to over 130 different forms of therapy. The possibility that there may be some underlying consistency and theoretical unity that ties together many of these seemingly diverse therapeutic approaches is an appealing one. The possibility that James's functionalism underlies eclecticism in psychotherapy will become more meaningful as we examine some of the details of his ideas.

James's Theory of Emotion

Almost every general introductory text in psychology will at some point (usually in a chapter on emotion) mention the James-Lange theory. For example, in the textbook *Invitation to Psychology* by Houston, Bee, Hatfield, and Rimm (1979), two pages are given to the James-Lange theory. Unfortunately in this and many other texts the theory is so oversimplified that it seems ridiculous, like some strange old-fashioned conception akin to the theory of humors or vapors:

> According to their theory, the emotions we feel are the result of messages we receive from our bodies when they react to emotion-producing aspects of the environment. . . . If the James-Lange hypothesis is correct, a unique pattern of physiological

changes should accompany each and every emotion. (Houston *et al.*, 1979, pp. 321–322)

This is not an accurate summary of the James-Lange hypothesis. James was concerned with three components of emotion: the perception, the actions in response to the perception, and the bodily feelings that followed the actions. He certainly did not believe that unique patterns of bodily feeling followed directly from a stimulus. James's own conception is quite assimilable into later theoretical and research emphases on the significance of set and setting in emotional arousal by such theorists as Schachter (1966). James's theory is also in line with recent research by Schwartz which shows that electrical activity in groups of facial muscles is distinctly patterned for different feelings and *precedes* any overt change in facial expression (G. E. Schwartz, Fain, Salt, Mandel, & Klerman, 1976). James's theory is also supported by the cross-cultural research on facial expressions that shows a uniformity of facial expressions across cultures for basic emotions such as happiness, sadness, anger, fear, surprise, and disgust (Ekman, 1971).

The clinical significance of his theory of emotion was brought out by James in his 1894 article "What Is an Emotion?" James advised,

> If we wish to conquer undesirable emotional tendencies in ourselves, we must assiduously, and in the first instance cold-bloodedly, go through the *outward motions* of those contrary dispositions we prefer to cultivate. (p. 201)

In the 1890 *Principles* James expanded on the above point:

> Our natural way of thinking about these coarser emotions is that the mental perception of some fact excites the mental affection called the emotion, and that this latter state of mind gives rise to the bodily expression. My theory, on the contrary, is that *the bodily changes follow directly the perception of the exciting fact, and that our feeling of the same changes as they occur is the emotion.* Common-sense says, we lost our fortune, are sorry and weep; we meet a bear, are frightened and run; we are insulted by a rival, are angry and strike. The hypothesis here to be defended says that this order of sequence is incorrect, that the one mental state is not immediately induced by the other, that the bodily manifestations must first be interposed between, and that the more rational statement is that we feel sorry because we cry, angry because we strike, afraid because we tremble. (James, 1890/1950, vol. 2, pp. 449–450)

For psychotherapists, the important theoretical point here is that feelings or emotions should not be considered apart from their expressions. The therapeutic target is not the feeling alone (as in extreme analytic existentialism) or the behavior alone (as in extreme behaviorism) but the percept–action–feeling unit. What James did was to define perception–expression–experience as the *unit* of emotionality. And, indirectly, as the basic unit of therapeutic concern.

What is seldom considered in a textbook discussion of the James-

Lange theory is the relevance of the theory for clinical work. In fact, most therapists practice within some application of the James-Lange model. Whether the therapist is an eclectic behavior therapist applying systematic desensitization methods or a humanistic therapist applying reflection of feeling methods, the goals are: (*a*) to help clients understand how their own actions are causing their discomfort and (*b*) to get the clients to try new behaviors leading to new feelings. Therapists believe that what their clients feel comes mainly from what their clients do (and this includes what clients say to themselves). To change feelings, therapists attempt to get clients to change their actions, their perceptions, and their thoughts.

The Jamesian theory clearly indicates why emotions and feelings are of such central importance in clinical work. It is *not* because they are especially dangerous or troublesome, as is popularly thought, but because *feelings can, and must, be used as conscious mediators of behavior and personality change.* If the percept–action–feeling sequence is generally true, then to change the way people feel therapists must help clients notice which percepts and actions lead to which feelings. From there, new actions and new perceptions can be tried that will lead, consciously, to new feelings.

The Clinical Level of Discourse

Many of James's ideas are relevant for psychotherapists: his discussion of habit acquisition and his arguments against the automation theory, his conceptualizations about the selectivity of attention, his thoughts about imagination and individual differences, his conceptualizations about the sense of reality, his discussion of ideomotor activity, his lengthy arguments about choice and purposefulness and the education of will—all are easily translatable into issues and practical concerns that occupy contemporary clinicians, but full discussion would require a book-length treatment. Instead, let us consider the overall level of theoretical discourse that James consistently used in all his writings.

It was this level of discourse that Allport (1961) pointed to as *the* major contribution of James's functionalism. James never slides into the metatheoretical language of multiple inferences characteristic of psychoanalytic theorizing. Nor does he become entwined in the technically remote object language that often is found in behavioristic theorizing. Even when discussing the problems of irrational, emotional processes or the processes of habit modification, his discussion is maintained at a level similar to that of everyday language—the same ordinary language most used by clients and therapists in sessions. It is precisely this level of discourse that Goldfried (1980) identifies as the most appropriate for the formulation of unifying strategies, strategies that cut across the particulars of technique and theory.

The central importance of the level of discourse used in psychological theorizing was argued at length by James's fellow functionalists John Dewey and George Herbert Mead. In his famous paper "The Reflex Arc Concept in Psychology" (1896) Dewey attacked the reductionism of the reflex arc analysis, which was widely espoused in the late 1800s, with its sharp distinction between stimulus and response. Dewey argued that behavior cannot be meaningfully reduced to its basic sensorimotor elements anymore than consciousness can be meaningfully analyzed into its elementary components. When this kind of analysis is undertaken, the behavior or experience loses all meaning for everyday life. All that remain are concepts in the minds of the theorists, concepts that are very far removed from the clinically interesting phenomena of subjective experience (anxieties, fears, hates, desires, insights, etc.) and actions in the real world.

John Dewey presented his arguments in forceful language:

> The conscious stimulus or sensation, and the conscious response or motion, have a special genesis or motivation, and a special end or function. The reflex arc theory, by neglecting, by abstracting from, this genesis and this function gives us one disjointed part of a process as if it were the whole. It gives us literally an arc, instead of the circuit; and not giving us the circuit of which it is an arc, does not enable us to place, to center, the arc. This arc, again, falls apart into two separate existences having to be either mechanically or externally adjusted to each other. (1896, p. 370)

What exactly is this functional level of discourse? John Dewey said clearly what it is not: too much reduction or too much abstraction leads to third-, fourth-, and higher order conceptualizations that make it difficult to return to the *common* sense and thought and feeling levels at which people actually experience and talk about their lives.

It is important to state that the functional level of discourse is not necessarily simple or uncomplicated. Surely no one could accuse James, or his fellow functionalists such as John Dewey and George Herbert Mead, of oversimplification. Mead, for example, consistently rejected the schematic descriptions of social behavior offered by the behaviorists:

> Social psychology is behavioristic in the sense of starting off with an observable activity—the dynamic, ongoing social process and social acts which are its component elements to be studied and analyzed scientifically. But it is not behavioristic in the sense of ignoring the inner experience of the individual—the inner phase of that process. (Mead, 1934, p. 7)

And elsewhere,

> The social act is not explained by building it up out of stimulus plus response; it must be taken as a dynamic whole—as something going on—no part of which can be understood by itself—a complex organic process implied by each individual stimulus and response involved in it. (Mead, 1934, p. 7)

The functional level of discourse always asks *what* is happening (around the person and in the person's experience) and *how* the person is responding. These primary and secondary levels can always be studied and clinically utilized even when the *why* of an experience or a response is complicated or obscure. It is always possible to focus on what people experience and how they respond, even when an explanation of why they have certain experiences and make certain responses is unknown. With these *what* and *how* levels of discourse every other kind of observation and abstraction (physiological, microbehavioral, microenvironmental, microphenomenal, and interpretive) can be used as a supplement to understanding.

Of course, functional psychologists and clinicians who work within the functional orientation share this level of discourse with novelists, journalists, songwriters, poets, historians, and street-corner psychologists, and this is desirable. It is this very commonness that allows functional psychologists to move back and forth easily between theoretical-clinical language and everyday language. Indeed, the practitioners of functional psychology sometimes seem to employ a criterion of "pop validity." If a concept cannot be understood and applied by the people it is designed to explain (themselves and their clients), then the truth value of that concept is limited. (There are, of course, limits to the application of this criterion just as there are limits to predictive and repeatability tests of concepts.) The criterion of "pop validity" is what James meant by the pragmatic test of the truth of an idea for an individual. At the functional level of discourse if individuals cannot understand or use an idea, that idea is not true for them—even though the concept may explain their behavior! It is this emphasis on a functional level of discourse that makes functional psychology so aligned with clinical work.

To be most effective, psychological concepts must be true for a person as well as true about the person. Many of the explanations of behavior and personality patterns and of inner experiences offered by psychoanalysts and learning theorists may be abstractly true, but not functionally useful for the people to whom they are applied.

In philosophy James is identified with "pragmatism" which he also called "practicalism" (see James, 1898, p. 526). In his 1898 essay on "Philosophical Conceptions and Practical Results" James asserts,

> Beliefs, in short, are really rules for action; and the whole function of thinking is but one step in the production of habits of action. . . . The ultimate test for us of what a truth means is indeed the conduct it dictates or inspires. (p. 527)

This philosophical emphasis is also a clinical emphasis. Over and over again therapists attempt to get their clients to test directly the truth of their beliefs and change them or keep them by connecting thoughts and feelings to actions and consequences. It is this consistent emphasis on practicality that most identifies the functional level of discourse.

Clinical Precursors

Now I will examine the more explicitly clinical versions of this functional approach. James and his fellow functionalists provided the rationale, but other figures in the late 1800s and early 1900s developed the specific clinical applications of functionalism.

The four forerunners of the modern functional orientation to psychotherapy that I will discuss here are Janet, Burrow, Taft, and Thorne. Many others could be considered, but these four are of especial importance: Janet because he was a contemporary of the founders of the two other major trends in modern psychotherapy, Freud and Pavlov, and created his therapy with full knowledge of their work; Burrow because he clearly recognized the need for psychotherapists to develop their own personalities beyond both their individual neuroses and shared social neuroses; Taft because she was the first psychotherapist to deliberately apply the label and ideas of James's, Dewey's, and Mead's "functional" psychology to psychotherapy; and Thorne because he explicitly developed and promoted "eclectic" therapy at a time when therapy and counseling were largely dominated by the conflicting camps of analysis, behaviorism, and humanism.

Janet (1859–1947)

Like Freud, Janet published his first major papers from the 1880s to 1909. Also like Freud, he used the hypnotic and cathartic approach to traumas in his early clinical work but later abandoned this focus on hypnosis and traumas. However, Janet eventually emphasized fostering mature modes of consciousness, while Freud emphasized understanding psychopathology.

Janet's psychotherapy was characterized by: (a) an unlimited variety of techniques (among them free association, which Janet called "automatic talking"); (b) the identification of subconscious "fixed ideas" that disrupted behavior and weakened consciousness (Janet coined the word "subconscious"); and (c) synthesizing methods to supplement analytic methods.

> Janet emphasized from the beginning that bringing the subconscious ideas into consciousness was not sufficient to cure the patient. . . . removal has to be supplemented by synthesizing treatment in the form of reeducation or other forms of mental training. (Ellenberger, 1970, p. 373)

Like William James (as well as Freud and Pavlov), Janet was very concerned with the various ways of mobilizing psychological energy and of the connections between psychological tension and subconscious energy drains. Like all the therapists who would follow him in the functional orientation, Janet emphasized that feelings are regulators of action and that abnormal states manifest a disorganization of these regulations. Janet defined psychological strengths by the perfection of action and psychological weakness by the imbalance of feelings and the mediocrity of actions.

Another characteristic that Janet and all later functional therapists share is the notion that psychotherapy can be put into perspective only if psychopathology is seen as "arrested development" within a total range of adult development from abnormal to normal to exceptional (an evolutionist model). He believed that the evolution of man is open toward the future. "We grow in time like plants in space" (Ellenberger, 1970, p. 394; see also Ey, 1968, p. 194).

Trigant Burrow (1875–1950)

This theme of continued evolution also is stressed throughout the writings of Trigant Burrow. If Janet can be characterized as largely "forgotten," then Burrow should be described as "never known." Despite the voluminousness of his writings (books, clinical articles, and research articles), Burrow remains almost totally obscure. Mention his name or the name of his therapeutic system "phyloanalysis" to 100 therapists and 99 will fail to recognize him. This obscurity was a great loss for theory and research in therapy because Burrow was truly innovative.

Consider these innovations:

1. In 1923 he founded the Lifwynn Foundation, a "social laboratory" to study the neurotic characteristics of the culture.

2. In 1924, he began psychophysiological studies of patterns of internal tension to identify defending and nondefending physiologically.

3. He stressed that therapists must continue to get therapy in order to break the limits of the therapist–patient roles:

> It does seem to me quite outrageous that psychoanalysts are themselves as neurotic and confused as their patients. . . . I think it quite perverts the aim of our work to pretend any longer that the neurosis is not a social condition and that we ourselves do not share equally with our patients in it. (Burrow, 1958, p. 82)

4. He used the examination of the "immediate moment" as the focus of therapeutic work, "it being the purpose of our laboratory work to observe only the present moment—that is the mood of the present moment as it relates to one's self and to others" (Burrow, 1958, p. 178).

5. He conceptualized that psychopathology and phylopathology were the encroachment of the symbol system on basic feeling processes, "a certain pathological image-substitution, existing socially, is as definitely the cause of mental disorder as the germ of tuberculosis responsible for the prevalence of this disease among us" (Burrow, 1958, p. 160).

Perhaps Burrow's greatest contribution and innovation was his recognition that most therapies are organized around theories and techniques but pay little attention to structure. By structure, is meant the context (physical, social, and psychological) in which the therapy takes place and the time frame of the therapy. Burrow shared with Taft a willingness to experiment with different settings and time frames for carrying out therapy. (See Burrow, 1958, and Syz, 1961.)

Throughout all these and other innovations was a broad philosophical perspective (which Burrow shared with Janet and James).

> Burrow conceived of man's present biosocial phase as a transitional stage in the development toward a type of existence in which human wholeness can be reached on a more native and culturally advancing level. As he expressed it: "Man is still early—too early to know how early he is." (Syz, 1963, p. 43)

Jessie Taft (1882–1960)

Although Jessie Julia Taft has not been forgotten or ignored as were Janet and Burrow, her influence has been largely confined to the field of social work (Smalley & Bloom, 1977). The functional approach to the practice of social casework was developed in the 1930s at the University of Pennsylvania by Jessie Julia Taft and her colleague Virginia Robinson.

Taft studied directly with John Dewey and George Mead when she did her doctoral work at the University of Chicago from 1908 to 1913. She drew upon their ideas and the ideas of William James throughout her career. She was the first system formulator in psychotherapy to apply the ideas of functional psychology and pragmatic philosophy to psychotherapy directly and deliberately.

She stressed, as did Burrow, that the psychotherapist has an

> obligation to continuous self-analysis and personal adjustment resulting in what we know as grown-up behavior. . . . Therapy as a qualitative affair must depend upon the personal development of the therapist and his ability to use consciously for the benefit of his client, the insight and self-discipline which he has achieved in his own struggle to accept self, life, and time as limited. (Taft, cited in Robinson, 1962, pp. 111, 175)

She also stressed the central importance of emotionality in personality and personality change: "There is no factor of personality which is so expressive of individuality as emotion, none so antagonistic to generalizations" (Taft, cited in Robinson, 1962, p. 140). Taft described therapy as "growth" through the medium of a "dynamic" relationship. "Therapy relates to the balance of forces in the organization of the personality" (Taft, cited in Robinson, 1962, p. 154). She assessed the value of therapy in the strongest possible language.

> The possibility of providing for the individual in need, an artificial growth-producing situation, is, in my opinion, the epoch-making psychological discovery of our era, a discovery that may yet be found to be more momentous for the future of civilization than the unlocking of the forces in the atom. (Taft, cited in Robinson, 1962, p. 175)

Frederick Thorne (1909–1978)

In 1950 Thorne completed the book *Principles of Personality Counseling,* which, in his words, "attempted to make an eclectic presentation of all known methods of counseling and psychotherapy" (Thorne, 1955, p. i). He attempted "to relate therapy to diagnosis with a clear statement of the indications and contraindications for use of all methods" (p. i).

Thorne's two major works, *Principles of Personality Counseling* (1950) and *Principles of Psychological Examining* (1955) were actually conceived before 1940. Thorne spent his entire career in psychology developing, reformulating, and expostulating the eclectic approach to therapy. Of all the therapists discussed in this chapter Thorne is the most self-consciously and persistently eclectic in orientation.

Thorne was forced into a student's form of underground eclecticism early in his studies because of the difference between the narrow point of view of the faculty and his own breadth of interests. He remarked, in a biographical chapter,

> My eight years on the Columbia campus . . . required me to give lip service to a behavioristic psychology which I didn't believe in and could not respect, so that I literally went "underground" and engaged in "bootleg" studies of psychodynamics

and psychopathology. By day I fulfilled the role of an experimentalist and did my
Ph.D. in psychophysics. . . . By night, I read Freud, Adler, Jung and other clinicians.
(Thorne, 1972, pp. 244, 245)

Thorne received both a Ph.D. and an M.D.; this background put all
of his eclectic formulations within the medical model. He always endorsed the medical sequence of testing and diagnosis—treatment, treatment assessment, treatment modification (if necessary), and follow-up.
Thorne, however, also was interested in counseling with healthy personalities and explicitly formulated ideas and methods of "psychological
fitness" training (Thorne, 1965).

During the period from 1945 to 1974, Thorne founded and served
as the editor of the *Journal of Clinical Psychology*. This journal served the
very important function of providing an outlet for case reports and
observations that were not acceptable to the research- and statistics-
dominated psychology journals of that time. A perusal of the early vol-
umes of Thorne's journal reveals a breadth of representation of theories
and methods that could not be found in any other journal of his time.

Summing-Up

What, then, do these four therapists have in common that would
allow us to attach the common label *functional* to their ideas and methods?
Despite their different emphases and aims and the very different contexts of their work (Janet, an academic clinician; Taft, a social worker;
Burrow, a renegade therapist conducting "social experiments"; and Thorne,
a journal editor and spokesperson for the eclectic position) the four
shared these ideas:

1. Feelings are the basic mediators of behavior change and personality change.
2. Conflict among affect systems, cognitive systems, and behavior
   systems is the crux and source of psychopathology.
3. Removing the conflicts requires a positive biopsychosocial model
   of how human beings can function optimally.
4. Psychotherapy must work simultaneously on easing tensions and
   building up energy.
5. Psychotherapists must work first, and continuously, on their
   own psychological health.

These propositions also can be found in nascent form in the psychological and philosophical writings of William James, George Mead,
and John Dewey. They are the guiding ideas or background ideas from
which all functional therapists work.

It is significant that neither of the textbook writers, Garfield (1980) and Palmer (1980), devote any attention to these historical precursors of contemporary eclecticism. Palmer does not cite Thorne, Taft, Burrow, or Janet at all and only once mentions William James. Garfield's text does briefly mention both Thorne and Taft but ignores James and the others completely; nor does Garfield credit Thorne with much influence on modern eclectic practice. Taft is cited merely as an advocate of time-limited therapy. In my view the ahistorical approach to eclectic theory building has very serious limitations. It is much harder to draw general eclectic strategies and practices from cross-combinations of therapeutic traditions that were originally noneclectic than it is to draw directly from eclectic precursors. It is something like trying to define American food as a cross of French, German, Italian, Chinese, and other cuisines, rather than identifying the core bread, meat, and vegetable tradition that was inherited from the British. Of course, both the "melting pot" analysis and the "line-of-descent" analysis are true, but a real appreciation of American eclecticism in eating habits requires that both be considered. The same is true for eclecticism in therapy.

Conclusions

From this historical overview it is now possible to specify further the eclectic therapy that is presented in this book. What is meant by eclecticism is functional eclecticism. Functional eclectic therapy is that tradition of therapy starting with James and Janet that emphasizes these common features:

1. Therapists must be open to ideas and techniques from any particular system (Open-minded Eclecticism).
2. Therapists need to look for underlying trends and principles that cross different systems (Unified Eclecticism).
3. Therapists should give equal attention to behaviors, thoughts, feelings, and social circumstances (Practical Eclecticism).
4. Although attention is given to possible unconscious determinants and to automatic behavioral contingencies most attention is focused on cognitions and behaviors that are under conscious control (Humanistic Eclecticism).

Are these guiding ideas relevant for all modern eclectic therapists? I would say not. Many modern eclectics would endorse most of these ideas but not all eclectics would subscribe to every proposition. Even so, functional eclecticism must be considered the core eclectic position around which all others diverge as peripheral viewpoints.

If the four common features of historical eclecticism are tied in to the modern survey results reported in Chapter 1 this overall conclusion tentatively can be drawn: *The majority of today's eclectic practitioners work within a framework of clinical functionalism.*

The argument I am making about functional psychology as the background theory for the practice of eclectic therapy is not generally known and accepted. Indeed, a 1981 computer search of the clinical psychology literature, using the National Institute of Health's bibliographic search service, failed to reveal a single reference for functional psychotherapy but numerous references for eclectic therapy. (The search terms used were: eclectic psychology/therapy/psychotherapy/counseling/psychiatry, and functional psychology/therapy/psychotherapy/counseling/psychiatry.)

Nonetheless, even though the functional psychology-eclectic therapy connection is novel and speculative, it is potentially very powerful. If functionalism is the magnet that has indicated a common direction for eclectic efforts, then more progress should be made, clinically and theoretically, if the lines of influence are made clear rather than left hidden.

The next four chapters will fill in the historical contributions made to clinical functionalism by James, Janet, Burrow, Taft, and Thorne. It is hoped that readers who are unfamiliar with the ideas and methods of these pioneers will come away from these reappraisals with a new appreciation of their significance for modern therapy.[2]

---

[2] A survey by Prochaska and Norcross (1983) of 410 members of APA Division 29 (Psychotherapy) revealed that "psychodynamic orientations have experienced renewed preference with eclecticism declining, suggesting a need for more integrative models of therapy" (p. 161). The eclectic orientation was the most frequent choice as the professed theoretical orientation at 30.2%; the psychodynamic was second at 18%. Only 4% of the eclectics chose atheoretical eclecticism while 31% selected technical eclecticism and 65% preferred synthetic eclecticism. In line with this direction of preference, a new book on *Eclectic Psychotherapy* (1983) by L.E. Beutler appeared with the subtitle "a Systematic Approach" and a book on eclecticism in counseling by Michael Cavanagh (1982) was published with the title *The Counseling Experience: A Theoretical and Practical Approach.* [Added in proof—Author.]

3

William James and the Harvard Line of Clinical Functionalism

Many of the most important contributors to modern psychotherapy (including Jung and Freud) were driven by efforts to solve their own emotional problems. Ellenberger calls this a "creative illness" (1970, pp. 444–450). Much of the power of James's theorizing emerged from his efforts to find ideas and methods that would help him personally.

For example, James's formulation of his theory about emotions and how they can be changed by positive actions was based upon his personal struggles with depression. The biographer G. W. Allen quotes from one of James's letters to a friend in 1866, "All last winter . . . when I was on the continual verge of suicide" (Allen, 1967, p. 124). James also reports on his depression in the *Varieties of Religious Experience*,

> I awoke morning after morning with a horrible dread at the pit of my stomach, and with a sense of the insecurity of life that I never knew before . . . for months I was unable to go into the dark alone. (James, quoted in Allen, 1967, p. 166)

To change these sometimes overwhelming feelings of dread and disaster James undertook to choose systematically which thoughts he would believe (the thoughts that led him to feel better) and how he would act on those thoughts ("Remember: Care little for speculation/ Much for the *form* of my action," James, quoted in Allen, 1967, p. 168). That he was successful in his self-therapy can be attested to by his lifelong productivity and by his reputation at Harvard, among the students he taught, for liveliness and good spirits.

Of course, James was not merely advocating a kind of "happy face" method of repression. He paid careful attention to all the nuances and subtle shifts within the stream of consciousness.

James on Consciousness

If Freud is forever associated with the theory of the unconscious and Watson, Pavlov, and Skinner with theories of behavior, then James's special position in the history of psychology is his theory of consciousness.

His theory first became widely known with the publication of the two-volume *Principles of Psychology* (1890/1950). To put James's ideas in historical perspective consider what had *not* yet happened in psychology:

- The American Psychological Association would not be formed until 1892. (James would become the third president of the APA in 1894.)
- Freud's *The Interpretation of Dreams* was not published until 1900.
- Watson's *Psychology from the Standpoint of a Behaviorist* would not be published until 1919.

William James's *Principles* began, "Psychology is the science of mental life, both of its phenomena and their conditions" (James, 1890/1950, p. 1). By "phenomena" James meant "feelings, desires, cognitions, reasonings, decisions, and the like" and by "conditions" he referred to any influences that could alter the phenomena such as aging, drugs, fevers, excitement, exhaustion, repetition, etc. He said that "the quest of conditions becomes the psychologist's most interesting task" (James, quoted in Allen, 1967, p. 3) and *"No mental modification ever occurs which is not accompanied or followed by a bodily change"* (p. 5) and, further, *"The pursuance of future ends and the choice of means for their attainment are thus the mark and criterion of the presence of mentality* in a phenomenon" (James, quoted in Allen, 1967, p. 8).

Chapter 9 of the *Principles* is titled "The Stream of Thought." In his shortened version, *Psychology: Briefer Course* (1892), James tended to use the two phrases interchangeably because he never narrowed "thoughts" to cognitions but always referred to consciousness as a mix of thoughts, feelings, and desires and images.

Rychlak has commented on the importance of James's conceptualization of consciousness, with its *equal* weighting of thoughts and feelings, for humanistic therapists:

> The intellectual list theorists have also taken the position that feelings do not enter into mentation, if indeed they exist at all. But for James, feeling relations are central to the course of thought. And here we observe a tendency that I think all humanists share, that is, to ascribe significance to something called emotion, feeling, or affection in human affairs. (Rychlak, 1978, p. 101)

James's choice of the "stream" metaphor conveys very well his emphasis on the affective in consciousness.

> Consciousness, then, does not appear to itself chopped up in bits. Such words as "chain" or "train" do not describe it fitly as it presents itself in the first instance. It is nothing jointed; it flows. A "river" or a "stream" are the metaphors by which it is most naturally described. *In talking of it hereafter, let us call it the stream of thought, of consciousness, of subjective life.* (James, 1890/1950, p. 239)

For clinicians one of the most significant sections of James's theory concerning "the stream of subjective life" is that dealing with "gaps" in consciousness:

> In all our voluntary thinking there is some topic or subject about which all the members of the thought revolve. Half the time this topic is a problem, a gap we cannot yet fill with a definite picture, word, or phrase, but which, in the manner described some time back, influences us in an intensely active and determinate psychic way. Whatever may be the images and phrases that pass before us, we feel their relation to this waking gap. To fill it up is our thought's destiny. Some bring us nearer to that consumation. Some the gap negates as quite irrelevant. Each swims in a felt fringe of relations of which the aforesaid gap is the term. Or instead of a definite gap we may merely carry a mood of interest about with us. Then, however vague the mood, it will still act in the same way, throwing a mantle of felt affinity over such representations. (James, 1890/1950, p. 259)

All of the phrases James uses to discuss these active gaps in consciousness are still much used by clinicians: *Felt meaning, lingering consciousness, feelings of tendency*, the *fringes, overtones* of consciousness are all phrases pointing toward what clinicians now call the preconscious or unconscious. James emphasizes the great importance of these *feelings* of *tendency*, "often so vague that we are unable to name them at all. It is, in short, the reinstatement of the vague to its proper place in our mental life which I am so anxious to press on the attention" (James, 1890/1950, p. 254).

In an interesting essay on "William James and the Stream of Thought" Rosenzweig (1968) presents a convincing case that William James's "stream of thought" discussion in the *Principles* directly influenced Freud's formulation of the association method and the basic rule of psychoanalysis. Even more interesting than the question of influence (or mutual influences on both men from Charcot, Janet, and other writers) is the contrast between James's and Freud's theories about the stream of consciousness.

For James, the unconscious was felt but unnamed. For Freud, the unconscious was neither felt nor named but causative. For James the unconscious was an active, positive tendency that could be brought into consciousness with regularity. For Freud the unconscious was a disruptive negative tendency that could be brought into consciousness only with difficulty. James focused on the use of felt meanings in consciousness. Freud focused on the hidden meanings outside of consciousness. James centered on the mechanisms of consciousness and the use of feelings as mediators of change; Freud centered on the mechanisms of repression and how repressed feelings prevent change.

In an essay on "Sources of the Stream of Consciousness" Strange (1978) discusses the significance of Morton Prince's functionalist conceptions of the unconscious which were derived from Janet and James, "His [Prince's] work is important in that it shows that a concept of the unconscious could be developed within the framework of American functional psychology. In time, however, Prince's original work on the unconscious was eclipsed by the ascendence of the psychoanalytic view" (Strange, 1978, pp. 21–22).

Hilgard is among the prominent contemporary theorists who urge a reconsideration of the James-Janet-Prince theories of consciousness and unconsciousness. The most important difference between the Jamesian and the Freudian unconscious is that the former can be observed and the latter can only be inferred.

> The deep unconscious of Freud . . . is often accessible only by way of its derivatives. According to Freud, dream interpretation . . . is a most important way to learn about the unconscious. . . . The communication with the unconscious, by these (dream inference) processes, is an indirect one. (Hilgard, 1977, p. 249)

Functionally oriented research on dreams (Hart, Corriere, Karle & Woldenberg, 1980; Karle, Corriere, Hart & Woldenberg, 1980) and clinical work with dreams has resulted in the last decade in new evidence that suggests that dream work or the mechanisms of repression can be undone directly in dreams so that latent affective content can become conscious without the need for indirect interpretations. This research is of course contrary to Freud's dictum that "what is essential in dreams is the process of the dream work" (Freud, 1933/1965, p. 8), but directly supports James's idea that gaps in the stream of consciousness can be filled in and thereby emerge into consciousness. This research will be discussed at length in Chapter 9.

In private correspondence James examined with great interest the new ideas of Freud and Jung about unconscious determinants of actions. Ernest Jones reports in his biography of Freud that James had said to Freud, "The future of psychology belongs to your work" (E. Jones, 1955, p. 57). However, in a letter to his friend Flournoy, James sounded less sanguine and more critical of Freud's psychology.

> I hope that Freud and his pupils will push their ideas to their utmost limits, so that we may learn what they are. They can't fail to throw light on human nature; but I

confess that he made on me personally the impression of a man obsessed with fixed ideas. I can make nothing in my own case with his dream theories and obviously "symbolism" is a most dangerous method. (Cited in LeClair, 1966, p. 224)

An unfortunate consequence of the earlier prevalence of Freud's views is that more research and theoretical attention has been directed at inferred mechanisms of repression than at the subjectively observable processes of consciousness. More theories focus on how feelings impede change than on how feelings and decisions aid change. A modern resurgence of the functional position among clinical psychologists could result in rapid development of knowledge about conscious mediators of personality change during the next several decades.

New Evidence Concerning James's Clinical Work

In a brief chapter that I wrote about "Functional Psychotherapy" for Corsini's *Handbook of Innovative Therapies* (1981) I remarked, "If we stretch the definition of 'therapist' a very long way we can even talk about William James as a therapist—a therapist who had only one patient, himself" (Hart, 1981, p. 2). It now turns out that William James did see patients and that he had a much more developed theory of abnormal behavior than has heretofore been known.

Dr. Eugene Taylor, the archivist for the William James papers at the Harvard Library of Medicine, has gained access to lectures and letters of William James that have not been published or generally known. Dr. Taylor remarks

Many of the early philosophers in the Boston School of Psychotherapy also saw patients. There is evidence, for instance, that James took several patients into his home for treatment. . . . His home office practice, while merely a temporary experiment, was probably modeled after the home-office practice of J. J. Putnam and Morton Prince. These were the days . . . before any psychiatric outpatient clinics existed, and while Prince and Putnam saw patients as a profession, James merely dabbled, since his main emphasis was teaching and writing. The episode is significant, if for no other reason than the fact that these bare handful of individuals were the only real live patients James saw in his career as a medical doctor and therapist. (E. Taylor, personal communication, 1981)

The most important unpublished lectures (Dr. Taylor is working on preparing them for print) for clinicians are the Lowell Lectures of 1896 on Exceptional Mental States. Taylor says of this work:

While he [James] had defined the nature of the stream of consciousness and the 'ultra-marginal zone' of awareness as early as his Baltimore Lectures on the Brain and Mind in 1878, and again in his *Principles* in 1890, where he outlined the general nature of the Subliminal, it was not until the presentation of [his 1896 lectures] that James

focused on the nature of subliminal consciousness, collecting all of his previous ideas
so widely dispersed into a simple coherent statement. (E. Taylor, 1980a)

E. Taylor evaluates the Lowell lectures in this way: "James played
an important role in the development of a uniquely American psychology of the unconscious that was later inundated by the flood of Freudian
psychoanalysis" (1979, pp. 1, 2).

The topics covered in the lectures were: dreams and hypnotism,
automatism, hysteria, multiple personality, demoniacal possession,
witchcraft, degeneration, and genius. James reviewed all the relevant
literature of the time including Breuer and Freud's writings on hysteria.
He argued that visual imagery, hypnotism, automatic writing, crystal
gazing, and speaking in tongues could all be used as tools for exploring
the unconscious.

The theory he devised to unify these various topics and methods
is described by Taylor,

> Evidence suggested, James said, the operation of two systems going simultaneously
> in the person, one conscious the other unconscious. The normally conscious state,
> which is aware of our everyday activities and is aware of itself has no knowledge of
> the hypnotic strata. The unconscious stream, on the other hand, contains innumerable
> possibilities for self-expression, some of which are bestial and archaic in nature, while
> others are far superior and wiser than our normal working awareness. Influencing the
> hypnotic strata for purposes of healing . . . could only come about when one self-
> consciously appealed to an awakening of this wiser and superior aspect within one's
> own personality. (E. Taylor, 1979, p. 6)

This formulation bears some resemblance to the theories of C. G.
Jung. James and Jung met only once, in 1908, when Jung and Freud
traveled to the United States to deliver the Clark lectures on psychoanalysis. However, Jung was very influenced by James's books. Taylor
evaluates this influence this way,

> According to Jung's own account, James' writings helped to shape his earliest for-
> mulations of psychological types; James was the guiding spirit in the direction Jung
> took in diverging from Freud over the nature of psychic energy; he influenced Jung's
> definition of science, and his views on the collective unconscious. Early on James
> impressed Jung with the importance of viewing personality as a holistic totality that
> quite transcends the bounds imposed on it by the rational mind. (E. Taylor, 1980b,
> p. 157)

In an address given at the 1936 tercentenary exercises at Harvard
University Jung ended his talk with this tribute,

> William James . . . psychological vision and pragmatic philosophy have on more
> than one occasion been my guides. It was his far-reaching mind which made me
> realize that the horizons of human psychology widen into the immeasurable. (Jung,
> 1969, p. 125)

James defined the "subliminal" as

> the operation of two simultaneously conscious and intelligent systems within the personality; primary consciousness, he said, being rational and logical in orientation, focused on needs and activities arising from daily encounters with external material reality perceived through the senses, which secondary consciousness was composed of enumerable streams of consciousness, some bestial and archaic, others equivalent but unknown to waking material consciousness, and still others that reflected the divine and transcendent within each of us, wiser and far superior to mere rational awareness. Recognizing that at any given moment we have the ability to actualize the bestial and underdeveloped . . . it was through our willful choices that we allowed the best that is within us to come forward. (James, cited in, E. Taylor, 1980a, p. 283)

Today, this seems like old stuff to most clinicians. But remember that these formulations were made *before* Freud developed his ideas of the ego and the id and long before the modern emphasis on growth tendencies by humanistic and transpersonal therapists such as Maslow, Rogers, and Assagioli.

James's ideas found their greatest immediate influence among the members of the Boston School of Psychotherapy. This group was made up, over the late 1800s and early 1900s, of such individuals as Morton Prince, J. J. Putnam, Hugo Munsterburg, Adolph Meyer, Boris Sidis, G. S. Hall, Josiah Royce, Isodor Coriat, August Hoch, and George Santayana.

Morton Prince established the Harvard Psychological Clinic, which was later directed by Henry Murray. Both Murray and Gordon Allport carried on at Harvard the tradition of personalism that was such a central part of William James's philosophy and psychology. (I will discuss and apply the work of Murray and Allport in Part III when a unified theory of clinical functionalism is presented.)

The tendency toward eclecticism was present very early in the Boston School; Taylor comments,

> The orientation of this "school" was by no means a carbon copy of James' ideas although James was undoubtedly a primary motivating force. Rather, the group as a whole *reflected a very open-minded and eclectic attitude toward psychotherapy and the unconscious, focusing on the therapeutic process but drawing from widely diverse fields of philosophy, neurology, experimental psychology, psychic research, religion, and faith healing*. This is one of the reasons why James equated clinical practice that is, the exploration of the unconscious, with the functional tradition in psychology. (E. Taylor, 1980a, p. 4, italics mine)

This "open-minded and eclectic attitude" which characterized the Boston School at the turn of the century can serve just as well to describe modern eclecticism.

It would be possible and useful to trace the links of James' clinical functionalism much more deeply and widely but for the purposes of this book a short account must be sufficient. However, before leaving this subject I want to quote Dr. Eugene Taylor again to show how fascinating historical tracings can become,

> Historical data on the background of James' interest in mental therapeutics shows an interesting link between Ralph Waldo Emerson's ideas on the stream of consciousness in the 1830s; J. J. Garth Wilkinson's early replication of experiments by Eliotson and Braid on hypnotism as a therapeutic agent; and James' eventual development of the "stream" metaphor, as well as his use of dreams, automatic writing, crystal gazing, and hypnosis as techniques for exploring the subliminal consciousness. There is also evidence that Emerson's references to the idea of pragmatism and later the profound influence of C. S. Pierce, influenced James' own ideas of functionalism. Pierce in particular played a much greater role in American Functionalism than is realized. Dewey introduced Adolf Meyer to Pierce's work when Meyer was at Chicago in 1893 or '94, and Meyer later gives credit to Pierce and James for the pragmatic emphasis Meyer placed on his psycho-bio-social model of treatment in psychiatry. (E. Taylor, personal communication, 1981)

A complete history of clinical functionalism will need to range very widely, into philosophy, political theory, and psychiatry to mention just three arenas that are beyond the boundaries of this book. But it is very important to keep in mind that the theory and practice that is described here as "modern eclectic therapy" derives from a very broad intellectual and social context. Just as recent studies of psychoanalysis have shown Freud's indebtedness to Judaism (Bakan, 1958), I am sure later studies of functionalism will show an American tradition going back to Emerson, Thoreau, and the pragmatic revolutionaries such as Franklin, Paine, and Jefferson in the late 1700s.

James's Ideas about Habits, the Self, and the Healthy Personality

One of the most attractive features of James's theorizing is how much he interrelates every psychological topic. He is the antithesis of the "nothing but" kind of theorist. Also characteristic of Jamesian psychology is the connecting of ideas and applications. James, no matter how abstract or abstruse the subject, always tries to find practical applications.

For example, in Chapter 4 of the *Principles* on "Habit" James discusses the enormous influence that repetition has on all organic behavior. In characteristically lively language he says,

> Every smallest stroke of virtue or of vice leaves its never so little scar. The drunken
> Rip Van Winkle, in Jefferson's play, excuses himself for every fresh dereliction by

saying, "I won't count this time!" Well! he may not count it, and a kind of Heaven may not count it; but it is being counted none the less. Down among his nerve-cells and fibres the molecules are counting it, registering and storing it up to be used against him when the next temptation comes. (James, 1890/1950, Vol. 1, p. 127)

He uses strong language to exhort readers to develop new positive habits,

Never suffer an exception to occur till the new habit is securely rooted in your life. . . . Seize the first possible opportunity to act on every resolution you make. . . . Keep the faculty of effort alive in you by a little gratuitous exercise every day. (James, 1890/1950, Vol. 1, pp. 123, 124)

These admonitions about habits are very far from the sophisticated contemporary learning theories; however, it is well established that behavior therapies are not really based upon learning theory (Breger & McGaugh, 1965; Brewer, 1974). Instead, they are practical programs for change, scientific by virtue of their concern with specified procedures and results, but definitely not theoretically derived applications.

The Self

James's chapter on "The Consciousness of Self" (Chapter 10 in the *Principles*) directly follows his more general chapter on consciousness, Chapter 9, "The Stream of Thought." For James the problems of consciousness and the psychology of the self were closely related.

James begins by defining the "constituents of the self" as: (a) the *material self* (the body, clothes, and physical possessions), (b) the *social self* (the recognition given a person by friends and acquaintances), (c) the *spiritual self* (the person's psychological faculties and dispositions, the inner or subjective being), and (d) the *pure ego* (the central self or self of all the other selves).

He goes on to define the feelings and emotions the different constituents arouse, "self-feelings," and the actions that the different constituents lead to, "self-seeking and self-preservation."

Although James's language seems rather quaint, especially his use of the term *spiritual self,* it is clear that he has devised a very useful therapeutic framework that involves different kinds of self-awareness and the interrelation among awareness, feelings, and actions.

On page 310 James formulates an anticipation of Rotter's and McClellands's social expectency theories complete with a formula:

$$\text{Self-esteem} = \frac{\text{Success}}{\text{Pretensions}}$$

He says, "With no attempt there can be no failure; with no failure no humiliation. So our self feeling in this world depends entirely on what we *back* ourselves to be and do" (James, 1890/1950, Vol. 1, p. 310).

On page 315 he makes a clear distinction between the present self and the ideal or potential self, and discusses the conflicts that arise between the different self constituents.

It is not hard to see James as the precursor of later therapeutic formulations about self-concepts, social self-concepts, and ideal self-concepts in the systems of Carl Rogers and George Kelly.

In another section of this chapter James sounds quite a lot like Albert Ellis discussing rational-emotive therapy or even Meichenbaum on cognitive restructuring therapy.

> To give up pretensions is as blessed a relief as to get them gratified. . . . Many Bostonians . . . would be happier women and men today, if they could once for all abandon the notion of keeping up a Musical Self, and without shame let people hear them call a symphony a nuisance. How pleasant is the day when we give up striving to be young—or slender! . . . Everything added to the Self is a burden as well as a pride. (James, 1890/1950, Vol. 1, p. 311)

Most of the last third of his chapter on the self is taken up with a discussion of pathological conditions and cases such as amnesias, delusions, multiple personalities, and possessions.

James summarizes his discussion of the self this way,

> The consciousness of Self involves a stream of thought, each part of which as 'I' can 1) remember those which went before, and know the things they knew; and[1] emphasize and care paramountly for certain ones among them as *"me"* and *appropriate to these* the rest. The nucleus of the "me" is always the bodily experience felt to be present at the time. (James, 1890/1950, Vol. 1, p. 400)

This emphasis on the felt and changing sense of self is almost identical to the contemporary formulation given by Gendlin in his manual on *Focusing*. The focusing technique (more of which will be presented in Part IV) is designed to be a general method of therapeutic training appropriate for a wide variety of therapeutic orientations and applications. In a personal communication about the degree of influence he had felt from James's functionalism Dr. Gendlin replied,

> I'm all for functional, my theoretical ideas make experiencing an interaction process inherently. I don't think experience is stuff inside a box. I took off from Sullivan who came from Mead and Dewey. (E. Gendlin, personal communication, 1979)

---

[1] For further information concerning James's clinical theories and his influence on clinical movements see Foster (1943), B. Ross (1978), D. Ross (1975), Spoerl (1942), High and Woodward (1980), and Watson (1977).

The Healthy Personality

A persistent theme in James's psychological and philosophical writings is his concern for the perfectability of the personality.

James very much believed in the value and necessity of psychological exercise. When discussing habits he advises,

> *Keep the faculty of effort alive in you by a little gratuitous exercise every day.* That is, be systematically ascetic or heroic in little unnecessary points, do every day or two something for no other reason than that you would rather not do it, so that when the hour of dire need draws nigh, it may find you not unnerved and untrained to stand the test. (James, 1890, Vol. 1, p. 126)

This tradition about the benefits of psychological exercise is a very old one in American and European thought (Benjamin Franklin and Emerson are just two of James's notable precursors). It has, however, never been developed fully in therapeutic applications, but runs throughout the thinking of the early clinical functionalists.

A little known fact about James's sphere of influence is that his ideas indirectly influenced the founding and organization of the Peace Corps. In the late 1930s a Camp William James was established which grew out of the interest among Harvard and Dartmouth students and professors in transforming the Civilian Conservation Corps (CCC) from a temporary relief program into a permanent national peacetime organization. Camp William James was a leadership camp within the CCC. It was disbanded because of World War II but later became the model for Vista and the Peace Corps (see E. Taylor, 1980a). The original Camp William James included an emphasis not only on leadership and communication but on various forms of personal inward discipline. Every camp for young people seems to be loaded with calisthenics, sports, and games but this was one of the first to emphasize psychological exercises.

In a little known paper on "The Religion of Healthy Mindedness" written about Walt Whitman, James elaborated on his own ideas about the connections between psychological health and happiness:

> If, then, we give the name of healthy mindedness to the tendency which looks on all things and sees that they are good, we find that we must distinguish between a more involuntary and a more voluntary or systematic way of being healthy-minded. In its involuntary variety, healthy mindedness is a way of feeling happy about things immediately. In a systematical variety, it is an abstract way of conceiving things as good. (James, 1964, p. 251)

William James sought to cultivate the involuntary kind of healthy mindedness and tended to distrust philosophical systems that posited everything as good.

On the practical side, in what might be called applied ethics, William James was a pivotal influence in the establishment of both Alcoholics Anonymous and the Mental Hygiene Movement of William Beers (see E. Taylor, 1980b). Both of these organizations placed a central emphasis on creating new habits from new beliefs and on the significance of moral choices related to new images of health.

Ethics and Therapy

James's concern with how best to live is at the very heart of his philosophy and, I contend, at the heart of all psychotherapy. He counseled a broad-minded, pluralistic ethics that recognized that the feelings and objects and ideas dearest and closest to one person might leave another person cold. Each individual must find his or her own best choices, again and again, throughout life. This credo can well be a guide for modern therapists who live in a society even more diverse than that of James. London (1964), Mowrer (1961), and other contemporary therapists have cogently argued that therapists must recognize the moral dimensions of psychotherapy. In no forerunner is this moral dimension more clearly or more fully explored than in the philosophical writings of William James.

In the book *Philosophy in America* the philosophers Anderson and Fisch (1939) evaluate James's significance for moral philosophy,

> James, placing thought and belief at the mid-section of the reflex arc, saw that because of the exigencies of action there were forced options of belief in which the evidence was not, and perhaps never could be, sufficient to determine a choice. Confinement of belief within evidence would result in a paralysis of action, whereas the function of belief is to facilitate it. The adventure of belief beyond evidence might uncover evidence that would otherwise remain hidden, and at least in the case of belief about a future which depended in some measure upon the will, it might actually create evidence in its own support. . . . Whereas classic empiricism had emphasized the blindness of non-evidential belief to negative evidence, James emphasized its generation of positive evidence. (1939, p. 523)

Neurosis might be grossly defined as the "paralysis of action" that comes from the inability to generate positive actions and feelings. Every clinician must be concerned with understanding how clients can be reengaged in the "adventure of belief" that is living.

William James as Therapist

To picture William James at work as a therapist will require some imagination. He wrote no case histories, consequently there is no specific information about the techniques he used or the clinical inferences he made or the advice he gave his clients.

However, from the archival information about what James read, from his letters, and from his own psychological and philosophical writings, a tentative profile of William James as a therapist can be constructed:

> He would very likely have made use of hypnosis, free association, cathartic techniques, history taking, and the "talking cure." He would have been concerned about his clients' feelings and emotions as well as their thoughts, symptoms, and life circumstances. He would have paid attention to conscious, subconscious, and unconscious determinants of psychopathology. In one way or another, he would have emphasized that each client's willful choice of certain beliefs and habitual actions creates repetitive moods and outcomes. He would have been very concerned that his clients learn to explore the subliminal side of their own awareness, both for protection against negative tendencies and for guidance toward emergent positive tendencies. He might have discussed religious and philosophical questions with his clients. Since he was a physician he could occasionally have made use of both mood changing and cathartic drugs. Finally, he would have counseled his clients to be concerned about their psychological health in general, beyond the removal of specific symptoms and complaints, and he would have encouraged them in programs of psychological exercise.

What emerges from this imaginary sketch of "William James—Psychotherapist" is a picture of an early eclectic. Psychotherapy has not progressed so far that William James would be out of place, with a crash reading course and a few workshops, among modern eclectic therapists.

Overall, Wilbert McKeachie's (1976) reassessment of James's importance for educational psychology can be applied equally to his significance for contemporary psychotherapy:

> *Talks to Teachers on Psychology* were for years the most useful advice on education available from psychology. . . . It many ways, James' advice seems less dated today than it did a generation ago. His sensible, rather cognitive approach would not be rejected by modern theorists with the amused disdain that S-R theorists of a generation ago would have shown. (pp. 821–825)

Modern psychotherapists have recovered from the one-sided theoretical excesses of both the psycboanalytic and the behavioral theorists. This generation of therapists has more in common with William James than with either Freud or Watson.

In summary, there are six major points of confluence and influence between James's ideas and modern therapeutic theories and practices.

1. James emphasized working on both the conscious and subconscious determinants of behavior and personality change.

2. James emphasized feelings as highly significant mediators of conscious personality change.

3. James stressed the importance of choice, will, and purposiveness in bringing about life changes.

4. James's theoretical level of discourse stayed very close to what could be used in everyday life.

5. James gave careful attention to all the nuances and subtleties within the "stream of consciousness." The acquisition of this sensitive inner attentiveness is, in itself, a central aim of most therapeutic endeavors.

6. James stressed the importance of psychological exercise and the cultivation of psychological health to offset the clinician's focus on psychopathology.

4

The Clinical Eclecticism of
Pierre Janet

William James and Pierre Janet had much in common: (a) both taught philosophy (although Janet moved from philosophy to medicine and psychology, while James's career moved in the other direction); (b) both had medical training; (c) both participated fully in the widest intellectual currents of their times (one of Janet's closest colleagues was Bergson); (d) both were academics; and (e) both came from upper middle class backgrounds that provided a significant range of intellectual and social contacts and financial stability.

However, the differences between their careers are of equal importance. Janet was primarily a clinician and secondarily a philosopher while James was primarily a philosopher and only tertiarily a clinician. Both wrote books about philosophy and psychology, but Janet's greatest contributions are centered around clinical case studies. James's contributions to clinical work are largely indirect, through his ideas about pragmatism and functionalism which influenced others.

Although James is well known by most students and clinicians, he is simply unknown as a theorist of relevance for therapists. For that reason, Chapter 3 provided only those details of his life and thought that are not generally discussed in books on the history of psychology. Janet is almost entirely unknown, either as a clinician or as an historical figure of importance in early psychology and psychiatry. Not until Ellenberger's *Discovery of the Unconscious* (1970) did the modern reevaluation of Janet's system of psychotherapy really begin.

Because many of the important clinical writings of Pierre Janet have not yet been translated into English, this chapter relies heavily upon the summaries and evaluations of his work provided by Ellenberger (1970) and Ey (1968).

Janet was born (1859) and died (1947) in Paris. His life spanned two world wars, plus the Franco-German war of 1870. The key dates of his life were: 1889, when he received his Ph.D., 1893 when he received his M.D., his marriage in 1894 to Marguerite Duchesne, and his Professorship of Experimental Psychology at the College de France in 1902 (which he held until 1935). Janet maintained an active clinical practice throughout his years of teaching. He was a contemporary and colleague of Alfred Binet, the inventor of the intelligence test. (In fact, both Janet and Binet competed for the teaching appointment at the College de France, which Janet obtained.)

Janet's Early Theories of Hysteria

To comprehend fully how unappreciated Janet is today among psychotherapists, it is necessary to comprehend the preeminence of French clinical work at the turn of the century. Freud went to study in France with the great French hypnotist Charcot. In 1895 when Breuer and Freud (1957) first published *Studies in Hysteria*, Janet had already written his medical dissertation in 1893 on *The Mental State of Hysterics* (see Ellenberger, 1970, p. 341). It is not surprising that Ey says,

> As the inheritor of a long French philosophical tradition greatly influenced by English and American ideas and work, Janet—like all Frenchman of that period—would not think of letting himself be influenced by anything coming from Germany. . . . Janet's systematic and rather suspicious misappreciation of Freud was, moreover, largely mutual on Freud's part. (1968, p. 177)

When Janet did attend directly to Freud's work he did not do so cordially. He believed Freud had borrowed extensively, without acknowledgement, from his own articles and his book on hysteria. When Janet did comment upon this publicly at the 1913 International Congress of Medicine in London he was caustic in his criticisms: first, he claimed priority for the cathartic method applied to hysterics through the clarification of traumatic memories and second, he criticized Freud's later methods of symbolically interpreting dreams and his theories of the sexual etiology of neuroses. In print Janet was also extremely critical of Freud's approach:

> He [Freud] granted the truth of the facts and published some new observations of the same kind. In these publications he changed first of all the terms that I was using; what I had called psychological analysis he called psychoanalysis; what I had called psychological system, in order to designate that totality of facts of consciousness and movement, whether of members or of viscera, he called complex; he considered repression what I considered restriction of consciousness; what I referred to as a

> psychological dissociation, or as moral fumigation, he baptized with the name of catharsis. But above all he transformed a clinical observation and a therapeutic treatment with a definite and limited field of use into an enormous system of medical philosophy. (Janet, 1924, pp. 41–42)

Janet goes on to discuss Freud's theories and methods for several pages and then concludes his criticism with the remark, "Psychoanalysis is today the last incarnation of those practices at once magical and psychological that characterized magnetism" (Janet, p. 46).

With the hindsight of 50 years it is possible to see that Janet and Freud, like James and Freud, often were working on different problems. Analysts are more interested in tracing the influence of the unconscious on pathology while functionalists are most interested in studying the influence of the subconscious and conscious on everyday life and on maturation.

Janet termed his methods "psychological analysis" and "psychological synthesis"; he gave equal weight to the tracing and release of symptoms and to cognitive re-education. His analytic methods in working with hysterics included hypnotic suggestion, "automatic writing," and "automatic talking" (both of these methods closely resemble Freud's method of free association).

Janet's case reports make it clear that he did far more than work toward simple abreactions; for example, in the case of Marie who suffered from blindness in the left eye, Janet remarks:

> I put her back with the child who had so horrified her; I make her believe that the child is very nice and does not have impetigo (she is half-convinced. After two reenactments of this scene I get the best of it); she caresses without fear the imaginary child. The sensitivity of the left eye reappears without difficulty, and when I wake her up, Marie sees clearly with the left eye. It is now five months since these experiments were performed. Marie has never shown the slightest signs of hysteria. She is doing well and is above all becoming stronger. Her physical aspect has changed thoroughly. I do not attach to this case more importance than it deserves, and I do not know how long it will last, but I found this story interesting as showing the importance of subconscious ideas and the role they play in certain physical illnesses, as well as in emotional illnesses. (Cited in Ellenberger, 1970, p. 364)

This excerpt shows clearly that Janet was using, under hypnosis, corrective abreactions and not simply reliving the traumatic scene. His method here resembles the directed daydreaming techniques used later by Desoille and Assagioli and to some extent the methods of Perls and Moreno.

Janet accumulated more than five thousand of his own case studies, all of which contained minute observations. Early in his career he formulated three guidelines for his work: First, to always examine his patients personally and not rely upon secondhand observations and to examine them without witnesses who might influence their responses (to avoid the errors of his mentor Charcot); second, to make an exact record of everything they said and did (Janet called this the "fountain pen method"); and third, to scrutinize the entire life history of the patients and their past treatments. In these precepts Janet very much resembles Thorne (see Chapter 6, and *The Principles of Psychological Examining*, Thorne, 1955).

In 1906 Janet delivered 15 lectures at Harvard University which were later assembled into a book titled *The Major Symptoms of Hysteria* (1929). I will quote at length from Janet's descriptions of the case of Marceline to give a full impression of his clinical astuteness:

> Long ago, in 1887, a young woman of twenty, whose name was Marceline, entered the hospital in a lamentable state. For several months past she had not taken any food; first because she obstinately refused to eat, then because she immediately vomited any food or drink one forced her to swallow. Besides, she no longer had any function of evacuation; she was incapable of urinating spontaneously, and sounding alone could cause her to discharge a few drops of urine. In these conditions, this young woman, who had reached the last stage of emaciation, seemed to have but a breath of life left; she remained constantly lying in her bed, being incapable of standing. Her mental activity was as much reduced as her physical activity; she was completely insensible on the whole surface of her skin and on all her mucous membranes; she heard very badly and saw but exceedingly little. Though she looked intelligent, she replied with great indifference to the questions put to her, and seemed to be in a serious state of stupefaction. As we did not succeed in nourishing her otherwise, we had to try the effect of hypnotic practice.
>
> After some attempts we easily caused her to enter into a singular state, which appeared momentary and artificial, but differed altogether from the habitual state in which we had constantly seen her since her entrance into the hospital. She looked quite transformed physically and morally. She was now capable of moving, she accepted any food, and had no longer any vomiting. Lastly, she urinated spontaneously, without difficulty. On the other hand, she had become sensitive over her entire body, and could hear and see perfectly; she expressed herself much better, with more vivacity, and showed a complete memory of all her anterior life. After having nourished her in this new state, we thought it necessary to awaken her, since this state was considered artificial. She immediately fell back into her preceding state. Inert, insensible, unable to eat or urinate, she simply presented one more disturbance; namely according to the law of somnambulisms, which you know, she had quite forgotten what had happened during the preceding period.
>
> Nevertheless, thanks to these artificial somnambulisms, we were able to nourish her and cause her to recover her strength. But it was always impossible to make her eat in the period considered normal, which we always brought back by awakening her. So that, tired of thus putting her to sleep at each meal, which was very long, we left her for whole days in the artificial state. The only result was apparently a great advantage, since all day she ate well, urinated completely, and presented more sensibility, memory, and activity. One day her parents, finding her in this fine artificial state, considered her cured, and took her out of the hospital.

Everything went well during the first days; but, after a few weeks, on the occasion of her menstrual period, she experienced a kind of upsetting, and awoke spontaneously, that is to say, she suddenly returned to the state of depression and stupefaction from which we had drawn her, but she presented, in addition, a forgetfulness bearing, this time, on whole weeks. She was very much bewildered at finding herself in her house without understanding how she had left the hospital, for she did not remember the events of the preceding days. Besides, she again refused to eat, and could not urinate. Marceline was brought back to me, and, in the presence of all these disturbances, which were well known to me, I could do nothing else but put her to sleep again, or rather bring her back to her artificial state.

Well, gentlemen, things continued in this way for fifteen years. Marceline would come to me in order to be put to sleep, enter into her alert state, and then go away very happy, with complete activity, sensibility, and memory. She would remain thus for a few weeks; then, either slowly or suddenly, in consequence of some emotion, fall back into her numbness, return to the state we had considered primitive and natural, with the same visceral disturbances. The forgetfulness now extended over whole years, and disturbed her existence completely. She would hasten to come to me to get herself transformed again. Things continued thus for years together, till the death of the poor girl, who succumbed to pulmonary tuberculosis. How are the two states of Marceline to be explained? . . . The essential phenomenon that, in my opinion, is at the basis of these double existences, is a kind of *oscillation of mental activity*, which falls and rises suddenly. These sudden changes, without sufficient transition, bring about two different states of activity; the one higher, with a particular exercise of all the senses and functions; the other lower, with a great reduction of all the cerebral functions. These two states separate from each other; they cease to be connected together, as with normal individuals, through gradations and remembrances. They become isolated from each other, and form these two separate existences. Here, again, there is a mental dissociation more complicated than the preceding ones. There is dissociation, not only of an idea, not only of a feeling, but of one mental state of activity. (Janet, 1929, pp. 86–92)

Janet, Freud, James, and most other theorists and therapists of their time were fascinated by hysteria. The reason was that hysterics showed more clearly and dramatically than other patients the dual nature of consciousness. Hysterics also demonstrated how little influence normal consciousness and the functions of normal consciousness (willing, thinking, planning, attending, etc.) had on the patient's symptoms. Hysterics seemed to reveal directly the underside or infrastructure of consciousness (what James called the "subliminal," Freud the "unconscious," and Janet the "subconscious").

The most famous single case study to convey the idea of dual consciousness was Morton Prince's *The Dissociation of Personality* (1905/1957).[1]

---

[1] For a discussion of the clinical study of multiple personalities in the United States consult Carlson (1981). He traces the use of the concept back to Benjamin Rush who wrote about his ideas and clinical findings in 1811 and 1812. Rush suggested that the mind may occupy two hemispheres.

Prince and Janet were close friends and colleagues. Prince received his
M.D. degree from Harvard in 1879; he was Professor of Nervous Diseases
at Tufts College Medical School from 1902 to 1912, from 1926 to 1929 he
was Associate Professor of Abnormal and Dynamic Psychology at Harvard. Prince was influenced by and in turn influenced both Janet and
James. (As mentioned in the previous chapter, he established the first
psychological clinic at Harvard and was an important member of the
Boston Group of Psychotherapists.) Prince's case study of "Miss Bea-
champ" was at the time more famous than Freud's and Jung's case
studies. His book established the fascination of the general public and
the media with multiple personalities which has continued to the present.

Prince's book was successful because he chose to present the medical and psychological disorders in the context of a full biography of the
patient. (He was the forerunner of the life study method of Murray,
Allport, and, more recently, White.)

Prince describes his method this way:

> In this study I have (a) traced the development of the different personalities which
> originated through the disintegration of the normal self, and (b) shown their psycho-
> logical relations to one another and to the normal self. By giving (c) a detailed account
> of the daily life of the personalities, after the manner of a biography, I have sought
> to show their behavior to the environment and the way in which a disintegrated
> personality can adapt itself to the circumstances of life, and how it fails to do so. . . . By
> departing from the customary way of treating these phenomena and introducing them
> in the course of a biography, I have been enabled to present them without removing
> them from their psychological setting. (Prince, 1905/1957, pp. v–vi)

Prince's method, which is paralleled in Janet's long case studies,
was necessitated by a theory of psychopathology that stressed that *symptoms are the restricted functioning of normal psychological processes.* To clearly
observe and understand restricted functioning it is necessary to comprehend a client's normal functioning.

Janet had proposed the concept of dissociation in his Ph.D. dissertation in 1889; the concept was derived from Jean Charcot's theories.
(Janet worked closely with Charcot and took over Charcot's laboratory
upon the death of his teacher in 1893.) Janet used the term *subconscious*
to refer to a level of functioning that was not usually in awareness but
could become conscious. Morton Prince used the term *coconsciousness* to
describe the splitting of normal consciousness into separate parts.

Hilgard is the most important modern theorist to revive the Janetian
concept of dissociation. He suggests that the Freudian concept of the
repressed unconscious and the Janetian concept of the dissociated subconscious are different but not wholly incompatible:

The two conceptions are compatible and can be integrated. . . . The first kind of repression overlaps with amnesia as it is studied in hypnosis. . . . If an actual historical incident—possibly some traumatic experience of childhood—has been forgotten, it may often be again brought to memory through free association. . . . According to the definition of dissociation as unavailable information subject to recovery, this kind of repression classifies as a dissociation. . . . In this [the second] kind of repression, the contents that are conceded have to be *inferred;* they are not recovered directly but are known only through their derivatives. (Hilgard, 1977, pp. 251–252)

One simple clinical implication of this distinction is that hypnosis and drug-induced abreactions and other uncovering methods of treatment will be effective for clients who mainly suffer from dissociations (such as battle traumas) but will not be effective for clients whose disorders are based upon repressed conflictual material arising from early childhood.

A second clinical implication is that clients who can be taught conscious positive functions to offset their neurotic tendencies are more likely to suffer from dissociative disorders than severe repressions.[2]

Janet was directly influenced by the work of the early Gestalt theorists. His concepts of dissociation, the narrowing of consciousness, and the influence of the subconscious context on thoughts and perception are all very similar to the Gestalt therapy developed by Fritz Perls (see Perls, 1948, 1969a). Both Janet and Perls give equal attention to the *uncovering* of the dissociated emotional contents and the assimilation or resynthesis of those contents.

Janet's Technical Eclecticism

In his *Principles of Psychotherapy* (1924), Janet applies everything from hypnosis to rest cures, from moral re-education to religious instruction,

---

[2] One of the most interesting commentaries on the ideas of Pierre Janet was provided by one of the founders of management and industrial psychology, Elton Mayo. In the dedication of his book on *The Psychology of Pierre Janet* (1952/1972) Mayo states that "In July, 1939, . . . Janet expressed to me his complete conversion to the view that his observations could well be applied to the better understanding of social and industrial situations" (p. v). Mayo and his colleagues at the Harvard University Graduate School of Business Administration pioneered in the use of the case study method in business, a method that Mayo found to be highly developed in the clinical work of Janet: "In the study of the particular situation . . . Janet's guidance has been found . . . most useful" (p. vii). An intriguing direction of thought would be the application of the argument made in this book (that the Janet-James style of functionalism and pragmatism underlies eclecticism in therapy) to the possibility that functionalism and pragmatism provide the background theory for eclecticism in management consulting.

from "talking cures" to "action programs." And even this book does not fully cover Janet's "prodigious ingeniousness." As Ellenberger comments, "one should read many of his short papers" to truly appreciate the range and inventiveness of Janet's clinical methods (see Ellenberger, 1970, p. 351).

The therapeutic methods applied by Janet to the great variety of cases he saw were so diverse as to be almost unteachable. Ellenberger comments on the "almost unlimited variety of his psychotherapeutic devices" (1970, p. 351). He quotes Dr. Ernest Harms who studied with Janet at the Salpetriere clinic,

> I was startled by the set up. . . . When I asked Janet what his therapeutic approach here was I received the strange reply: "I believe those people, until it is proven to me what they say is untrue." I had just faced a young man who avoided stepping into any shadow because, in shadows, roamed Napoleon who wanted to draft him into the army. Beside him was a woman of past 70 who feared persecution from the Mayor of Paris, who wanted to make love to her. I found it difficult to see any truth in such fixed ideas. Janet noticed my perplexity. . . . "You see these people are persecuted by something, and you must investigate carefully to get to the root." What he wanted to make me see was that one ought not to discard persecutional fantasies as ridiculous or view them only symptomatically; one ought to take them seriously and analyze them, until the causal conditions were revealed. (Ellenberger, 1970, p. 351)

On the other hand, Janet was extremely perspicacious and did not take the symptoms and complaints of his patients at all literally: "Most frequently, psychotics are acting. Don't believe one-fourth of what they say. They try to impress you with their grandeur or their guilt, in which they themselves believe only half-heartedly or not at all" (cited in Ellenberger, 1970, p. 351).

Faced with this kind of practical flexibility and with the seemingly infinite variety of techniques that Janet invented and adopted it is, perhaps, not too surprising to find that he had very few students for a therapist and writer of such international stature.

Janet's direct line of influence was largely confined to France. Among his most prominent students was Henri Baruk who was to become a leader of French psychiatry from his position as director of the national mental hospital Charenton which he held for almost 40 years. (Baruk was also the teacher of Ellenberger.) Baruk described Janet as "a brilliant and captivating speaker and one of our great clinicians, a marvelously gifted and warmly humanitarian man, rare in every sense of the word" (Baruk, 1978b, p. 137). These are glowing words, but they seem more descriptive of an artist than of a scientist and clinician. Functionalism has always stayed very close to the artistic, inventive side of clinical work—a characteristic that makes it difficult to learn and to teach.

One of the difficulties of the eclectic approach, for students, is that it is open-ended. It is much easier for a student therapist to apply one basic technique over and over, with variations, than to apply a great variety of techniques. Also, it is much easier to apply a single-level conceptual approach than a general, multilevel theory such as the clinical theory of Janet. One way around these difficulties is developed in Part IV where a manual is provided for a series of therapeutic sessions based upon the general eclectic theory drawn from Part II and spelled out in Part III. By applying the manual as a guideline, student therapists can perhaps gain the benefits of therapeutic variety and eclecticism without getting lost. After all, student therapists cannot very well "wait for more experience"; they must "do something" every session.

Of course, if Janet had been merely a talented inventor of techniques he would not warrant a full chapter in this book. He would be similar to a virtuoso pianist, renowned in his time but forgotten when the next era of virtuosi emerges. But Janet was much more than a virtuoso therapist, he was a composer, a theorist who devised a comprehensive theory that allowed him to apply a vast range of techniques consistently and coherently.

Janet's General Theory

Janet defined neuroses generally as disorders of the various functions of the organism characterized by arrested development, without deterioration of the functions themselves. He discriminated between hysteria, which is characterized by (a) the narrowing of consciousness and (b) the dissociation of psychological functions, and psychasthenia (or obsessions), characterized by (a) the reduction of psychological energy and (b) the exaggeration of inferior functions such as doubts and anxieties. From this definition it is clear that Janet's understanding of psychopathology must depend upon a wide understanding of the *normal* functions of consciousness and behavior. In contrast to Freud, who focused on tracings of the particular pattern and causation of the psychopathological disorder, Janet focused on understanding "the various functions of the organism." In this effort he eventually arrived at a table of the hierarchy of symptoms in relation to the hierarchy of psychological functioning.

Through the years Janet developed several revisions of the hierarchy of functions. His most elaborate formulation divided nine tendencies or functions into three groups:

   I. The Lower Functions
     1. Reflexive tendencies
     2. Perceptive tendencies
     3. Sociopersonal tendencies
     4. Basic intellectual tendencies
  II. The Middle Functions
     5. Immediate actions and assertive beliefs
     6. Actions and beliefs
 III. The Higher Tendencies
     7. Rational tendencies
     8. Experimental tendencies
     9. Progressive tendencies

Janet commented, "If one considers the order of frequency and the speed with which psychical functions are lost in the sick, one observes that they disappear more quickly when their coefficient of reality is higher, and that they persist longer when their coefficient of reality is lower" (cited in Ey, 1968, p. 188).

Baruk, his student and colleague, later extended these observations into experiments with drugs and observed, "bulbocaynine produced no catatonia in the lower vertebraes, which possess no initiative, but only in birds and mammals, which do have initiative and lost it under the effects of this drug" (Baruk, 1978b, p. 40). He also observed that "drugs in small or moderate doses affect the psyche, whereas in large amounts their consequences go beyond that and bring about changes in the neurological system and the structural design of the brain, and lead to paralyses, contractions, or epilepsy" (Baruk, 1978b, p. 59).

Janet placed effective and novel action at the top of the hierarchy, followed by attention, habitual actions, memories, imagination, emotional reactions and, at the bottom, useless muscular movements.

For Janet, as for James, feelings are viewed as regulators of actions. Abnormal conditions indicate a disorganization of the regulators. Psychopathology always indicates a lack of balance and organization in the affects. Unbalanced feelings lead to a regression of action.

Janet placed special emphasis on voluntary action and directed attention, the functions most disturbed by psychopathology and most important in normal functioning:

> These two operations, voluntary action and attention, converge by their own activity to form a synthetic operation. . . . *The formation of the mind in the present moment.* There is a mental faculty which we might call "presentification." (Cited in Ey, 1968, p. 187)

Throughout his clinical and philosophical writings Janet emphasizes the mental operations that allow human beings to grasp reality in the moment; nothing is more psychologically real than the present moment in the stream of consciousness. Psychopathology is most clearly evidenced by gaps in consciousness, gaps that limit the effectiveness of voluntary action and attention.

Both James and Janet emphasize the crucial nexus of the present moment and present functioning (the stream of consciousness with functioning in reality). They also both make use of the concept of psychological energy or "psychological tension." In *Les Neuroses* (1909, p. 363 cited in Ellenberger, 1970, chap. 6) Janet says, "The tension of reality with action and belief (demanding the highest degree of tension) is a phenomenon of high tension; reverie, motor or visceral agitation can be considered as the phenomena of low tension." Janet then goes on the relate observations he made concerning the speed of visual perception under various psychological disorders and expresses the hope that eventually these fluctuations in tension will be related to brain physiology. (Interestingly, the first crucial psychophysiological experiments concerning the effects of psychopathology on visual functioning were conducted by the functionalist pioneer discussed in the next chapter, Trigant Burrow.)

Psychological tension may be defined as the person's present ability to apply his or her psychic energy at a higher level in the hierarchy of functions. For example, when awakening from a nap in a hotel room could the person quickly shift to an accurate and effective perception of what to do and how to do it if a fire alarm were ringing? The person who immediately returned to sleep or the person who begins to yell "fire" would not be functioning in an optimum way.

When teaching patients and students about psychological tension Janet liked to use the analogy of psychological energy to psychological economy. When dealing with any neurotic patient, Janet advised, the first concern should be to evaluate thoroughly the patient's resources and expenditures. The therapist must then consider, equally, three directions of treatment: increasing the patient's psychological income, decreasing the patient's expenditures, and liquidating old debts that deplete the resources.

In his famous essay on "The Energies of Men" originally published in 1907 James discusses the work of both Janet and Prince. He makes the important point that it is not only psychopathological patients who suffer from psychological energy fluctuations but normals as well: "We are each and all of us to some extent victims of habit-neurosis. We have to admit the wider potential range and the habitually narrow actual use. We live subject to arrest by degrees of fatigue which we have come only from habit to obey. Most of us may learn to push the barrier farther off, and to have perfect comfort on much higher levels of power" (James, 1907/1962, p. 675).

What Janet called "progressive tendencies" represent the highest levels of individual and innovative functioning. One of Janet's favorite expressions was, "We grow in time like plants in space." He believed, as did James and Bergson, that the evolution of human beings is open toward the future. At the level of the progressive tendencies a person contributes to both his own development and to the development of humanity.

In James and Janet can be recognized the early conceptualizations of the human potential movement that was developed 70 years later in the work of such humanistic psychologists as Carl Rogers, Abraham Maslow, and Roberto Assagioli. One enduring feature of functional therapy and functional psychology is the effort to understand psychopathology by understanding positive or maximal functioning. The functionalists tend to use the study of suprafunctioning just as much in their approach to therapy as they do the study of pathological and normal functioning.

Janet, and later his disciple Dr. Leonhard Schwartz, developed a testing method for the combined evaluation and training of psychological functioning that in many remarkable ways anticipated the modern cognitive behavioral emphasis on task-specific testing and the interactionalist position in personality assessment. The underlying principle of their psychotechnic training was to teach the patient to perform a complete action that requires a high degree of voluntary attention and action. The method, which is repeated with many variations, proceeds in four steps:

1. First measure the level at which a patient is able to achieve a certain prescribed action.
2. Then have the patient execute a complete task of that kind, first slowly and carefully, then more quickly but always perfectly, continuing until the task can be conducted with no difficulty.
3. Then shift the patient to work of a higher level.
4. Finally, find whole groupings of similar activities that will constitute good investments of psychological energy for the patient.

Janet remarks, "The completed and terminated act heightens the psychological tension of the individual, while an incomplete and unachieved act lowers it" (cited in Ellenberger, 1970, p. 384).

What is remarkable in these early functionalist techniques and concepts is that they anticipate so many bridgings between modern camps such as cognitive therapy and humanistic therapy. Part of this tendency toward eclectic bridging arises, I believe, from the conceptual level that Janet and James used to explain psychological functioning. By linking *consciousness, gaps* in consciousness, and *levels* of functioning they direct their focus at the *forms* of behavior. Patterns of behavior are always linked, in the functionalist approach, with a level of consciousness and level of reality sensing. The functionalists avoid both the overly molecular analysis of S-R behaviorism and the overly speculative analyses about unconscious mechanisms required by psychoanalysis. As it turns out, this conceptual "middle way" provides the broadest road for clinicians to apply to therapy.

For Janet psychopathology is a failure of development, a kind of immaturity. Ey remarks,

> His entire psychopathology is based on the idea of a *development*, of a psychosocial *autogenesis* of the psychic being. It is the alteration of this functional structure which, by not attaining maturity or maintaining itself at a normal level, produces a collapse of the behavior patterns and of the feelings which constitute the neurotic symptoms. (1968, p. 194)

Janet was concerned early on with what became ego psychology and, later, self psychology in psychoanalysis.

The Problem of Intentionality

By setting up his hierarchy of functions in terms of "tendencies," which are dispositions to action, Janet assigned priority to the problem of intentionality. Of all the large unfinished problems facing contemporary psychology and clinical psychology, the problem of intentionality is perhaps the most crucial just because it has been neglected for so many years. The behaviorist position dismisses concerns about intentionality because its focus is on automatic contingencies. The analytic position undermines concerns about intentionality through its focus on unconscious motivation.

Clinicians must be concerned with intentions—what they are and how they work. They also must be concerned about the conditions that cause a paralysis or malfunctioning of the functions of choosing, willing, and planning. Every client who comes to therapy arrives at the therapist's office, basically, because he or she is unable to carry out choices effectively. Most alcoholics, at some level, want to stop drinking; addicts want to stay off drugs; phobics want to act without fear or despite their fears; obsessives want to stop their unproductive thoughts. In all of these clinical conditions, and in most others, the patients *want* to function better. Many even have some specific plans but cannot carry out either their desires or their plans. Intentionality, and disturbances of intentionality, are at the core of psychopathology no matter what the etiology, symptoms, or circumstances.

Janet's "theory of tendencies" discusses the dangers of inferior functions that diminish the organism's sense of reality. "Assertive beliefs," in Janet's system, are beliefs that attach to whatever is thought or imaged. (These inferior functions are similar to Freud's primary process thinking.) Such beliefs can only be offset by the operation of a higher function "reflection" which, Janet says, "reproduces within ourselves the discussion of an assembly" (cited in Ey, 1968, p. 193).

At the highest levels of development the functions

> are characterized by a particular distribution of strength: They do not limit themselves to the use of accumulated strength in the inferior tendencies, they draw their strength from a special reserve in order to add it to the ideas which are not strong in themselves. A man of character is capable of executing his decisions, his promises, his commitments, even if this decision affords him no actual satisfaction. Morality consists of choosing one's duty. There must be a reserve of special strength to make a man capable of executing an action in this manner. (Janet, cited in Ey, 1968, p. 193)

Janet is clearly talking about something quite different from sublimation. He is arguing for a psychology of morality, based upon a consciously sensed moral imperative that derives energy from the higher progressive function rather than directing energy from lower functions.

Baruk flatly states that "Psychiatry is an essentially moral discipline" and bemoans the fact that "the evolution of psychiatry has caused the moral aspect to be neglected in favor of purely technical solutions" (1978b, pp. 56, 57). There is no doubt that the best way for young therapists to make names for themselves is to concentrate on techniques and limited concepts. The young therapist who becomes deeply involved in philosophical and social concerns will, most likely, be viewed by his or her more straight-line colleagues and superiors as fuzzy-headed and impractical. But, if Baruk and Janet and James and the other functionalist pioneers are correct, morality is the heart and soul of therapy.

Baruk developed a test of moral conscience that he called the "Tsedek" after the Hebrew word meaning charity and justice. The test contains 15 items that describe hypothetical situations involving conscience in which the individual must weigh personal feelings against social necessity and moral obligation.

Here are two examples of items from the test:

1. In a time of emergency, food is in short supply. Rationing is based on the following rules: Very large portions for persons in good health who can work and produce, very small rations for the aged or ill who can contribute nothing. Is this fair?
2. A backward child who does not know how to defend himself is bullied by his schoolmates. Those who would like to help are afraid to do so, lest they be bullied in turn. How would you judge them?

In interviews conducted with his colleague Bachet, Baruk found that between 80% to 90% of normal subjects had a very clear feeling of the difference between right and wrong. They did not believe one human being had a right to sacrifice another. Different types of moral judgment were discerned, from simple emotional judgments to unjust and double judgments. Some subjects gave what Baruk described as "well-rounded" or "synthesized" judgment: "Instead of looking at the test situations from a single point of view, or considering what was practical against what was not, these subjects joined heart to intelligence" (Baruk, 1978b, p. 225). Baruk's observations of levels and types of morality conform closely with Janet's theories. (In Chapter 12 in the section on "Psychological Fitness" the modern research and theory of Dabrowski, which shows definite confluences with the theories and observations of Janet and Baruk, will be reviewed.)

For Janet, as for James, when moral psychology is extended to its limits it becomes a search not only for the role of morality in indiviual's lives but for a "science of peace," a way to help the nations and peoples of the world live together in justice and harmony. The great unsolved problem of therapy is connected to the great unsolved problem of humanity.

Janet (1930) contributed a short autobiography to Murchison's first volume of *A History of Psychology in Autobiography*. He said of himself, "At the age of eighteen I was very religious, and I have always retained mystical tendencies which I have succeeded in controlling. It was a question of conciliating scientific tastes and religious sentiments, which was not an easy task. The conciliation could have been affected by means of a perfect philosophy satisfying both reason and faith. I have not found this miracle, but I have remained a philospher" (Janet, 1930, p. 123). In Janet, as in James, this fundamental concern with the wider meanings of life became most clearly expressed in a theory of the role of will and belief in psychological development, what Janet calls a "psychology of conduct" (p. 132).

Conclusion

As the ideas and clinical studies of Pierre Janet continue to be reappraised and, hopefully, assimilated into the general eclectic approach of modern times, we can expect that Ey's conclusion about Janet's work will become more widely appreciated: "The work of Pierre Janet does not belong only to the past" (Ey, 1968, p. 195).

5

The Iconoclastic Eclecticism of Trigant Burrow

There are two kinds of history: popular history and critical history. The first might be called surface history; it is taught in schools and preserved in calendars; it is always organized around single dates, names, and places—"In 1492 Columbus sailed the ocean blue." Critical or scholarly history looks more deeply into influences and conditions and numbers of people. From critical history we learn about the multitude of influences and cross-influences that shaped the past and continue to emerge in the present. We learn about inconsistencies and discrepancies and mixed, tentative historical interpretations. Popular history tends to be fixed while critical history always is being reformulated as new influences are discovered and new interpretations are offered and as happenings in the present give a different weighting to what is more and less important.

The popular history of psychotherapy still places Freud as the discoverer of the unconscious and the founder of modern therapy. However scholarly evaluations by Whyte (1962) and Ellenberger (1970), to name just two, have shown that there were many competing theories of the unconscious before Freud and that the tradition of somnambulistic healing in the 1700s and 1800s provided a significant precursor to modern therapy. In my view, the modern shift toward eclecticism among therapists is likely to bring about a reassignment of historical weightings so that Trigant Burrow, who is now largely unknown and ignored, will be reappraised and found to be of great significance for contemporary therapy.[1]

[1] I thank Mrs. Alfreda Galt, secretary of the Lifwynn Foundation, for supplying information and publications about phyloanalysis. For readers who want more information about Burrow's writings and research and information about the current activities of the Foundation its address is: 30 Turkey Hill Road South, Westport, Connecticut 06880.

Burrow's total obscurity is, in some ways, hard to comprehend. He authored, between 1909 and 1950, almost 70 articles and chapters and published four books. In 1911 he helped to found the American Psychoanalytic Association and in 1925 he was its president. During his lifetime Burrow carried on an unusually large correspondence with the most famous intellectual figures of the time, including Freud, Jung, Adler, D. H. Lawrence, Sherwood Anderson, Adolf Meyer, C. K. Ogden, and Count Korzybski.

The quick answer for Burrow's obscurity might be that he simply had nothing enduring to add. Or it might be argued that he delimited the range of his influence because of the inaccessibility of his writing style. This second possibility is certainly plausible. Sentences full of such terms as *phyloanalysis, ditention, cotention,* and *organismic morphology* are not likely to attract a wide readership. But why was Burrow's work ignored by most professionals?

My own opinion is that Burrow's contributions were real and important but were much too advanced for his time. He provides a classic example of a thinker who was offering a paradigm shift (Kuhn, 1977) that was too far ahead of his contemporaries to receive serious consideration. After all, psychoanalysis was still struggling for professional recognition when Burrow was stating, "Psychoanalysts are themselves as neurotic and confused as their patients" (Burrow, 1958, p. 82). Burrow was a man going against the zeitgeist not with it. There is ample evidence that he was not merely ignored but was professionally attacked and ostracized. In 1933 this former president of the APA was dropped from membership and was then refused regional membership in the New York Psychoanalytic Association.

One characteristic of critical history is that it is always being rewritten. Just as Boring's history books and papers essentially wrote applied psychology out of importance in the 1920s, by overemphasizing laboratory experimentalism (O'Donnell, 1979), so did the early histories of clinical psychology and psychiatry write off Burrow through their overemphasis on individual psychoanalysis and its variations. It should be obvious that critical history is sometimes no more objective than popular history; it is simply more detailed and complex. Indeed critical history often is used to elevate one paradigm to importance and submerge others. In short, history serves a modeling function for the present and future as much or more as it serves to chronicle events from the past. (That is why I am spending so many pages early in this book to offer a different perspective on the history of therapy. I want to offset popular impressions and argue against some of the accepted scholarly interpretations of the field.)

Some Facts about Trigant Burrow

Before going on to describe Burrow's basic ideas, methods, and findings, I will briefly mention some of the key events of his life. He was born September 7, 1875. He received his M.D. from the University of Virginia in 1899 and his Ph.D. in 1909 from Johns Hopkins in experimental psychology. At Hopkins he studied with Dr. George Stratton and Dr. Knight Dunlap and was directly exposed to functionalism through Professor James Mark Baldwin and Dr. Adolf Meyer. In later years Burrow identified a philosophical seminar he took with Baldwin as the turning point in his professional life.

> Professor James Mark Baldwin was speaking of the field of mental disorders, and I recall his mentioning the names of Charcot, Janet, Forel and other prominent European psychiatrists. But he said that none of them had as yet "ignited the spark" requisite to bring about an understanding of the basic course of mental disease. This interested me, and I remember that I then and there recorded the pledge to devote my life's work to the effort to contribute what I could towards igniting this spark necessary to throw light on the nature of abnormal mental conditions. (Burrow, 1958, p. 17)

At age 29, in 1904, Burrow married Emily Sherwood Bryon; they had two children (John and Emily) who later were to assist Burrow in his work. When Freud and Jung came to the United States to lecture in 1909 Burrow met them and was exceedingly impressed with their ideas. Between 1909 and 1910 he packed his family off to Zurich where he studied and underwent a personal analysis with Jung.

Later, when Jung split from Freud, Burrow avoided siding with either of them, although he was theoretically more sympathetic to the position of Freud on the personal unconscious rather than Jung's on the collective unconscious.

When Burrow returned from Europe he established a very successful private practice of psychoanalysis in Baltimore and served on the psychiatric staff at Johns Hopkins and at Meyer's Phipps Psychiatric Clinic. As mentioned earlier, Burrow was a founding member of the American Psychoanalytic Association and, later, in 1925 president. He delivered 15 papers to the Association between 1921 and 1927. He also presented 24 papers to the American Psychopathological Association during the period 1913 to 1944. Even before founding the American Psychoanalytic Association Burrow was an active member of the American Psychological Association; he often contributed papers to the psychological journals. Trigant Burrow was among the first professionals to be fully trained in both psychoanalysis and experimental psychology. His publications span medical, psychoanalytic, sociological, clinical, and experimental journals.

By 1921 Burrow had become disaffected with the techniques and concepts of traditional psychoanalysis. He gave up the security of his private practice and professional life to embark upon a social experiment. In 1923 Burrow and his psychological assistant Clarence Shields established Lifwynn Camp, with about 20 other people, to study group analysis. In 1927 they organized the Lifwynn Foundation to carry on the work of group analysis. A few years later, in 1929, they undertook a series of psychophysiological studies that intersected the work of their social laboratory. This group work and physiological research, along with writing and lecturing, occupied Burrow until his death in 1950.

Anyone reading this chronicle of Burrow's life will be startled by the discontinuity that appeared in 1921. It is astounding to hear of a man giving up his financial stability (and along with that the stability of his home life) to engage in a "social experiment." Burrow was precipitated into this drastic move by an astonishing personal event that arose in the course of his analysis of Mr. Clarence Shields in 1918. Burrow described the incident this way:

> Having years ago been "analyzed" in preparation for my work in psychopathology, I had for years duly "analyzed" others. It unexpectedly happened one day, however, that while I was interpreting a dream of a student–assistant, he made bold to challenge the honesty of my analytic position, insisting that . . . the test of my sincerity would be met only when I should myself be willing to accept from him the same analytic exactions I was now imposing upon others. As may be readily judged such a proposition seemed to me nothing short of absurd. . . . Needless to say I had heard this proposal from patients many times before, but while my reaction to the suggestion in the present instance was chiefly one of amusement, my pride was not a little picqued at the intimation it conveyed. So with the thought that in the interest of experiment it could at least do no harm to humour for a time the waywardness of inexperience, I conceded the arrangement. (Burrow, 1958, p. 45)

It would be easy to dismiss this "arrangement" as an example of the analytic errors that counter-transference can provoke. However, it is also interesting to note that Freud and Jung frequently engaged in mutual dream analysis, and according to Jung (1961), part of the personal reason for their breakup was Freud's unwillingness to reveal fully his associations to all of his dreams.

Whatever the interpretation of Burrow and Shields's mutual analysis, it became the basis of Burrow's lifelong involvement with social analysis and led to his abandonment of individual analysis. "I saw what has been for me the crucial revelation of the many years of my analytic work—that, in its individualistic application, the attitude of the psychoanalyst and the attitude of the authoritarian are inseparable" (Burrow, 1958, p. 45).

Once both Burrow and Shields fully accepted the resistances and urges to dominate that they shared in the role of the analyst,

> The direction of the inquiry was completely altered. The analysis henceforth consisted in the reciprocal effort of each of us to recognize within himself his attitude of authoritarianism and autocracy toward the other . . . and its replacement by a more inclusive attitude toward the problems of human consciousness (Burrow, 1958, p. 46)

In a few years Burrow and Shields expanded their reciprocal analysis from a group of two to a group of more than 20. They clearly shifted the focus of analysis from intrapsychic blocks and defenses to interpsychic blocks and defenses. In many ways their efforts can be seen, historically, as the precursor of the T-group experiments of Lewin and his colleagues and the much later encounter group explorations of the 1960s.

Throughout his life Burrow attempted to get Freud and other analysts to see group analysis as complementary, not antagonistic, to individual analysis. In these efforts Burrow was completely unsuccessful. Burrow wrote to Freud in 1927:

> No one knows better than you that it is not possible for the psychoanalyst to win acceptance from his individual patient through mere theoretical discussion and explanation but only through his own affective experience with the method and disclosures of psychoanalysis. In the same way I cannot stand opposite my hearers and explain unconscious *social* processes which are secretly concealed within their own social personality when in their affective life *they do not wish these unconscious social processes explained.* (Burrow, 1958, p. 162)

It is not surprising that at a time when Freud and other analysts were struggling to have psychoanalysis accepted as a legitimate medical and investigative tool they would be unreceptive to a method that called into question the objectivity, range, and effectiveness of their methods. Clearly, Burrow's social laboratory does not provide a model for treatment that is likely to become popular with practitioners accustomed to the medical, authoritarian, doctor–patient model. Burrow recognized this limitation and, consequently, never offered his social analysis or social laboratory approach as a treatment model. Instead he always insisted that mutual analysis was a mode of investigation that could provide insights, ideas, and methods that might be revised and applied in more traditionally structural treatments. This brings up a very large issue, the treatment versus discovery issue, which will be discussed at length in Part II under the topic "Role Models for Therapy." Suffice it to say, for now, that in every orientation to therapy, including psychoanalysis, the issue of whether the therapist is treating the patient or mutually exploring and searching for psychological reality is a primary consideration that influences the structure, content, and process of therapy. Burrow is of especial interest in the history of eclectic therapy because he offers such a radical departure from traditional therapeutic modes.

The Concept of Primary Identification

Even before Burrow dropped individual analysis and embarked upon his social analysis experiments he had formulated a novel challenge to basic Freudian theory. He described the discovery this way:

> In the midst of my psychoanalytic work I suddenly came upon what appeared to me a phase of organic sensation and awareness that antedated the infant's earliest objective appreciation of its surroundings. (I remember so well the moment, and the patient— a teacher, by the way, and a highly subjective woman.) I called it the organism's *primary subjective phase* and spoke of the infant's *primary identification with the mother*. . . . There was no doubt with me that there existed between the infant and maternal organism a *tensional rapport* . . . a total physiological continuity in sensation and reaction that underlay the entire developmental life of the organism and that was quite different from the tensional modifications brought about with the infant's adaptation to its environment *and to its mother* through the process of outer objective awareness (the employment of symbols). (Burrow, 1958, pp. 41, 42)

Burrow first reported on his concept and clinical observations at a meeting of the American Psychoanalytic Association in 1917; the paper was titled "The Preconscious or the Nest Instinct." He followed up the paper with three publications about the theory in *The Psychoanalytic Review* (Burrow, 1914, 1917, 1918).

These papers contain anticipations not only of Freud's ego, id, and superego formulations but also the ego psychology of Horney, Hartman, and Fromm in the 1930s and, most importantly, Kohut's (1977, 1978) self-psychology which is so important for psychoanalysis in the 1980s. What Burrow argued was that narcissistic psychic disturbances were primary and that oedipal conflicts were secondary. In Burrow's theory the inception of "introverted mental states" could be traced to disruptions of the primary preconscious bond between mother and child, not to later sexual conflicts with the parent of the opposite sex.

The pathology of primary identification occurs when the child, and later the adult, continues this identification and substitutes his or her feelings for the mother for real perceptions of the mother, himself or herself, and of the world. The feeling image is perceived as reality. During intrauterine life it was reality for the child to feel a part of the mother and this closeness of feeling naturally continues for some time after birth. At the feeling level the newborn children identify with the mother's feeling response to them, which may be mostly positive, mostly negative, or mixed. This primary feeling response can dominate the child's later life, if it is not replaced by equally powerful object perceptions. The psychopathology of this continued primary identification, narcissism, can take many forms: the child may so focus on this one kind of feeling to such an extent that he or she may preclude development of normal emotions toward the opposite sex or toward other people in general. Narcissistic children and adults come to look upon themselves as all-sufficient deities, acting in the world solely in response to their own choices and goals.

Burrow's theory has received some recognition from historians of psychoanalysis. Clarence Oberndorf in his *History of Psychoanalysis in America* (1953) cites among the four "most noteworthy and original American contributions before 1920 . . . Trigant Burrow's emphasis on a 'primary subjective phase' in the infant chronologically preceding the Oedipus situation" (p. 153). However Burrow was never accorded much recognition by the later ego and self theorists in psychoanalysis. In a 1949 letter he remarked rather harshly about these unacknowledged borrowings,

> I have not myself read either Fromm or Horney, but a good many people have spoken
> of what they felt was the tendency of these authors to borrow rather freely from my
> thesis. Harry Stack Sullivan helped himself lavishly to my material. I knew him at
> Hopkins and he received through the years all of my reprints. (Burrow, 1958, p. 584)

Burrow tried repeatedly to persuade Freud to examine the phenomena and concept of primary identification seriously (see, for example, Burrow's letter of 1925, cited in Burrow, 1958, pp. 94–98) but without success. Freud wrongly insisted on aligning Burrow's concept with those of Jung and did not examine the idea carefully. Indeed it is only now, almost 70 years later, through the work of Kohut, that the concept of primary identification is taken seriously by the majority of psychoanalysts. (Unfortunately, Kohut does not cite Burrow in his major writings.)

Kohut's work offers a partial bridging between analytic theories of the unconscious and humanistic theories of the self. This tentative bridging is to be found, much earlier, in Burrow's formulations. In a 1949 letter to Carl Rogers, Burrow commented:

> I especially like your emphasis upon the study of the organization of the self as basic
> to the understanding of personality. The pervasiveness which you assign to the self
> in its influence upon human behavior is a generalization with which our results are
> in close agreement. (Burrow, 1958, p. 553)

As his experiences of group analysis were deepened and clarified Burrow eventually arrived at a formulation that linked the concept of

primary identification drawn from individual analysis with his observations of the social neurosis and socially shared image illusions drawn
from group analysis,

> The community occupies the central position within the social unconscious that the
> mother-image occupies within the individual unconscious. . . . But if the social image
> represented by the community possesses the same underlying psychology as the
> mother-image, then this social image can have no more relation to the reality of the
> social organism than the image of the mother has to the reality of the mother-organism.
> (Burrow, 1958, p. 75, cited from a paper read in 1924)

What Burrow has done is link the Janetian concept of dissociation
and the subconscious with Jamesian ideas of the self and the preconscious and both with the George Herbert Mead's concepts of self and
society.

Burrow did not extend his ideas about primary identification to
explanations of the clinical phenomena of hypnosis, but they do provide
a possible explanatory tool. The rapport that most hypnotists, including
Janet, consider necessary for deep hypnosis could be said to depend
upon the hypnotic subjects' regression to a state of primary identification
where the preconceptual "tensional rapport" is temporarily reestab-
lished. The hypnotist, then, occupies the role of the mother, not so
much perceived as an object, but assimilated as a subject. Since this
level of consciousness is primary all dissociated contents of consciousness become accessible; the dissociation takes place only in object or
symbolic consciousness. This explains how elements of consciousness
that are out of communication in ordinary consciousness become accessible to one another, and to the hypnotist, during deep hypnosis. Primary organic consciousness then becomes the background for all consciousness, it is the essential source that William James sought to make
accessible to consciousness.

It would be inaccurate to give the impression that Burrow deliberately developed his approach to therapy by focusing on the ideas and
methods of Janet, James, and the other clinical functionalists. That is
not what happened. He was very well acquainted with the formulations
of Janet and Charcot and with the ideas of functionalism (he corre-
sponded frequently with John Dewey). But Burrow was much more
directly involved in psychoanalysis than in, for example, the Harvard
line of clinical functionalism. Burrow's connection to functional psychology is similar to Perl's connection to gestalt psychology. Both men
practiced long and successfully as psychoanalysts, but when they sought
to enlarge their approaches, both drew upon ideas from experimental
and general psychology rather than from their clinical contemporaries.
Interestingly, both Perls and Burrow eventually arrived at a community

based structure for their therapy. Also of interest is that both men focused on the problem of perception and attention in their clinical work. Perls described his therapeutic development this way:

> Two years ago I read a paper at the American Psychological Association. I claimed all individual therapy to be obsolete, and pointed out the advantages of the workshop. . . . Now I'm slowly coming to the insight that workshops and group therapy also are obsolete, and we are going to start our first Gestalt Kibbutz next year. (Perls, 1969, pp. 73–74)

Unfortunately, there were no growth centers such as Esalen when Burrow organized his social laboratory in 1923. His Camp Lifwynn might be considered the prototype of both the modern humanistic growth center and of the community based forms of experiential treatment advocated for psychotics by Laing (1967). Because there was no professionally accepted model, as there is now, for the community based programs offered at Camp Lifwynn, Burrow necessarily worked outside rather than alongside the professional movements of his time. To understand fully this important theoretical linkage more information about Burrow's methods of group analysis and his findings is needed.

Group Analysis

Burrow regarded all of his work on group analysis as a development of the theory of narcissism in its societal implications,

> As this organismic conception of consciousness is relativity itself within the subjective sphere, its encompassment can no more be apprehended within the scheme of evaluation represented by Freud and his predecessors than the relativity of the physicists can be apprehended on a static Newtonian basis. (Burrow, 1958, p. 75)

On his side, Freud considered Burrow to be overblown in both his goals and methods. At one time Freud sarcastically remarked about Burrow's group analysis, "Does Burrow think he is going to cure the world?" To which Burrow replied, rather overenthusiastically, "I most certainly do" (Burrow, 1953, p. 120).

Burrow believed that the "social neurosis" that he was studying and attempting to alleviate through group analysis was so widespread that only an epidemiological approach, similar to the hygienic and vaccination approaches to the treatment of the plague and smallpox, would ever be successful:

> The early years of our group researches convincingly demonstrated that "normal" social behavior is not biologically healthy social behavior . . . man as a global community or voice suffers from a *social neurosis*. . . . Perhaps an analogy from the

field of medicine might be helpful . . . early students of diseases endemic to the tropics brought back with them accounts of communities in which the natives, without exception, regarded the incidence of intermittent chills and fever as a condition natural to their kind as a tube or group. . . . They accepted the various symptoms of their infection as a matter of course. After all, the persistence of the symptoms of malaria among them day in and day out was their habitual experience, both as individuals and as a social community . . . the same element of basic anxiety, of guilt, of conflicting motivations, of emotional projection, of wishful thinking and feeling, of predjudice and self-bias determines the behavior of normal and neurotic alike. (Burrow, 1953, p. 26)

This sweeping thesis of universal social pathology can be compared to Freud's thesis concerning infantile sexuality. Both assertions are inflammatory, controversial, and easily dismissed as outlandishly speculative. On the other hand, both Freud and Burrow offer many clinical observations and careful arguments to support their speculations. Obviously, the social undesirability of an explanation of human behavior should not prevent scientists from seriously evaluating a theory. Burrow commented, "Our observations indicate that the usual and accustomed in the field of man's behavior do not represent a criterion of health" (Burrow, 1953, p. 6).

Burrow's theory and method of group analysis began with a focus on the immediate moment. Like Janet and James he was trying to explain gaps in consciousness. Burrow, in discussing his work with a former patient, contrasted his earlier psychoanalytic focus on the past with his phyloanalytic focus on the immediate present:

It happened he came to me after I had abandoned the older psychoanalytic basis of technique. With my altered approach all the reminiscent material upon which I had formerly set so much store has now been completely thrown into the discord, and my entire work with Mr. O. consisted simply in *training him to detect in the immediate moment* the obvious discrepancy between his observable mood and his alleged mental content indicated by his presumably "direct" statements. (Burrow, 1958, p. 122, author's italics)

Part III will discuss in detail the reasons a functional therapist must focus constantly on noticeable discrepancies between expressions and apparent experiences. For now I want just to point out that it is the central clinical focus of all functional therapies. (Similarities between Burrow's focus and the later clinical emphases of Rogers, Perls, Reich, and other humanistic-analytic therapists are evident.)

Burrow observed and conceptualized the gaps in consciousness to be due to the interference of self-images. In effect the person who loses awareness of the immediate moment is perceiving his or her own fantasy world rather than the real world:

> In the sense in which I now view our nervous disharmonies a certain pathological
> image-substitution, existing socially, is as definitely the cause of mental disorder as
> the germ of tuberculosis is responsible for the prevalence of this disease among us.
> (Burrow, 1958, p. 160)

Elsewhere, Burrow again comments on the significance of the present moment, "for in our finding the immediate moment is the focal point of our human pathology" (Burrow, 1958, p. 178). Burrow identifies two characteristics of this pathology: there is wishful affect and disturbed attention. As in the functional theories examined in previous chapters, Burrow emphasizes the centrality of feeling. Indeed Burrow regarded his phyloanalysis as basically a science of feeling.

> Our experimental studies indicate that when man adapts a technique which dissipates
> his conditional concerns with the projective affects . . . the fullness and continuity
> of his feeling life will be restored. These studies give full support to the position that
> inherently the feeling-processes of individuals are continuous and consistent with one
> another. (Burrow, 1953, p. 66)

Despite this optimistic statement about human nature, Burrow was certainly not an optimist concerning social relationships. In many ways he anticipates the behavioristic critiques, such as Skinner's *Beyond Freedom and Dignity* (1971), which point up the social illusions and personal automatisms hidden behind social-political precepts and images, *"Whether in individual or nation, it is not one's thinking that determines his pattern of reaction, but one's pattern of reaction that determines his thinking"* (Burrow, 1953, p. 212). However, Burrow's solution to this social neurosis is not a program of social conditioning and control but a program of corrective experiencing: "It is imperative that man recover his inner sense of his disorder—that he somehow get back into the *feel* of the deviate internal stress we find to be the inseparable somatic accompaniment of his superficial affects" (Burrow, 1953, p. 213). And, " 'application' in this field means training in the expression of feeling" (Burrow, 1958, p. 176). Burrow believed, as do all functionalists, that disordered functioning is not only perceptible to others but can be noticed by the disordered person. He believed in the accessible unconscious: "I do not think the unconscious is primarily deep at all. I think the whole story is on the surface and in full view at every moment. We simply do not commonly possess a technique for observing its outstanding obviousness" (Burrow, 1958, p. 178).

Burrow used different terms to describe pathological disturbances of the immediate moment: the *dissociative factor, retropathic feeling, autopathic feeling.* All his terms referred to the displacement or substitution of direct perception, thinking and doing; indirect psychological processes provoked by feelings and centered around symbolic images take over for direct functioning:

> This self-enfoldment, this retroversion of the individual upon his own image has seriously dislocated processes that are basic in mediating man's relation to man. It has muddied the springs of native feeling and thinking and has distorted the primary coordination of man's organism as a species. The self-reverting, self-conscious type of behavior expressed as "face" constitutes a functional impasse in human inter-relations. This dissociative factor which I shall describe as *autopathic* or *retropathic*, exerts a profoundly deleterious influence upon the behavior of man. (Burrow, 1953, p. 173)

Much of Burrow's work is a gold mine of possibilities for the clinical researcher. For example, one can hypothesize that what Burrow calls retropathic behavior in defense of face or self-image should be directly discrimnable, in photographs, from orthopathic, direct behavior. If photographic analyses such as those applied by Ekman (1972) and others to the identification of emotional expressions were applied to the study of disordered feeling gaps it should be possible to identify directly autopathic emotional expressions and discriminate them from orthopathic emotional expressions.

Burrow described the goal of group analysis this way:

> My aim has been only to discriminate between wishfully conditioned habits of feeling and thinking . . . and feeling and thinking that is the expression of direct biological incitements. In contrast to the intellectual approach to human problems, this whole process of group-analysis with us has been a somewhat unusual one. There has never been any mental observation—never any "thinking things out." There was the observation of an inter-relational habit of feeling and thinking that was throughout artificial and the constant challenge of this functional artifact in our behavior as a community. (Burrow, 1953, p. 47)

Unfortunately, there is no record on film or tape of these group analyses and no published transcripts. Nor are there published reports by "outside observers." Burrow insisted that the phenomena under observation, disordered feelings, could be noticed only by participant observers and that films and transcripts would be useless since the basic material, the feelings, would be missing from the recordings.

Burrow's colleague Hans Syz gives a similar description of the focus of group analysis:

> Burrow's emphasis was on working directly with feeling and behavior as they can be experienced internally and observed externally. A subjective or experimental element entered his formulations in that specific bodily sensations as actually felt in oneself and sensed in others were included in his statements. (1963, p. 62)

Fortunately, beginning in 1924 Burrow and his co-workers shifted their efforts from an exclusive focus on group analysis to detect and correct gaps in social functioning to a search for the physiological substrata underlying gaps in consciousness and functioning.

Psychophysiological Findings

After years of daily group analysis Burrow and his colleagues were able to identify two kinds of attention, which he termed "ditention" and "cotention." They observed that certain sensations or feelings regularly accompanied one form of attending and were not present during the other: "This sensation was not at all clearly outlined at first as to location or quality. It lasted for only a few seconds, and was not sharply defined or vivid; nor had it the quality of either pleasure or pain. There was merely my conscious recording of a barely perceptible sensation of pressure, stress or tension seemingly within the anterior cerebral zone. I could in no way account for this reaction, but it is quite unthinkable that such a subjective sense or sensation . . . could ever have come to awareness had there not been the interuption of the social interests and distractions that ordinarily occupy man's projective trends" (Burrow, 1953, pp. 245, 246). This vague sense seemed to accompany the effort to eliminate narcissitic or ditentive attending and replace it with cotentive or realistic attending.

It is interesting that Burrow makes the point that, without the preparation of the group analytic work, this vague, transitional, subjective sense would not be detectable. To a greater extent than is sometimes realized, psychotherapy consists of setting up conditions that allow for the perception of inner experiences that otherwise would be overlooked. The functionalist emphasis upon the subliminal, rather than the deep, unconscious is exemplified by this search for the conditions that will make visible the previously invisible processes of the stream of consciousness.

Armed with the observation that the transition between ditention and cotention was marked by a discriminable sensation of tension, Burrow and his co-workers took on the task of identifying the measurable physiological correlates of ditention and cotention. Their efforts were successful; in effect, they accomplished the first physiological identification of defensive and nondefensive behavior. Burrow summarized their general findings:

> Our instrumental studies have centered chiefly on oculomotor behavior, respiratory reactions, and brain-wave patterning in the ditentive and cotentive mode of the organism's adaptation . . . the chief findings . . . were: (1) A marked and consistent

slowing of the respiratory rate in cotention as compared with ditention, the decrease in rate in cotention being accompanied by an increase in the thoracic and abdominal amplitude of the respiratory movements. (2) A reduction in number of eye-movements in cotention. This reduction during cotention occurs not only when the eyes are closed, or when they are directed straight ahead and no specific task or stimulation is imposed, but also under a wide variety of stimulus conditions. (3) A characteristic and consistent alteration in the brain-wave pattern during cotention. This alteration consists of a reduction in alpha-time and a general diminution in cortical potential, which is most pronounced in the motor regions. (Burrow, 1953, pp. 394, 395)

Modern commentators such as Pribram (1962) and Sulloway (1979) have rightly pointed out the significance of Freud's early psychophysiological speculations. But, incredibly, Burrow's early psychophysiological research has been totally ignored. If Burrow's findings from the late 1920s and early 1930s could be replicated the field would need to recognize him as the first clinical researcher to discover physiological correlates for defensiveness (and for subconscious processes). The advances in biofeedback research during the last decade make it all the more important that Burrow's findings be given a second look. If they hold up it should be possible to apply biofeedback methodology to directly teach an awareness of ditention and cotention and to aid in the shift from the ditentive mode to the cotentive.

Burrow and his co-workers, in the later years of their work, did try to teach cotention directly. Here is Burrow's prescription:

To induce cotention it is necessary to secure quiet conditions, as for example when you take three quarters of an hour of rest on returning from work in the afternoon. If with the eyes closed you will let yourself become aware of your eyes as organs in your head, you will close out all the restless images that make of us such mental gadabouts. In the effort to hold the eyes steadfast, in the absence of any point to focus upon, you necessarily develop an increasing awareness of the muscles about the eyes that maintain them in a position of equilibrium. As you first undertake this experiment you will probably become drowsy and will fall asleep, but you will have fallen asleep in a healthy posture as far as your eyes are concerned. I don't know whether you know that all thought is accompanied by fine eye-movements or tremors. So that in regaining control of the movements of these eyes you automatically eliminate mental images or thought. It is this procedure that brings you back to your own organism, to your basic physiology, to the condition that was native to you as an infant, and native to your race in its infancy. In first undertaking cotention you will find it difficult and you will find every excuse for not continuing it. Thinking, especially emotional thinking, is so much a habit with you now, as with the rest of people, that it is easier to be pushed on by this habit than to let go of it. (Burrow, 1958, pp. 435–436; this passage is from a letter Burrow wrote to his son John in 1942; for another description of the procedure see Burrow, 1953, pp. 372–373)

Burrow did know of the research work of Jacobsen, the creator of the "progressive relaxation" method now so widely used in behavior therapy, and it is probable that Burrow's research and ideas influenced

Jacobsen's research and applications. However Jacobsen's (1974) procedure is very much narrowed and redirected so that it became more of a time-out method to interrupt neurotic behavior rather than a reeducative mode of attention.

A Biological Model of the Mind

Burrow believed that the perceptual disordering evident in ditention was a result of the faulty biological preeminence given to words and images as a result of human evolution:

> We see ditention as a functional brain-disorder affecting man throughout. It is a disorder of function that interrupts man's sense of his unity and solidarity as a species and, instead, sets each individual . . . over against every other individual. . . . This ditentive mechanism involves the private assumption by each of us that he possesses a valid "right" or perogative, and that other people are right only in the measure in which they agree with him. (Burrow, 1953, p. 51)

According to Burrow the evolution of the cortex gave to the human species not only the boon of symbolic facility but the possibilities for distortion through symbolic projection:

> The development of speech or the word constituted, of course, a tremendous asset for man socially and economically but, at the same time, owing to a *faux pas* in his evolution, the acquirement of the symbol and of language exacted of man a very onerous toll. For concomitant with the use of this handy instrument of symbol-projection as applied by man to external objects, the mechanism of symbolic projection . . . reverted upon its inventor and in so doing came to apply itself unconsciously to man himself. Because of this projective attitude of individuals of the species toward one another, this partitive mechanism gradually came to muddle very seriously man's primary relationships interindividually. . . . His symbol-usage encroached upon the phylum until the coordination uniting the species as an organismic whole was largely superseded socially by a purely projective or affecto-symbolic interrelationship of individuals to one another. (Burrow, 1953, pp. 295–296)

In Burrow's theory, basic neurotic dysfunctioning occurs whenever, under pressure from the affect centers of the brain, the symbolic centers begin to substitute projective perceptions for actual perceptions. The normal processes of thinking and perception are sidetracked, "The affect-object loses perspective because attention has been deflected into purely interpersonal involvements" (Burrow, 1953, p. 205).

This psychobiological theory of Burrow anticipated by several decades the modern triunal theory of brain function developed by MacLean (1973, 1978) and popularized in recent years by Sagan (1977) and Koestler (1979). Koestler, in his book *Janus*, described the central thesis in these words: "Under favourable conditions, the two basic tendencies—*self-assertion and integration*—are more or less equally balanced, and the holon lives in a kind of dynamic equilibrium within the whole—the two faces of Janus complement each other. Under unfavorable conditions the equilibrium is upset, with dire consequences (Koestler, 1979, p. 58).

Much has been made, in psychology and the popular press, about the two hemispheres of the brain and the differences between language-dominated, left-side, serial functioning and image-dominated, right-side, wholistic functioning (see Ornstein, 1975). But the more fundamental brain division, for clinicians, is the up–down not the right-left division. The up-down division concerns the connections between the affect centers and the symbol centers. Faulty functioning of these up-down connections results in the substitution of narcissistic perceiving, thinking, and doing for realistic functioning.

The reestablishment of cotentive functioning, according to Burrow, cannot be achieved through words *or* images. The only possibility is to reestablish a stability of feeling and to recognize the presence of ditentive functioning and discount it when it occurs. Koestler is so dismayed by the biological and social immensity of the effort to reestablish balanced functioning that he eventually concludes that the only possibility is the discovery and worldwide application of a new psychoactive drug that can be administered to the populace at large.

Whatever the cure, it is clear that both Burrow and Koestler are talking about how to offset a kind of species-specific moral insanity. Burrow words it this way:

> A significant shift in man's emotional behavior has taken place within his organism, with a concomitant modification in neuromuscular function. It is always the *function* that I am talking about. It is always the displacement of the total by the partitive pattern of behavior, individual and phylic. My theme is the misplaced identity throughout man, as a species, caused by the inadvertent channeling of feeling or affect into the circumscribed symbolic area. When I speak of the "third brain," I am speaking of this affecto-symbolic reaction-pattern that has become functionally separated from the organism's pattern of behavior as a whole—the whole pattern, phylic and individual. (Burrow, 1953, p. 100)

This displaced functioning unit, the "third brain," is what Burrow elsewhere calls the "I-personae." It is the false sense of self that substitutes for a realistic intra- and inter-psychic sense of self. It is the dissociated sense that produces the narcissism leading to the kind of moral insanity that says "my way is always right." On page 191 of *The Neurosis of Man* Burrow (1949) cites James's essay on "The Moral Equivalent of War." In the widest scope of their theories both James and Burrow were concerned with the general neurotic qualities in human beings that lead to social breakdowns and social strife. Psychotherapy, in their view, necessarily becomes community therapy.

Summary

Of all the theorists chosen to exemplify the variety of ideas and methods that contributed to the history of functional eclecticism no one diverges more from the mainstream of therapy than Trigant Burrow. His work could be dismissed as the esoteric odyssey of a cult leader; his co-workers could be dismissed as uncritical followers; his writings rejected as jargon-filled vanity communications. But these dismissals would be a mistake and a real loss to the field of therapy.

Trigant Burrow's contributions stand as a test of commitment to an unusual therapy structure.[2] No one has traveled farther away from the traditional therapist–client model of therapy while, at the same time, attempting to verify his ideas and methods with scientific observations and reports. He is like some strange Marco Polo of the mind; whether he discovered a new land or merely reported a novel group fantasy is still unknown.[3]

---

[2] Having personally participated in a community-structured therapy (Hart, Corriere, & Binder, 1975), I can attest to both the extreme difficulties and the real possibilities that surround such group endeavors. My own group experiment dissolved, after nine years, because of a failure to solve successfully the core problem of power within the community. Burrow and Shields and their co-workers persevered for more than 25 years!

[3] Among the prominent nonprofessionals who gave serious and laudatory attention to Burrow's writings was D. H. Lawrence. See Lawrence (1921/1960).

6

The Functional Therapy of Jessie Taft and the Systematic Eclectic Therapy of Frederick Thorne

Jessie Taft

The functional school of social casework became widely known in the 1940s. At that time a schism existed in social casework practice between the "functional school," founded by Jessie Taft and Virginia Robinson, and the majority of social casework practitioners who adhered to a "diagnostic school" based upon Freudian theory.

Taft was born in Dubuque, Iowa, in 1882. She graduated from Drake University in 1904 and from there she went to the University of Chicago where, in 1913, she received a Ph.D. At Chicago she was directly exposed to the ideas of functional psychology through her studies with John Dewey and George Herbert Mead. And, importantly, it was at the University of Chicago that she met her lifelong friend and colleague Virginia Robinson.

In a letter written in 1908, Virginia Robinson said of her new friend,

> Jessie Taft has been a strong rock for me. She is so frank and sincere and free from conventionality that she compels you to a like frankness, and you find yourself telling her things in the most natural, matter-of-course manner. Things get straighter when you talk to her, too. She sees things in such a clear, straight way without warping them. (Robinson, 1962, p. 30)

Apparently Jessie Taft already possessed, as a young student, many of the qualities she would later describe as desirable for a dynamic therapist.

Jessie Taft was deeply responsive to her teachers at Chicago, especially George Herbert Mead. She said of him, "His wisdom was not to be measured in minutes of listening to him but in a lifetime of realizing the significance of his ideas" (cited in Robinson, 1962, p. 36). Jessie Taft set for herself the professional task of developing "a satisfactory view of emotion from functional psychology" and a social theory of the self that could be used in applied psychology.

She went from Chicago to New York where she worked in the mental hygiene movement with psychologists, social workers, and psychiatrists. She became director of the Child Study Department of the Children's Aid Society of Pennsylvania in 1918. In that position she gained recognition as a therapist and consultant and as a teacher of social workers.

With her friend Virginia Robinson she developed the psychologically oriented curriculum at the Pennsylvania School of Social Work. In 1934 she became a full-time professor of social casework at the university where she continued until her retirement in 1952. At the school's 50th anniversary in 1959 Jessie Taft received a special citation for her contributions to the program. Under the leadership of Virginia Robinson and Jessie Taft the School of Social Work at Pennsylvania had become the most significant and controversial school in the United States.

Apart from her background in Chicago functionalism, the other major influence on Jessie Taft's thinking and practice came from her exposure to Otto Rank. She first met Rank at a meeting of the American Psychoanalytic Association in 1924 and was immediately impressed by his personality and his thoughts, "for the second time in my life I have met a genius" (cited in Robinson, 1962, p. 121).

She took courses from Rank at the New School for Social Research and went through a personal training analysis with Rank, "not due to any conscious personal need or any lack of professional success, but to the deep awareness of being stopped in professional development. I knew that I had not the basis for helping other people, however deep my desire" (cited in Robinson, 1962, p. 124).

Jessie Taft worked closely and productively with Dr. Rank until his death in 1939. During that time she translated several of his writings into English (including *Will Therapy and Truth and Reality*, [Rank, 1945]). In 1958, after her retirement she wrote an appreciative biographical study of *Otto Rank* (Taft, 1958).

A valuable perspective on the history of eclectic therapy could be written simply by developing the thesis that psychoanalytic outcasts and innovators such as Rank, Adler, Burrow, and Reich found a home in America for their ideas and methods within the broad functional tradition of psychology. Writing about her participation in a 1930 seminar with Rank, where it became clear that he had irrevocably broken from the Freudian camp, Taft remarked:

> As I look back I believe that I was perhaps the only one (in the seminar) for whom the transition came easily and naturally. I had no medical ties and no stake in Freudian psychology. I had been brought up on pragmatism and the thinking of George Herbert Mead and John Dewey. For me there was nothing to lose. (Cited in Robinson, 1962, p. 128)

For Jessie Taft, combining Rank's will therapy with functional psychology and the enforced pragmatism of social casework, there was a great deal to gain.

Taft's Basic Theoretical Ideas

The *Encyclopedia of Social Work* lists three defining characteristics of functional social casework that differentiated it from diagnostic casework. (1) The functional school works from a psychology of growth; it is client centered not problem centered. (2) Casework is viewed as a method of administering some specific social service. (3) The caseworker focuses on processes of helping, not predetermined goals. The functional school identifies the purpose of all social work as the release of human potential in individuals, groups and communities.

> The psychological base for functional social casework practice is a view that the push toward life, health, and fulfillment is primary in human nature, and that a person is capable throughout his life of modifying both himself and his environment according to his changing purposes. . . . This viewpoint does not deny the irrational, the unconscious, and the powerful and potentially crippling effects of life experiences, especially early experiences and relationships in the immediate family. (Smalley & Bloom, 1977, p. 1283)

These emphases on growth, self-fulfillment, and the importance of conscious, willful choices are similar to the emphases found in other functional theorists. Functional casework is based upon a growth model of personality rather than a model that stresses merely compensations or reactive adaptations. As in other functional approaches, feeling is given a primary place in functional casework: "The role of feeling and response to feeling in furthering productive engagement is accepted as primary in the practice of casework" (Smalley & Bloom, 1977, p. 1289).

The growth and individuality emphases that Taft incorporated from functional psychology are also found in the work of Rank. In her biography of Otto Rank, Taft quotes from a 1929 talk he gave at Yale University:

> But neither Freud, nor Jung, nor Adler sufficiently considers the creative part of our personality, namely, that which is not purely biological as Freud sees it, nor purely racial as Jung conceives it, nor yet purely social as Adler thinks, but which is purely individual. (Cited in Taft, 1958)

Casework is frequently stereotyped as a rather drab and bureaucratic activity, so Taft's theoretical position was all the more striking and controversial with its emphases on choice, will, individuality, growth, and creativity.

Although Taft was a very effective writer her career led her to be more involved with teaching, therapy, and administration than writing. Most of her published writings are rewrites of speeches and case presentations. Consequently she was less of a systematist than James, Janet, and the other functional therapists covered in this section of the book. She was more concerned with the use of ideas than their conceptual elaboration and ordering. In many ways she was a therapist's therapist who exerted more influence through the force and integrity of her personality than through the originality or scope of her theories. As a theorist she was a creative borrower. The potency of her use of the ideas she applied to her therapeutic work will be evoked in the subsequent quotations from her therapeutic writings.

Taft's Dynamic Functional Therapy

Taft labeled her specific therapeutic approach "Relationship Therapy."

> The term "relationship therapy" is used to differentiate therapy as I have experienced and practiced it from psychoanalysis or any process in which either the analytic or the intellectual aspect is stressed or the immediacy of the experience denied or confused with history. (Taft, 1961, p. xvi)

Her only complete book on her therapy is *The Dynamics of Therapy in a Controlled Relationship,* originally published in 1933. The bulk of the book consists of two case studies (one of a 7-year-old boy, John H., one of a 7-year-old girl, Helen P.) plus an introductory chapter on "The True Element in Therapy" and a concluding chapter on "The Forces That Make For Therapy." She uses the word *therapy* in preference to the more widely used term in casework, *treatment,* because it implies less manipulation. Taft points out that there is no verb for therapy in English; therapy, for her, is viewed as a process going on and the therapist serves that process. (There is a colloquial verb for therapy; "to therapize" is an ironic and sarcastic verb to describe the kind of counselor who is overbearing and pontificating.)

Taft made use of Rank's time-limited scheduling of therapeutic sessions to bring out for her clients the essential time binds of living: "One might fairly define relationship therapy as a process in which the individual finally learns to utilize the allotted time from beginning to end without undue fear, resistance, resentment or greediness (Taft, 1933/1962, p. 17).

Jessie Taft uses simple everyday language to describe the phenomena of therapy. In her view, the basic block to growth in and out of therapy is fear.

> The source of failure in living lies primarily in fear as a quantitative factor, and the effect of this fear upon the balance which is required to accept and maintain conflict inherent in the life process on a comparatively constructive basis, at least sufficiently so for growth to go on. (Taft, 1933/1962, pp. 283–284)

The basic conflict she refers to is similar to the conflict specified by Burrow, that between independence and dependence, between the need to be self-functioning and the equal need to realistically and emotionally merge and share with others. In neurosis self-functioning becomes rigid and impenetrable or narcisstically unreal, in growth there is a realistic balance between self-reliance and reliance upon other people.

In Taft's relationship therapy there is an acute awareness that the success or failure of therapy depends upon what the therapist is, not what the therapist knows:

> In the last analysis therapy as a qualitative affair must depend upon the personal development of the therapist. . . . To make case work therapeutic, incidentally or deliberately, one must *be* a therapist. (Taft, 1933/1962, p. 21)

This emphasis on the personal qualities of the therapist is especially important in relation to feelings:

> I do not consider the therapeutic process a rational or intellectualized affair for the therapist any more than it is for the patient. . . . The therapist above all must be able to be, what the patient is not for a long time, spontaneous and aware of his own slightest feeling response. (Taft, 1933/1962, p. 118)

Taft's persistent, central focus on the therapist's personal feeling characteristics has been developed in modern humanistic therapies such as those of Axline and Rogers. In several sources (Evans, 1975; Hart, 1970a) Rogers has acknowledged his indebtedness to both Rank and Taft.

One of the ironies of modern eclecticism is that the functionalist and humanistic stress upon desirable personality characteristics of the therapist, such as empathy and congruence, are now widely accepted by therapists of many persuasions. Unfortunately it is sometimes implied that a person can be empathic simply by trying hard or by learning simple techniques such as reflecting feelings. This is roughly as effective as a large corporation's efforts to create a good working atmosphere by posting signs that say "Be Courteous and Friendly to Your Fellow Workers" or "Customers are People Too."

Jessie Taft is more willing to live with ambiguity and openendedness than most theorists and practitioners.

> Therapy is a process in which a person who has been unable to go on with living without more fear or guilt than he is willing or able to bear, somehow gains courage to live again, to face life positively instead of negatively. How is this possible? If one thinks of an exact scientific answer to the question, I must confess that I do not know; that, at bottom, therapy of this kind is a mystery, a magic, something one may know beyond a doubt through repeated experiences but which in the last analysis is only observed and interpreted after the fact never comprehended in itself or controlled scientifically any more than the life process is comprehended and controlled. Yet is is possible to describe it theoretically in philosophic or psychologic terms although one realizes that the description will be of no value to any patient and of no immediate avail to any therapist who must play his part at the moment without rehearsal or prompting. (Taft, 1933/1962, p. 283)

This therapist and patient for one knows exactly what Jessie Taft is saying! In intellectual terms it is the old controversy between the therapy-as-art advocates and the therapy-as-applied-science advocates. In this chapter Jessie Taft and Frederick Thorne represent opposite poles of the controversy: Taft is the artist par excellence while Thorne is the epitome of the applied scientist who seeks to diagnose and treat. Nonetheless, both theorists share in the functionalist eclectic tradition. A strength of the eclectic position in therapy is that it makes room for these contrasting styles of thinking and doing therapy.

Taft shares with Burrow a deep distrust of the limits of nonparticipant observation as a way to understand the essential processes of therapy. Taft agrees with Burrow's reasons for not allowing observers, transcripts, or films of his group analysis sessions. For both of them therapy sessions partake of many of the qualities of dreams. Like a dream a therapy session is vivid and real to the emotionally involved client and therapist. But dreams are often pale and incomprehensible to awakened dreamers and boring to uninvolved listeners. (The surest bromide for insomnia is to tell the insomniac a long, detailed dream!)

Another therapeutic emphasis that is found in Taft and other functional therapists and in later humanistic therapists is the focus on the feeling moment in the present. Out of the feeling moment come emergent qualities that do not need to be constructed by the therapist. In the last sentence of her therapy book Taft writes,

> For relationship therapy, like life, utilizes the forces already within the human being and therefore, in so far as it is effective, is never finished while the individual survives

but continues to develop in time, the inevitable medium in which man creates, no less than the symbol of his final limitation. (Taft, 1933/1962, p. 296)

Frederick Thorne

The contrast between the careers of Jessie Taft and Frederick Thorne was striking. Taft was always immersed in professional and university affairs; she worked closely and productively with collaborators and received many honors from her colleagues and admiring students. Thorne had no binding affiliations, no close working colleagues and, despite the prodigiousness of his writings, no real followers. He remained a kind of lonely lighthouse keeper throughout his career; his lighthouse was the *Journal of Clinical Psychology*, which he founded in 1945 and edited until 1974. He remained editor emeritus until his death in 1978. All of his books were self-published and distributed through the Journal of Clinical Psychology Press.

In a posthumously published editorial opinion on "Unfrocking phoniness and pretensions" he wrote,

Quite truthfully, I spent much of the first 50 years of my life trying to be something I was not . . . the key to my reconciliation with my real Self was the recognition that true worth cannot be granted by fiat, but only earned by genuine accomplishment. (Thorne, 1979, p. 921)

Frederick Thorne was born in 1909 and in a biographical essay published in 1972 started the chapter with this sentence, "My troubles literally started at birth in a difficult forceps delivery with head lacerations" (Thorne, 1972, p. 241). He then went on to chronicle a history of childhood difficulties that included: nutritional problems, physical underdevelopment, respiratory disorders, severe myopia, and severe stammering and stuttering. Along with these problems Thorne experienced a difficult home life with his mother. "My whole life has been greatly influenced by a continuing double-bind relationship with my mother which continued until her death, even though she was senile in a nursing home" (Thorne, 1972, pp. 242–243).

Thorne received little or no help with his physical and family problems until he discovered for himself at age 15 a shelf of psychology and psychiatry books in his local library. He says, "From that time on, I avidly read anything psychological I could get my hands on. . . . I took every available psychology course motivated basically by the need for self-understanding" (Thorne, 1972, p. 244). This theme, the search for self-understanding, carries throughout Thorne's life; indeed, the title of his biography is *Toward Better Self-Understanding*. Of course, this theme has been significant for many psychotherapists, including Freud, Jung, James, and Adler but the search for self-cure dominated Thorne's career. He received his Ph.D. in experimental psychology from Columbia in 1934 but immediately went on to study medicine at Cornell University, where he was awarded the M.D. degree in 1938. Thorne remarked, "It should be stressed that even after completing my medical educa- tion . . . my primary interests were in the field of clinical psychology which I regarded as basic to psychiatry" (Thorne, 1972, p. 250).

Thorne's interests were primarily in teaching and research in clinical psychology but he was completely frustrated in his efforts to secure an academic position. On top of that frustration he wrote a *Handbook of Clinical Psychology* for the Mosby handbook series only to have the sole copy of the manuscript get lost in the mails.

During World War II Thorne worked as a psychiatric examiner for the Selective Service System and then went on to develop a lucrative private practice in southern Vermont. He did have the opportunity to do some psychiatric teaching at the University of Vermont and at Bran- don State School but never was able to secure an academic position in clinical psychology. So, Thorne created his own forum in the field, the *Journal of Clinical Psychology*, in January 1945. He commented, "In the early 1930's it was practically impossible to get a paper accepted on clinical topics by the APA or published in an APA journal" (Thorne, 1972, p. 252).

This publishing project came to dominate Thorne's career.

> Within five years, the publication business grew to such size as to be come my principal source of support and to require my full-time attention as publisher, writer, editor, and researcher. I began to expand by adding monographs, books, and tests to our line. (Thorne, 1972, p. 253)

He had created his own kind of "University of Clinical Psychology" and from his position as editor, publisher, and writer sallied forth to do battle with the many foes of clinical psychology and to develop his own statement of systematic eclectic therapy.

Just as Taft reinterpreted Rank within the framework of functional psychology, so did Thorne adapt the teachings of Alfred Adler:

> My interest in eclecticism stemmed from two important sources. At Columbia, I was influenced profoundly by Robert S. Woodworth (probably the first great American eclectic) who introduced me to the term and whose interests had the broadest spectrum. Also at Columbia, I first met and during 1929 and 1930 took a course under Alfred Adler, who also impressed me deeply. Adler's individual psychology dealt with a very wide range of phenomena ranging from biological inferiority to style of life and existential concerns—in fact, no other teacher ever impressed me as being so com- prehensive as Alfred Adler. (Thorne, 1972, p. 255)

In the conclusion to his biography Thorne says,

> My most creative moments have come in moments of frustration and conflict. . . . My greatest successes and my greatest failures have been due to the same traits and motivations. I like to think of myself as an iconoclast with all the profits that original thinking can bring and all the losses of popularity which stepping on other people's cherished beliefs can bring. (Thorne, 1972, p. 271)

Thorne's Basic Theoretical Ideas

Thorne used several different labels to describe his therapeutic and theoretical approach, including "integrative" and "directive," but his central emphasis was always on eclecticism. "Our inspiration comes from the life of Sir William Osler, who is known as the founder of the modern system of eclectic medical practice" (Thorne, 1968, p. v).

In the *Principles of Personality Counseling: An Eclectic Viewpoint* Thorne asserts the need for an eclectic orientation that would "integrate and relate the positive values of newer viewpoints with traditional methods" (1950, p. 22). He goes on to specify eight characteristics of an eclectic system of psychotherapy: (1) compilation of all known psychotherapeutic techniques, (2) operational definitions accompanied by transcripts, films, and tapes of each method, (3) evaluation of functional dynamics, (4) relating therapy to psychopathology (5) establishing indications and contraindications for each method, (6) establishment of criteria of therapeutic effectiveness, (7) statistical analyses of long term records, and (8) validation through prognostic predictions and follow-ups. These are ambitious standards but Thorne diligently sought to carry them out. One characteristic of Thorne's eclecticism is his tendency to be programmatic, that is, he outlines and enumerates rather than deductively or empirically arriving at principles and descriptions. For example, his list of 8 characteristics easily could be collapsed into 4 or extended into 10 and there is no indication about to what extent most eclectic practitioners agree with or share these eclectic characteristics. In other writings Thorne enumerates "15 things to relax tension," "12 objectives of case handling," and a "22 category biological classification of feelings and emotions." These programmatic categorizations are more common in clinical medicine than in psychology. It is likely that this writing style did little to attract adherents to Thorne's eclecticism, particularly during the height of psychological hypothetical-deductive theorizing in the 1950s.

Elsewhere Thorne argues against "rag-tag eclecticism" and argues that the primary organization and integration of the relevant data of clinical psychology are inherent in the nature of personality. In his book

Personality: A Clinical Eclectic Viewpoint Thorne offers 97 postulates about the nature of personality beginning with:

POSTULATE I. PERSONALITY IS A CLINICAL CONCEPT WHICH HAS NO VALID MEANING APART FROM THE ACTUAL STATUS OF WHAT A PERSON IS AT SPECIFIC MOMENTS AND IN SPECIFIC SITUATIONS OF EXISTENCE. . . . This specific study of *personality statuses* can be accomplished only by appropriate clinical methods, of which trained introspection and the direct personal encounter are the most important. (Thorne, 1961, p. 1)

Thorne articulates a theme that runs persistently through clinical functionalism, viz. that the basic subject matter of clinical work is different from the basic subject matter of general psychology,

Psychology, then, may be regarded as the general study of human behavior while personality refers properly only to persons. . . . In terms of our clinical, eclectic approach to the study of personality states, it is postulated that the raw data of personality must be taken in their "giveness." (Thorne, 1961, p. 2)

What Thorne did was to apply James's concept of the stream of consciousness and Janet, Adler, and Meyer's concept of the life flow, life-style, or life chart to the clinical study of personality. He arrived at a conception of the fundamental unit of personality as ever-changing states or "personality statuses,"

POSTULATE 6: THE PHENOMENOLOGICAL APPROACH IS THE MOST VALID METHOD FOR PERSONALITY STUDY. The phenomenological method for personality study uses the *person-to-person encounter* in which one person experiences another, attempting to place himself in the position of the other. . . . POSTULATE 7: THE FUNDAMENTAL UNIT OF PERSONALITY STUDY IS "THE PERSON EXISTING IN (BEING) AND MEETING (COPING WITH) HIS ENVIRONMENT." AND THE FUNDAMENTAL UNIT OF THE CLINICAL METHOD IS "TWO-PERSONS-EXISTING-IN-A-WORLD" AND "ENCOUNTERING EACH OTHER EXPERIENTIALLY," WITH THE CLINICIAN USING ALL HIS TRAINING AND EXPERIENCE TO ENTER THE WORLD OF THE CLIENT AND EXPERIENCE WITH HIM. . . . The study of personality thus becomes the study of phenomenal behavior data defining the status of a person at a specific time and place. (Thorne, 1961, pp. 8–9)

Thorne follows James in according the "sense of self" as the central datum in consciousness.

POSTULATE 37: THE SELF IS THE CONTINUING CONSCIOUS AWARENESS OF BEING A SEPARATE PERSON. (Thorne, 1961, p. 102)

He discusses ego functioning as the awareness and concerns of the self with itself.

Thorne was very influenced by his former mentor at Columbia, Prescott Lecky. He did a revised version of Lecky's book *Self-consistency:*

A Theory of Personality (1945) and made self integration "the central drive or need, since higher behaviors are impossible except in integrated states" (Thorne, 1972, p. 259). In Thorne's usage the concept of integration is inseparable from the approach of eclecticism. "The term *integrative psychology* may be assigned to the eclectic viewpoint which seeks to relate the interactions of the subfunctions to the basic organization of the entire personality as a whole" (Thorne, 1955, p. 6).

Thorne drew upon Janet and James's concept of "ideomotor action" (the tendency of motor activity to follow immediately after thoughts of action) to specify why the clinician must be concerned with the contents of consciousness (Thorne, 1955, pp. 332–334). In Postulate 20 of his personality theory he puts forth the proposition that the decision process is more important than the motor action because the act is only the last step of a whole decision-making process. He argues, as did Dewey, that failure to understand the dynamics of the decision process may result in a failure to comprehend the personal meaning of what the person is doing. Many young students of behavior therapy have learned to their chagrin that rotely compliant behaviors have quite different therapeutic consequences than personally chosen behaviors.

The last postulate in Thorne's treatise on personality states: "POSTULATE 97: ULTIMATELY, PERSONALITY STATUS CAN BE UNDERSTOOD CLINICALLY ONLY IN TERMS OF THE MEANINGS AND SIGNIFICANCES OF GLOBAL 'PERSON' FUNCTIONINGS" (Thorne, 1961, p. 217). Thorne meant by this something close to the gestalt emphasis on wholes and contexts. "The proper topic for personality study is the person working out his life in the world" (Thorne, 1961, p. 183). Person functionings are embedded in lower psychophysiological levels of organization and integration but achieve their dynamic significance only in terms of phenomenal qualities and existential implications. General psychology can study part functions such as perception, learning, motivation, etc., but only clinical personality study reveals global person functionings.

Thorne was truly eclectic as a theorist and did make an effort to be comprehensive.Consequently any brief, selective summary of his ideas, such as this, cannot convey the full range of his thought. The quotations I have included in this section of the chapter tend to make him sound rather humanistic and existential. Other selections from his writings quoted in the next section sound extremely behavioristic; still others sound quite psychoanalytic.

A good example of the way Thorne attempts to unify psychoanalytic, behavioristic, and humanistic concepts is his theoretical discussion of the ego. He defines ego as "a constellation of self-centered attitudes organized about a conscious awareness of self" (Thorne, 1955, p. 453). Ego structure reflects the relative permanence of ego attitudes and includes the concepts of real self, ideal self, and social self. Thorne then goes on to discuss developmental–observational studies of maturation and the possibility of a maturational sequence from egoism to altruism. In his discussion of the significance of values in personal development and for therapy Thorne closely resembles James, Janet, Burrow, and Taft (as well as later functional theorists such as Allport): "In our opinion, values provide the reference points about which men organize their lives" (Thorne, 1965, p. iv).

Thorne's Eclectic Therapy

It is apparent that Thorne was very influenced in his mode of theorizing by the model of clinical medicine. However he was saved from an overreliance on the doctor–patient model which stresses diagnosis, symptomatic treatment and theories of pathology by the extensions he gave to his theories into counseling and popular psychology.

In a very significant monograph he published in 1965, titled *Tutorial Counseling: How to be Psychologically Healthy,* Thorne argued that personality growth must be a goal of all people and that psychologists need to develop skills and theories that aid psychological health.

He puts forth the proposition that "psychological health, as a whole, depends upon the degree to which any person succeeds in actualizing his potentials in learning to cope with all the standard situations of life, living actively and creatively, and acting out many roles well" (Thorne, 1965, p. 155).

Thorne defines tutorial counseling as, "a special method of personality counseling based on the systematic attempt to impart psychological information pertinent to all areas of life adjustment (Thorne, 1965, p. vii). In the book Thorne covers the achievement of psychological health in many different life areas: sex, work, marriage, friendship, leisure, and recreation. He also devotes chapters to topics such as "Psychological Values," "Enriching Conscious Experiencing," "Maximizing Intellectual Resources," "Self-Actualization," and "Handling Emotions." He states emphatically that "psychological health is more than the absence of mental disorder. It is a positive status involving full-humaneness, full-living, complete self-actualization and the most active possible existence" (Thorne, 1965, p. 15).

Thorne found out, as had James and Janet before him, that the attempt to guide and describe psychological health took him beyond the role models typically used in counseling and psychotherapy. At various places in *Tutorial Counseling* he uses business, coaching, teaching, exploring, and artistic models to explain psychological growth. The health–sickness model is just too narrow by itself to account for personality growth.

One model or image that Thorne relies upon repeatedly is the fitness–coaching model. He argues that psychological fitness requires diligent exercise and conditioning just as does physical fitness:

> *Fitness*, either physical or psychological, involves a state of being maximally prepared to cope with the demands of life. Analyzed operationally, fitness usually is considered to involve the following factors:
>
> (1) Theoretical knowledge and practical experience, so that a person is oriented to the nature of the problems faced.
>
> (2) Intensive training and practice under real-life conditions of increasing stress and pressure for maximum performance.
>
> (3) Conditioning processes in which physical and psychological resources including intellectual performance, emotional control and level of motivation are brought to peak efficiencies.
>
> (4) Maintenance of fitness by avoiding harmful or debilitating factors. (Thorne, 1965, p. 14)

The idea of psychological fitness was certainly latent in the theories of James, Janet, Burrow, and Taft but in Thorne's eclectic functionalism the concept is carefully developed. Psychological fitness ideas and techniques will be further developed and applied in parts III and IV of this book. The great significance of the fitness idea is that it makes explicit the differences and similarities between rehabilitation goals in therapy and fitness or actualization goals.

In one of his last books Thorne uses the title *Psychological Case Handling: An Eclectic System of Counseling and Psychotherapy* (1968) to describe the range of ideas and techniques he surveyed. "Case handling," for Thorne, was a broader term than "therapy." He defines "psychological case handling" as "a generic term referring to all the operations conducted by competent psychologically-trained personnel in helping clients to get along better in life" (Thorne, 1965, p. 23).

The range of techniques and ideas applied by Thorne to psychological case handling were extremely wide. He includes chapters on "Symptomatic Therapy," "Supportive Therapy," "Reassurance," "Conditioning and Behavior Therapies," "Suggestion," "Persuasion," "Pressure, Coercion and Punishment," and "Life Management Analysis."

In line with his emphasis on "personality statuses" as the basic unit of personality study Thorne makes "moments" the basic unit of clinical case handling.

> The existential locus . . . is the psychological state of the moment. If any person has enough moments of highly actualized psychological states, self-enhancement is achieved and life is successful. Hence anything which contributes to moments well spent contributes to self-actualization in general. . . . The eclectic approach to life management attempts to consider all factors contributing potentially to self-actualization (maximal integration) or conversely, causing failures of integration. (Thorne, 1968, p. 13)

Thorne's focus on states and moments contains the same theoretical and practical focus that pervades all functional theories: "State measurements basically are concerned with *change*, with the evolving process of what the person is *doing* in the world. The basic question underlying state measurements is 'How is the person doing?' " (Thorne, 1968, p. 45). Thorne criticized behavioristic and psychoanalytic theories for their focus on "what" and "why" questions that ignored the complexities of clinically evaluating how a person is doing:

> An important defect of behavioristic or psychoanalytic theories is their lack of existential referents, in the first instance due to the mechanistic and largely chance determination of environmental stimulation, and in the latter case because of determination by the hydraulics of the unconscious. The requirements of discovering the existential referents of psychological state make it necessary to conduct longitudinal studies of the stream of conscious experience (psychological states) in which both intrinsic and extrinsic organizing factors are properly represented. (Thorne, 1968, p. 49)

It is interesting that Thorne's style of psychological examining, his use of diagnostic tests, and his application of special-purpose records for quantitative evaluation of cases closely resembles the methods used in modern cognitive behavior therapy. Unfortunately he is never identified as a forerunner of cognitive behaviorism nor is he acknowledged as an important influence on the trends toward eclecticism in behavior therapy.

A good example of Thorne's quantitative approach (which he drew from Meyer) is his "time investment analysis." He explains:

> Prevailing patterns of organization . . . probably are most directly reflected in terms of time invested in various activities. . . . Indeed, a simple tabulation of how time has been spent during any day (or other pertinent time interval) provides a diary or record of life. . . . *Time* is more closely related to existential realities than psychology has traditionally given emphasis to. Time is literally life. (Thorne, 1968, p. 128)

Thorne argues against the traditional trait emphasis of personality theory. Every clinician, he advises, must find out the specifics of each client's daily use of time. Prescriptive tasks and exercises can then be used to bring about changes in the way time investments are made.

Thorne also argues for the use of miniature situational techniques to sample clients' response repertoires.

Whatever assessment method is applied the goal is always to evaluate the personality states, which Thorne calls "the real referents of psychology" (Thorne, 1968, p. 46). For Thorne, the psychological state is the crucial nexus of all therapy; it is the beginning and end point of his systematic eclectic therapy:

> We contend that all psychological operations and measurements refer only to psychological states existing at the moment. All that can be measured or studied is the psychological state of the person at any time and place. Psychodiagnosis refers only to the psychological state (mental status) at the time of study. Psychotherapy deals only with the psychological state of the client at the moment case handling is carried out. (Thorne, 1968, p. 46)

Conclusions to Part II

By this time, after meandering through a variety of theories and techniques and a wide-ranging discussion of historical influences and cross-influences, it no longer may be clear what an eclectic therapist is or isn't. This apparent confusion is helpful, I believe, because some boundaries separating analytic, behavioral, humanistic, and other orientations are more historical and accidental than real. If it is difficult to tell whether Sullivan, Rank, Reich, Rogers, or Perls should be classified as a functionalist that is all to the good, because they did not classify themselves, they simply thought and wrote about clinical problems.

One of the values of the historical approach is that a new context can be created that gives old ideas a new look and new ideas a reference in the past. From the perspective of functional eclecticism, for example, the ideas of the ego analysts are wholly intelligible. With the exception of Jung, most of the dissident analysts who split from Freud to develop their own theories (Rank, Reich, Adler, Horney, Fromm, Hartman, etc.) placed more of an emphasis on ego functioning with less emphasis on unconscious determinants. Their shift in emphasis fits well within the functionalist position that stresses consciousness while not ignoring subconscious and unconscious influences on actions, thoughts, choices, and feelings.

The following six points are those which all functional eclectics more or less share in their approaches:

1. The immediate moment is the focus of clinical concern, with gaps in consciousness considered to be of especial significance.
2. Feelings are regarded as conscious regulators of behavior.

3. The self-concept and related images of the self are always carefully examined.
4. Willful choices, plans of action, and philosophical and moral concerns must be included within the scope of therapy.
5. Models of growth and health are given at least as much weight as models of psychopathology.
6. Any technique or idea that works can be used; a pragmatic attitude toward the tools of therapy is endorsed.

With these points in mind it should be possible to roughly categorize any theorist as to his or her affinity for the functionalist position.

III

Theory

7

A Paradigm for Modern Functional Eclecticism

Theories are used to explain well-defined sets of observations and experimental results and to organize subtheories. The field of psychotherapy and counseling is too underdeveloped for comprehensive theory building. The so-called big theories in the field are not really used as theories in the same way that the fields of physics, chemistry, and biology develop and use theories. Therapy theories (such as psychoanalytic theory and cognitive behaviorism) are more accurately described as orientations or paradigms rather than explanatory theories. The function of an orientation is to define what questions, phenomena, methods are important (and indirectly to define what can be ignored.) But the statement "this is important, this needs to be observed and explained" is not the same as a complete theoretical explanation. Freud's theory of repression, for example, is not a theory; it is a statement saying "something called repression exists and is important for clinical work, here are some ways to observe its manifestations and some partial explanations." Scholars have shown that Freud actually offers half a dozen or more *different* definitions and explanations of repression (Mackinnon & Dukes, 1964; Madison, 1961). Psychoanalysis stands out from other therapeutic orientations not because it offers a satisfactory theoretical explanation of repression but because analysts say such an explanation is necessary. A paradigm or orientation is like a choice of directions to explore, some explorers want to go west, some southwest, some north, and so on. Actual theories are the master maps of numerous explorations in which the similarities and differences between repeated observations of the same terrain are reconciled.

Unfortunately, disputes in psychology sometimes resemble the silly arguments between easterners and westerners about which is better or worse, New York City or Los Angeles. Let us agree at the beginning that the choice of an orientation or paradigm, like the choice of where to live, is not made on scientific grounds.

The only special advantage of the orientation offered in this book is that it suggests several directions of travel can be compatibly explored. We do not have to counsel everyone to "go West young man," we can say "go West or North or East or South."

In their text on *Personality and Personal Growth* Fadiman and Frager (1976) include a chapter on "William James and the Psychology of Consciousness." It is unusual for James's ideas to be considered at length in books on personality or psychotherapy. He is everybody's neglected grandfather, mentioned briefly and then passed over. Fadiman and Frager discuss his position carefully because they give a central place to the psychology of consciousness in the study of personality and they attempt to use this central focus on consciousness to define an eclectic metatheory. They say of James:

> James' works are free of the arguments that currently divide psychological theorists. He acknowledged that different models were necessary to understand different kinds of data and was concerned more with clarifying the issues than with developing a unified single approach. James' philosophies prefaced the development of the field of psychology; he anticipated Skinner's behaviorism, existential psychology, Gestalt theory, and the Rogerian self-concept. (Fadiman & Frager, 1976, p. 191)

Their argument, of course, is the same one developed at length in parts I and II of this book: James provided the background metatheory for modern eclecticism. My addition to the argument is that James should be combined with other functional eclectics such as Janet, Burrow, Taft, and Thorne; when this linking is accomplished there is a foundation for a modern paradigm of clinical functionalism. How does one come up with a whole that is greater than the sum of the parts? Multiply the parts instead of summing them; by multiplying and variously combining the ideas of the major functional theorists reviewed in Part II it may be possible to arrive at a new, modern paradigm for clinical functionalism.

Role Models

A beginning exercise that can be used with graduate classes in psychotherapy and counseling is to ask the students to brainstorm as many role models for therapy as they can imagine. The instructions for the exercise are:

Try to think of as many role models for therapy as you can. Don't defend the models or criticize, just generate as many as you can. We'll critically discuss and evaluate them later.

What typically happens is that the students do produce a dozen or so models but these are divided into "serious" role models and "silly" role models. The serious ones always include: doctor-patient, scientist-subject, and teacher-student. The wild or silly role models can include anything and everything, such as dog trainer-dog (the student who offered this suggestion did not specify who was to be the dog, the therapist or the client), witch doctor-native, and painter-painting. What is "serious" about the first group of role models is that students take them seriously and what is "silly" about the second group is that the students do not consider them important.

As step two of the exercise, ask students to justify each role model and discuss its advantages and disadvantages. In this stage some surprising points emerge. The first is that there are often just as many negative characteristics cited for the "serious" role models as for the "silly" ones. The second point that emerges is that some of the apparently "silly" role models turn out to be surprisingly interesting and compelling. For example, the student who facetiously presented the trainer–animal model actually knew a great deal about dog training. She pointed out that trainers vary in their approaches, some emphasize reward-punishment, others emphasize the relationship between the trainer and the animal and the necessity for getting the animal's attention and understanding. She was able to cite several specific training techniques that might be of value in therapy.

The upshot of all this discussion is that the usually accepted doctor-patient, teacher-student, and scientist-subject roles are seen to be open to numerous criticisms and limitations and some of the seldom used models are seen to be of considerable value.

As a third stage of this exercise the class then can consider how the history of psychotherapy and counseling might have been different if nontraditional role models had been used. Specifically, the students can be asked to imagine how the history of therapy (techniques, theories, and structures) would have been changed if other role models had been taken as central to defining the role of the helper and helpee. Then go on to consider a great many role models seriously including: coach-athlete, attorney-client, experimenter-subject, manager-employee, minister-church member, master artist-artist, political representative-constituent, engineer-project client, occupational therapist-patient, business representative-customer, caseworker-client, and parent-child.

Out of all this discussion may come what is for many graduate students their first recognition that the traditional models implied by theories of therapy are not the only useful models and, secondly, the realization that every theory of therapy has an implied role model attached to it. This, for the students, is often the beginning of a true receptivity to eclecticism. If students can recognize something of value in role models that are not encompassed by the existing theories then, of course, they are more willing to take an eclectic position about the range of theoretical possibilities. This broadening is important because single role-model orientations to therapy usually have attracted *more* attention in the development of psychology than multiple role models. In an *APA Monitor* interview, Ernest Hilgard commented,

> Of psychology's heroes, I suppose William James is the figure that has appealed to me most, because of his breadth and warmth. I was always very much impressed by Robert Woodworth. People who are as broad as Woodworth aren't as visible as people who take a strong, fixed position. Freud was kind of a tyrant but that helped make him conspicuous, in contrast to Pierre Janet, who had very similar ideas. . . . We don't need unified theory. Most unified theories tend to peter out. . . . What really is sustained in the long run is an approach which favors curiosity and open-mindedness. (Cited in Bazar, 1981, p. 14)

The first level of a paradigm for clinical eclecticism is to consider the wide range of useful role models for the client–therapist relationship. This is similar to the first level of the clinical examination of personality that must begin with an assessment of the personality images used by the client (see Chap. 12). If a therapist does not recognize that the role model she or he is using is only *one* of several viable choices, then the therapist's range of technical and conceptual eclecticism is immediately limited. Genuine functional eclecticism *begins* with a plurality of role models.

This means, for one thing, that the Boulder conference scientist–practitioner model that has been officially endorsed for the training of clinical psychologists is too narrow. The Boulder model firmly embeds the therapist within the doctor-patient and applied scientist roles. One of the negative consequences of this role narrowing is that typically most Ph.D. clinical psychologists know very little about areas of psychology (such as sports psychology and industrial psychology) that do *not* closely fit the applied scientist model. In contrast, most counseling students end up knowing very little about areas of psychology that *do* fit the applied scientist model and depart from the implied teacher–student model most utilized in counseling.

If one accepts the argument that a plurality of role models is desirable for the therapist–client relationship, then a very wide range of areas of knowledge opens up to the therapist both within psychology and beyond it. For example, the chapters on technique in the manual section of this book will include adaptations from biology, etiology, public policy research, management, religion, and other areas of human concern. These techniques, imported from other fields, will be seen to be just as applicable to the task of therapy as the more home-built techniques developed within clinical, counseling, and medical psychology.

Two Positive Examples of the Benefits of Role Model Plurality

More than 35% of all doctorates awarded in psychology in 1980 were in the clinical area; more than 9% were in counseling. In contrast, only 2% of the doctorates were in the field of industrial psychology. This statistic perhaps explains why so few clinical and counseling psychologists know much about management, organizational and industrial psychology; the organizational speciality has little influence within the field as a whole.

It is unfortunate, in my estimation, that clinical and counseling students are not exposed to management theories and practices because the level of discourse used in organizational psychology is much closer to the level of discourse found in therapeutic psychology than is the level of discourse in, for example, the experimental psychology of learning.

Many of the ideas and methods of management psychology can be directly translated into therapy terms; consider, for example, these passages from Peter Drucker's book *People and Performance:*

> The first test of any business is not the maximization of profit but the achievement of sufficient profit to cover the risks of economic activity and thus avoid loss. (Drucker, 1977, p. 89)

There is a close analogy between the widespread fallacy of profit maximization in business and the equally widespread fallacy of symptom relief in therapy. If the terms *therapy/business, symptom relief/profit,* and *change/economic activity* are interchanged Drucker's statement becomes:

> The first test of any therapy is not the maximization of symptom relief but the achievement of sufficient relief to cover the risks of change and thus avoid loss.

Elsewhere Drucker says of the management task in business, "But it requires building on strength to make weaknesses irrelevant" (Drucker, 1977, p. 84). This passage does not even require a shift of terms, only a shift of context from the business setting to the therapy setting.

In another passage Drucker says:

There are three different dimensions to the economic task: (1) the present business must be made more effective; (2) its potential must be identified and realized; (3) it must be made into a different business for a different future. (Drucker, 1977, p. 101)

If "economic task" is translated into "therapeutic task" and "business" into "personality," then Drucker's advice frames an orientation that is very close to the eclectic position in therapy.

As another example of the useful application of the management paradigm to therapy consider the Johari Window. The Window was developed as a framework to help managers understand leadership by Joseph Luft (1970, 1969) and Harry Ingham and named after the first names of the authors. The concept was further developed and applied by Paul Hersey and Kenneth Blanchard (1977).

According to the Johari framework there are some attitudes and behaviors engaged in by leaders that they know about themselves, this is a *known to self* area of personality. At the same time part of the leader's personality attitudes and style are *unknown to self.* From the point of view of others there are areas of the leader's personality *known to others* and *unknown to others.* Assembled together, the Johari Window resembles Figure 1.

When applied to therapy this framework provides a useful conceptualization of the therapist–client relationship, a conceptualization that closely fits the functionalist eclectic orientation (see Figure 2). Without commitment to a theory of repression or the unconscious, several functional tasks of therapy become simply to: (1) Let the client know what the therapist knows, (2) let the therapist know what the client knows, and (3) explore to find out what neither the client nor the therapist knows. By increasing the client's awareness and the therapist's awareness and decreasing the regions of blindness, unnecessary privacy, and vagueness, therapy should show progress. Successful therapy should bring about a change in the areas occupied by awareness, mutual awareness, and communication (see Figure 3).

A particular value of this model is that because it was developed outside the clinical context it does not rely on theory-tied techniques such as interpretation or free association. Instead, the interventions that

	KNOWN TO SELF	UNKNOWN TO SELF
KNOWN TO OTHERS	PUBLIC	BLIND
UNKNOWN TO OTHERS	PRIVATE	UNKNOWN

Figure 1

	KNOWN TO CLIENT	UNKNOWN TO CLIENT
KNOWN TO THERAPIST	PUBLIC	BLIND
UNKNOWN TO THERAPIST	PRIVATE	UNKNOWN

Figure 2

alter the Johari Window are conceptualized in terms of feedback and disclosure. No commitment is made to a theory of active repression to explain the presence of "the unknown." This model exactly fits James's model of consciousness–subconsciousness.

There is perhaps nothing more valuable for students (and teachers) of counseling and psychotherapy than the attempt to translate theories and methods from other fields. The act of translation itself is similar to the translation of novels from one language to another; the translator is made aware of the limits of expression within a single language and the common sentiments across languages. Just as language sophistication leads to cosmopolitanism so does the study of multiple fields lead to eclecticism.

The Dangers of Role Model Narrowness

As an example of how role model narrowness leads to therapeutic and theoretical rigidity consider the use of systematic desensitization in cognitive behavior therapy. Early developments in behavior therapy were based on the double-pronged argument: (1) that traditional insight therapies were ineffective (Eysenck's 1952 argument) and (2) that the application of learning theory and research to the tasks of therapeutic behavior change would provide many effective techniques. The role

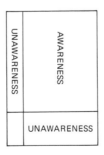

Figure 3

model espoused for the therapist was that of the applied behavioral scientist or behavioral engineer. The therapist–client relationship was seen as an extension of the experimenter–subject relationship.

The most popular technique to emerge from this behavioral paradigm was the technique of systematic desensitization developed by Wolpe. Wolpe defined behavior therapy in these words,

> Behavior therapy, or conditioning therapy, is the use of experimentally established principles of learning for the purpose of changing unadaptive behavior. Unadaptive habits are weakened or eliminated; adaptive habits are initiated and strengthened. (Wolpe, 1969, p. vii)

He defines systematic desensitization as

> the breaking down of neurotic anxiety-response habits in piecemeal fashion. A physiological state inhibitory of anxiety is induced in the patient, who is then exposed to a weak anxiety arousing stimulus. The exposure is repeated until the stimulus loses completely its ability to evoke anxiety. Then progressively "stronger" stimuli are introduced and similarly treated. This technique, which characteristically employs relaxation as the anxiety-inhibitory state, has made it possible for the first time to exert direct control over a great many neurotic habits. The therapist has been enabled to treat those habits in almost any order that he chooses, and as far as he chooses. (Wolpe, p. 91)

Wolpe is certainly optimistic about the scope of his treatment procedure and confident about its learning-based rationale. He goes on, following the passage quoted above, to describe how systematic desensitization was developed from laboratory studies of experimental neuroses in cats. Wolpe stresses the importance of having an effective counteranxiety response (feeding in cats, relaxation for humans) and the necessity to recondition by starting with weak anxiety-provoking stimuli and then progressing to stronger and stronger stimuli (this is called establishing a stimulus hierarchy). His book is filled with graphs showing "stimuli in a continuum" and "units of anxiety."

The first logical difficulty with Wolpe's method is that, in a therapeutic situation with humans, subjects are seldom exposed to actual anxiety-provoking stimuli, instead they are asked to *imagine* anxiety provoking scenes. Unfortunately the learning theory that Wolpe purports to be applying does not include any formal explication of the processes of imagination. (Indeed, in the narrower behavioral learning theories imagination and other subjective processes are not admitted into the realm of phenomena that are to be explained.) What Wolpe is applying is not a theory but an analogy. Of course there is nothing at all wrong with the use of analogies; indeed, it is the level of discourse that therapists use most. What is objectionable is the sleight-of-hand attempt to pass off a schematic analogy as a systematic theory. Elevating a paradigm to the level of a theory conveys the misleading impression that much more is known about the processes and applications than is really known.

However, even if this logical difficulty is disregarded, Wolpe's theory and method of systematic desensitization encounters many difficulties. An analogy is only as useful as the closeness of the parallel between one set of events and the analogous set of events. Recent evidence suggests that anxious human beings do not at all respond like anxious cats in cages.

The first line of evidence is provided by Wolpin who, in a remarkable series of experiments, has shown that neither relaxation nor a hierarchy of gradual presentations of anxiety-provoking stimuli are necessary to bring about appreciable reductions in anxiety responses.

The first of Wolpin's experiments came about serendipitously—he took advantage of a student's foul-up. Wolpin had been training a student to apply the systematic desensitization procedure to a woman client who had a phobic fear of snakes. The student, carefully following instructions, had spent seven sessions teaching the client a relaxation procedure and building up a descriptive heirarchy of fearful snake stimuli ranging from looking at a glass case five feet away containing a small dead snake to putting her hand inside a glass case and touching a small live snake. But, during the eighth session the student took the client through the entire heirarchy in one gigantic session. The student did not understand that deconditioning sessions were to be spread out over time. Remarkably, the phobic woman responded positively and was able to fondle and play with two large snakes after the session. Twenty-three days later, in a follow-up session, she again was able to fondle and play comfortably with the large snakes. A therapeutic change had been effected but the two basic principles of systematic desensitization had been violated. Wolpin remarks, "It may be that the rapid deconditioning was made possible because of the excellent relationship that was obtained and the consequent high degree of trust on the part of the patient" (Wolpin & Pearsall, 1965, p. 111). Unfortunately, in Wolpe's analogue model of systematic desensitization no provision is made for relationship factors.

Wolpin decided to follow up on his curious accidental finding and conducted a series of experiments in which he found that: (1) Tensing conditions worked just as effectively as relaxation conditions and (2) progressing from the top down in a hierarchy worked just as well as progressing from the bottom up. (See Jacobs & Wolpin, 1971; Wolpin 1969; Wolpin & Kirsch, 1974; Wolpin & Raines, 1966) These findings directly counter what Wolpe says about how systematic desensitization *must* work according to applied learning theory. A reasonable interpretation of these data is that systematic desensitization is not a learning technique at all but a persuasion technique. When systematic desensitization works it does so not because of the successful application of learning methods but because a ritual of persuasion has been followed that both the client and the therapist believe and trust.

Some theorists have argued that *all* of learning theory when applied to human beings is an elaborate persuasion technique. In a comprehensive review of the research literature on human learning, Brewer (1974) asserted "There is no convincing evidence for operant or classical conditioning in adult humans." In his conclusion to the chapter he states:

> A more natural and internally consistent interpretation of these experiments is that all the results of the traditional conditioning literature are due to the operation of higher mental processes, as assumed in cognitive theory, and that there is not and never has been any convincing evidence for unconscious, automatic mechanisms in the conditioning of adult human beings. (Brewer, 1974, p. 27)

Experiments such as Wolpin's and critiques such as Brewer's gradually have forced most "behavior therapists" to become "cognitive behavior therapists." Additionally, as cited in Chapter 1, most contemporary behavior theorists actually are eclectic or multimodal in their approaches. Since the only viable models of cognition and consciousness that were developed in the history of psychology came from the functionalist tradition, most eclectic cognitive therapists actually are practicing a form of functional eclecticism.

The fact that many therapists still apply systematic desensitization in the belief that they are doing reconditioning simply attests to the power of single role models for practitioners. For many therapists the role of the applied scientist is a highly attractive one and they cling to the image and trappings of the role despite evidence that they are actually doing something quite different from what the model says they are doing.

Even the expanded definitions of modern cognitive behavior theory tend to align themselves with a narrow role model for the therapist and a very narrow specification of the therapy process. There is no real harm in narrowness if it is made explicit by saying "let's see how far we can extend this simple analogy." The danger of narrowness arises when therapists actually believe that the narrow analogy defines the entire domain of the field.

As an example of pseudobroadening consider the argument made by Goldfried and Davison in the opening chapter of their influential book on *Clinical Behavior Therapy* (1976). They begin by rejecting the early reliance of behavior therapy on learning theory and conditioning as too limited. They also reject the definition of behavior therapy tied to a school of concepts and techniques.

> Instead, we believe that behavior therapy is more appropriately construed as reflecting a general orientation to clinical work that aligns itself philosophically with an experimental approach to the study of human behavior. (Goldfried & Davison, 1976, pp. 3, 4)

Having correctly specified that behavior therapy is a "general orientation" and not a developed theory, these authors then immediately narrow the orientation back to the old, familiar applied-scientist role:

> The assumption basic to this particular orientation is that the problematic behaviors seen within the clinical setting can best be understood in light of those principles derived from a wide variety of psychological experimentation and that these principles have implications for behavior change within the clinical setting. (Goldfried & Davison, p. 4)

Instead of behavior therapy being applied learning theory, it is now applied experimental psychology. We are immediately drawn back into the illusion that there is more to behavior therapy than an orientation or paradigm. It is, Goldfried and Davison claim, the application within a clinical setting of principles derived from psychological experimentation. This sounds impressive. Unfortunately the "principles" that they apply in the clinical chapters are simply analogies between clinical and experimental situations. This kind of scientific puffery leads to the ritualized clinical behavior that was observed in examining Wolpe's systematic desensitization method. Clinicians actually end up with a lower level of knowledge than would have been attained simply by studying the clinical method for itself with no pretensions to a basis in experimental theory.

The fact is, the claim that cognitive behavior therapy is based upon experimentally derived principles makes no more sense than the claim that the government operates according to the principles of applied economics and political science. There are no established "principles of social science" that have the genuine status of derived theoretical propositions similar to those found in, for example, the principles of hydraulics. When "principles" are used by politicians to justify policies, they are simply defending belief systems and rituals of action. The same is true for therapists.

Summary of the Multiple-Role Argument

The founders of clinical functionalism were divided in their allegiances to different role models for therapy. Janet stayed very close to the doctor–patient role model but also used the philosopher–student model; Thorne started with the doctor–patient and applied scientist model but was forced to go beyond them by his own psychological fitness theories. Taft aligned herself with the caseworker–client role model but so redefined the role of the caseworker that, at times, she seemed to be using the broadest role model possible, human being to human being. Burrow, like Taft, believed most in the expertise of experience rather than the expertise of training; he most often used the role model of community member to community member. James, typically, was the most diverse in his use of role models. He ranged all the way from the traditional teacher-student, doctor-patient, and applied scientist models to the philosopher model in which both the therapist and the client were involved in a common search to define and live what is true, beautiful, and right.

Imagine the difference in psychotherapy and counseling if graduate students were trained mainly in the arts rather than the social and biological sciences. What if Dostoevski and Vonnegut replaced Skinner and Pavlov as the mentors for therapeutic guidance? What if theses were novels, plays, and poetry? It is at least plausible that the sensitivity, insight, and human responsiveness needed by a therapist could be taught just as well or better (if it can be taught at all) through the arts rather than the sciences. To repeat, it is an accident of history that the clinical sciences came to dominate the training of therapists. After all, the earliest therapists of ancient Greece were more aligned with art, religion, and philosophy in their healing rituals than with science. There is no reason to suppose they were less effective in their healing rituals than systematic desensitizers. This argument is made with full recognition that clinical psychology, psychiatry, counseling, and social work are all too much embedded within clinical traditions to shift significantly the role models they teach their students. Nonetheless, every eclectic therapist should recognize the clinical role for what is is, just one among many possible roles that a therapist can use.

Late in his life Ernest Hemingway was asked, "Who would you say are your literary forebears—those you have learned the most from?" He gave an answer that greatly surprised the interviewer:

> Mark Twain, Flaubert, Stendhal, Bach, Turgenev, Tolstoi, Dostoevski, Chekhov, Andrew Marvell, John Donne, Maupassant, the good Kipling, Thoreau, Captain Marryat, Shakespeare, Mozart, Quevedo, Dante, Vergil, Tintoretto, Hieronymus Bosch, Brueghel, Patinir, Goya, Giotto, Cezanne, Van Gogh, Gaugin, San Juan de la Cruz, Gongora—it would take a day to remember everyone. . . . I put in painters, or started to, because I learn as much from painters about how to write as from writers. . . . I should think what one learns from composers and from the study of harmony and counterpoint would be obvious. (Plimpton, 1963, pp. 227–228)

If Hemingway and other writers can improve the craft of writing by opening themselves to the influence of artists and composers, therapists surely can improve their therapy craft by learning from novelists, coaches, grandmothers, grandfathers, managers, priests, and many other human actors in the dramas, melodramas, and comedies of everyday life.

8

The Feeling Moment and the Dynamics of Expression

This chapter makes a radical shift from the level of theorizing presented in the preceding chapter. Chapter 7 was concerned with the general role model that therapists have in mind when they approach the task of therapy. Therapists' role models reflect the general theory of practice that guides all their activities.

In this chapter the smallest units of the therapeutic process are considered—the critical moments or events within each therapy session. Do such units exist? What are they? What makes them critical? How are critical events recognized and used by therapists? How are these critical events ordered into a meaningful continuity within a session and across sessions?

The beginnings of answers to these questions are contained in the writings of an even earlier founder of functional psychology, Charles Darwin.

Darwin and the Expression of Emotions

The psychology historian Duane Schultz identifies Charles Darwin as one of the most important "antecedent influences" on the development of the functional point of view:

> There were several functional psychologies, each differing somewhat from the others. All, however, showed an interest in the functions of consciousness. Because of this emphasis on the functioning of an organism in its environment, functionalism is vitally concerned with applied psychology. . . . Darwin's influence . . . brought about a pronounced change in the goal of psychology. . . . Darwin influenced some psychologists to consider the functions that consciousness might serve. (Schultz, 1960, pp. 85, 89)

Darwin's two best-known works, *On the Origin of Species* (1859) and *The Descent of Man* (1871), both emphasized the similarity between the mental processes of human beings and those of animals. He also stressed the survival value of conscious mental responses to the environment.

For clinicians, however, Darwin's most important book was *The Expression of the Emotions in Man and Animals,* published in 1872. In this book Darwin extensively reviewed the parallels between emotional expression between humans and other animals and suggested that the changes in gesture and posture characteristic of the dominant emotions could be understood in evolutionary terms. He argued that emotional expressions were vestiges of movements that had served some practical function.

In a chapter discussing the "Darwinian Evolution of Certain Aspects of Mind," the psychiatrist Margaret Reinhold says,

> Evolving mind made a contribution to the survival of the species as did evolving body. . . . Those aspects of mind that are understandably of value to survival included not only instinctive reactions, but the affect accompanying and intensifying such reactions. . . . In man, unconscious (instinctive) reactions may be examined by conscious mind. A certain degree of conscious control of instinctive reaction then becomes possible. (1978, pp. 166, 167)

In his concluding remarks to *The Expressions of the Emotions,* Darwin says,

> The movements of expression in the face and body, whatever their origin may have been, are in themselves of much importance for our welfare. They serve as the first means of communication between the mother and her infant; she smiles approval and thus encourages her child in the right path, or frowns disapproval. We readily perceive sympathy in others by their expression; our sufferings are thus mitigated and our pleasures increased; and mutual good feeling is thus strengthened. The movements of expression give vividness and energy to our spoken words. They reveal the thoughts and intentions of others more truly than do words, which may be falsified. . . . The free expression by outward signs of an emotion intensifies it. He who gives way to violent gestures will increase his rage; he who does not control the signs of fear will experience fear in a greater degree; and he who remains passive when overwhelmed with grief loses his best chance of recovering elasticity of mind. These results follow partly from the intimate relation which exists between almost all the emotions and their outward manifestations; and partly from the direct influence of exertion on the heart, and consequently on the brain. Even the simulation of an emotion tends to arouse it in our minds. (Darwin, 1872/1965, pp. 364, 365)

This passage contains a wealth of ideas for the clinician: First, emotional communication is identified as basic for the development of the infant; it can be inferred that disturbances of emotional communication will have serious, long-lasting consequences. Second, emotional expression is posited as the basis for the contact or empathic response among human beings, disturbances of expressiveness will result in serious disturbances of social contacts. Third, emotional expressions are claimed to reveal thoughts and intentions more truly than words alone; they are harder to falsify and should be examined carefully by the clinician looking for the congruence or incongruence between what is said and what is experienced. Fourth, emotional expressions are the basis of emotional control; to change how a person feels the clinician must change what and how the person expresses. The last point, of course, is the central argument of the James-Lange theory of emotions that was discussed in Chapter 2.

It should be obvious that modern eclectic therapists are in essential agreement with the points made by Darwin in 1872. For Darwin, James, Janet, and all the other functionalists, consciousness, emotionality, expressiveness, and adaptability are closely interrelated. The critical moment or unit within a therapeutic session must in some way revolve around disturbances and emergences in emotional consciousness and expressiveness.

The Feeling Moment

Among the modern researchers who have followed the Darwinian focus on the importance of emotional expressiveness Paul Ekman and his colleagues stand out for the quality and quantity of their work. Ekman has established that facial expressions for at least six emotions (sadness, anger, surprise, happiness, fear, and disgust) are distinct and are consistently recognizable across cultures. In the same research it was also found that although emotional expressions were cross-cultural, emblematic expressions were culturally determined and not transferable from culture to culture. (See Ekman, 1971, chap. 4, for a brief summary of this research.)

Other research by Ekman and his colleagues (Ekman & Friesen, 1975) established that true emotional expressions happen very quickly in a few seconds or fractions of a second in contrast to emblematic expressions that are consciously controlled, "held" by the person for four seconds or more. Because of the rapidity of facial emotional expressions it is very easy to get sequential blends of expression within a few seconds. For example, a person talking about his mother's death might move very quickly within a two second span from expressions of disgust to anger to sadness.

Montague and Matson report on therapy research that applied the techniques of facial affect scoring to films of therapeutic encounters:

> That facial expressions may be not only overlapping but also contradictory was discovered by researchers in the process of running films of therapeutic encounters at slow motion, when it became apparent that there was more going on facially than met the naked eye. The films revealed very subtle expressions which appear and disappear so rapidly as to pass undetected in normal interaction. Specifically, when films were run at four frames (rather than the normal 24) per second, two and a half times as many changes of expression could be observed. . . . It was speculated that these micro-momentary flashes of expressions represent emotions which slip out unbidden from behind the mask, as it were, and are quickly suppressed or censored, accordingly, they are often inconsistent with what a person is "trying to say". . . . One patient, saying nice things about a friend, had a seemingly pleasant facial expression; slow motion films revealed a wave of anger cross her face. (1979, pp. 68–69)

Research by the psychiatrist Mahl (1956) on the effects of white noise on free associations has demonstrated that subjects who cannot hear their own voice because of the blocking effect of the noise through headphones frequently will begin to subvocalize in the pauses between their regular vocalizations. These unintended subvocalizations are often more emotional and contradictory to the content or emotionality of the normal vocalizations.

Another very different but parallel kind of research on affect and expressiveness comes from the field of advertising. In a little known book called *The Responsive Chord* Tony Schwartz (1974) reports on the effects of sounds on radio and television advertising. Mr. Schwartz created more than 5,000 radio and TV spots and his library of recorded sounds is still used widely in the industry. The entire basis of Mr. Schwartz's success was the discovery that people could detect and emotionally respond to sound effects. Over and over again it was found that listeners would accept artificial sounds but responded with much more positive affect and attention to natural sounds. Schwartz says, "I have no interest in *sound effects*. I am solely interested in the *effect of sound* on people" (T. Schwartz, 1974, p. xiv).

If radio and TV listeners and watchers are sensitive to unnatural sights and sounds, then it seems reasonable to conclude that personal contacts are also constantly monitored for naturalness and believability. However, in ordinary social transactions people will accept many visual and verbal "special effects."

In the therapeutic situation therapists are not willing to accept the same kinds of gaps, contradictions, and emblematic expressions that are used in routine social interaction. What is special about the therapeutic setting is that the therapist changes both the rules and the pace of the communications. For the ordinary rule which is "you must make social and intellectual sense" the therapist substitutes the rule "you must make emotional sense." The ordinary pace of conversation is designed to accomodate cognitive communications. Affective communications follow a different tempo, they are sometimes slower, sometimes faster.

By changing the rules of communication and varying the dynamics of expression the therapist can create *feeling moments*. A feeling moment is created whenever a therapist detects a mismatch between *what* is said and *how* it is expressed, and then brings this mismatch to the client's attention.

The art of therapy involves noticing the mismatches, selecting which mismatches to point out, and working with the client to resolve a mismatch once it is brought into awareness. As every inexperienced therapist knows, every minute of therapeutic interaction provides an abundance of material. The problem is to choose what to change and what to let go. Novice therapists sometimes feel, once they are sensitized to listening and looking for feeling–expression mismatches, as though they are in a time warp—too much happens too fast, It will be necessary to discuss other levels of therapy to orient the therapist in knowing what to do with feeling gaps and feeling moments, but the first emphasis must be to attune young therapists to these basic units of the therapeutic transaction.

From the discussion developed so far it is now possible to explain what it means when therapists talk about "intuitive listening," "empathic listening," or "listening with the third ear." Therapists must not only "listen with the third ear" but "see with the third eye." That is, they must listen and look affectively to perceive gaps and micro-expressions when there is a mismatch between what is said and how it is said. Therapists use this special perceptiveness to then help the client achieve emotional consistency and full expressiveness in place of emotional inconsistency, chopping, and withholding.

It should also be clearer now why the functional tradition emphasizes the *visible* unconscious. It is not necessary to infer the unconscious when gaps and mismatches can be easily perceived. The therapeutic task becomes, as James clearly recognized, elucidating the vague and filling in the gaps. Of course, once this task of elucidation through expression is undertaken it may eventually lead to very obscure and surprising emotional contents. Nonetheless, the primary phenomena of functional therapy are tbe *visible* gaps and mismatches not invisible dynamics that must be inferred.

There is no presumption, within functional theory, that the content of gaps or feeling moments is repressed or suppressed. Basically what is *in* a feeling gap is simply unknown, whether the gap represents an emergent feeling or a pushed-down feeling or some combination is not known.[1]

The difference between working with emergent feelings and repressed feelings will be discussed at length in Chapter 12. For now, I want to stress the point that a functional therapist must apply both a growth model and a psychopathology model to understand and work with feeling moments. Either model by itself is insufficient and misleading. Any feeling moment may represent the emergence of something new in the client's experience and expression repertoire or it may represent the "return of the repressed"—something old from the client's past that is now reemerging. Both the emergent and the reemergent are important for effective therapy.

The tendency, among analytic therapies, has been to emphasize repressed kinds of feeling contents. Among directive counselors and cognitive-behavioral therapists the tendency is to stress the acquisition of new emotional skills. In functional eclectic therapies both sides of the therapeutic growth cycle are considered: the reintegration of past emotional experiences and the integration of new emotional experiences. Both start from the recognition of feeling moments.

The Affective Drive

Why is it important to make what is vague clear? Why not let the gaps and mismatches stay as they are? Why is it desirable to reduce the affective incongruities that a person exhibits? The first answer to these questions is a clinical empirical one: Therapists have observed that clients feel better and function more effectively when they can clearly express how they feel. Mixed-up feelings are stressful and the clear expression of a feeling, even a painful feeling, is experienced with relief. But why? The answer to this question must be tentative and speculative, but clinical observations and research on emotional expressiveness both suggest

---

[1] Several years ago I conducted a series of experiments that demonstrated that the well known feeling-of-knowing or tip-of-the-tongue experiences that people often have about names, telephone numbers, and other sought-after memories can be studied precisely and experimentally (Hart, 1965, 1967). The basic conclusion drawn from these nonclinical experiments was that subjects could very often accurately monitor which memory gaps were fillable and which were not. In other words, the feeling-of-knowing experience was a useful guide to memory retrieval efforts. The significance of affect tags for learning, memory, and retrieval are now more actively being studied by experimental psychologists. See Bower (1981) for a discussion of research on "mood-state-dependent memory" and the influence of emotion on cognitive processes.

the possibility that there is an affective drive toward clear and complete emotional communication just as there is a cognitive drive toward clear and complete perception and understanding of the environment.

Organisms can tolerate perceptual deprivation but suffer from it; animals prefer environments that are interesting and often will choose to explore and find out about their environment over food, sex, or even the avoidance of pain.

The "cognitive drive" refers to the impulse to collect and organize information. As Harlow's (1950, 1971) experiments indicate, monkeys have a desire to receive sensory stimulation without any further reward. He concluded that monkeys enjoyed mental stimulation and he referred to cognition as a basic drive. White (1959) calls the cognitive drive "competence motivation" and argues that organisms have a drive to master their environments through exploration, manipulation, and understanding.

Gaps and mismatches of expression leave the organism affect deprived just as surely as the gaps and mismatches of perception leave the organism cognition deprived. As we come to know what we mean by talking, so do we come to know what we feel by expressing. *Talking about* feelings is not the same as expressing feelings. A basic emphasis within the functional approach is that neither behavioral compliance nor intellectual understanding are acceptable substitutes for expression. Understanding is not sufficient to satisfy the affective drive.

If this crucial point is not recognized, a therapist will recognize and point out "feeling moments" only to smother the feeling in pillows of talk. Intellectualizing therapists are unwilling to shift from the cognitive mode into the affective mode.

A therapist must, of course, also pay attention to the content of what is expressed as well as the gaps in expression. But that skill is already available to most people from ordinary social interactions. What is special about therapy and the therapy situation is that both the therapist and the client agree to look at what is usually overlooked. The role models that facilitate this special kind of interchange are all characterized by the label *sensitive*. Sensitive parent–child, sensitive husband–wife, and sensitive friend–friend relationships require attention to what is not expressed as well as what is expressed. This kind of sensitivity to the subconscious side of interactions contrasts with literal-minded insensitivity which looks only at what is said.

The Dynamics of Expression

During the 1960s and 1970s the arguments between the behavioral and linguistic theorists about the acquisition and use of language filled the pages of many books and journals. Psycholinguistics, unfortunately, has very little to say about the expressive, emotional side of human communication. More has been contributed about emotional communication by ethologists than linguists. Despite their popularity, books on body language do little more than provide dictionaries of body positions and gestures, similar to dream dictionaries that purport to relate symbols to emotional messages.

In fact the grammar, syntax, and rhetoric of affective communication are largely unknown. Any "principles" that are enunciated have the status, at best, of hypotheses rather than proven generalizations.

The therapist working with feeling moments who wants to aid the client's movement toward complete expression of a feeling will find as much guidance in books on drama, poetry, rhetoric, and film as from the scientific literature.

Here are some rough generalizations about how to work with expressions to reveal emotional meanings:

1. Vary the loudness of the expression; ask the client to say something louder or softer.
2. Vary the tempo of the expression; ask the client to speak faster or slower.
3. Vary the emphases in the expression; ask the client to stress different words.
4. Change the movements that accompany the expression; ask the client to move faster, slower, more smoothly, more unevenly, and change the form of the gesture.
5. Change the position of the body; ask the client to take different postures.
6. Change the direction of the delivery; have the client move closer, farther away, to the side, etc.
7. Vary the number of times an expression is made; some emotional expressions sound very different the tenth time they are delivered by the client.
8. Substitute nonsense words or sounds for the original words and work with the dynamics of the sounds. This device can take the client completely away from the mismatched words and allow the feeling to come through. After the feeling is clearly felt new accurate words can be fitted to the expression.

All of these dynamics are familiar to poets, songwriters, speechwriters, and advertisers. Surprisingly, they are seldom directly taught to students of therapy. The reason for that neglect is that therapists and teachers of therapy too frequently focus on understanding and discovering the *cognitive* meanings of the client and not the *emotional* meanings. The statement

"I'm not hungry," for example, has a simple cognitive meaning that will be readily understood by anyone. However if the therapist detects that there is a mismatch between what is said and what is felt the best way to elucidate the hidden emotional content is to work with the dynamics of expression (have the person repeat the statement, say it louder, change the gestures, say it softer, etc.) rather than ask the individual to explain. An explanation in reply to the question, "What do you mean when you say 'I'm not hungry'?" will stay at the same emotional level or even go farther away from the emotional content. In contrast, direct work with the dynamics of expression does not add irrelevant content. Instead, the submerged or contrasting emotional expression can begin to surface.

An example. There is a danger in giving examples of feeling moments and therapeutic work with the dynamics of expression. It takes a truly great novelist to evoke strongly the feelings behind words on paper; and a novelist uses many pages to set the context for dialogue. In a short therapy sample the interchanges between a client and therapist all too easily can sound flat and emotionally trivial. But, with these forewarnings, here is a short transcription of a part of a session.

The client is a 32-year-old woman who came back for two emergency sessions with a therapist she had seen in individual therapy for a year and a half. They had not met together for nine months. She was distressed because of some things people in a group therapy setting had said to her (she and her spouse had continued to go to biweekly group sessions with another therapist after ending their individual therapy sessions). This transcription begins about half way through the session:

> C: It's not fair for me to want to come running to you when I don't feel good.
> T: Not fair?
> C: Yeah not fair at all.
> T: What's not fair?
> C: You get all the shit and none of the flowers.
> T: You're supposed to bring me flowers?
> C: No but I want to. You are really special to me. I really value what you gave me before. I don't think I'll ever feel hopeless and helpless again. I know how it feels to be helped.
> T: You want help now?
> C: Yes I know I do . . . but . . .
> T: I want you to say "It's not fair to want to come running when I don't feel good."
> C: It's not fair to want to come running when I don't feel good.
> T: Louder.
> C: (She repeats the expression and begins to cry.)

T: Say it like a question.

C: (She repeats the statement as a question, and continues to cry.)

T: Now say it with your eyes closed and say it softly; whisper.

C: (This time the repetition reveals more yearning and wanting in the voice.)

T: Now I want you to say just the second part, "I want to come running when I don't feel good."

C: (This declarative statement is delivered with crying but there is more support behind the voice.)

T: Open your eyes.

C: Hi.

T: Hi . . . What you're saying is very important. Can you feel it?

C: Feel what?

T: Can you experience the feeling behind those words?

C: Oh yes, I *do* want to come running when I don't feel good. . . .

This session continued for another half hour with talk about what is "fair" and what is not and some brief discussion about the meaning of this kind of emotional expression from the client's past. No attempt actually was made to take the client into the old feelings because she seemed able to integrate the new, direct emotional expression without a further exploration of her early experiences with her father and mother. When the session ended the client and therapist agreed to schedule only special sessions, when the client felt she needed them, rather than meet on a regular weekly schedule. The therapist explained that he could make this arrangement because of the current flexibility of his activities; if his schedule changed he would need to make other arrangements.

This brief transcription with an experienced client might make the exploration of feeling moments seem a little too easy. What is missing are resistances. How and when resistances are dealt with will be discussed in Chapter 12.

Reich and the Need for Emotional Expression

Among the many therapeutic traditions that indirectly have used the Darwinian approach to emotional *expression* as necessary for the organism can be included: the humanistic therapies, psychodrama, the encounter group therapies, and the body therapies. Of these various therapies none exhibited a clearer understanding of the necessity for emotional expressiveness in the therapy situation than that of Wilhelm Reich.

I discussed in several sections of Part II how theorists who split from mainline psychoanalysis often found a receptive home for their ideas and methods in functionally oriented therapies. The reason was that most neo-analytic theorists placed more importance on ego functioning and consciousness in their system than did Freud. However there is also another type of theoretical schism from Freudian theory that fits into functional theory when the Darwinian roots of the theory are clearly understood. The body therapies of Ferenczi, Gros, and especially Reich are completely aligned with the notion that it is not sufficient to experience a feeling or image cognitively but that *expression* must be a concomitant of the experience.

This point was never fully clarified by James, Janet, and the other functional pioneers. Sometimes they seem to be saying that experience and recognition of a feeling are enough; at other times they imply experience must be coupled with expression for therapeutic effectiveness. Only when the clinical side of functional theory is clearly connected to Darwin's arguments about emotional expressiveness are the therapeutic directions made clear. Of all the functionalist pioneers, Burrow most clearly recognized this necessary alignment. Unfortunately Burrow himself became too much of an outcast from the professional mainstream to offer a haven of respectibility and acceptance to Reich, as Taft did for Rank. (There is no historical evidence that I know to suggest that Burrow and Reich were familiar with each other's work.) Nonetheless their theories and methods are very similar in two significant ways:

1. Both stressed that ordinary normal life was often affectively insane or disordered.
2. Both based their methods on rebalancing the affective side of the organism and undermining the false use of the affect system by the symbol system.

Reich first gained notoriety by establishing adolescent sex clinics. He argued that since all hysterical disorders were dysfunctions of sexuality the best way to treat and prevent hysteria would be to teach and encourage people to have fuller, satisfying sexual experiences. In this post-Kinsey and post-Masters and Johnson age of modern sex therapy, Reich's approach seems mild and reasonable. But in the early 1900s his sex clinics were extremely controversial.

His major theory of practice, which definitely divided him from traditional analysis, was put forth in the book *Character Analysis,* first published in 1933.

Reich argued that it is not necessary for the therapist to wait for slips of the tongue, blocks in free associations, or dreams in order to identify resistances. Resistances, he argued, are everpresent as soon as the therapist shifts attention from the content of an interaction with a client to the form or style of the client's way of being:

> The character resistance expresses itself not in the content of the material, but in the formal aspects of the general behavior, the manner of talking, of the gait, facial expression and typical attitudes such as smiling, deriding, hautiness, overcorrectness, the *manner* of the politeness or of the aggression, etc.
>
> What is specific of the character resistance is not *what* the patient says or does, but *how* he talks and acts, not *what* he gives away in a dream but *how* he censors, distorts, etc.
>
> The character resistance remains the same in one and the same patient no matter what the material is against which it is directed. (Reich, 1960, p. 66)

Rephrasing Reich's points into the functionalist language of this chapter, he is saying that the ways a person avoids expression, avoids feeling moments, and covers over gaps in consciousness are consistent regardless of the content of the feeling that is covered over. Every person acquires consistent dynamics of repression to cover over their dynamics of expression.

Reich goes on to specify how character resistances must be handled therapeutically, not through words but through actions:

> *The living expresses itself in movements, in expressive movements* . . . the words which describe emotional states render, in an *immediate* way the corresponding expressive movements of living matter. . . . In order to arrive at a true evaluation, one has to ask the patient *not* to talk for a while. . . . For as soon as the patient ceases to talk, the bodily expression of emotion becomes clearly manifest. After a few minutes of silence, one usually comprehends the outstanding character trait, or more correctly, the plasmatic emotional expression. While the patient, during his talking seemed to smile in a friendly manner, now, in silence the smile turns into an empty grin the mask-like character of which will soon become obvious even to the patient. (Reich, 1960, pp. 148, 149, 150)

From what Reich is claiming here it is perhaps possible to understand why Burrow and Reich both so completely distrusted the ability of outside observers to assess what is "going on" in a therapy session that is devoted to revealing character resistances and releasing emotional expressions behind frozen, but socially acceptable interpersonal exchanges. By working with the form or function rather than the content of an expression the body therapist may seem to be engaging in nonsense. That is because the grammar of affective communication and the grammar of cognitive communication are so different.

For example, in cognitive communication it makes no sense to use silence to communicate *more*. Cognitive information is imparted only in spoken or written units. But affective communications are conveyed silently as well as verbally. Reich says, *word language very often also functions as a defense:* the word language obscures the expressive language of the biological core. . . . By disclosing the pathological forms of expression we learn to know human biopathy in a depth which is inaccessible to the therapeutic techniques working with word language. Unfortunately, the biopathy, with its disturbed expression of life, is outside the realm of language and concepts. (Reich, 1960, pp. 150, 151)

The functional therapist's efforts to understand gaps in expression and help the client fill in those gaps involves more than work with words. Expressive words, expressive gestures, and expressive postures are all targets of therapeutic work. To make the gaps visible to the client the therapist often must change the dynamics of the expression, by freezing emblematic expressions, replaying micro-expressions, and changing the tempo of the interchanges. In the same way that motor performance can be improved and motor errors revealed by the use of slow-motion and fast-scan video feedback so does the functional therapist act as a kind of motion director to reveal expressive gaps and inconsistencies. (In this activity actual video feedback is very helpful in the therapy setting; this method will be described in the Manual, Part IV.)

Reich goes on to discuss the biological basis of empathy and its rootedness in emotional-expressive identification between organisms:

We comprehend the expressive motions and the emotional expressions of another living organism on the basis of the identity of our emotions with those of all that is living. We comprehend the language of the living *immediately* on the basis of the functional identity of the biological emotions. (Reich, 1960, p. 172)

What Reich has done here is the same thing that Burrow and James did: Emotional expressiveness is identified as the biological core of person to person, people to people, and species to species communications. The clinical significance of this Darwinian thesis is clear: The therapist must create feeling moments that will help the client to attend to those gaps or distortions that disrupt the primary biological basis of the therapist–client contacts.

Readers who are familiar with Reich's career will know that he went on from these observations, made at what I have identified as the functional level of discourse, to chemical, cellular, and energetic observations and speculations about "orgone energy." These extensions of Reich's theory never have been carefully evaluated. Reich himself was pursued by the Food and Drug Administration and eventually died in federal prison. He was jailed and all his writings and devices were banned because of what the government contended were his false claims about the curative effects of orgone. Reich was convicted on a contempt of court charge because he refused to recognize the authority of the courts to decide a scientific issue. Whether this phase of Reich's career represents quackery or persecution cannot be known at this time. It resembles the current scientific controversies surrounding laetrile and other unorthodox treatments for cancer.

Nonetheless Reich's functional methods of character analysis and his perceptive application of the Darwinian thesis about emotional expressiveness to clinical work can be utilized by modern eclectic therapists who need make no judgment pro or con about Reich's orgone theory.

Alexander Lowen (1958) and Stanley Keleman (1971) have developed the pre-orgone stages of Reich's therapy into an effective set of techniques, called bioenergetic therapy, which will be used in Part IV of this book.

Reich uses the term *functional* repeatedly in his theoretical formulations. Of course I do not want to argue simplistically that every therapist using the term *functional* is a "functionalist." That would be similar to saying that every philosopher who ever used the term "existence" was an "existentialist."

What matters is how a term is used. Reich's clinical usage is very similar to James's, Janet's, and Burrow's. Of central importance to it is the willingness to relate internal and external phenomena, experiences, and observations. Reich states very clearly,

> *Self-perception is an essential part of the natural life-processes.* It is not nerves here, muscles there and vegetative sensations in a third place; rather the processes taking place in the tissues form an indivisible *functional unity* with their perception. . . . We have to distinguish clearly between functional thinking and mechanistic thinking which cuts things apart and will never grasp living functioning. Let us put down four important principles of a functional concept of nature:
>
> 1. Every living organism is a functional unit; it is not merely a mechanical sum total of organs. The basic biological function governs every individual organ as it governs the total organism.
> 2. Every living organism is a part of surrounding nature and functionally identical with it.
> 3. Every perception is based on the consonance of a function within the organism with a function in the outer world; that is, it is based on vegetative harmony.
> 4. Every form of self-perception is the immediate expression of objective processes within the organism (psychophysical identity). (Reich, 1960, pp. 218, 219)

What Reich says in this quoted passage is an extension of Dewey's argument against the reflex-arc concept discussed in Chapter 2. Reich pushes the Dewey–James argument about the centrality of emotional consciousness to its limits. What he, Darwin, Dewey, James, Burrow, and all the other functionalist theorists assert is that the emotional side of human nature is essential for the perception of reality. Emotions and feelings are not merely the necessary preoccupation of clinicians when they dysfunction, but full and accurate emotional perception and expression are required to function in the world of biological reality.

Conclusions

In the preface to the 1965 edition of Darwin's *The Expression of the Emotions in Man and Animals*, Konrad Lorenz states, "I believe that even today we do not quite realize how much Darwin knew" (Darwin, 1872/1965, p. xiii). Therapists should give special emphasis to Lorenz's judgment of Darwin. There is no other historical source besides Darwin that provides such a persuasive rationale for the centrality of emotional expression in human functioning.

Within the functional orientation the basic unit of therapy is the feeling moment. A feeling moment comes into existence whenever the therapist makes the client aware that a gap or emotional inconsistency exists between experience and expression. A feeling gap represents a break in intrapersonal and interpersonal contact. Contact cannot be sustained or improved unless feeling gaps are completed through expression. To explain how feeling moments can successfully be brought to completion we will next look at the functional theory of dreams and dream work in therapy.

The consequences of defining the feeling moment as the critical unit for psychotherapy are several:

1. The process of therapy is specified as an emotional-cognitive-action process. Awareness, feeling, and expression all must be involved to complete a feeling moment.
2. Because of their evolutionary link to the needs of biological survival, feeling moments are much more than therapeutic curiosities. Just as an organism will not long survive if it leaves significant gaps in its perception and understanding of the external environment, neither can an organism function effectively if it leaves many gaps in its inner emotional awareness and expressiveness.
3. Therapists must be capable of much more than guiding the way clients understand their emotions, they must guide them to effective emotional expressions.
4. Since expressions are actions, therapy becomes action oriented rather than merely introspective.
5. True emotional expressions are necessarily spontaneous, which means that the content and direction of every therapy session will be essentially unpredictable. An effective therapist must be extremely flexible. Therapy that focuses on feeling moments shares more of the qualities of street theatre than it does the qualities of a staged performance.

6. Whether a feeling moment will lead to the reemergence of repressed feelings or the emergence of mature feelings is unknown when the therapist and client first approach a feeling gap. Therefore, the client and the therapist must be open to both possibilities.

Overall, it is the full experiencing of feeling moments that contributes largely to both adaptation and satisfaction in life.

9

A Functional Theory of Dreaming

The emergence of feeling moments into consciousness and the use of expression dynamics to aid this emergence is the working level of functional therapy. At times it is both possible and desirable to think about each therapy session as "nothing but" a series of feeling moments. The therapist working at this level does nothing but follow the stream of feeling consciousness wherever it goes and uses expression dynamics to further the flow whenever it becomes narrowed, diverted, or affectively inconsistent. But this level of work is too molecular by itself to orient the therapist fully within a session or across sessions. It is necessary to move up a level to understand how feeling moments and expression dynamics are organized into molar personality characteristics that can be targeted for therapeutic intervention.

Therapists who attempt to practice strictly at the molecular event level would be overwhelmed by the sheer number of moments that occur in a single session and would have no way of choosing or ordering the critical events that occurred; each feeling and each expression of feeling would be weighted equally. Progress in therapy typically implies some movement. When this expectation of progress or of personality change is included in the therapist's conceptual framework, a theory of personality organization and change must then be added. If feeling moments are taken as the basic critical units of therapy, then personality characteristics that describe the progression from less integrated to more integrated feelings are the natural target dimensions of personality for the functional therapist.

In this chapter a functional theory of dreaming will be presented that shows how responsiveness to feeling moments and the dynamics of feeling expression can be organized into personality dynamisms.[1] By a "dynamism" is meant a fluctuating personality characteristic related to emotional perceptiveness and expressiveness. (Dynamisms do not have the status of traits or dimensions of personality; they are much less stable and much more situation specific. A person's level of functioning on any emotional dynamism can vary not only with the situation but with the emotion. For example, some people readily express anger but rarely express sadness.)

Dreams never have been a major or even a secondary focus of functional theory. So most of the theory will be drawn from research and clinical work with dreams and daydreams from the last 15 years. The reason I am choosing to locate this next level of clinical theorizing within the context of dreams is because the way a person dreams provides a very clear picture of how effectively he or she expresses and experiences feelings. For the dreamer there are no outer distractions, there is nothing to perceive, to understand, to cope with, or to model coming from the outer environment. Therefore, the way a dreamer responds to feeling moments in dreams is largely self determined.[2] Also, because the cognitive drive to explore and to understand is diminished at night, the affective drive to complete feelings is in the ascendancy. Dreams are primarily affective experiences and only secondarily concerned with cognitive processing. From the functional perspective dreams provide clear pictures of how much awareness the dreamer shows of feelings and in what ways the dreamer responds from feelings. Dreams, then, are regarded

---

[1] Portions of this chapter were reprinted earlier in Karle, Hopper, Corriere, Hart, and Switzer (1980) and Hart, Corriere, Karle, and Woldenberg (1980). For further details about research on the functional approach to dreams see these references and the specific research reports cited in them. This chapter concentrates on theory.

[2] A major controversy within the field of personality in the last two decades has been the trait versus situational issue. Are typical responses most determined by general characteristics within the person or by demand characteristics of the situation? The eclectic position that has developed out of this controversy is called interactionalism; sometimes traits are prepotent and sometimes demand characteristics are prepotent, and sometimes there is an interactional effect—the research must determine which condition exists through experimentation. (See Pervin, 1978, for a review of this position.) What I am suggesting here is that dreams are likely to show emotional traits more clearly than waking experiences because situational demand characteristics are diminished. (They are of course not eliminated, but are supplied in the dream by the dreamer's memory.) The only way to determine whether the personality dynamisms revealed in dreams are traits of emotional expressiveness is to look at a series of dreams and examine the consistency or inconsistency across dream, fantasy, and waking experiences.

as pictures of feelings and moving pictures of the ways a person responds to feelings.

As mentioned, there is no ready-made set of ideas, observations, and case studies to draw upon in constructing a functional theory of dreams. None of the functionalist pioneers, not James, nor Janet, nor Burrow, nor Taft, nor Thorne developed a functional theory of dreaming to compete with analytic theories of dream interpretation.

Nor did the later academic functionalists develop a theory of dreaming. A clear example of the failure of functionalists to offer alternative approaches to dreaming is found in the work of Gordon Allport. It was Allport who, along with Henry Murray, brilliantly carried on the Jamesian tradition of functional eclecticism at Harvard. Allport's book on personality, published in 1937, virtually created the modern field of personality theory and research and gave the field a distinctively functionalist bent. Nonetheless, even in the 1961 edition of his book, Allport has only one entry in the subject index and only one sentence in the text about dreams. That sentence is: "Dreams, for example, often reveal the primary process in spite of repressions that operate during waking hours" (Allport, 1937/1961, p. 147). By adopting the Freudian perspective on dreams and by accepting Freud's language about "primary processes," Allport indirectly cedes the entire field of dreaming to the analysts. (This is all the more peculiar for Allport to do because, as we shall see later in this chapter, he had in his research repertoire a very effective technical approach that easily could have been applied to a functional study of dreams.) When functionalists such as Allport and Murray did work with fantasy materials they focused on daydreams rather than dreams, presumably because fantasies were assumed to be more accessible to conscious control and reporting than dreams.

Because the functionalists did not offer an alternative explanation for dreams or alternative ways to work with dreams (and most behaviorists ignored dreams and other mental contents entirely), the analytic approach to dreams became almost the only approach available to clinicians. The analytic emphasis on the inference of underlying, unconscious dynamics from dream symbols and free associations became the standard method of clinical dream work. For therapists the choice was: apply one of the varieties of analytic interpretation to dreams or not work with dreams at all. That is perhaps why even in the work of modern-day heirs of the functionalist tradition such as the humanistic therapist Carl Rogers there is no systematic clinical attention given to dreams. The notable exception to this generalization about humanistic therapy is the work of Fritz Perls, but Perls worked clinically, from a combination of psychoanalysis

(Freud and Reich) and psychodrama, not from functional psychology.

What this lack of a direct functional tradition in dream theory means now is that any effort to construct such a theory must be explicitly developed from and contrasted with the dominant analytic dream theories. Accordingly, I will begin this chapter with a critique of dream theory from a functionalist perspective.

Critiques of the Interpretive Approach to Dreams

Freud

The influence of Freud's theoretical views on the nature and function of dreaming has been enormous. Although they marked a significant advance in the understanding of dream phenomena, they also were limiting. They created a preoccupation with the content and interpretation of single dreams rather than the ongoing, variable dream processes. Further, by stressing the determinative power of early childhood experiences, Freudian theory overlooked the importance of present waking behavior on dream life and the potentiality for basic shifts in affect.

From the analytic perspective the primary approach is to interpret the content of dreams. Freud was able to advance dream theory by treating dreams as meaningful and *personal* communications. He formulated a theory and a method that allowed the sometimes confusing, bizarre, and seemingly nonsensical expressions that occur in dreams to be deciphered into their hidden meanings about a dreamer's wishes and inner life.

Freud expressed the central idea of his theory in the first major work, *The Interpretation of Dreams* (1960). Chapter 3 is titled "A Dream is the Fulfillment of a Wish." It is his succinct definition of a dream. Because a dream is the fulfillment of a wish, all dreams become meaningful once we discover the hidden wishes that are disguised by the dream symbolism. Freud goes on to argue this in the *New Introductory Lectures* (1933/1965):

> What has been called the dream is the text of the dream or the *manifest* dream, and what we are looking for, what we suspect, so to say, of lying behind the dream, we shall describe as the *latent* dream thoughts. . . . We have to transform the manifest dream into the latent one, and to explain how, in the dreamer's mind, the latter has become the former. (pp. 9–10)

The normal dream contains a visible text (manifest content) and an invisible cause (latent content). Freud admits that this dream form is incomplete because some transforming and explanation are necessary to make the latent content apparent. In *A General Introduction to Psychoanalysis* (1953) he comments:

> *The process by which the latent dream is transformed into the manifest dream is called THE DREAM-WORK;* while the reverse process, which seeks to progress from the manifest to the latent thoughts, is our work of interpretation; the work of interpretation therefore aims at demolishing the dream work. (p. 179)

The discovery process, or interpretation, changes the dream from its symbolic form to its real form and the wishes are disclosed. A dream in its real form, according to Freud, has a clear *meaning*. It is a *meaningful* communication.

Freud used the following dream to illustrate his theory and method. It is often discussed in the literature as his "Irma Dream." He later related, "This is the first dream I submitted to a detailed interpretation." We can contrast very clearly the functional approach to working with dreams to the Freudian approach using this specimen.

Dream of July 23rd–24th, 1895

A large hall—numerous guests whom we were receiving—among them was Irma. I at once took her on one side, as though to answer her letter and to reproach her for not having accepted my "solution" yet. I said to her: "If you still get pains, it's really only your fault." She replied: "If you only knew what pains I've got now in my throat and stomach and abdomen." I was alarmed and looked at her. She looked pale and puffy. I thought to myself that after all I must be missing some organic trouble. I took her to the window and looked down her throat and she showed signs of recalcitrance, like women with artificial dentures. I thought to myself that there was really no need for her to do that. She then opened her mouth properly and on the right I found a big white patch; at another place I saw extensive whitish grey scabs upon some remarkably curly structures which were evidently modeled on the turbinal bones of the nose. I at once called Dr. M., and he repeated the examination and confirmed it. . . . Dr. M. looked quite different from usual; he was very pale, he walked with a limp and his skin was clean-shaven. . . . My friend Otto was now standing beside her as well, and my friend Leopold was percussing her through her bodice and saying: "She has a dull area low down on the left." He also indicated that a portion of the skin on the left shoulder was infiltrated. (I noticed this, just as he did, in spite of her dress.) . . . M. said "There's no doubt it's an infection, but no matter, dysentery will supervene and the toxin will be eliminated." . . . We were directly aware, too, of the origin of the infection. Not long before, when she was feeling unwell, my friend Otto had given her an injection of propyl, propyls . . . propionic acid . . . tri-methylthylamin (and I saw before me the formula for this printed in heavy type). . . . Injections of that sort ought not to be made so thoughtlessly. . . . And probably the syringe had not been clean. (Freud, 1960, p. 107)

Freud proceeds to analyze the dream by first recounting the events of the previous day that were partially represented in his dream and then by giving his associations to each of the elements of the dream. For example, his mention of the final image of the dream is as follows:

And probably the syringe had not been clean. This was yet another accusation against Otto, but derived from a different source. I had happened the day before to meet the son of an old lady of eighty-two, to whom I had given an injection of morphine twice a day. At the moment she was in the country and was suffering from phlebitis. I had at once thought it must be an infiltration caused by a dirty syringe. I was proud of the fact that in two years I had not caused a single infiltration. (Freud, 1960, p. 118)

He concluded his interpretation with this summary:

The dream fulfilled certain wishes which were stunted in me by the events of the previous evening (the news given me by Otto and my writing out of the case history). The conclusion of the dream, that is to say, was that I was not responsible for the persistence of Irma's pains, but that Otto was. Otto had in fact annoyed me by his remarks about Irma's incomplete cure and the dream gave me my revenge by throwing the reproach back on to him. The dream acquitted me for the responsibility for Irma's condition by showing that it was due to other factors—it produced a whole series of reasons. The dream represented a particular state of affairs as I should have wished it to be. *Thus its content was the fulfillment of a wish and its motive was a wish.* (Freud, 1960, p. 114–115)

Freud intended this dream and its interpretation to show that dreams are wish fulfillments, not necessarily to demonstrate the dynamics of his theories in action. But this example encompasses the fundamental way in which Freud saw dreams—as symbolic messages about wish-messages. The dream analysis ends with an understanding.

Freud's basic thesis is that dreams are wish fulfillments. But wishes are feelings that have not been expressed fully. Because of this, the wish–fulfillment theory does not take into account the dynamics of affect expression. Dreams are taken as fixed messages, not as mutable forms of expression. This approach bypasses the dynamic shift from passive, incomplete, symbolic nonexpression to active, complete, and direct expression. The theory and the dream on which it is founded are the same in that they both are fixed without allowing for movement toward expression and nonsymbolism.

An extremely interesting personal account of the benefits and limits of the psychoanalytic interpretive approach to dreams is now available in Dr. Abraham Kardiner's book *My Analysis with Freud* (1977). Kardiner reports a pivotal dream in the analysis, which Freud very subtly and accurately interpreted, concluding with "[you] remained submissive and obedient to him in order not to arouse the sleeping dragon, the angry father."

Kardiner comments:

My immediate reaction was to accept Freud's interpretation. It was not until many years later that I understood the basic error committed here by Freud. The man who had invented the concept of transference did not recognize it when it occurred here. He overlooked one thing: *Yes, I was afraid of my father in childhood, but the one*

whom I feared now was Freud himself. He could make me or break me which my
father no longer could. By this statement he pushed the entire reaction into the past,
thereby making the analysis an historical reconstruction. (p. 58)

Such a therapeutic error would be less likely to occur within the
functional approach to dreams because the focus is on *how* the dreamer
functioned in his dream and in his life not on what caused the dream.
Of course within the functional approach, the sources of arrested
functioning can be examined, not merely to trace the causation of symbolic
functioning, but to help the patient to develop a more satisfying level
of functioning. To do that the patient would need to express his real
feelings in the present, to the therapist and others in his life.

The basic thesis of functionalism is that dreams are attempts to
complete feelings that were left incomplete. Obviously this emphasis
overlaps Freud's thesis because wishes are incomplete feelings. But the
functional theory includes the wish-fulfillment theory as a special case.

And then there is the one about a man who tells his analyst, "Last night I had this
dream about keys and locks." And the analyst interprets the dream for the patient,
to show him that he was symbolically dreaming about sexual intercourse. So the next
day he reports another dream, this time about having sex with his wife, and he quickly
adds, "But I know I was really dreaming about keys and locks."—Anonymous

While this well-worn clinical joke oversimplifies both what analysts
do and what dreamers report, it poses several important questions about
dreams. First, what is the function of dreaming; what does dreaming
about locks and keys accomplish for the dreamer *while* he dreams? Second, when is a dream symbolic, and when is it "real" or directly representational? When are we dreaming about sex and when do we dream
about locks and keys? Third, where do symbols originate? Are they
mysterious products of an unknown nighttime physiological mechanism
or do they originate in the process of the dreamer's daytime experience?
Fourth, do nonsymbolic dreams occur? And fifth, if they do occur, is it
possible to shift from symbolic to nonsymbolic dreaming *within* a dream?
Can dreams become nonsymbolic without outside interpretation? Is the
analysis necessary or even beneficial in the above story?

In fairness, I should say that Freud's answers to these questions
were limited because they are not his questions. However, part of the
task of advancing a research area is to give new answers to old questions;
the other is to ask new questions. Freud did this himself when he posed
and answered the critical question, "Can nonsensical dreams be interpreted
to make sense?"

What is the function of dreaming? Freud argues that during sleep,
dreams do what has not been done in waking—they have a compensatory

function. His answer to this question often has been shortened in quotations and paraphrases to say: dreams protect sleep. But his fuller answer is more significant and more general:

> Dreaming has taken on the task of bringing back under control of the pre-conscious the excitation in the unconscious which has been left free; in so doing it discharges the unconscious excitation, serves it as a safety valve and at the same time preserves the sleep of the preconscious in return for a small expenditure of waking activity. (Freud, 1960, p. 579)

Freud believed that dreams compensate for unresolved excitation to the unconscious, making it conscious in a new form. Because this new form exists at a lower level of excitement it allows sleep to continue. Although some energy, such as tossing and turning, murmuring, movement, etc., is utilized in return for this compensation, it is small in comparison to the amount of energy that is discharged through this "safety valve." Dreams not only protect sleep, they "protect waking" as well.

In the functional approach dreaming is a natural releasing activity in which feelings that were not expressed or not expressed fully during the day try to come to completion through expression. Symbolic dreams give a partial release, while more functional dreams move toward a full release. Dreaming is expressive as well as "compensatory."

Dreaming is not the "guardian of sleep," but the "agent of feeling." Sleep does not need "protection." This is too confining a concept. People can have as much and sometimes more excitement and feeling at night as during the day. With the shift into a functional mode of dreaming, nighttime experiences become "vehicles of expression" that can show the dreamer psychological possibilities not yet experienced in waking. Dreaming becomes a powerful experience, sometimes prospective in feeling *and* meaning. Dreams are prospective in the sense that they arise from the dreamer's heritage for complete expression in his past and his intellectual and physical capability to expand his range of expression into new adult forms.

When are dreams symbolic? Except for children's dreams and very trivial and infrequent adult dreams, Freud would say that dreams are always symbolic because the dream work mechanism, or censor, is always converting direct wishes into direct symbols. He says there are no "innocent dreams"—dreams that are directly expressive. "What we dream is either manifestly recognizable as psychically significant (rare or nonexistent), or it is distorted and cannot be judged until the dream has been interpreted (the usual case) (Freud, 1960, p. 182).

In the functional view dreams are symbolic when the dreamer has not completed his feelings in his waking life; they are nonsymbolic when he has. Nonsymbolic dreams, far from being "trivial" or "innocent," are the best indicators that a person is living his feelings.

Where do symbols originate? Although Freud devotes most of his description to dream work mechanisms such as displacement, condensation, and secondary revision, he never gives a clear statement about where these mechanisms of distortion originate. Dream work could be an existing and healthy part of our neurophysiology.

Symbols arise from two sources. First, they are the result of the translation from words, perceptions, and actions in waking life to the pictures or images of dreaming. Freud treats this case adequately. Secondly, they result from the disordering or mixing of feeling components that occurs when feelings are not completed. Here Freud is vague; he never specifies whether the dream work mechanism is pathologically acquired. The functional view asserts that it is; emotional disorders are not caused by dream censors or dream work mechanisms intrinsic to the dreamer. The mechanisms are caused by the *external disordering* that children and adults undergo. These mechanisms of disordering or distortion (such as substitution) are learned. Dreaming is naturally distortion-free.

Children have more intense dreams than adults, and more "nightmares," because they have more intense feelings during the day. At the beginning stages of disordering they are unable to symbolize enough of the feelings left incomplete during the day to avoid experiencing them at night. There is ample evidence that children's dreams alter from almost nonsymbolic expressions of feeling to indirect, symbolic withholdings of feelings as they get older (cf. Foulkes, 1981; Foulkes, Larson, Swanson, & Rardin, 1969; van de Castle, 1970). There also is evidence that the way children talk about their feelings becomes more and more abstract and impersonal as they get older and learn the adult forms of nonexpression (cf. Lewis, Wolman, & King, 1971). Adult symbolization has both a present cause, the way our expressions were disordered during the day, and a past antecedent, the origin of that disordering in the past.

Can dreams be nonsymbolic? Freud recognizes that nonsymbolic dreams can occur, but his evaluation of their significance is limited to using them as proof for his theory of dreams as wish-fulfillments:

> The dreams of young children are frequently pure wish-fulfillments and are in that case quite uninteresting compared with the dreams of adults. They raise no problems for solution, but on the other hand are of inestimable importance in proving that, in their essential nature dreams represent fulfillments of wishes. (Freud, 1960, p. 124)

In the functional view nonsymbolic dreams imply something far more significant. If disorder can lead to progressively more symbolization, then, conversely, reordering leads to progressively less symbolization in dreaming. The movement toward complete expression of matched feelings in waking leads to functional dreaming. The following type of dream begins to emerge with increasing frequency:

> I am talking to N. (wife). She and I are fighting and I feel myself going away from her and me. I stop fighting and say to myself "I want." She has to feel how she feels—I want. And then I feel my *own* body. I feel I *want*. (Dreamer's emphasis)

Although the dream does not represent a complete expression, such as verbalizing "I want," it does present a shift in awareness and clarity from symbolism (fighting) to real feeling (wanting).

Can symbolic to nonsymbolic shifts occur within a dream? Freud does not recognize the possibility of shifts from symbolic to nonsymbolic dreaming within a dream. Dream censorship is not overcome except indirectly, through the post-dream counterwork of interpretation. He would say that once the dream work mechanism is engaged, it stays engaged. He does not recognize the possibility that dream work mechanisms can be overcome.

For the functionalist this shift is the goal. Without this goal in mind, therapeutic work with dreams becomes bogged down in endless hunts for the meanings of symbols. In actuality this disengagement can be striking and the hunt quite short:

> I dreamt I was in a scary unknown house with many scary creatures. I have finally begun to open doors and fight my way through the rooms—the house changed into the house I used to live in in Detroit.

The following dream contains clear functional shifts in the dreamer's processes. The dreamer had just returned from a week-long visit with his family. In a therapy session upon his return, he talked about how he had expressed more than he had any previous visit, but that he did "put up with things I really didn't need to. . . . I had acted like I did as a child." In the dream he had after the session, he noted that he "acted the way I really am now."

> In kitchen with parents. Mother wants to talk to M. (my brother). She says quietly, "M . . . M." Then she shouts "M.! M.! very angrily. She starts to leave. I am aware of no particular feeling. Then I begin to get angry. I see my father stabbing M. in the shoulders for answering my mother angrily. I begin to yell at them, and as I yell, I realize they have no sense at all hurting my brother. He wasn't doing anything wrong. I realize they are like children and I am an

adult. I can really feel my anger all through my body. I enjoy the powerful feeling. My parents run away and stay at a distance, outside the kitchen.

By citing this type of functional dream I am applying Maslow's strategy of seeking the exceptional "good case" instead of the more typical clinical strategy, which is to examine pathological deviations from normality. (Consult Maslow [1954] *Motivation and Personality* for a discussion of his important paradigmatic experiments on "peak experiences.") This strategy of seeking the exceptional gives us a perspective on "normal" dreams that places them on a continuum of disorderedness. Normal dreams are normally diɔordered; they are not the optimal mode of dream life. It is this vision of new possibilities from observing undisguised dreams that forms the essence of the functionalist's disagreement with Freud.

The argument is that undisguised dreams are natural and that what are usually called normal adult dreams are disordered; this leads to a very optimistic view of daytime behavior—it can become less symbolic and more real.

In functional feeling expansion there is a shift from existing *in* an image (a) to more feeling awareness *about* the image (b). Sometimes a temporary image expansion is necessary to guide a person before he can go beyond and behind images into direct feeling expression. Thus image expansion (c) occurs, although it is not always necessary. What is necessary is a third shift that involves functional expansion and image contraction in order for transformation from symbolism to realism to occur (d) There is movement ultimately not toward more feeling *through* images but toward more feeling without images through nonsymbolic expression. This contrast between image expansion and image contraction may seem to substitute the extra-mundane for the mundane. But the intensification of feeling brought about by such a transformation would be anything but dull; it would be a revivification of the dreamer's waking and dreaming life.

The value of symbols. The fact that image expansion sometimes precedes image contraction points to a basic relationship between feelings and images, or, more broadly, between feelings and symbols. The primary emphasis in the functional approach is ɔn recognizing and altering the emotional traits of the dreamer, the shift from symbolism to realism is a secondary emphasis but there is a correlation: more effective emotional functioning eventually leads to more realistic dreams.

It is, however, very often the case that more symbolism is the next step toward less symbolism. The best way out of an image trap might be to expand the image, like a balloon, until it bursts. In a therapy session a patient often is helped to exaggerate an image is is "living *in*" until he can have feelings *about* what living from such an image does to his life. For example, someone who lives from the image "I cannot show everything I feel" may be pushed to express the exaggerated image "I cannot show anything I feel." The first image seems reasonable to him; he is unconscious of its effects on his life. The second image soon seems crazy. By feeling the restricting consequences of the second image on his body and his life, he will begin to feel the consequences of the first image.

One of the values of symbolic dreams is that they show, in pictures, how absurd seemingly rational images can be. The image "I can't show anything" might be represented with the dreamer being attacked by enemies while his friends are all around him. Perhaps only one word would be necessary to save him and he is frustrated because he is unable to make a sound. This type of dream often has a great impact on the dreamer.

Another value of increased symbolism is shown in what Jung (1974) referred to as numinous images. A numinous image is an expanded image that reflects increased general feeling that allows the dreamer to have a feelingful perspective on his life. It symbolizes a direction for the dreamer to pursue in waking that will lead to transformation.

The value of such symbolic dreams is very great. Movement from one level of feeling to another is not accomplished with one simple expression of feeling. The consequences of a simple therapeutic session may take many months to "live out." It is the same for dreams. The numinous dream provides a symbol for the dreamer's new way of living. The symbol functions to help him *remember* how he can be. A powerful symbol is required to overcome the inertia of old habits of nonfeeling. Therefore, far from always being "bad," a symbol or image that works for the dreamer, rather than against him, can counter the inertia of *forgetfulness*.

A point stressed by Janet, Burrows, Dewey, Mead, and other functional theorists is that effective personality change requires social motivation and social support.

As Mead (1934) stressed, "The individual's consciousness depends on his taking the attitude of the other toward his own gestures" (p. 47). A symbol "always presupposes for its significance the social process of experience and behavior in which it arises" (Mead, 1934, p. 89). This means that dreams and dream symbols, one of the most private of our inner experiences, are socially derived and require social interaction if they are to be changed. The shift from interpretive to functional analysis is a shift from a psychological to a socio-psychological emphasis. When a therapist works with a client's dream functionally he or she is essentially inviting the client to be more public and less private, and thus to remove the protective need for distorting symbols. Working with dreams is more complicated when more resistances and defenses (and symbolism) are present. But working with defenses, resistances, and symbolism from dreams is no different than working with these tendencies in waking. (This subject will be discussed in Chapter 12.)

Clinical Examples of Functional Dream Work

The therapist who wants to use the functional approach will first have to make clear the difference between interpreting a dream's meaning and evaluating how the dreamer functioned in a dream. Most clients are predisposed to interpret their own dreams, getting them to do something different will require a clear explanation of how and why the functional approach differs from the interpretive approach.

Here are some instructions that are usually helpful in orienting clients to take a functional approach to their dreams:

The Daily Use of Dreams. There are three basic starter questions that can be applied to any dream to alert you to the way you function. Question One is "How do I feel in this dream?" Be sure you start by asking this question immediately so that you will not be led away from the feelings of the dream into a preoccupation with figuring out the symbols. Question Two is "Am I the main character in this dream?" This question will orient you to pay attention to how you are and what you do. After all, no one else can influence you or force you to dream a certain way, so if you are dreaming of yourself as a spectator or victim you need to become aware of the role you are creating for yourself. Question Three should be applied when you are not satisfied with how you feel or how you were in the dream; ask yourself, "How could I change this dream so that I would feel better?" Actually make up some new endings or new actions that you can imagine for yourself that make the dream feel better.

By asking these questions and taking an active attitude toward dreams in the morning, the dreamer is preventing "dream hangovers" from dominating the way he or she feels during the day and also helps prepare for a transformative or realistic dream at night.

Notice that these methods are applied in the morning. They should *not* be applied at night before going to sleep in an effort to control dreams. The programmatic approach to dreams usually just results in a disruption of sleep; it is not the same as the functional method which works in the morning to change the way a person responds from dreams.

The Long Term Use of Dreams. One: When a dream seems particularly powerful or important to you write it down in a dream journal. Don't try to write down every dream or you will make hard work out of something that should be easy and natural. Two: Be sure to talk about your important dreams with friends just as you would talk about anything else of importance that happened to you. Three: Begin to ask those same three questions ("How do I feel?," "Am I the main character?", and "How could I change this to make myself feel better?") about situations in your life as well as about your dreams. You will then begin to connect your nighttime world of feeling with your daytime world. And you will see that the way you act in the real world is closely connected to how you are in the dream world.

After clients are accustomed to these basic instructions they can be deepened:

If you want to apply the functional approach to your own dreams, you can now go beyond the three starter questions. The functional analysis of dreams focuses on looking at how you were functioning and how you could function. Specifically you can ask yourself, for any dream:
"How expressive was I in this dream?"
"How active was I in this dream?"
"How clear was I in this dream?"
"How much feeling did I experience in this dream?"
"How much contact did I make with other people in this dream?"
It is the activity of paying attention to these functional dynamics that is of importance, not how accurately you evaluate yourself.

Later, clients can be given an even more general understanding of how dreams fit into their waking lives:

One way to understand dreams is to look at dreaming as a form of emotional exercising that each of us does every night. This understanding is in line with the functional emphasis on *how* we dream rather than *what* we dream. It is more important to know how fast and how far someone jogs and how long it takes for their pulse to return to normal than it is to know where they ran or what they saw while jogging. In the same way it is more important to know how effectively you function in your dreams than what you dream about. Once you remember your dreams you can follow this simple exercise to help you work with your dreams.
If I were more active in this dream then . . .
If I were more expressive in this dream then . . .
If I felt more in this dream then . . .
If I were clearer in this dream then . . .
If I made more contact in this dream then . . .
If you ask yourself those five simple questions for each dream you remember, you will begin exercising your dream personality.

By teaching clients to ask these new questions about dreams, the functional therapist actually is educating clients in the functional approach. One of the great advantages of the functional method of working with dreams is that it is comparatively straightforward and easily understood. Clients can apply the functional method to their own dreams after a short period of training. (See Hart & Binder, 1976, for sample training programs with families.)

Within a session the way a therapist works with dreams is simply to first get the client to pay attention to how he or she functioned in a dream (functional dynamisms) and then to try out different increases or decreases in functioning on the different personality dimensions. Here is a short sample of therapeutic work with a dream from an experienced client, who had been exposed to the functional approach to dreams for several months.

T: Tell me the dream.

C: It's still vivid: I was wandering around on the street, just walking with no particular direction in mind. There were many other people around; I could see them but was only vaguely aware that they were around. I was in a state of general malaise. J. stopped me and talked to me about being lost and directionless. He talked directly to me, looking intently into my eyes. I noticed being there with him, being on the street and seeing other people around, and feeling my body and particularly my feet on the ground. As J. talked to me I got increasingly more feeling, mostly sadness. I felt drawn to him and moved toward him. I became even more sad and started crying and telling him how it is for me just to wander around. I felt very settled by his talking to me, soothed by his voice and the words he was saying to me. Then he said, "You need this a lot. You need someone to talk to you like this all the time." I stayed with J. for a long time listening to him and enjoying my sad feeling.

T: How do you feel telling me the dream now?

C: I get the same sad feeling I had in the dream.

T: What would happen if you let that sad feeling increase?

C: I don't know. . . . I'd feel more I guess.

T: Go ahead, remember the dream feeling and let it increase.
   The client is silent for a few minutes and then says:

C: I don't like feeling lost and vague.

T: Go ahead say that again.

C: I don't like feeling lost and vague!

T: Again.

C: I don't like feeling lost and vague!

T: Do you feel sad?

C: Well, underneath, on top I just feel lost and vague.

T: Go underneath. What would you say to me from underneath?

C: I do feel sad. I need someone to talk to before I can feel it.

T: Say that—"I need someone to talk to."

C: I need someone to talk to . . . (crying)

T: That's right K., you can't feel much unless you have someone to share the feeling. You tell yourself that in the dream very clearly.

(From here the client and therapist go on to discuss parallels between the dream feelings and defenses and waking feelings and defenses.)

This dream work comes through very clearly mostly because it was relatively clear to begin with; there was very little symbolism and distortion. About all the therapist needed to do was give the client a chance to repeat and feel some of the emotional expressions in the dream and then connect them to his waking life.

The therapist helped the client increase his feeling level by first allowing him to express the defensive feeling and then the wanting or direct feeling. The interweaving of work with feeling moments, expression dynamics, and personality dynamisms emerges very easily in this dream.

Principles of the Functional Approach to Dreams

Implicit in the critique of the analytic and other theorists in the preceding section were a group of guiding ideas or principles that the functionalist applies to clinical work with dreams. These ideas do not always contradict analytic ideas. Indeed, the functionalist emphasis on work with functional dynamisms and the analytic emphasis on revealing the latent meanings behind dream symbols are not clinically contradictory. The eclectic clinician can apply both approaches. However, the functional predilection is toward *first* working with what is obvious and available to consciousness and then proceeding toward subconscious and unconscious dream meanings. This small difference in what is done first and what is done later makes for very large differences in clinical style. The functional therapist necessarily stresses expression and activity while the analytic therapist tends toward understanding and insight.

Modern dream researchers have been decidedly critical of Freudian dream theory. For example, Fisher and Greenberg (1977) in a book titled

The Scientific Credibility of Freud's Theories and Therapy argued that: (1) There is no research evidence that dreams contain hidden wishes, (2) there is no empirical evidence that free associations to dream symbols clarifies the information contained in the dream, and (3) the manifest content of dreams in itself consistently reveals the personality and attitudes of the dreamer. In a survey of 132 different research modes of dream analysis Winget and Kramer (1979) reported that if images or styles of functioning characterize a person's dreams the same styles and images will be found in waking fantasies. Although dreams emerge at night from a special state of consciousness, they are not discontinuous in their characteristics with material from waking consciousness.

Unfortunately, the results of modern dream research have not been systematically applied to clinical work with dreams. Clinicians need more than scattered research results; a schema for the application of research findings to dreams in a clinical setting is required. The formulation outlined in this section provides one kind of alternative to the typical interpretive approach.

Although handwriting analysis is seldom used by modern therapists, it is a subject that provides a good introduction to the differences between interpretive and functional analyses of dreams. In typical and traditional handwriting analyses the sign approach is utilized. Certain characteristics of the person's writing are related to certain personality characteristics, for example, the ways the *i*'s are dotted (or not dotted) and the ways *t*'s are crossed. This approach is analagous to the fixed symbol interpretation of dream contents. "A high extended *t* cross means" . . . is the same kind of reasoning as "A cave means. . . ."

In a very interesting research study conducted in the early 1930s Allport and Vernon departed from the diagnostic sign approach to handwriting analysis and studied handwriting as just one kind of expressive movement. In their book *Studies in Expressive Movement* (1933/ 1967) they reported that three dimensions of expressive movement could be used to describe differences in handwriting between people and to identify intraindividual consistencies. These three dimensions were: *emphasis* (how much pressure the writer applies and how strong a mark is made); *area* (how much space does the writer occupy), and *centrifugality* (the extent to which the writer maintains a smooth coherent line vs. a spread out, less coherent line). Individuals maintained the same place on these dimensions whether they were writing on paper with a pen or in a box of sand with their toe.

Allport and Vernon comment, *"Our argument is that wherever reliability or internal consistency is found, we have a presumption of some kind of harmony or integration in the expressive behavior of the subjects"* (1933/1967,

p. 97). The functional approach to dreams can follow the same sort of tactic as that applied by Allport and Vernon to the study of handwriting. That is, look not at special sign–symbol meanings but at how a person performs on general dynamisms of expression. In other words, the functional analysis of dreams looks at *how* the dreamer functions expressively in the dream rather than *what* the dream symbols mean. The crucial thing to do from the functionalist approach is to evaluate how well or how poorly the dreamer functioned in the dream.

Five basic dynamisms of functioning in dreams have been identified that relate meaningfully to clinical work. Each of the five evaluates some aspect of how well the dreamer responds to the emotional moments in the dream. The five dynamisms were evaluated in a variety of research studies that indicated that dreamers were consistent from dream to dream and from dream functioning to waking and fantasy functioning. Studies also indicated that dreamers could improve their level of functioning over time. (See Hartshorn, Corriere, Karle, Switzer, Hart, Gold, & Binder, 1977; Karle, Hopper, Corriere, Hart, & Switzer, 1980.)

The Functional Scales

The five basic personality dynamisms are:

1. *The feeling dynamism* refers to the individual's overall feeling level or emotional tone.
2. *The activity dynamism* refers to the specific physical actions an individual takes in response to various events and emotional interactions.
3. *The clarity dynamism* measures the level of awareness the individual has.
4. *The expression dynamism* measures how the individual verbalizes feelings about events and interactions.
5. *The contact dynamism* defines the degree to which an individual moves toward people.

The first dynamism scale, *Feeling*, is used in a broad sense, the category definitions are:

5. *Intense:* The feeling dominates the dream; feeling overrides all else in the dream, e.g., prolonged crying, screaming, anger, terror, dreams of danger, life threatening, extreme feeling situations, intense reliving of childhood feelings, ecstasy.
4. *Strong:* Definite feeling, more than what is usually evident in normal waking life, but feeling does not dominate entire dream.

3. *Moderate:* There is some feeling. The feeling is not vague and in the background but does not dominate or even greatly influence the dream picture.

2. *Slight:* The dream itself evokes some feeling response in the scorer. The feeling, however, is vague and in the background.

1. *No Feeling:* Dreams about things or events that remain affectively neutral. The dream has no effect on the scorer; there is no obvious content that might evoke feeling.

The second dynamism scale, *Activity,* is about the actions of the dreamer. It measures the quality of the dreamer's actions (not the quantity of general activity). The scale definitions are:

5. *Fully Active:* Dreamer's activity in response to dream events is complete. His or her activity is dominating, striking, totally responsive, initiates action, frequently changes consequences of dream.

4. *Clear and Direct:* For the most part the dream feelings and actions make sense in themselves. The picture is clear and direct but not complete. Minor distortions.

3. *Somewhat Clear and Direct:* The dreamer has a general idea of what is going on in the dream feelings and actions. But there is an incomplete development of dream picture. Some elements may be distorted.

2. *Unclear and Indirect:* There is much distortion but it does not completely obscure the dream picture. The dream picture is unclear. There is incomplete development of dream picture. Feelings and events are disconnected. Very little idea of what is happening, no idea why.

1. *Completely Confused:* The dream picture is incoherent. Distortion dominates. Events and feelings have no relationship. Many elements are hazy and undefined. No development of dream theme.

The fourth dynamism scale, *Expression,* is about how intensely the dreamer shows his or her feelings about the dream events or interactions. It has to do with the quality of the dreamer's expression. The scale definitions are:

5. *Intense:* Prolonged and complete expression of feelings. Expression completely dominates the dream. The dreamer continues to express even in the face of obstacles. Total expression. Striking and definite. Dreamer is not confined in any of his expressions by any of the events or characters.

4. *Strong:* Expression that takes preference over all other dreamer activities but is not prolonged or does not dominate the entire dream.
3. *Moderate:* Definite but not striking expression. Clearly does not dominate the dreamer's activity and is only part of the overall dream picture.
2. *Slight:* Some expression but relegated to a minor feature of the dream. The dreamer's expression is not a striking feature of the dream.
1. *No Expression:* No outward manifestation of any type of dreamer expression of feeling and thoughts. There is no manifest display of internal dreamer situation.

The fifth dynamism scale, *Contact,* refers to how much contact with other people the dreamer makes in the dream. The scale points are:

5. *Full Contact:* The dreamer moves toward friends and others in the dream. There is no avoidance of emotional contacts. The dreamer actually touches other people in the dream.
4. *Strong Contact:* Movement toward others is strong but not always complete.
3. *Moderate Contact:* There is more movement toward than away.
2. *Slight Contact:* There is more movement away than toward. Strangers predominate.
1. *No Contact:* No other people in dream or all movement is away from physical contact with others.

These five scoreable dynamisms of emotional functioning in dreaming are not considered to be either exhaustive or independent. There may well be other dynamisms that would be useful to evaluate. Nor is it assumed that these are unitary dynamisms; they might be collapsed into fewer functional characteristics. What is asserted is that this way of analyzing dreams, in which the dreamer's emotional functioning is evaluated before the dream symbols are interpreted is an effective alternative to the typical clinical approach to dreams.

Conclusions

The functional theory of dreams that I have sketched in this chapter contrasts sharply with several analytic preconceptions that have gained general acceptance among clinicians. First, the functional theory does not assume that dreams offer more access to unconscious processes.

Instead, dreams are conceptualized as giving more access to feeling consciousness. Cognitive awareness and feeling awareness both are forms of consciousness. The functionalist does not accept the analytic theorist's tendency to assign feeling processes to unconscious realms. According to functional theory the grammar of thought and the grammar of feeling are different but they are both accessible to awareness and control. Furthermore, both feelings and thoughts, in the functionalist conceptualization, have conscious, subconscious, and unconscious determinants.[3] Functional theory does not assume that dreams are the "royal road to the unconscious." If anything, dreams are the royal road to more feeling consciousness.

Second, functional theory does not assume that dreams have a compensatory function for the personality. In terms of feeling moments, the dynamics of expression, and the five functional dynamisms, dreams parallel waking. A person functioning at a higher level in waking will function at a higher level in dreaming. The reason dreams are sometimes misconstrued as providing a compensatory function to waking consciousness is because waking is so frequently identified with thinking, perceiving, and acting, not with feeling. The person who completely ignores feeling moments during the day will seem to have been plunged into a maelstrom of feeling at night. But this is only relative, the feeling repressor is not experiencing more feeling in dreams than the feeling experiencer but only more feeling than he or she notices during the day.

A shift in the level of theorizing and level of clinical work from a molecular focus on feeling moments and expression dynamics to personality dynamisms was made in this chapter through the study of dreams. In the functional approach to dreams the focus is on *how* the dreamer functions emotionally not on the content of the dream or the interpretation of dream symbols. A functional dream analysis begins with the dreamer's self-assessment of how he or she functioned in the

---

[3] Among contemporary personality theorists the English philosophical psychologist Gooch (1972, 1973) is one of the very few to specify that dreaming is a different form of consciousness, not primarily a manifestation of unconscious mechanism. He points out that signs of dreaming can take place in decorticate animals and assigns to the cerebellum the physical origin of dreams. He also speculates, somewhat in the style of Koestler, that the cerebellular affective consciousness must be synthesized with cerebral cognitive consciousness for full human functioning. An interesting finding that supports this assignment of the cerebellum as the center of affective consciousness is research showing that every feeling experience tends to show a motor discharge in the cerebellum and that every motor discharge from the cerebellum shows a feeling discharge in the midbrain. See Scott, Karle, Switzer, Hart, Corriere, and Woldenberg (1978) Karle, Hopper, Corriere, and Hart (1977), and Karle, Hopper, Corriere, Hart, and Switzer (1977) for psychological research on sleep and dreams related to the functional theory.

dream on the five dynamisms: expressiveness, clarity, feeling, contact, and activity. Then the dreamer considers which functional characteristics might be increased or decreased. Next, the dreamer looks at parallels between the dream profile and similar functional profiles from waking life. Functionalism stresses (1) conscious meaning of the dream as the central meaning; (2) direct expression of feelings as primary and symbolic expression as secondary; (3) a parallelism between waking functioning and dream functioning (in contrast to the compensation or safety valve hypothesis). To change dream function the dreamer must change waking functioning.

Functional analysis of dreamer personality processes does not preclude interpretive analyses of what a dream means. However, the functional hierarchy of taking what is available to consciousness first, what is vague or subliminal second, and what is repressed or unconscious last is applied to dreams in the same way it is applied to fantasies, waking reports, and therapy experiences.

10

Adult Growth and the Goals of Therapy

"Do therapists aim to help their clients feel less badly or feel better?" This may seem to be a simple question with an obvious answer—"both." But in fact most clients want to "feel better" in the sense of getting rid of their painful symptoms. That is why tranquilizers are the number one, two, three, and four most prescribed drugs in the United States (with sleep-inducing drugs close behind).

Imagine two therapists who could absolutely guarantee their therapeutic results and who decided to take advantage of the new laws regulating advertising by professionals. Therapist A advertises that he can cure clients of their painful symptoms, especially anxiety and worry. Therapist B advertises that he can help clients feel better and function more effectively. Who would become rich and famous? It would not even be a close contest; therapist A would need to open branch offices in retail stores to handle all of his customers. Most clients come to a therapist when they feel badly and want to get back to normal. Very few clients go to a therapist when they are feeling well and doing well in order to expand their lives. This situation is so common that clients and therapists often accept it unquestioningly. Consequently, the majority traditions in therapy, psychoanalysis and behavior therapy, always have followed the medical model of cure and symptom relief rather than alternative models. Only the functional school and the modern humanistic heirs of the functional tradition have consistently argued that therapy is a search for growth rather than a cure for illness.

The functional theory of dreaming and functional methods of working with dreams were constructed from a Maslowian model of the peak dream. Instead of basing the theory upon the analysis of malfunctioning, attention was directed to specimens of effective dreaming. This approach, which uses the healthy specimen rather than the pathological specimen, can be extended far beyond work with dreams. It is an essential characteristic of the functional eclectic theory of therapy, extending back to James and Janet.

The difference between emphasizing feeling more and functioning better as a goal of therapy versus the goal of feeling not-so-bad is a major one with important consequences. I will argue in this chapter than an eclectic therapist must give *equal* weight to both goals. To neglect one or the other is to fail to align clinical practice with fundamental research knowledge.

Research on Happiness, Success, and Satisfying Life Styles

There is a large body of relevant research on what makes people feel good and what makes for a satisfying life. Peculiarly, this research is largely ignored by therapists and counselors. Students of counseling and psychotherapy know much more about categories of psychopathology than they do about profiles of success and satisfaction. This curricular omission is a serious one for both clients and therapists since it leads to one-sided concentration on psychopathology rather than a dual concern with eupsychic and pathopsychic factors.

In 1958 the Joint Commission on Mental Illness and Health issued a monograph by Marie Jahoda on *Current Concepts of Mental Health* (Jahoda, 1958). She surveyed the literature and criticized the most common definitions of mental health—"normality" and the "absence of mental disease"—as inadequate. She then identified six approaches to a concept of positive mental health that emerged from a variety of theoretical approaches:

1. Attitudes of an individual toward his or her own self
2. The individual's style and degree of growth, development or self-actualization
3. Integration
4. Autonomy
5. Perception of reality
6. Environmental mastery

It is significant that Jahoda begins and ends her book with citations from the functional theorist Adolf Meyer, "At the beginning of this report stands a statement by Adolf Meyer contrasting two approaches to the field of mental health: the Utopian way, which leads to moralizing, and the scientific way, which leads to experimentation and deliberate action" (Jahoda, 1958, p. 109). She concludes her book with a plea for more research on the *positive* characteristics of mental health.

Bradburn's Research on Psychological Well-Being

The first major study of the quality of life experiences was carried out in 1957 by the Survey Research Center of the Institute for Social Research (see review by Campbell, 1981). This national survey was requested by the National Commission on Mental Illness and Health. The study had a mental illness orientation but included one question asking the 2,460 respondents to indicate how "happy" they were—"very happy," "pretty happy," or "not too happy."

In 1961 Norman Bradburn of the National Opinion Research Center initiated a program of research focusing on happiness and mental health rather than mental illness. I will discuss Bradburn's work at length because of the excellence of his research and the significance of his findings for the theory and practice of eclectic therapy. I believe Bradburn is one of the most important but least recognized researchers in modern clinical psychology. His work provides one of the rarest of the rare kinds of research in social science—a successful replication of interesting and valuable findings.

Bradburn states the basic tone and thrust of his research immediately, in paragraph 1, on page 1, Chapter 1 "On Psychological Well-Being":

> The research reported in this volume is an attempt to apply a social-psychological perspective to the study of mental health in normal populations. It is *not* concerned with the diagnosis of psychiatric cases, whether treated or untreated, but rather with the problems that ordinary Americans face in the pursuit of their life goals. The fundamental question that underlies the study concerns the most fruitful way to understand the psychological reactions of normal individuals to the stresses and strain of everyday life. Thus, our research focuses on the relationship between an individual's life situation and his psychological reactions to that situation. (Bradburn, 1965)

Later, in the same introductory chapter, Bradburn traces the concern with psychological well-being as a dependent variable to William James. He agrees with the historian Howard Mumford Jones that the appearance of William James's *Principles* in 1890 had the greatest influence on changing the terms of the philosophical, social, and psychological discourse about happiness. From James on, the discussion of happiness and well-being was firmly connected to psychology and as a psychological concept was closely tied to problems of social adjustment. Regrettably, the Jamesian emphasis on conscious assessments of well-being was offset by the "influence of Freudian theory, which has made psychologists particularly distrustful of self-reports of subjective feelings and sensitive to the distorting influences of defense mechanisms" (Bradburn, 1969, p. 8).

In the pilot study conducted by Bradburn and Caplowitz they interviewed 2,006 adults from four small Illinois communities. The respondents were interviewed for 90 minutes about their behavior and attitudes concerning work, family, self-definition, satisfaction, dissatisfaction, and personal crises (Bradburn, 1965). Questions included:

> Taken all together, how would you say things are these days—would you say that you are *very happy, pretty happy,* or *not too happy?*
> During the past few weeks were you treated badly by anyone?
> In general do you have enough energy to do the things you would like to do?

The results of the pilot study were clear-cut in showing that valid and reliable measures of happiness could be obtained from self-reports. The most important finding was that psychological well-being is the resultant of each individual's position on two *independent* dimensions, one of positive affect and one of negative affect:

> It was clear that these two dimensions were independent of one another, making it impossible to predict an individual's score on the negative affect dimension from any knowledge of his score on the positive affect dimension and vice versa. On the other hand, both dimensions were related in the expected direction to overall self-ratings of happiness or subjective well-being. The best predictor of the overall self-rating was the discrepancy between the two scores; the greater the excess of positive over negative affect, the higher the overall rating of psychological well-being. (Bradburn, 1969, pp. 9, 10)

One general comment that can be made about Bradburn and Caplowitz's findings is that they provide convincing evidence for sophisticated explorations of subjective reports and argue against simplistic, one-shot questions concerning a complex feeling such as happiness. Subjective reports are often denigrated as useless or misleading when what should really be criticized is the adequacy and depth of the interviewer's questions.

Bradburn uses the example of a married couple who are arguing. Knowing that the man is arguing with his wife or even knowing that he argues frequently with his wife does not give much information about his overall sense of happiness or even his overall sense of marital happiness. Only if additional knowledge is obtained about the relative frequency of his positive and negative marital experiences would it be possible to predict the man's self-assessed state of marital happiness. And only if additional positive and negative affect information from other areas of his life were collected could an interviewer begin to predict the man's overall sense of well-being.

The followup study conducted by Bradburn surveyed more than 2,700 adults in settings that included suburbs and inner cities. Subsamples were re-interviewed in waves, some of which included four separate interviews (the last interview took place almost a year after the first).

The results confirmed the pilot study's findings about the dual structure of psychological well-being. The results also supported the reliability and stability of the measures of positive and negative affect.

Bradburn comments on what happens when subjects are asked general questions about feeling states, questions that mix positive and negative affect components:

> In effect, what the respondent is doing when asked whether he feels particular ways "often" or "seldom" is to average out his experiences over the long hand and give us a report of the way he feels most frequently . . . he performs the arithmetic that we perform when we subtract the time-focused reports of negative affect from those of positive affect. (Bradburn, 1969, p. 230)

Therapists should keep this in mind when listening to their clients or when questioning clients about their experiences. The lesson of Bradburn's research is that the total level of life satisfaction cannot be predicted from specific negatives or specific positives.

As Bradburn points out, neither can the quality of a person's life be predicted from the quantity of reported experiences:

> In addition to the fact that people differ on the number of pleasant and unpleasant experiences, they differ in the number of feelings they report. Some people either have many more experiences that produce affect of one kind or another, or they are differentially sensitive so that they report more affect. Further differences in the quantity of affect are not related to the quality; that is, people who report a lot of feelings are not happier than those who report few feelings. (Bradburn, 1969, p. 226)

This finding on the lack of relationship between quantity and quality of experiences deserves further study, if only because it runs counter to ordinary expectations about the "richness of life" and the "quality of life." The implication for a therapist is that clients who report many positive experiences are not necessarily better off than those who report very few. Everything depends upon the ratio of positives to negatives. In any given single session it would be easy to be misled.

The overall implications of Bradburn's research for clinical theory and practice are significant:

First, any therapy that aims to increase the client's well-being must be concerned with *both* positive factors and negative factors.

Second, therapists should try to educate client's about the real relationship between positive and negative factors since client's are usually predisposed to concentrate only on removing or lessening the negatives.

Third, since it is the *excess* of positives over negatives that contributes most to a sense of happiness, satisfaction, or well-being it might be possible to develop a safety margin of positive activities in different life areas that would allow the individual to withstand stress and negatives in times of personal crisis. This notion of a safety margin of positives over negatives resembles the physical fitness strategy that is becoming increasingly accepted by physicians and the general public. Perhaps the parallels between physical fitness and psychological fitness can be meaningfully extended and taught to both therapists and clients. This possibility will be explored in the next chapter.

Other Related Research on Happiness

One line of research that shows remarkable parallels to Bradburn's was conducted by industrial psychologists studying work satisfaction. Herzberg, Mauser, and Snyderman (1959) proposed a model to explain job satisfaction that identified two factors: "satisfiers" and "dissatisfiers." Such factors as low pay, disagreements with supervisors, and poor environmental conditions were related to job dissatisfaction but their absence did not lead to job satisfaction. The presence of such factors as challenging work, job responsibility, and chances for self-development led to job satisfaction but their absence was not associated with job dissatisfaction. (For additional, related research summaries on job satisfaction see Zaleznik, Christensen, & Roethlisberger, 1958.)

Another line of research is provided by Flanagan's investigation of the factors that contribute to the "quality of life." He found that "the largest correlation coefficients with overall quality of life were material comforts, health, work, active recreation, learning and creative expression" (Flanagan, 1978, p. 143).

Related research is provided by Fozard and Popkin's work on "optimizing adult development." Their general argument is that "if psychosocial environments were better designed to accommodate the changes in human needs over the life-span segments between 20 and 65 years, people could adapt more easily to the problems of aging as well as enjoy their old age more" (Fozard & Popkin, 1978, p. 975). They suggest that programs of treatment to help older adults must include both attempts to deal with negative affect (depression, anxiety, low self-images) and positive affect (motivation and pleasurable social contacts).

Reported life satisfaction of older adults who had lower levels of activity was generally less than that for older adults who had higher levels of activity and social contact.

Vaillant reported a 30-year longitudinal study of mental health and the connection between mental health and physical health. He found that sustained personal relationships were more important in aiding adaptation to life circumstances than the presence or absence of traumatic events. Vaillant concludes his report with this forceful statement:

> Mental health *exists*. Contrary to popular belief, lucky at work means lucky in love; lack of overt emotional distress does not lead to headache and high blood pressure but to robust physical health; and those who pay their internist the most visits are also most likely to visit psychiatrists. Inner happiness, external play, objective vocational success, mature inner defenses, good outward marriage, all correlate highly— not perfectly, but at least as powerfully as height correlates with weight. . . . Not only do I now believe that mental health is tangible, but I believe that it exists as a dimension of personality. . . . Effective evaluation of long-term therapy, especially of psychotherapy, may be better achieved by charting a patient's move along a continuum of positive external behaviours than by focusing on the presence or absence of individual symptoms. (Vaillant, 1977, pp. 373–374)

Vaillant's longitudinal findings about mental health are generally paralleled by the longitudinal analyses of the Terman high IQ subjects by Sears (1977). Sears reports that work satisfaction and work persistence were best predicted by feelings of satisfaction, ambition, and good health expressed as early as age 30, while family life satisfaction and success in marriage were predicted by good childhood social adjustment, good mental health in later years, and a positive attitude toward parents. Sears found, as did Vaillant, high consistency of expressive feelings about work, health, and self-worth from age 30 to age 60. Also highly consistent was the importance the most successful subjects placed upon achieving satisfaction in their family life.

Goleman (1980) reports on other analyses by Sears of the data into the characteristics of the "most," "middle," and "least successful" of the high IQ groups. He found that the A's when compared to the C's were characteristically a livelier group, both more activity oriented and more physically oriented.

When these longitudinal findings are combined with Bradburn's sample survey findings, there is evidence for both the dual and independent positive-negative affect model of life satisfaction but also for the high correlation of the positives. That is, a person who is high in marriage positives is also likely to be high in work, play, and social positives. (Related survey findings are reported by Kane, 1977, Shaver

& Freedman, 1976, and the California Department of Mental Health, 1979.)[1]

Theory and Research on Adult Stages of Life

The survey research investigations briefly reviewed in the previous section tended to move from empirical findings to theory. The investigations reviewed in this section tend to proceed from theory to research. The three theoretical directions that have most influenced the investigation of adult life stages are: the psychoanalytic, the humanistic, and the functional. Of course these three traditions are interwoven not independent.

Psychoanalytic Stage Theories and Research

Freud's clinical observations and theories were directed toward explaining persistent conflicts and fixations. However, his first two famous co-workers, Adler and Jung, were much more concerned with positive stages of growth. Adler emphasized that all problems in life can be grouped under three main life areas: work, friends, and sex, and that successful solutions require a focus beyond the self. Jung stressed that

---

[1] Therapists who look into this area of research will soon find that there are contributions from numerous fields including sociology, survey research, social psychology, industrial psychology, and political science. Additionally, although survey questions and procedures overlap, there are conceptual differences between theorists and researchers who emphasize relative deprivation, happiness, need satisfaction and level of aspiration, or global measures of well-being. My discussion concentrates on Bradburn's research because I believe his affect–balance measures and concepts fit so well within the functional theoretical framework. I agree with Campbell, himself one of the leading contributors to survey research on happiness and life satisfaction, who says Bradburn's "is perhaps the conceptually cleanest statement describing happiness available" (Campbell, 1976, p. 8). For a comprehensive picture of the many surveys and replications on happiness, well-being, and satisfaction readers must consult a variety of sources. Begin with the Gurin, Veroff, & Feld (1960), and Bradburn (1965) references. Then go on to Cantril (1965), Cantril & Roll (1971), Bradburn (1969), Campbell (1981), Veroff, Douvan, & Kulka (1981), Veroff, Kulka, & Douvan (1981). For a sampling of Gallup, Harris, and Life Insurance Surveys, see Norbeck (1980). Another line of relevant research takes the multifactorial personality assessment approach to the measurement of healthy personalities. See Heath (1965) and Cattell (1973) for a sampling of these approaches. Taken together, these survey research and personality assessment studies include tens of thousands of subjects across many cultures.

the entire second half of life, as contrasted with the first half, is preoccupied with a wider psychic development, beyond the ego.

Levinson, one of the modern empirical investigators of life stages who works within an analytic framework, identifies Erikson as the synthesizer of analytic stage theories, who acts as a bridge between Freud, Adler, and Jung.

> On the psychological side, our thinking about adult development thus grows out of an intellectual tradition formed by Freud, Jung, and Erikson. This tradition includes Rank, Adler, Reich and other socially oriented depth psychologists. In recent years, these sources have been used by Ernest Becker, Robert Lifton and others in creating a broader approach to adult life in society. The schisms that for so long have divided the various schools of depth psychology, and have restricted the scope of each viewpoint, are perhaps beginning to be outgrown. The absurdity of the old sectarian struggles is evident. The present study will, we hope, contribute to the emergence of a more integrative, non-sectarian approach. (Levinson, 1978, p. 5)

Levinson is clearly making a plea for eclecticism and theoretical broadening. His research studied 40 men between 35 and 45 years old, executives, hourly workers, academics, and novelists. The basic research tool was the in-depth interview. Each tape-recorded interview lasted an hour or two at weekly intervals for 10 to 20 hours over a span of two to three months. Follow-up interviews were conducted two years later. The content of the structured research interview was directed at the identification of significant life patterns. As part of the interview procedure five pictures were used from Murray's Thematic Apperception Test. (Murray and Allport's functional methods of life assessment interviewing influenced all stage researchers and Murray's classic research with the OSS and at the Harvard Clinic has been used repeatedly as a model for studies in this field.) Levinson's essential method was to elicit life stories from the interviews, construct biographies, and develop generalizations based on the biographies.

Levinson and his co-workers found five life stages that they could identify clearly and that occurred in a fixed sequence with a relatively low variability in the age at which every period begins and ends. These periods were: pre-adult—15 to 20 years, Early Adulthood—15 or 20 to 40, middle Adulthood—40 to 60, late Adulthood—60 to 80, Late-late adulthood—80 to 90.

Because of the ages of their sample participants Levinson concentrated on the Middle Adulthood period. The core finding of the research was that *"the life structure evolves through a relatively orderly sequence during the adult years"* (Levinson, 1978, p. 49), with alternating stable periods and transition periods.

The primary task of every stable period is to build a life structure: a man must make certain key choices, form a structure around them, and pursue his goals and values within this structure. . . . Each stable period has additional tasks of its own which reflect its place in the life cycle and distinguish it from the other stable periods. . . . The primary tasks of every transitional period are to question and reappraise the existing structure, to explore various possibilities for change in self and world, and to move toward commitment to the crucial choices that form the basis for a new life structure in the ensuing stable period. (Levinson, 1978, p. 49)

Levinson found that these life periods were different from both normal development of ego functions and from the occurrence of unresolved complexes. Failures to make a life transition successfully do happen but these failures show up in a reduction in the overall level of life satisfaction, not in a freezing at an earlier level of adult development. Levinson also distinguishes among the life period, the successfulness of development in a life period, and the marker events (such as marriage, promotions, loss of job, etc.) that take place during different life periods.

A related series of studies on men and women were conducted by Lowenthal, Fiske, Thurnher, and Chiriboya (1976). Their overall findings were quite similar to Levinson's concerning the orderliness of life periods. Related life stage investigations were conducted by Gould (1978); he carried out detailed clinical interviews with men and women, using life period categorizations similar to those discovered by Levinson. Gould organized his observations around life "assumptions" that were accurate at one period of life but become false for later periods:

The arbitrary internal *constraints* of adulthood were once the internal *standards* of childhood . . . they are our windows onto the world, the point of view we use to interpret reality and choose actions . . . we must become self-defined, flexible and free; we must live closer to our impulses and further from the rigid rules of childhood in order to feel alive. (Gould, 1978, pp. 321, 322)

Gould identified four major false assumptions which adults must undo:

1. "I'll always belong to my parents and believe in their world."
2. "Doing things my parents way, with willpower and perseverance, will bring results."
3. "Life is simple and controllable. There are no significant coexisting contradictory forces within me."
4. "There is no evil or death in the world. The sinister has been destroyed." (Gould, 1978, pp. 5, 6)

The "structures" that Levinson writes about and the "assumptions" that Gould explores are both personality images or components that must reach awareness before they can be successfully changed. (In Chapter 12 I will discuss personality images and the ways they can block or further growth.)

In a very successful popularization of the work of Levinson and Gould, the journalist Gail Sheehy wrote about *Passages: Predictable Crises of Adult Life* (1976). Her work is especially important because she made the life stages theory of Erikson and derived research well known to many prospective therapy clients. People entering counseling or psychotherapy could now conceptualize their concerns and goals within a growth model rather than a sickness model.

In a follow-up to her best-selling book, Sheehy herself undertook a research survey. With the collaboration of several news magazines she obtained more than 60,000 life history questionnaires. From these completed self-reports she then identified and interviewed people who had very successfully developed their lives through several life crises. Sheehy calls these people "pathfinders." She found that there were striking similarities among blue-collar, white-collar, and professional groups on the five self-descriptions most closely linked to well-being. These were:

1. My life has meaning and direction.
2. I have experienced one or more important transitions in my adult years, and I have handled these transitions in an unusual, personal or creative way.
3. I rarely feel cheated or disappointed by life.
4. I have already attained several of the long-term goals that are important to me.
5. I am pleased with my personal growth and development. (Sheehy, 1981, p. 22)

She found that pathfinders had a willingness to risk change and undertake genuine acts of courage in making transitions from one way of living to another. This result is in line with findings of the University of California San Francisco Human Development Program that reported that "The sense of well-being, was far more likely to be associated with the sense of past and future change in goals and behavior patterns than with continuity" (from Lowenthal Fiske, 1980; cited in Sheehy, 1981, p. 77).

The work of Sheehy and other writers about life stages tends to blend well-being interviews and questions with life-history interviews and questions. A similar blending of analytic stage theories and empirical life satisfaction research is found in previously cited research of Sears and his colleagues at Stanford. A book edited by Sears and Feldman called *The Seven Ages of Man* (1973) reports at length on the developmental data related to physical, cognitive, and personality growth. One of the salutory features of developmental theories and research is that they tend to bring together a variety of theoretical approaches around common observations and issues. This will be evident in the discussion of humanistic approaches.

Humanistic Theories and Research

Humanistic psychology, as the self-proclaimed "third-force" alternative to behaviorism and psychoanalysis in psychology, is closely identified with theories that highlight positive, life-long growth and creativity rather than early determinism and psychopathology. All of the major humanistic theorists—Assagioli, Jourard, Perls, Maslow, and Rogers—were very concerned with developing a theoretical approach that both studied and promoted individual development. Growth centers were founded and flourished in the United States and elsewhere near major metropolitan centers mainly through the contributions of humanistic psychologists who sought to create institutions outside the traditional, formal centers of learning, new institutions that could emphasize affective and personal learning rather than technical and cognitive learning.

However, the humanistic psychologists tended to be much less concerned with studying stages or periods of adult growth and much more concerned with identifying the kinds of motivational and interpersonal conditions that contributed to growth. They also studied experiential processes that characterize highly creatively functional persons.

Perhaps the best known of all the humanistic growth theories is Maslow's. He occupies the position within humanistic psychology that Erikson occupies within analytic psychology; that is, his theories have stimulated an amazing amount of research and numerous clinical applications. Both Maslow's and Erikson's theories also have become known to the general public.

Chapter 3 in Maslow's *The Farther Reaches of Human Nature* (1971) is titled "Neurosis as a Failure of Personal Growth." This theme, that neurotic psychopathology is the consequence of failing to take the risks of growth and change, runs throughout Maslow's work and that of most other humanists. Maslow labels the withdrawal from the challenge of growth as the "Jonah complex." Just as Freud points to the negative psychological consequences of failing to make a childhood psychosexual adaptation, so Maslow points to the clinical consequences of fixation at an early stage of adult development.

For Maslow and most other humanistic theorists the drive to "self-actualization" is as powerful in the life of the adult as are the drives toward sexuality, exploration, and independence in the life of the adolescent. Maslow's famous "hierarchy of needs" discriminates between "deficiency motivation" and "being motivation." Needs extend from physiologic needs (hunger, thirst, fatigue, etc.) to safety needs, to belongness and love needs, to esteem needs, to the need for self-actualization. The self-actualizing person experiences many "peak experiences" as his or her higher needs are met and also moves toward the realization of goals or values beyond himself or herself.

Maslow's picture of the self-actualizing person was not based upon research but drawn from clinical and historical studies. It is clear, however, that Maslow's "self-actualizers" resemble the empirical descriptions of Sheehy's "pathfinders" and also the descriptions by Sears, Bradburn, and others of individuals who score exceptionally high on scales of well-being.

In a recent empirical study of "peak performances"—behaviors exceeding a person's normal level of functioning—the psychologist Gayle Privette questioned 45 men and 75 women to see if there were elements common to peak experiences in widely different fields such as sports, art, and science. She found three distinctive characteristics: clear focus, spontaneity and feelings of strength, and vitality. Privette (1981a) found sharp differences between peak and average experiences on these characteristics.

Rogers's "fully-functioning" person closely resembles Maslow's "self-actualizing" person. For Rogers, therapists should be mainly facilitators of their clients' own tendencies toward self-development. The characteristics that Rogers specifies as necessary and sufficient for personality change are: (a) contact between two or more persons, (b) the clients are experiencing a discrepancy between self-images and experiences, (c) the therapist is congruent or genuine, (d) the therapist experiences unconditional positive regard for the client, and (e) the therapist communicates empathically with the client. (See Rogers's chapters in Hart & Tomlinson, 1970.)

Rogers then specifies the process, or the moment-by-moment experiential happening, that takes place when clients go through psychological growth. The basic characteristic of this change process is that the person begins freely to recognize, accept, and follow new feelings. The individual "begins to drop the false fronts, or the masks, or the roles, with which he has faced life. He appears to be trying to discover something more basic, something more truly himself" (Rogers, 1961, p. 109). In short, the person becomes a self-actualizing or more fully functioning person. (The steps of this process in which false images are given up for new choices, actions, and experiences will be discussed at length in Chapter 12.)

Among all the humanistic theorists the one who was perhaps most concerned with developing a comprehensive theory of personal growth and health was Jourard. In his book *Healthy Personality: An Approach from the Viewpoint of Humanistic Psychology* he makes a very clear statement about the difference between growth and change and the difference between defending and growing:

> Growth of the self is a change in the way of experiencing the world and one's own being. Not all change is experiencing growth, however. One can speak of growth only when the changes enhance the person's ability to cope with challenges in his existence. Some alterations in experience, as occur in psychosis, make effective action impossible; they may be described as regression rather than growth. . . . Growth is change, but change in the direction of greater awareness, competence, and authenticity. . . . Growth in consciousness makes it possible for a person to see connections between ways of behaving and their consequences for well-being. . . . Growing will go on throughout a person's life span . . . if he has courage (and the encouragement) to accept, and not respond reflexively with mechanisms of defense. (Jourard, 1974, pp. 191, 197)[2]

If these humanistic ideas and clinical emphases seem reminiscent of the functional writings of James, Janet, and Dewey, it is no accident. Humanistic psychology was, in many ways, a reassertion of the functional perspective in the 1950s and 1960s within academic psychology that had become dominated by behaviorism and a clinical psychology dominated by psychoanalysis. The third force was the re-emergence of the unifying eclectic spirit of William James. All of the humanistic theorists drew extensively from the ideas and the style of discourse exemplified by James and Dewey. There is, however, also a direct line of influence on developmental psychology extending from the functional pioneer Galton through James, Hall, and Baldwin then through Murray and Allport right up to contemporary developmental psychologists.

---

[2] Despite the humanist's emphasis on growth, creativity and self-actualization, humanistic psychologists are not cockeyed optimists. Maslow, Rogers, and other humanistic theorists are well aware that self-actualization must take place in an environment and that some environments are so depleted or oppressive as to stifle growth. There is ample evidence to show that both physical health and psychological health are closely correlated to economics. Professor Harvey Brenner of the Johns Hopkins School of Hygiene comments:

> The long-term trends in economic growth and changes in employment are the main issues in mortality. . . . Suicide is the best economic indicator we have. . . . It is an indication of failure.

Brenner's research indicates that when the unemployment rate jumped just 1.4% in 1970, the number of mental disorders increased 100%, alcoholism jumped 30 to 35%, the suicide rate went up 15 to 25%, and heart attacks and strokes went up 15 to 25%. Brenner asserts that the relationship is so clear that "unemployment can be used as a constant for predicting mortality rate. The economy can be used to determine length of life." (See Minkoff, 1980, for a journalistic report of Brenner's and related research.)

Direct-Line Functional Theories and Research

As was indicated in Chapter 2, the functionalists broadened the definition of psychology to include comparative, industrial, educational, and *developmental* psychology. The foremost early contributor to the functionalist study of child and adult development, aside from Darwin, was his cousin Francis Galton (1822–1911). Galton was fascinated by the study of individual differences and was particularly interested in the study of genius. He argued that individual greatness followed family lines with a frequency of occurrence too great to be explained by environmental influences. In Galton's first psychological work on *hereditary genius,* published in 1869, he reported on the biographies of 977 eminent men and their sons (Galton, 1908). In later books he developed additional statistical and graphical techniques (including the method of correlation) to analyze the measurements and observations he continued to collect on genius. In Galton's research can be found the early prototype for both the Terman-Sears studies of genius and the later survey studies of well-being. Galton also pioneered in the use of twins for psychological investigations, the study of imagery, and the use of word associations and mental tests. The catholicity of his interests can be matched by only one other early psychologist, William James. Galton matched James's liking for words with an equally intense liking for numbers and gave to developmental psychology the distinctively empirical, statistical bent it has maintained in psychology right up to the present.

Galton's influence on functional developmental psychology was most visible in the works of Cattell, Hall, and Baldwin. Of these three James Cattell (1860–1944) most exemplified the Galtonian spirit of measurement. Cattell was interested in collecting norms on simple individual differences, such as reaction time, as well as more complex measures of mental performance; he also continued the tradition, begun by Galton, of studying eminence in science. (In 1894 Cattell and Baldwin established the *Psychological Review,* and in 1895 he acquired the weekly journal *Science.* Because of his involvement with these and other successful publications, Cattell became less known as a scientist and more known as a publisher and editor.)

Baldwin's contributions to developmental psychology bear more resemblance to the French psychologists Janet, Simon, and Piaget than to the English or German. James Mark Baldwin (1861–1934) sought to create a genetic epistemology. He theorized that cognitive development proceeds in infancy through epochs or stages, starting with reflexive processes, then into sensorimotor and ideomotor stages, and progressing into symbolic and ideational transformations.

A recent review of two of Baldwin's pre-1900 books in the *Journal of Contemporary Psychology* by the historian of developmental psychology Robert Cairns was titled "Developmental Theory Before Piaget: The Remarkable Contributions of James Mark Baldwin" (1980). Cairns states "Baldwin outlined for American psychology its first—and most influential—theory of psychological development" (Cairns, 1980, p. 438).

G. Stanley Hall (1844–1924) was less interested in measurement than Cattell and less interested in specifying mechanisms and stages than Baldwin. His distinctive contribution to developmental psychology was to define the scope of the various fields of study. His first work focused on the child, his middle works on the adolescent and young adult, and his later works on old age. His two-volume *Adolescence* (1904) and the equally massive two-volume work on *Senescence* (1922/1972) essentially defined the fields of adolescent and geriatric psychology. (Lewis Terman was one of the prominent developmental psychologists who studied with Hall.)

In *Senescence* Hall identifies five stages of human development: childhood, adolescence, middle life (24 or 30 to 40 or 45), senescence, and old age or senectitude. His stages and his observations of middle life and senescence resemble those of contemporary researchers but are much less detailed. In Chapter 7, "Report on Questionnaire Returns," Hall describes the responses his subjects gave to questions such as: "How do you keep well?," "What duties do you feel you still owe to others or to self?," and "In what do you take your greatest pleasure?" He found that many of his subjects continued to show great industry and changeability throughout senescence, a condition he refers to as an "Indian summer." He argues that the special function of elders in society is to preserve moral standards and give a perspective to living.

The real flowering of the developmental approach to adults for clinicians came in the work of the two functional psychologists at Harvard who followed James, Munsterberg, and Prince: Henry Murray and Gordon Allport. In their writings and research on adult development can be found many ideas and methods that are still relevant for the contemporary eclectic therapist. Murray's work essentially anticipates the later adult developmental studies of Levinson, Gould, and others, while Allport's formulations anticipate the growth theories of modern humanistic-existential therapists.

Both Murray and Allport attempted to blend case study and biographical methods with measurement methods. Because of this blending of subjective and objective approaches, their works are of special value to contemporary eclectic therapists who are at home in both traditions.

Henry Murray succeeded Morton Prince as director of the Harvard

Psychological Clinic in 1929; he was 36 at the time. He had switched to a concentration on psychology rather late in life, at about age 33. This career switch was definitely influenced by Murray's association with Jung in 1926. Prior to that time he had received an M.D. at Columbia University (in 1919), a surgical internship, a Ph.D. in biochemistry at Cambridge University, and had published 21 articles on embryology and medicine. Like Thorne, Murray felt more influenced by medicine in his approach to therapy and research than by psychology: "From medical practice I derived the 'multiform method' of assessment, coupled with the belief that it should be possible for a group of trained collaborators using a wide variety of methods to make a reasonably complete examination, formulation, and appraisal of a whole person as an ongoing order of differentiated functional variables" (Murray, 1981, p. 10).

Murray makes the typical functionalist assertion about the importance of critical events, "concrete reality is to be found only in the momentary" (1981, p. 20). He also clearly puts the functioning, changing individual at the center of psychology's concerns: "The point of view . . . is that personalities constitute the subject matter of psychology, the life history of a single man being a unit with which this discipline has to deal" (Murray, 1938, p. 3).

In 1938 Murray published the first of his researches to apply the multiform method to the assessment of life histories. *Explorations in Personality* reports on 2 1/2 years of research with 51 college-age men. With characteristic eclecticism Murray dedicated the book to Morton Prince, Sigmund Freud, Lawrence Henderson, Alfred North Whitehead, and Carl Jung. The long list of Murray's collaborators on this study reads like a "Who's Who in Personality Research." It includes Robert White, Jerome Frank, Saul Rosenzweig, Nevitt Sanford, and Rickers-Ovsiankina.

In some ways the conceptual framing of the research was more important than the findings. Murray describes what he calls "the long unit" for psychology: "Because of the meaningful connection of sequences the life cycle of single individual should be taken as a unit, the *long unit* for psychology. . . . This proposition calls for biographical studies" (1938, p. 39). This is the unit that preoccupies all psychologists interested in adult growth. The editor of Murray's papers, Edwin Shneidman, comments that

> one of Murray's chief disaffections with traditional psychoanalytic theory—remembering that, in the round, he holds it indispensable for a profound understanding of man— is that it focuses too much on the pathological and abnormal aspects of man and this cannot be a complete psychological system. . . . Murray's redress for this condition is to accentuate the supranormal, the good, the talented, and more, to focus on man's

capacity for proaction . . . and man's important capacity to be creative. (Murray, 1981, p. 272)

Murray's eclecticism spanned a concern with (1) conscious, subconscious, and unconscious determinants of action, (2) with subjective and objective viewpoints of biographical events, (3) with projective and objective tests, and (4) with anthropological, sociological, and psychological descriptions of human functioning. This broadmindedness led to the formulation of what is perhaps the widest definition, ever, of personality research, "Every man is in certain respects (a) like all other men, (b) like some other men, (c) like no other men" (Murray, 1981, p. 235). Murray's *Explorations in Personality* (1938) and his later *Assessment of Men* (1948) are filled with questionnaires, psychological test results, situational assessments, biographies, autobiographies, and observations from diverse conceptual viewpoints. His later writings include psychohistorical studies of Melville and other historical figures. In Murray's work the modern therapist can find almost every clinical tool put to work in an integrated way.

The same catholicity is found in the work of Murray's colleague at Harvard, Gordon Allport. Both men centered on the study of lives and used every research and conceptual tool available to elucidate how a life could be described and explained.

Allport clearly states the guiding questions that formed his approach to studying personality, "How should a psychological life history be written? What processes and what structures must a full-bodied account of personality include? How can one detect unifying threads in a life, if they exist?" (Allport, 1950, p. 377). The first question, "How should a psychological life history be written?," can be said to permeate all developmental studies of adult growth. Toward the end of his career in personality research Allport confessed "I still do not know how a psychological life history should be written" (Allport, 1950, p. 377). Allport accepts the Jamesian insight that there is no single answer to the question; there is no best way to describe a personality any more than there is one best way to live. The therapist who accepts this humbling conclusion will move a long way toward being able to think about clients more effectively and flexibly.

Allport greatly influenced psychologists to make use of personal documents (diaries, letters, and autobiographies) in personality research (see Allport, 1942, 1965). He also was interested in the use of both objective tests and subjective reports.

One of Allport's most important concepts for the developmental psychologist to keep in mind is that of the "functional autonomy of motives." Motivations that developed to fulfill needs of one kind at an earlier stage of development may continue to motivate behavior and choices at a later stage of behavior but fulfill different needs. One master need that develops at a later stage in life is to find patterns and meaning in one's life history:

> We prefer to say that the essential nature of man is such that it presses toward a relative unification of life (never fully achieved). . . . Among them are man's search for answers to the "tragic trio" of problems: suffering, guilt, death. We identify also his effort to relate himself to his fellow men and to the universe at large. . . . As a consequence of this quest—which is the very essence of human nature—we note that man's conduct is to a large degree proactive, intentional, and unique to himself. (Allport, 1937/1961, p. 252)

Conclusions

What kind of summing up can be made of the research and ideas drawn from the diverse traditions covered in this chapter? The first conclusion is that there is more agreement than disagreement among the many theoretical approaches to adult development. All agree that adults *do* continue to develop and that failures to make transitions from one life stage or period or life crisis to another are as damaging for adults as earlier childhood developmental lapses. Adult growth is not just an extra or a luxury but a necessity; the failure to risk and change in adults will lead to significant decrements in well-being.

Most of the traditions also agree, more or less, with the conceptualization of happiness as a dual function of pluses and minuses. Happiness cannot be achieved just by eliminating the negatives, nor can negatives be predicted from positives or vice versa; happiness depends upon the affective overbalancing of positives to negatives. The consequences of this for therapy are that therapists must concentrate as much upon building up positive potentials as diminishing symptoms. Assagioli, one of the most persistent voices for eclecticism within the humanistic-existential school of therapy states the general goals of therapy this way:

> One might say in brief that the various tasks and aims of a complete synthetic treatment are: First, the discovery and elimination of the direct causes of the trouble and consequently the subsequent healing of the symptoms. Second, the elimination of the conditions—physical, psychological and environmental—which might determine the reappearance of the troubles. Third, the elimination of the consequences of the illness. Fourth, helping the patient to make a constructive use of the drives existing in him, which otherwise might produce new inner conflicts and/or antisocial behavior. Fifth, to arouse and utilize to the utmost all his latent gifts and possibilities and particularly the higher ones latent in the superconscious. (Assagioli, 1964, p. 2)

The third conclusion is that adult developmental studies (perhaps more than any other area of psychology, certainly more than child or clinical or abnormal psychology) are dominated by the eclectic functional perspective. The groundwork established by Galton, James, Cattell, Hall, and Baldwin was extended by Murray and Allport and today provides the context in which most clinical and research investigations of adult growth take place. The dominant characteristic of this research is a commitment to the study of individual lives, using whatever measuring tools and concepts are useful.

11

Psychological Fitness

A Model for Personality Exercise and Change

The eclectic therapist can make very good use of the research and ideas reported in the previous chapter. First, and most basically, therapists will be alerted to pay attention to what their clients say about the quality of their lives. (This is not as obvious as it seems, too frequently both therapists and clients forget to ask and answer general questions such as: "Are you happy?" What makes you feel happy?" and "What makes you feel bad?") Second, the knowledgeable therapist will give equal attention to positive and negative factors. Third, the eclectic functional therapist will understand that what clients can consciously report about positive and negative feelings eventually may lead to more reports of experiences that were in the background. Fourth, the functional therapist will begin with what is most conscious and accessible to positive change and then work toward less conscious and less accessible life areas. (The therapist, wherever possible, works with client strengths, not weaknesses.) The therapist will be helped by the fact that positives can overbalance and offset negatives and by the possibility that positive strengths may interact and multiply.

In this chapter and the next a model will be developed to explain how therapists can work with clients to promote positive personality characteristics and diminish negative ones. Chapter 11 develops a model of psychological fitness[1] (what fitness is and how to promote it); Chapter

[1] The first prominent functional psychologist to develop an explicit program of psychological fitness training was Joseph Jastrow in his book *Keeping Mentally Fit: A Guide on Everyday Psychology* (1928). Jastrow included chapters on "Keeping Happy," "The Psychology of Sport," and "Choosing and Holding Your Job." He made use of the analogy between mental and physical training: "Physical training helps you to make the most of

12 explains defenses and details how fitness models interact with pathology models.

Research Connecting Psychological Health to Physical Health

In an investigation by Dr. Lisa Berkman of the California Department of Public Health of 7,000 older adults it was found that psychological activity ratings could predict mortality rates independently of such ordinary health factors as smoking and obesity. People who were less psychologically active and had fewer social contacts were two and a half to three times more likely to die prematurely (Berkman, 1977). This is just one research among dozens that points up the significance of psychological factors for physical health.

In a survey of related research that focused on psychological factors related to strokes and heart attacks Dr. James Lynch concluded: *"The lack of human companionship, the sudden loss of love, and chronic human loneliness are significant contributors to serious disease (including cardiovascular disease) and premature death"* (Lynch, 1977, p. 181). In a popular book designed to educate the public about the need for psychological openness and the health dangers of psychological rigidity the anthropologist Ashley Montague (1981) refers to "psychosclerosis" (hardening of the mind).

Research on the Type A personality's proneness to heart attacks is well known. The Type A person is someone who is characterized as engaging in a never-ending competitive struggle to achieve more and more in less and less time. Even when the Type A person exercises and maintains a well-balanced diet he or she (most often he) is much more likely to suffer from premature cardiac disease and death than the non-Type A person. Furthermore these personality styles have been found to be extraordinarily difficult to change. Like the lung cancer victim who keeps smoking, Type A heart patient keeps running on the treadmill of competition (see Friedman & Rosenman, 1974).

The five leading causes of death in the United States are: cardiovascular disease, cancer, violence (accidents, homicide, and suicide),

---

your muscle skill; mind-training teaches you how to make the most of your mental skill . . . . The practical purpose of it all is to keep you mentally fit" (Jastrow, 1928, p. 22). Jastrow established the psychology laboratory at the University of Wisconsin in 1888; he had obtained his Ph.D. from Johns Hopkins in 1886 (the first from that institution granted in psychology), studying under G. S. Hall; Clark Hull was Jastrow's most famous student at the University of Wisconsin.

and respiratory and digestive diseases, all of which show strong correlations with life-style personality characteristics. Over the past 80 years there has been almost no change in life expectancy for adults. The individual of age 40-plus had essentially the same chance of living to age 70 in 1900 as does the person of the same age today. Only a pronounced change in life-style is likely to give an adult a greater life expectancy.

Lynch introduces his survey of mortality statistics with this comment:

> An entire generation has been raised to believe that dieting, exercise, innoculations and other forms of preventive care are *the* means to avoid disease and premature death. The idea that another crucial element influencing well-being is the ability to live together—to maintain human relationships—seems strangely "unscientific" to our age . . . human relationships *do* matter. They are desperately important to both our mental and physical well-being. The fact is that social isolation, the lack of human companionship, death or absence of parents in early childhood, sudden loss of love, and chronic human loneliness are significant contributors to premature death. (Lynch, 1977 pp. 3, 7)

From the survey statistics of Bradburn and others discussed previously, it can be said that unless negative social-psychological factors are offset by positive factors people are living at risk. The numerator of life's positives must exceed the denominator of negatives. This psychological arithmetic would seem almost too obvious to be mentioned if it were not for the fact that it is so frequently ignored in practice. There is no widespread awareness of how and why people should take care of their psychological fitness.

Dr. Robert Taylor, a coordinator of research with the Office of Preventive Services in the California State Department of Mental Health, states:

> Health is not primarily about disease or its prevention but how a life is put together. . . . Human biology has unique aspects equal to those of human personality; neither can be meaningfully averaged. It has been estimated, for example, that certain so-called normal features of human anatomy reproduced generation after generation in standard textbooks do not apply to more than 15% of the population. Each person must confront the admonition "know thyself" in the realm of personal biology. . . . Dreams, breathing patterns, muscle tension, emotional sensations—they carry personal messages from a biological substrate; messages which are essential to preventing disease and promoting health. (R. Taylor, 1979, pp. 6, 9)

Taylor's statement provides a solid clue about what must be involved in psychological fitness—*to be psychologically fit a person must be sensitive to inner experiences and take actions in response to this inner sensitivity*. In the same way that a person who is physically fit does not ignore personal biological messages, the psychologically fit person does not ignore personal psychological messages. Psychological fitness involves both awareness and action. A person who feels lonely, for example, if psychologically fit would recognize when the loneliness reaches a magnitude that needs to be offset by companionship and would discriminate feelings of loneliness from feelings of privacy and solitude.

Lynch accurately ties the search for a theory of psychological fitness to the functional theories of Darwin and James:

> William James, one of America's foremost philosophers and the architect of the modern American system of education, accurately foresaw that Darwin's theories would lead to the emergence of a new faith system: a belief in the ability of scientific techniques to abolish grief, loneliness and sadness just as they had already eliminated some of mankind's dreaded physical diseases. (Lynch, 1977, p. 189)

But James's search for a mind cure was based upon a delicate balance between objectivism and subjectivism. It was a balance that was very much upset by the ultraobjectivity of behaviorism and the ultrasubjectivity of psychoanalysis.

Fitness must begin with the individual who takes responsibility for his or her own psychological fitness. This is the first lesson of the psychological fitness approach that therapists must convey to clients: "You must take over; know what helps you to feel good and what leads to feeling bad and do something about it." Clients who come away from a series of therapy sessions without taking on the responsibility for monitoring and achieving their own psychological well-being might be better off taking a series of vitamin injections.

One of the most famous recent cases of a person taking on responsibility for his own physical and psychological health was published in the best-selling book *Anatomy of an Illness as Perceived by the Patient* by Norman Cousins (1979). In 1964 Mr. Cousins suffered a very serious attack of a disease of the connective tissue (ankylosing spondylitis) which quickly left him bedridden, immobile, and in extreme pain. His doctor's prognosis was that Cousins would be crippled for the rest of his life.

Cousins reasoned that perhaps his attack had been brought on by exposure to extreme stress over a short period of time. From his familiarity with Selye's theories of stress Cousins postulated that if the negative emotions he had been experiencing had produced negative chemical changes in his body perhaps positive emotions could produce offsetting and restorative positive chemical changes. With the cooperation of his doctor, he moved out of the hospital and into a hotel where he could arrange to view comedy films.

Cousins quickly discovered that the laughter he experienced when watching the comedies left him feeling less pain, more mobile, and more able to sleep. Also, chemical tests of his blood showed significant drops in sedimentation rate. Cousins continued his regimen of laughter, rest, and ascorbic acid and within a few months was able to return to his editorial work at the *Saturday Review.* Within a year he was relatively pain-free and was able to play tennis, golf, ride a horse, and play the piano.

He concluded from his experiences:

> that the will to live is not a theoretical abstraction, but a physiologic reality with therapeutic characteristics. . . . What was significant about the laughter . . . was not just the fact that it provides internal exercise for a person flat on his or her back—a form of jogging for the innards—but that it creates a mood in which the other positive emotions can be put to work, too. In short, it helps make it possible for good things to happen. (Cousins, 1979, pp. 44, 145–146)

Cousins's remarks point very clearly toward the psychological fitness approach of this chapter: *Psychological fitness involves psychological exercising, emotional jogging, which puts the positive emotions to work in a way that offsets negative emotions and improves the general level of personality functioning.*

At an interview Professor Albert Marston of the University of Southern California and the author conducted with Norman Cousins to relate his research on laughing in response to funny movies with our own studies on crying in response to sad movies, Cousins remarked, "Medical treatment must be the add-on. Psychotherapy is the basic treatment. Patients must have someone who believes in them" (Hart, 1980). After his success with the book *Anatomy of an Illness as Perceived by the Patient,* Cousins became a professor in the University of California, Los Angeles's Program in Medicine, Law, and Human Values. In that position he tries, among other things, to teach the medical faculty and students about the importance of positive beliefs, choices, and human values in healing—not an easy task.

In our own research on the laboratory study of sadness and crying (Marston, Hart, Hileman, & Faunce, 1983) we found that most subjects (college students) could let themselves cry in response to excerpts from a sad film (*The Champ,* with Jon Voight, Faye Dunaway, and Ricky Schroder). Additionally, those subjects who did cry usually experienced a pleasurable release of tension. In other words the full experiencing of sadness, through expressive crying, did not lessen feelings of happiness.

Analogies between Physical Fitness and Psychological Fitness

If there truly is something that might be called emotional jogging or personality exercise it might be worthwhile to look at physical jogging and physical exercise to get some ideas about how psychological fitness might be developed to parallel physical fitness.

Americans have greatly increased their levels of physical exercise in the last two decades. According to the 1979 Perrier Survey of Fitness in America, which was conducted by Harris on a sample of 1,510 adults (and a subsample of 180 runners), 59% of the population are involved in some form of exercise; 15% are "high actives" who engage in 306 minutes or more of vigorous exercise weekly. Almost all of the parents surveyed (93%) believed it was vital for their children to exercise and stay in top physical shape. The number of people who actively participate in sports and regularly exercise had doubled from the previous decade. Such a finding reflects a major shift in attitudes toward exercise and physical fitness and in behaviors. In 1979 there were 17 million joggers, 21 million doing calisthenics, 34 million exercise walkers, 26 million swimmers, 20 million cyclists, 20 million bowlers, 6 million tennis players, and 14 million golfers. Those figures have mostly increased since that time.

Of course there is still room for improvement. Harris found that 23% of the general public said that nothing would get them involved in any form of physical activity, not even direct orders from their doctors with the warning that they would be severely at risk for premature death without regular exercise. Nonetheless, it is clear that the majority of Americans are fitness minded. Today major companies compete for executives by including health clubs in the package of executive benefits. Similar in-house fitness centers are provided for employees. The *Wall Street Journal* reported on one study showing that employees who participated in aerobic exercise classes were absent from work an average of one day per year, compared with six days a year for nonparticipants (Guenther, *Wall Street Journal,* 1981).

It is interesting to reflect on what it took to bring about the fitness ethic among modern adults. Consider jogging—it was not very long ago, in the 1950s, when the idea that adults would be running all over the country without being chased would have seemed ridiculous. The only people who ran regularly were children and athletes.

If one person can be identified who brought about the jogging craze it would be Bill Bowerman, track coach at the University of Oregon and former Olympic coach. In 1962 Bowerman toured New Zealand with the University of Oregon's world record four-mile relay team. There he met Arthur Lydiard, the New Zealand Olympic coach who had come up with the idea of combining conditioning with companionship by slow cross-country running in organized groups or running clubs. Bowerman was amazed to find that not only current and former athletes were running in these clubs but citizens of all ages. To Bowerman the entire countryside seemed to be alive with runners every weekend and holiday.

Bowerman returned to the United States determined to start a similar running movement here. He was joined by the cardiologist Dr. W. E. Harris and in the early 1960s they conducted a number of controlled running programs with adults aged 25 to 66. Bowerman and Harris found that the cardiovascular benefits of the programs were great and that the participants continued enthusiastically. The two men began advertising and lecturing to similar running groups throughout the United States. In 1967 they published a book, *Jogging,* which set forth the practices and benefits of the sport in a very appealing way. (Think how little response they would have achieved if the book and program had been called *Long Slow Running.*)

The authors recommended jogging with these words:

> Jogging is a graduated program of moderate exercise which can be adapted to men and women of varying ages and levels of fitness. . . . Jogging is a simple type of exercise, requiring no highly developed skills. Its great appeal is that it is so handy. Almost anyone can do it anywhere. (Bowerman & Harris, 1967, p. 5)

Bowerman and Harris made the point that jogging could be vital for a person's life and health but also that it was fun and easy. They listed the benefits of jogging as: its safety, participants look and feel better, they lose weight, they build endurance and confidence. In addition, jogging can be done alone or with others. At one point in their book (which includes progress charts, pacing charts, and instructions for starting jogging clubs) they advise "Train, don't strain" and "Make haste slowly." Elsewhere they advise new joggers to run no faster than they can while maintaining an easy conversation with a friend.

As they say, the rest is history. Today there are entire industries that are indebted to Bowerman and Harris. Some refinements have been added about pulse testing and equipment but jogging is still being practiced by millions in the same form that was recommended by Bowerman and Harris. If psychological fitness exercising is ever to be practiced as widely, devotedly, and beneficially as physical fitness exercising it will certainly require a formulation that makes it seem as simple and "natural" as jogging.

Consider whether there might be some useful analogies between physical fitness exercises and psychological fitness exercises:

First, although the best forms of physical exercise seem simple and natural, such as jogging, they are actually social inventions that must be understood and advertised before they come to be widely adopted. The same will certainly be true for psychological exercise programs.

Second, the basic principle behind physical exercise as a preventive measure is that the cardiovascular system builds up a greater range of responsivity through a progressive exposure to mild stresses. In this way, activity that might be a great stress for a beginning runner, for example, running a mile in eight minutes, eventually becomes easily attainable. To build up the personality system's responsiveness, a similar progression from mild to moderate stress would need to be scheduled.

Third, the exercise activity must be inherently pleasurable even though there is some strain. People would not continue to exercise for long if there were not short-range as well as long-range benefits. The same immediate benefits will need to be present in psychological exercise programs.

Fourth, the image of exercising needs to be generally accepted. Physical fitness has a high image value. Psychological fitness will not become a goal for many people until it possesses a similar attractiveness. The association of psychological fitness with older terms such as *mental health* tends to detract from its positive appeal since these terms are inevitably associated with efforts to prevent mental illness. It would be like calling jogging "antistroke therapy."

Analogies between Therapy and Coaching

One of the real advantages that comes from developing the psychological fitness approach to therapy is that the therapist's role model is broadened greatly. In Chapter 7 the eclectic emphasis on applying a variety of role models to therapy was discussed. The same theme can be explored more specifically in relation to the psychological fitness approach. Fitness is much more easily aligned with the activities of a coach or trainer than with those of a physician or healer. Therapists who want to teach clients about psychological fitness methods and concepts will find more guidance in examining the approaches used by tennis coaches, golf coaches, ballet coaches, art instructors, and gym instructors than from learning theories or classroom educational theories.

The practical, results-oriented eclecticism of coaching as a model of training has been more widely appreciated by business educators and trainers than by therapists. In the book *Coaching, Learning and Action,* published by the American Management Association, Lovin and Casstevens (1971) apply the coaching model to leadership training, supervision training, personnel management, and teacher training. They make the important point that learning for adults is related to problems and skills, not the enforced coverage of subject matter, and such learning must conform to the adult learner's self-images and intentions. They review a number of strategies of coaching: changing the environment, manipulating rewards and punishments, prescribing and supervising key skills that need to be mastered, encouraging joint planning, controlling the rate and amount of the responsibilities the trainee takes in, and coaching the extremes—concentrating on strengths and weaknesses.

Lovin and Casstevens apply a four-step learning process to the coaching task in business: (1) the trainee must have a sense of lacking something that is needed; (2) there must be some understanding of what would fill the need; (3) the trainee must make a decision to obtain what is needed; (4) guided action is then required to acquire the needed skill, knowledge, or ability. When these steps are followed the authors argue that coaching becomes a genuine growth process.

Another prominent management consultant who has applied the coaching model to business training situations is Ferdinand Fournies. In his book *Coaching for Improved Work Performance* (1978) Fournies advocates that trainers conduct a "coaching analysis" followed by face-to-face "coaching sessions." The coaching analysis involves: identifying the unsatisfactory performance, finding out if the person knows the performance is unsatisfactory, finding out if the person knows what should and can be done, exploring to find out if there are obstacles beyond the trainee's control, looking at whether negative consequences follow good performances of a skill or positive consequences follow poor performances, and checking to see if the performers could simply do it if they wanted to perform fully.

Fournies's face-to-face coaching sessions involve five steps that are somewhat similar to those of Lovin and Casstevens: *Step one*, getting agreement a problem exists; *Step two*, mutually discussing alternative possibilities; *Step three*, mutually agreeing on actions to be taken; *Step four*, following up to insure action is taken and performed correctly; *Step five*, clearly recognizing the achievement of a successful action.

Lovin and Casstevens's and Fournies's approaches are both very practically oriented eclectic packages. They include a blending of humanistic and behavioral methods; their translation into therapeutic applications within a fitness model is easily achieved.

Another theorist whose ideas have been widely used in both management human resource development programs and in general adult education programs is Malcolm Knowles. In his book *The Adult Learner:*

A Neglected Species (1978) Knowles argues that most learning theories and programs are based upon pedagogy (the education of children) not andragogy (the education of adults). He traces the development of a distinctive adult education movement back to Edward Lindeman, who was strongly influenced by John Dewey: "It was the artistic stream, which seeks to discover new knowledge through intuition and the analysis of experience, that was concerned with *how* adults learn" (Knowles, 1978, p. 28). Lindeman founded the American Association for Adult Education in 1929 and the *Journal of Adult Education.*

Although both Lindeman and Knowles drew heavily upon illustrations from education in the arts as a model for adult education, they might just as well have drawn from sports learning. In both sports education and arts education there is the same emphasis upon apprenticeships, self-directedness, direct experience, immediacy, and mutual planning.

Readers whose images of coaching and sports are restricted to old memories of unpleasant drills in grade school and high school physical education classes may wonder at the desirability of coaching as a model for therapy. But the kind of coaching referred to in this chapter is that given by talented professionals to willing student athletes. Coaching, in the sense used here, is just one form of adult education.

In the 1950s Cyril Houle began a line of investigation at the University of Chicago that has been extended by Allen Tough at the Ontario Institute for Studies in Education. The research focused on in-depth interviews with adults who were identified as "continuing learners." (In a way they were the educational counterparts to Sheehy's "pathfinders.") Tough found that continuing adult learners engaged in a large amount of self-directed education:

> Almost everyone undertakes at least one or two major learning efforts a year, and some individuals as many as 15 or 20. . . . It is common for a man or woman to spend 700 hours a year at learning projects. . . . About 70% of all learning projects are planned by the learner himself, who seeks help and subject matter from a variety of acquaintances, experts and printed resources. (Tough, 1971, p. 1)

Most of these learning activities would certainly qualify as forms of psychological exercising that contribute to adult psychological fitness.

Knowles includes in his book an extensive annotated bibliography on adult development and also reviews many theories of therapy for their implications for adult education. A similar degree of coverage of adult development and theories of therapy can be found in many books on coaching and sports psychology. It appears that, although adult and sports educators have made good use of therapy theories and research, therapists have made little or no use of ideas and methods drawn from sports and adult education. The reason for this one-way intellectual traffic is that most theories and techniques of therapy center around a concern with psychopathology. Sports and adult education, in contrast, center around concerns with excellence and growth.[2]

This theme of excellence as the goal of sports performance has been explored by several philosophers who write about sports. Weiss in *Sport: A Philosophic Inquiry* (1969) identifies the pursuit of excellence and the admiration of excellence as the essential motivating features of athletics for both participants and spectators. Weiss discusses components of outstanding athletic performances—speed, endurance, strength, accuracy, and coordination—but describes all the components as features of excellence. A similar analysis is found in *Man, Sport and Existence* (1967) by Slusher:

> The practical participation in sport is one of doing. . . . The *understanding of being* is clarified by sport. It affords man direction in his attainment of being. The man of sport soon learns that fundamental concepts of modern life do not necessarily bring about authentic conceptualizations of being. . . . Sport is *not* a supplement to life but rather an essential concomitant to that that we attribute to existence. (Slusher, 1967, pp. 4–6)

Thus, sport shares with art and education the essential quality of providing an activity that clarifies the subjective meaning of life. Excellence does not exist outside the individual's definition of what he or she strives to achieve. The sense of realizing, through action, possibilities that were only mental intentions and expectations before the individual's effort to realize them is the essence of a "sense of fitness." This means that fitness is always relative. Literally, it refers to the fittingness of an activity with an intention, not to the achievement of an external standard. What might be an outstanding feat of excellence for one person could be a failure for another. The person who does not clearly establish goals and take actions designed to realize them will have no sense of fitness at all.

---

[2] Two remarkable biographical books about adult education and adult self-development are John Holt's *Never Too Late* (1978) and Herbert Kohl's *Half the House* (1976). Holt's book is subtitled *My Musical Life Story*; it tells how he learned to play the cello at age 40: "To become a skillful musician has become perhaps the most important task of my life" (Holt, 1978, p. 1).

Kohl focuses on two questions: "Is it possible to live a healthy life in an unhealthy society? and Is it possible to change oneself in midlife despite one's education and the practical pressures to survive?" (Kohn, 1976, p. ix). Both Kohl and Holt give resoundingly positive answers to these two questions. Their books are worth a ton of clinical case studies about adult development.

In the preface to a recent anthology on *Psychology in Sports* the editor, Richard Suinn, remarks,

> First, training, as opposed to therapy, is the orientation. The programs are designed to enhance strengths rather than to treat emotional conflicts. Second, these programs emphasize self-control or self-regulation models. This means that athletes are trained in techniques that can be self-initiated and permit better self-control over psychological and physical states. Third, some programs aim at improvement of performance without the traditional limitation that psychology should deal with psychological factors rather than physical performance factors. . . . Finally, the programs all appear to reflect techniques developed on something more than trial and error experiences. (Suinn, 1980, p. xi)

The characteristics that Suinn ascribes to sports psychology programs could just as accurately be applied to psychological fitness programs *in* therapy.

What Is Psychological Fitness and Psychological Exercising?

It has taken this much buildup and background discussion to get around finally to the task of defining terms. Definitions offered earlier would have been too narrow. Sports, coaching, exercise, and fitness are considered in relation to therapy from a special perspective—the perspective that they are fundamentally activities that seek to clarify and maintain a sense of excellence and personal meaning.

The possible analogies between physical and psychological fitness are suggestive but the basic questions remain. Is there a condition that might be called psychological fitness and an activity that could accurately be termed psychological exercising?

In order to answer these questions satisfactorily it is necessary to discriminate between psychological movement and psychological space vs. physical movement and physical space. Obviously some psychological activities can and do take place in observable physical space, as when two people have a lively, close, and satisfying conversation. But more important in defining psychological exercise effects is the special notion of psychological space and psychological movement.

Psychological space and movement exist in a subjective realm. The crucial feature of all psychological exercise is that the person is acting from personal meanings and intentions. Without some subjective sense of meaning and goal directedness any form of psychological activity soon will lose its emotional meaning and its exercise efficacy. When a strong sense of meaning and purposiveness is present even the simplest activities can be repeated and extended for long periods of time.

Everyone has experienced the immediate pleasure and vigor that comes from making a decision, even before the decision is carried out. For example, deciding to go on a diet or socialize more or study a new subject can bring an immediate feeling of vigor and pleasure even before the actual activities of dieting, socializing, or studying are begun. Psychological movements (decisions, experiences, feelings, and actions) take place in a subjective psychological space that overlaps but is not identical with physical space. The consequences of psychological movement can be felt *before* any physical activity takes place.

Indeed, the effectiveness of behavior is evaluated not by its effect on physical space but by its degree of match with the psychological space of expectations and intentions. This theory is essentially James's pragmatic theory of reality. It is essential to have this formulation in mind when thinking about psychological fitness and psychological exercise. Without it, the therapist and client will end up using a mindless form of psychological calisthenics external to the client's own desires and goals. The fitness exercises will become a ritual to be performed within a belief system.

What is personally important in a fitness exercise (or in a sports or arts performance) is not the act alone, but the act in relation to a goal and ideal. The exercise is defined by the purpose of the person doing it. Sports and the arts, at their best, are *acts of will* that involve the total human being—body, mind, feelings, and spirit—in action.

A modern theorist who has argued for the theory of intentionality in the study of personality and personality change is Joseph Rychlak. He argues that psychologists have been overawed by the classical emphasis in the physical sciences on material, formal, and efficient causes. Aristotle's fourth kind of causation, purposiveness or intentionality, is essential to put first in evaluating psychological activities.

> This (introspective) self-seeking or self-directing side of behavior is what free-will advocates have tried to capture over the centuries—not without some confusion. We can see in the constructs of Marcus Aurelius, Descartes, Ducasse and William James the common view of human nature as being capable of self-control through consent or dissent. (Rychlak, 1977, p. 37)

> In formulating theories of behavior, phenomena which may be said to move "for the sake of something" (Aristotle's definition of final cause)—a principle, an aspiration, a goal—carry a self-direction which we have traditionally taken as the mark of intelligence. *Concepts of mentality demand the use of a final cause construct.* (Rychlak, 1968, p. 224)

Similar approaches to a philosophy of science for psychology and personality can be found in Polanyi (1966), Maslow (1966), and Hudson (1972).

The reason that excursions into the philosophy of science are necessary to define adequately psychological fitness and psychological exercise is that it would be misleadingly easy to take an objectivist position and define fitness in terms of external norms; exercise would then be defined as activity that improves a person's position on a normative curve.

However, within the functionalist conception of psychological fitness the individual's norms are primary, the social norms secondary. It is the individual's sense of movement toward what is better or more desirable that defines her or his quality of life. *Psychological fitness* is the attainment and maintenance of a self-defined high quality of life. Psychological exercise is any activity that enhances the individual's psychological fitness. Clearly, as with physical fitness and physical exercise, there can be both incidental and special kinds of exercising. A person who runs on the job (a cross-country mailman) is getting exercise without setting aside special time for exercising. A sedentary office worker will need to set aside special time for physical exercise.

Any activity that moves the person beyond ordinary physical functioning and limits can provide exercise, and any activity that moves a person beyond ordinary personality functioning and limits can provide psychological exercise.

People are psychologically fit when their positive self-evaluations of different life areas outweigh negative self-evaluations. Psychological exercise can be any activity that builds up positives or diminishes negatives. Since a person might be more fit in some life area than in others, it is possible to have an accurate sense of psychological fitness in one life area, such as work, and a psychological sense of negative functioning in other life areas, such as play or sex. The greater a person's level of psychological fitness in all life areas the more resistant he or she will be to the negative psychological effects of stressful external events.

This concept of psychological exercise relates to the James-Janet concept of psychological energy or tension. When a person is psychologically exercising she or he will experience an increase in psychological energy. For persons unfamiliar with this kind of energy increase the exercise experience may seem somewhat unsettling. In the same way that physical exercise increases cardiorespiratory functioning beyond familiar limits, so does psychological exercise increase personality functioning beyond comfortable limits. The temporary increase in energy or tension that at first seems threatening or discomfiting eventually will be accepted as desirable and pleasurable.

Psychological exercise also relates to the many nonspecific placebo effects that occur in therapy. Therapists frequently encounter "therapy hoboes," clients who wander from one form of therapy to another, experiencing some temporary benefits from each kind of therapy but eventually the beneficial effects lessen and the client moves on to search out yet another kind of treatment. It is quite possible that many subjective therapy effects that are attached to a specific kind of treatment—hypnosis, catharsis, dream interpretation, encounter, and so on—are really nonspecific exercise effects. What is actually happening is that the client uses the goal-setting and technique of the therapy as an exercise but since it is not recognized as such the client moves on once the technique loses its novelty.

The psychiatrist Jerome Frank is one of the most persistent theoreticians to argue for the point of view that much of therapy consists of the effects of persuasion and placebos. In his classic book *Persuasion and Healing* (1974) Frank states, "It is likely that the lack of clear differences in improvement rate from different forms of therapy results from features common to them all" (Frank, 1974, p. 22). One feature common to all therapies is that they provide concentrated opportunities to undertake new forms of psychological exercising. Unfortunately very few therapies identify the techniques used as exercise techniques and there is, consequently, no appreciation by the clients of the need for psychological exercise once they leave the therapeutic setting.

In a more recent book on *Placebo Therapy*, which extends Frank's arguments, Fish asserts that "some of the most important processes which take place in . . . therapy are unrelated to . . . theoretical orientation" (Fish, 1973, p. viii). He goes on to describe the significance of the "healing ritual" as an activity that transcends any particular technique of theory. The healing ritual consists of:

> First, the therapist explains the healing ritual persuasively, in terms of the patient's beliefs. Next, the patient undergoes self-cure. Finally, the process of self-cure allows the patient to shift from the mentally ill role to that of a psychologically unencumbered individual. (Fish, 1973, p. 44)

Within the psychological fitness framework it would also be desirable to translate Fish's healing ritual into a broader fitness perspective. Clients could then be led to evaluate their psychological fitness regularly and undertake self-directed exercise programs to improve and maintain desirable levels of psychological fitness.

One Program of Psychological Fitness Training

Given the broadness of the definitions of psychological fitness and psychological exercise it is obvious that many different specific programs of fitness training can be devised. The one sketched in this section is just one among many. It is a program that has been used by therapists in many different settings. The program asks participants to assess their psychological fitness in several of the different life areas found to be significant for happiness by Bradburn (1969) and Campbell (1981) (work, play, sex, and relationships). Participants then are asked to evaluate their overall personality functioning on the five personality dynamics described previously in the chapter on dreams—*expression, activity, clarity, feeling, and contact.* Next, participants evaluate their personality dynamics in relation to the specific life areas. The result is a profile of self-reported happiness ratings and personality evaluations that can be used as the basis for fitness exercises.

Fitness exercises can be self-constructed or therapist-constructed and can focus on content changes within a life area or on personality focused on one of the dynamics or both.

For example, a person who rates himself as dissatisfied about his relationships with friends and low in the contact dynamic could plan to talk twice as much every day with friends for a week just to see how this increased activity would feel. The therapist would ask the client to keep an exercise chart showing when and with whom the exercise was done each day. If the exercise seemed too difficult to do the amount would be scaled back.

The easiest way to construct exercises from the five personality dynamics is to ask the client to go one up or one down in one of the characteristics. For example, "How would you sound if you went up one step in expressiveness? Try it out now with me. How would you sound if you went one step down from your typical level? Try it." After experiencing these one-up–one-down exercises in a session the client can then target certain times or situations for similar exercise outside the session.

A popularized version of this program was described in the book *Psychological Fitness* (Corriere & Hart, 1979), which included a 21-day exercise schedule for readers who wanted to try the psychological fitness approach. The manual section of *Modern Eclectic Therapy* describes fitness exercises that therapists can use during therapy sessions (and as assignments).

The premises of this psychological fitness approach are these:

The personality needs to be exercised just as definitely and regularly as the body. Without exercise that involves assessing and improving one's life satisfactions in different life areas and stretching the limits of personality functioning the person will become less able to cope with stress.

Personality growth and change is necessary throughout a person's lifetime. The balance of strengths and weaknesses for one age level cannot be utilized with other age levels.

The most effective personality change comes about by focusing on strengths and weaknesses rather than just weaknesses.

Psychological fitness cannot be obtained or maintained without contact. Research shows clearly that a satisfying, happy life cannot be achieved without satisfying contacts with other people. Many psychological exercises involve improving and extending social skills.

Psychological exercising consists in enhancing positive emotions and decreasing negative emotions through planned periods of change either changing one's activities in life areas or changing one's modes of personality functioning. Keep in mind that the new "activity" might be in the direction of less activity; e.g., a person who is very high in activity and feeling level and contact in most life areas might set up a relaxation period or rest period at work and at home when she or he could be quiet and alone. Manuals that focus on one specific technique of relaxation are well known: for example, those by Benson (1975), Jacobson (1974), and Luthe (1969).

An essential feature of the psychological fitness approach is that people be taught these basic premises directly. The approach is both educational and experimental. By understanding the psychological fitness premises clients gain a new perspective on therapy; the therapeutic endeavor becomes one of developing a new attitude toward psychological health and the client takes on responsibility for his or her own psychological fitness.

Research studies of subjects who participated in psychological fitness training programs and in therapy programs that used the psychological fitness orientation demonstrated that participants would make significant personality changes by carrying out psychological exercise routines. For example Karle, Hart, Corriere, Gold, and Maple (1978) showed that subjects could make significant positive changes toward increasing self-actualization on the Shostrom Personal Orientation Inventory along with significant increases in extraversion scores and decreases in neuroticism scores on the hard-to-change Eysenck Personality Inventory.

The most important kind of psychological fitness change, however, always must be a self-assessed and self-evaluated one. People can learn to give themselves "psychologicals" regularly and then do something through exercise programs to improve or maintain their psychological fitness.

The advantages of this particular fitness and exercise program are *not* in the particular content areas or personality dynamics that are targeted. Other life areas and other personality characteristics very well could be used as the bases of fitness exercises. What participants in this program do learn is that *any* life area can be a source of increased fitness if they decide to try increasing their levels of satisfaction in that area and take action. Also, they learn that *any* personality characteristic can be viewed as changeable and can be a target of exercise efforts. This fitness orientation inculcates a freer attitude toward problems and difficulties in life. Shyness is not a permanent personality defect, nor is anxiety, nor is worrying or pessimism—they are viewed as changeable targets for fitness efforts. Zimbardo's (1977) programs to teach shy adults and young people to be more comfortably sociable and outgoing are a good example of the fitness approach. Similarly, a record of job dissatisfaction is not a pattern that need be repeated forever; instead people can build up new job skills as directly as they might build stronger muscles. The Trower, Bryant, and Argyle (1978) social skills training program is another good example of the fitness approach.

Other Programs of Psychological Fitness Training

The program described in the previous section is just one among many that are available. With the opening up of psychology to humanistic self-help programs, social skills training programs, Eastern psychology, and practical cognitive-behavioral programs of change that has taken place in the 1960s and 1970s there are now many excellent sources for people to draw upon and for therapists to utilize. What is needed, and what this chapter has tried to provide, is a theoretical and historical framework (the psychological fitness perspective of functional therapy) that can encompass a diversity of practical programs.

The SAGE Program

The SAGE (Senior Actualization and Growth Exploration) program was initiated by the writer-psychologist Gay Gaer Luce and colleagues in 1974. The program began with one core group of 12 older people as participants (ages 63 to 72) who agreed to attend one group meeting and one individual meeting weekly for at least six months. The purpose of the meetings was to find activities and exercises that might improve the quality of life of older people. By 1979 SAGE had grown to a staff of 25 in the original Oakland-Berkeley area and 8 core groups of participants. Additionally there were two dozen SAGE groups in other major cities, all coordinated by the National Association for Humanistic Gerontology.

In her book *Your Second Life* (1979) Luce describes many of the psychological exercises that were found to be effective with older people and the philosophy of growth that developed within the program. The program's starting premises were:

1. There is a purpose to old age.
2. People need special conditions for deep growth.
3. Growth and well-being are enhanced by increasing pleasurable experiences.
4. Each person will develop unique growth patterns.
5. In some ways older people may develop faster than younger people.
6. Many of the stress-related ailments of age are reversible.
7. Thoughts and feelings create feelings and influence bodily responses and life-styles.
8. Old age can be a time of release from the inhibitions and habits learned in childhood.
9. Old age, with its closeness to death, can be a time of immersion in truth and reality. (pp. 7–8)

These useful premises relate closely to the psychological fitness premises and to the functional philosophy of this book. In numerous instances Luce makes the point that psychological exercise benefits increase with practice.

The exercises used in the SAGE program included everything from participative listening to crying techniques to goal setting to self-image evaluations to massage, diet, and jogging. What all the techniques had in common was that they were designed to respond to the specific and changing needs of the participants. The overall thrust of psychological exercising is simply to teach people to pay attention to their personal (physical and psychological) needs.

The Austen Riggs Activities Program

A very different, but related, program of psychological fitness training was described by Joan Erikson in her book *Activity, Recovery, Growth* (1976). The Austen Riggs Center is an institution for disturbed adults located in Stockbridge, Massachusetts. The average age of the patients is 23 with a range from 17 to 43, and the average stay in the Center is 400 days.

Joan Erikson organized the activities program around the psychoanalytic growth model of her husband, Erik Erikson. The basic premise of the program was that "Activity—action—is the vital component of all change. Without change, recovery . . . is illusory. Without activity and change which is life itself, there is no growth" (Erikson, 1976, p. xi).

In contrast to the SAGE program which was based upon humanistic-existential psychology and exercise focused, the Austen Riggs program was analytically based and content focused. The program included participation in drama, art, nursery school, garden and greenhouse, and patient activities planning groups according to the needs and preferences of the patients. Nonetheless in both programs there is a clear fitness philosophy that permeates the outlook of the staff and participants. In a postscript to his wife's book Erik Erikson remarks,

> At stake here is the nature of the various conditions for an inspired active state: from the ego's activated adaptability and heightened sense of reality, to the mobilized condition of the whole person-in-action, and, finally, to the mutual actualization of individuals in which all communality depends. (Erikson, 1976, p. 263)

Other Programs

There are a great many other psychological exercise programs and exercise books available to therapists and to people who want to explore their own directions of psychological fitness improvement. However, many of these programs are not called exercise or fitness programs. For example, Perls, Hefferline, and Goodman's *Gestalt Therapy* (1951), Luthe's *The Creativity Mobilization Technique* (1976), and Assagioli's *Psychosynthesis* (1965) are essentially exercise manuals written from the humanistic perspective. Lazarus's *Multi-Modal Behavior Therapy* (1976) and Meichenbaum's *Cognitive-Behavior Modification* (1977) are exercise manuals written from cognitive-behavioral perspectives. Only Assagiolis's book (1965) is specifically labeled a "manual of techniques."

It is likely that many more psychological exercise manuals will be written in the future and that many programs of psychological fitness enhancement that are either activities-content focused or personality-exercise focused will be developed.[3] Alvin Toffler, author of *The Third Wave* (1980), predicts that professional and paraprofessional therapists increasingly will turn their attention to "life-organizing" activities rather than indepth therapy:

> We probably need fewer psychotherapists burrowing mole-like into id and ego, and more people who can help us, even in little ways to pull our daily lives together. . . . Some psychiatrists today perform a life-organizing function. Instead of years on the couch, they offer practical assistance in finding work, locating a girl or boyfriend, budgeting one's money, following a diet, and so forth. We need many more such consultants, structure-providers, and we need feel no shame about seeking their services. (Toffler, 1980, p. 393)

---

[3] Like any other exercise or improvement program, psychological fitness exercises can be done to excess. A helpful antidote to the overuse of psychological self-help programs is *The MAD Guide to Self Improvement* (DeBartolo, 1979).

12

Therapeutic Change

Models of Integration and Reintegration

Overview

Because this is a pivotal and complicated chapter, which concludes the theoretical summary and leads into the practical guidelines of the manual, it will begin with an overview of the several arguments and points to be considered.

Chapter 8 presented the critical importance of feeling moments in therapy. In this chapter the general significance of feeling and emotion in bringing about therapeutic change will be explained. Chapter 9 presented the five personality dynamisms that can be used to work functionally with dreams, fantasies, and memories. In this chapter it will be explained how these dynamisms are used to translate either defenses or positive impulses into participative emotions. It is this practice of making feelings and emotions into participatory, expressive acts that uniquely defines the therapeutic situation. Only in therapy are significant feelings repeatedly translated from inner experiences into visible expressions. This translation process works to unfreeze defenses and to expand proactive impulses. Additionally, every experience-to-expression translation is an exercise activity that contributes to the client's psychological fitness. (These specialized emotional exercises are largely confined to the therapeutic setting.)

Feeling-to-expression exercises are micro-events that can be related to two kinds of macro-processes: a four-step integration process and a four-step reintegration process. Particular attention will be given to Dabrowski's theory of positive disintegration to explain how the growth process and the defensive process interact.

A secondary argument, which will be explored, is that the therapeutic growth process shares many features with the general creative process as seen in the arts and sciences. Koestler's theory of creativity will be summarized and compared to the functional theory of therapeutic change.

Why Therapy Is Difficult

Therapy is hard because clients are resistant to change and defensive about fully revealing their emotional experiences. If it were not for defenses and resistances therapy would be very easy indeed. All the therapist would need to do would be to assess the client's desired areas of life development and plan, with the client, a program of self-directed psychological exercises and life changes leading to improvement. Going to a therapist would be very much like going to a hairdresser or ski instructor. A clear goal would be matched with definite procedures to attain the goal and both the client and therapist would be able to see whether the desired changes were forthcoming.

To an extent this kind of directed growth activity does go on in therapy; models of coaching and fitness training provide useful guidelines for carrying out this side of the therapeutic endeavor. However, no matter how clear-cut the goals and how direct the exercises and assignments for achieving them, it will not be long in any therapeutic transaction before progress is stymied. The client seemingly cannot or will not carry out the activities he or she agrees upon. It is at this point that the straightforward fitness and growth approach breaks down and the therapist must shift from a growth model to a pathology model in explaining and guiding the therapy. The purpose of this chapter is to explain how growth models and psychopathology models interact and how the process of personality integration is complemented by the processes of disintegration and reintegration.

A Model of Integration

The goal of functional therapy is personality change. Obviously, not every prospective client who comes for therapy is really a candidate for personality change. Therapists must, in Thorne's phrase, think very broadly about "case handling," and not try to do therapy with everyone. For some clients support, reassurance, and a return to their previous level of less-distressed personality functioning is the real goal of the therapist. However, even with clients who desire personality change in order to feel better and function more effectively, there will be a difference between therapy that works mainly on building up strengths and therapy that deals directly with defenses and resistances. Often, a good amount of change can be achieved simply by working from a fitness or growth model and ignoring areas of dysfunctioning. In effect, the dysfunctioning in one life area is offset by improved functioning in other life areas. For example, a person whose marital relationship is suffering because of the increased pressures of a job layoff might be helped to locate a new job without ever discussing directly the marital problems.

The often used distinctions between counseling and psychotherapy, or between short-term and long-term therapy, or between supportive therapy and depth therapy revolve around the extent to which basic personality change is attempted and the extent to which defenses, resistances, and repressed materials are uncovered. However, as we shall see, these familiar distinctions often gloss over a basic question: When *must* a therapy work directly with dysfunctioning and when can a therapist simply concentrate on improving functioning? To answer this question a specification of the process of growth or change is needed. Then the answer to the question becomes obvious—a therapist *must* work with dysfunctioning when the client is unable to make positive changes.

When working with growth or integration the therapist can ignore problems, symptoms, and complaints unless those dysfunctionings make it impossible for the person to carry out the steps of the change process. A four-step model of the integration process is used in functional therapy. The therapist helps to make the client aware of each step in the process, then both the therapist and the client will know when a step is missing or incomplete.

The four steps are: the Need step, the Choice step, the Action step, and the Image step. A person who completes all four steps has made a meaningful personality change.

The Need step of the growth process involves helping the client isolate, recognize, and verbalize a need or want. The process of satisfying needs and wants is one of the main jobs of the personality. The personality is the bridge between the biological experience of the need and the actions that must be taken to satisfy the need. Clearly needs and wants are different from problems. When a client makes the shift from stating needs as problems (which is a personal application of the medical model) to a personal declaration of what he or she needs (or wants), significant room has been made for personality development.

The Choice step of the process of integration is an extension of the recognition of needs and wants. Once a personal desire has been felt and stated, the client is encouraged to respond to his or her needs as an important reality. Choosing one's own needs requires an affirmation of inner-directedness. The person can't remain outer-oriented ("The world must [or won't] fulfill my needs"). A shift to an inner-orientation involves taking on responsibility for fulfilling one's own needs and wants as much as possible ("I can try to fulfill my needs"). All needs and wants are important; they all add to the ratio of positives to negatives in a person's life. The choice may be as small as "I want this and not that for dinner" or as large as "I want to feel more deeply with my wife." The therapist's task in this Choice step is to help the person feel what it is like to affirm personal needs.

The choice step is followed by the Action step. Once a person has admitted a need and chosen the need as a real value in his or her life then new actions can be tried to fulfill that need. The therapist may teach the client how to behave in new or more functional ways or may simply be a sounding board for the effectiveness of the ways that the client tries.

The last step in the growth process is the Image step. Awareness of a new need, choosing that need, and acting to fulfill that need eventually will result in a new personality image. The new image (e.g., "I am a person who feels deeply with my wife") functions to integrate a great many experiences and actions. The person now conceives of himself and guides his life, when it is relevant, from this image. The new image replaces old images (e.g., "I'm too busy to feel much with my wife") and will self-define the person in a world that contains a multitude of possible wants, choices, actions, and images.

The complete four-step integration process (Need-Choice-Action-Image) will be repeated again and again throughout a person's lifetime. Because needs and wants change, no set of personality images can be sufficient for a lifetime. The integration process goes on inside and outside the therapy situation. All that is unique to therapy is that therapists can directly and conceptually teach clients to be aware of the growth process. People are in the process long before they come to therapy and long after they leave it.

Exactly what the therapist need do to further this process of integration will vary from client to client and session to session. In the next section of this book a structuring of therapy sessions according to this four-step integration model (and the four-step reintegration model to be described) is presented. The therapist can work with feeling moments, expression dynamics, and personality dynamisms and apply innumerable techniques to create exercise effects—keeping in mind that everything in therapy rests upon a natural growth process. Indeed, the most fundamental of all psychological exercises is simply admitting needs, making choices, acting in new ways, and accepting new images into the personality. Unless these fundamental psychological activities are consciously carried on and monitored, no satisfactory level of psychological fitness is possible.

The first place to look for dysfunction is in failures to grow. Defensiveness or resistances are most clearly manifest when a person refuses to become aware of new needs and wants, or choose them, or act on them, or change personality images to accomodate them. If the four-step integration process is conceptualized as a cycle going from Needs and Wants-to Choices-to Actions-to Images, then dysfunctioning consists of a reversal of the clockwise cycle to a counterclockwise cycle. Instead of choosing and acting from needs and wants the dysfunctioning person begins to allow old images to dictate how he or she will act, what he or she will choose and what needs and wants can be satisfied: Images-to Actions-to Choices-to Needs and Wants. This means, in effect, that only old needs and wants can be satisfied because the person's old images are determining actions, choices, and even the awareness of what is needed and wanted. Since it is extremely unlikely that old needs and wants will match current needs and wants, the person caught in a reverse cycle is bound to be dissatisfied but may not know why. Only awareness of how the old personality images are blocking the emergence of new awareness and functioning will lead to a clearing away of the block or resistance. It is at this stage, when old images effectively block the natural growth process, that therapists must shift from a growth model to a pathology model in their work.

The Process of Disintegration

Disintegration refers to the breakdown of personality images and functioning. The process of disintegration can be positive if it results in further growth, or negative, if it results in a return to stasis or to a lower level of personality development. One of the great puzzles of therapy is found in the fact that disintegration can be positive. Several theorists, including Laing (1967, 1969), have discussed the possibility that personality disintegration as seen in psychoneuroses or even psychoses, can be a positive phenomenon leading to growth. In general, however, this possibility is not theoretically developed in most approaches to therapy.

The most thorough development of a theory of disintegration is found in the work of Kazimerz Dabrowski. Dabrowski was a professor in the Polish Academy of Science and Director of the Institute of Children's

Psychiatry and Mental Hygiene. He was the author of over 50 articles and 4 books in Polish, French, German, and Spanish before one of his books *Positive Disintegration* (1964) was translated into English. Dabrowski is now located at the University of Alberta and his work is becoming better known in the United States.

Dabrowski received an M.D. at the University of Geneva Medical School in 1929 and a Ph.D. in experimental psychology from the University of Pognan in 1932. His ideas relate directly to the historical tradition of functionalism; in 1931 he attended the lectures of Pierre Janet in Paris. He is one of the few modern theorists who is conversant enough with Janet's theories to disagree with him and modify his ideas:

> The inner conflict in neurosis, described by Jung as pathological, seems to play a principal role in development, while Pierre Janet's "reality function" plays a synthesizing part in adapting the individual to reality. Janet regards the absence of "reality function" in the inner structure as a cause of psychoneurosis. The theory of positive disintegration implies that the "reality function" undergoes major transformations during development. (Dabrowski, 1964, p. 104)

This is an intriguing idea—that the accurate *perception of reality is tied to the continual development of personality.* Perceptions that were adequate at one stage or time of personality growth become inadequate in other times. The temporary breakdown of personality and functioning may lead the way to a changed level of reality sensing and matching level of personality reintegration.

The symptoms or complaints that accompany psychological stress may be signs of efforts toward growth:

> It seems probable that certain forms of maladaptation to one's self and to reality, hypersensitivity, lability of psychic structure, and even certain symptoms of internal discord such as self-criticism with a strong emotional accent are elements indispensable in man's development . . . we may find in nervousness, neurosis, and many other disintegration processes hidden germs of positive intellectual and character development. (Dabrowski, 1964, pp. 104–105)

The entire catalogue of symptoms and signs of human misery— guilt, shame, depression, remorse, anxiety, indecisiveness, fearfulness, tension, and so on to delusions and hallucinations—*may* signal the effort to move from a lower to a higher level of personality organization. Unfortunately, whether the disintegration will be positive or negative cannot be clearly discerned or predicted. The advantage of the therapeutic interaction is that a therapist can guide the person toward a positive, controlled disintegration (this process will be described in the next section on reintegration). A disadvantage of therapy is that the therapist may overcontrol through his or her efforts to maintain or quickly achieve positive functioning and thus abort the natural process of disintegration.

According to Dabrowski's theory, higher levels of personality development are characterized by self-education or auto-therapy. The person undergoes the disintegration in his or her own unique way that leads to a unique pathway out of the disintegration and a unique new personality organization.

Dabrowski's theory, unlike those of Erikson or Kübler-Ross, does not focus on specific crises or stages of disintegration–reintegration, but on the *process* of adaptation to personal crises. This approach results in a definition of mental health more as a process than as a set of characteristics:

> The concept of mental health must be based upon a multidimensional view of personality development. Higher levels of personality are gradually reached both through adaptation to exemplary values and through disadaptation to lower levels of the external and internal environments. Development proceeds through the transformation of one's type, the widening of one's interests and capabilities, and the gradual approach toward one's personality ideal through the process of positive disintegration and the activity of the third factor. [The "third factor" in Dabrowski's schema is the inner impulsion toward growth.] This development moves . . . from what is simple to what is complex, and from what is automatic to what is spontaneous. Mental health is the development of personality toward a more elevated hierarchy of goals set by the personality ideal. In this definition, mental health means the continual striving toward further personality development. (Dabrowski, 1964, pp. 124–125)

Dabrowski's formulation, if taken seriously, forces a theoretical expansion away from the clear-cut definition of well-being or mental health in Bradburn's terms as a positive ratio of positives to negatives. (Remember that according to Bradburn's research there was no differences between the rated well-being of people who had few life elements in their ratings or those who had many; in other words there was no difference between simple and complex life organizations.) If Dabrowski is correct, then there will be times in a person's life when he or she must give up a satisfying but simple balance of positives to negatives and actually go through a period of disintegration (a period when negative experiences overbalance positives) in order to develop toward a richer, more complex and, eventually, more satisfying reintegration and rebalancing.

When Dabrowski's theory of disintegration is applied to the Need–Choice–Action–Image cycle it can be understood as the breakdown of the Image that is driving the cycle counterclockwise and countering growth. The person may experience, during the disintegration, disruptions of any function in the cycle: personality images may seem unreal or unrelated, actions may be indecisive or overly driven, choices may be inconsistent and conflicting, the perception of needs or wants suspended, and whole areas of the person's life (e.g., sexuality or relationships) may be deprived.

In his book *Personality-Shaping Through Positive Disintegration* (1967) Dabrowski states his basic thesis clearly:

> *Personality* . . . is a name given to an individual fully developed, both with respect to the scope and level of the most essential positive human qualities, an individual in whom all the aspects form a coherent and harmonized whole, and who possesses, in a high degree, the capability for insight into his own self, his own structure, his aspirations and aims (self-consciousness), who is convinced that this attitude is right, that his aims are of essential and lasting value (self-affirmation), and who is conscious that his development is not yet complete and therefore is working intensively on his own improvement and education (self-education). (Dabrowski, 1967, p. 5)

This is certainly an idealized conception of personality, Dabrowski distinguishes between individuality (all the distinctive positive and negative characteristics of the person) and personality (which refers only to the positive organization and development). Like Janet, James, and Burrow, he links personality development to philosophy and culture. The true development of the individual personality adds to the culture as a whole.

That is why, in Dabrowski's view, the fundamental approach to the development of personality is self-education or auto-therapy: "This is so because it is only when an individual attempts to understand and experience, even in a way that is incomplete and intuitional, the main problems of individual and social life, that he reveals a deepened attitude toward more important realities in his environment" (Dabrowski, 1967, p. 146). The prevalence of self-help is sometimes forgotten by therapists. Whether the growth is through the direct process of integration or the indirect process of positive disintegration many more people change, really change, by helping themselves than by getting help from therapists. Even in straightforward kinds of changes—such as stopping smoking, losing weight, working more efficiently, or exercising more—people change themselves much more frequently than they get help from physicians, pastors, or therapists.[1] Therapists should always keep in mind that, at best, they are merely advising in the natural process of growth and personality development that is going on all around them. Aside from this cautionary implication, Dabrowski's theory of positive disintegration has three other significant implications for the practicing

---

[1] According to the Surgeon General's Report on *The Health Consequences of Smoking* (1982), 75% of all regular smokers want to stop but do not or cannot. Of those smokers who have stopped, 95% did not participate in an organized program; they stopped on their own.

therapist. (The real answer to the old therapist joke "When are you going to stop practicing and start doing something?" is "Never!")

First, therapists should be wary about labeling symptoms and complaints as undesirable and acting quickly to ameliorate them. The person very well may be undergoing a process of positive disintegration that requires time to work itself through. The best intervention may be the least intrusive one.

Second, within a therapy setting, the therapist who finds a client stalled or fixed at one level of personality organization, organized around one or more personality images that are blocking the natural growth cycle, may decide to instigate a controlled process of disintegration. Within the terminology of this book a controlled therapeutic process of positive disintegration is called a reintegrative process. The purpose of this process is to make the client aware of the defensive nature of an image (and the thoughts, habits, and feelings attached to that image) that is preventing growth.

The Process of Reintegration

Personality images may or may not match momentary feelings. If, during a therapy session, the therapist notices frequent mismatches between what a client expresses and what he or she seems to be experiencing then the therapist may decide to counter the image that is sustaining the mismatch. For example, a woman whose self-image is that of a "loving wife" might be so inflexibly attached to her image that she maintains a "loving" demeanor even when she is obviously upset and angry about something her husband said to her. Her image acts as a defense or resistance to cover over the perception and expression of her underlying feelings. Defenses and resistances always function to substitute more acceptable feelings and expressions (more acceptable to the personality image) for unacceptable feelings and expressions. In other words, defenses and resistances are substitutes consistent with the personality image but inconsistent with the feelings of the moment. With resistances the substitution is more or less conscious, the person is *suppressing;* with defenses the substitution is subconscious, the person is *repressing.*

The process of reintegration can involve four steps; however, not every step occurs every time. It is possible to go from step one to step four while skipping two and three. Nonetheless, a full process of reintegration involves these four steps: Counteraction, Catharsis, Proaction, and Reintegration.

There are innumerable ways that a therapist can counteract an image that has become dysfunctional. The most straightforward way of proceeding is simply to point out the mismatch between the apparent feeling and what the client is saying: "Even though you are talking about loving your husband you look and sound angry." This kind of functional interpretation may well be resisted—"Well, I don't feel angry." The therapist can then work with the resistances, applying the same methods of working with expression dynamics and personality dynamisms that would be applied to an emergent image. Working with feeling moments is always dynamically the same whether the feelings are suppressed, repressed, or merely unknown. For example:

> T: Say that again only louder.
> C: "I don't feel angry!"
> T: Keep saying it, say it five times.
> C: (Client repeats five times.)
> T: Now imagine that you are saying that to your husband five times.
> C: (Client repeats again but in a flat voice.)
> T: Try saying "I'll go flat to keep from being angry."
> C: (She does and then she and the therapist talk about the process of going flat, when it happens, and what it means.)

Counteraction takes place by the therapist instructing clients to increase or decrease personality dynamisms and dynamics of expression, often with reference to a defensive image. All resistances and defenses are maintained within a certain narrow set of expressive parameters. So the counteractive process, by not allowing these parameters to stay fixed, begins to undermine the image. When counteraction begins to occur clients experience some stress. A kind of temporary disintegration takes place because the person starts to express things incompatible with the old image but does not yet have a new personality image to accommodate the new ways of functioning.

The counteractive step often leads to an emotional release. In this cathartic stage the client expresses the emotions that have been held in by the old personality images (e.g., "I don't like being nice all the time . . . that's not love"). Sometimes the catharsis may be an extended abreactive catharsis in which the client reexperiences times in his or her past when the old image was instilled to block feelings. The skilled therapist can use this stage to help the client distinguish between the past environment that demanded the old images and the new environment that requires new images and new levels of functioning. The major requirement of the catharsis step is that the client maintain a real level of contact with the therapist sufficient to allow the exploration of times in the past when contact was missing or distorted.

In the proactive step the client moves from a focus on reexpressing feelings that were blocked in the past to *the expression of similar or related feelings with the therapist in the present*. Here the client is helped to explore new feelings and develop new expression skills that eventually will lead to new personality images. At this stage the person who has just undergone a temporary disintegration has no idea if the images and ways of behaving that are being given up will lead to something more satisfying. All that he or she knows is that the old way of being no longer seems to be enough.

In the final step of the reintegration process the person ends up where he or she would have been all along if the old personality image had not distorted the individual's perceptions—at the top of the Need–Choice–Action–Image cycle. The person is now ready to start off open to new wants and needs that were blocked by the old image. The reason for calling this cycle a reintegration process is because it puts the person back into the cycle of integration. As a result of the controlled disintegration of a dysfunctional personality image the person is now open to thinking, feeling, and acting in new ways.

It is important to emphasize that this process of reintegration is necessarily an emotional process. The feelings and emotions that emerge may be mild or intense but they will be real and involving.

Another feature of reintegration is that the client experiences a kind of dual consciousness in which the sense of reality attached to the old image is suspended. This allows the person to experience the specific resistances and defenses attached to the old image without believing them in the same way they would be believed and acted on outside the therapeutic setting. A sort of playacting takes place during reintegration. By exaggerating the expression of the old image beyond its usual expression parameters the person is actually freed from attachment to the image. Indeed, during counteraction and catharsis and proaction the person may experience how much self-inflicted distress comes from efforts to maintain the old personality image. In ordinary circumstances the self-inflicted distress is hidden because the defense or resistance is not experienced in a concentrated way. When clients actually experience what their own resistances and defenses feel like, they are then much more willing to give them up.

The rather abstract terms Counteraction–Catharsis–Proaction–Reintegration were used to describe this four-step process because it is an artificial process. Although Dabrowski makes it clear that disintegration (both positive and negative) occurs outside the special circumstances of therapy, this full four-step process of positive disintegration would very rarely occur without the direction and presence of a therapist. The process of integration is described in simple, common terms (Need–Choice–Action–Image) because it occurs naturally and frequently in ordinary adult development. The full four-step process of reintegration that is described does not usually occur outside the therapeutic setting.

In his two-volume work *Theory of Levels of Emotional Development* (1977) Dabrowski collaborated with Michael Piechowski to develop a system for rating different levels of personality from interview and autobiographical materials. Like other functional theorists, Dabrowski and Piechowski make emotional development integral to personality development. Their approach to the study of basic emotional reactions differs from that of Ekman, Izard, and others who emphasize discriminating types of emotions and emotional expressions:

> We are concerned with the developmental differentiation of emotional functions and associated expressions of behavior. We have previously stated that the differences between *levels* of an emotional expression are greater and more significant than differences between particular emotions. (Dabrowski & Piechowski, 1977, Vol. 1, p. 119)

This discrimination leads to a wonderful but bewildering complexity for the therapist who must discriminate not only different emotional expressions but their highly significant meanings in relation to different levels of personality organization. The expression of happiness or disgust or anger or sadness or fear may be common to both higher and lower levels of personality but their meanings will be quite different.

Dabrowski and Piechowski take the by now familiar functionalist position that feeling is even more important than symbolism in directing personality development: "Emotional processes assume a guiding, directing and transforming role. And even though the capacity for symbolic thought is considered to be the distinctive trait that makes man human, we must stress that the capacity for feeling is, perhaps, even more fundamental" (Dabrowski & Piechowski, Vol. 1, p. 6).

The most detailed discussion of affective cognitive functioning from both the psychological and psychophysiological points of view in the history of functional therapy is found in Burrow's writings (see Chap.

5).[2] He recognized empirically and theoretically that pictures and the symbols attached to personality images can interrupt direct perception (both internal perceptions and external perceptions). The workings of the symbol system become derailed. Instead of aiding perception and action in reality, image-attached symbols falsely mediate between the historical person and the present. In effect the individual functions out of phase or out of time; the personality images act as a filter rather than as an efficient map. The person is trying to be the image rather than simply functioning.

To undercut symbol driven and image dominated perceiving a more basic level of functioning, feeling, is used. Symbols will be answered with more symbols, and pictures with more pictures. But feelings can disrupt both personality pictures and thoughts. This disruption is experienced as disintegration. As Dabrowski points out, only psychopaths are insulated from this kind of disruption. Psychopaths are trapped in a simple form of primary integration that, because of their inaccessibility to feelings, resists most kinds of disintegration. They do not suffer from full negative disintegration but neither do they have the possibilities of positive disintegration. They can neither descend into the psychic inferno nor ascend into psychic heaven; they stay at the first level of either adaptation or disadaptation.

In his portrayal of Gary Gilmore in *The Executioner's Song,* Norman Mailer describes how Gilmore killed two men to keep from killing his girlfriend who had jilted him. This represents an extremely primitive way of handling overwhelming feelings. Gilmore described his state of mind as,

> I can't keep up with life. . . . All week long I had this unreal feeling, like I was seeing things through water, or I was watching myself do things. Expecially this night, everything felt like I had this unreal feeling, like I was watching at a distance what I was doing . . . had this cloudy feeling. I went in and told the guy to give me the money, and I told him to lay down on the floor, and then I shot him. (Mailer, 1979, pp. 293, 378)

---

[2] The development of a therapeutically relevant neuropsychological theory of feelings and personality change, even the outline of such a theory, is far beyond the scope and competence of this book's author. At a minimum a comprehensive theory would have to integrate ideas about the vertical, evolutionary organization of the brain, related research about the role of the right and left hemispheres in cognitive and personality functioning, research on autonomic tuning and rebalancing, research and theory about ditention and cotention, holographic models of neuropsychological storage and access, and many, many modern findings about the various areas of the brain, their functions and interrelationship. On top of all this the theorist would have to assimilate all the modern research about brain chemistry and the specific links between various brain chemicals and various levels of psychological functioning.

Gilmore describes, very clearly, the defensive image of unreality that covered over what must have been his intense feelings of rage and hatred toward his girlfriend. The image "I love her and can't hate her or hurt her" effectively blocked Gilmore from acting out toward his girlfriend but at the cost of displaced actions and flattened feelings in the real world. It was mentioned earlier how reintegration involves a kind of playacting in which the client suspends belief in a defensive image enough to express the defense directly and fully to the therapist. Further playacting is involved if the client expresses feelings from the past (while clearly being aware of the present) and expresses feelings toward the therapist that were covered over and inadmissable in the past (all the while knowing that the therapist is not the real target of the feelings). The kind of mock expressions that are involved in counteraction, catharsis, and proaction are very important because they prepare the person to start to make new, real expressions of needs and wants in the present. Therapy time, during the reintegration cycle, becomes a meta-time that is not past and not present but between the two psychological time periods.

By now it should be clear that the functional therapist's model of feeling processes and ways of working with feelings are very different from the approaches taken in many other modern therapies. For example, the approach to working with feelings found in many humanistic encounter groups is quite contrary to the approach used by functional therapists. Often in humanistic encounter groups and sensitivity groups there is an explicit encouragement to "say your feelings" or "be open to your feelings" that may seem superficially similar to the functional focus on feelings.

However, it should be clearly understood that admonitions such as "say your sadness" or "show your anger" when applied grossly do nothing more than alert people to categories of feeling. The tasks of noticing and selecting certain feeling–expression mismatches, creating feeling moments, using expression dynamics, and varying personality dynamisms are not specifically understood or used by many group leaders who "work with feelings" and encourage group members to "share feelings." All too often what people share are not feelings but feeling flags. Different flags or emblematic expressions are run up the pole and displayed when it is suggested that expressing sadness or expressing anger or expressing tenderness are to be focused upon.

An example of this kind of feeling flag method is found in the book *How Do You Feel: A Guide to the Emotions* by Wood (1974). The book consists of many short chapters in which therapists and group members talk about what it is like to feel Accepted, Affectionate, Afraid,

Angry . . . Hopeful, Hurt, Inferior, and so on, to Shy, Superior, Suspicious, and Trusting.

Here is a sample passage:

> How does it feel to be accepted? . . . good, warm, comfortable, relaxed. It feels secure, important; takes away demands and expectations. With acceptance I give myself the opportunity to be with someone without demands or with a great lessening of demands on me. (Wood, 1974, p. 18)

It may well be useful for people to read about the many different blends of feeling and meaning that different people use to define different feelings. But this process of verbal description is entirely different than the process of expression, especially the process of discovering the contents of feeling moments. Describing a smorgasbord of feelings the way Wood's contributors do is very similar to writing restaurant reviews—writing the review is very different from eating. Describing feelings involves people in discursive talk rather than expressive talk. It teaches *nothing* about how to get in touch with feeling moments. The subtitle of Wood's book is "A Guide to Your Emotions." More accurately, it should be called "A Guide to Talking Humanistically About Your Emotions." There is nothing wrong with discursive feeling talk but it has no more connection to expressive talk than talking about sports, politics, or the Civil War.

Ekman's research on the facial expression of emotion demonstrated that true emotional *expressions* are very rapid, less than a second in length; emblematic expressions are signals or flags that are consciously held for four seconds or longer (see Chap. 8). What Wood's contributors are doing is describing emblematic, that is, consciously directed, held, feeling poses. The person who attends encounter groups where this kind of feeling communication is stressed learns only how more consciously to direct and display feeling emblems.

For some kinds of clients (e.g., hysterics) encouragement to label and display more feeling emblems is actually harmful. The reason is that hysterics are already excessively focused on displays of feeling. They need to stop displaying emblems and begin to be surprised again by the directions and contents of their own feelings.

In effect what a functional therapist does when working with defenses or resistances is to convert them into highly stylized emblematic expressions. That is, during counteraction, the client is instructed to hold a resistant expression for a long period of time (10 seconds, 30 seconds, or longer). By consciously holding the posture or facial expression far beyond the time frame in which it is typically used, the client makes the resistance: (a) less automatic, (b) less reasonable, (c) more noticeable, and (d) more amenable to change. The change sought is to reveal the true emotional expressions that are behind the resistance; these can never be known in advance. What the functional therapist does is use the client's well-practiced ability to hold emblematic expressions and apply this ability to break down resistances. Resistances are made into exaggerated emblematic expressions to get to the fleeting emotional expressions that are behind the cognitively frozen postures and verbalizations. This is the opposite of the style used by Wood and others in which thoughts and feelings are made into emblems.

Creativity and Change

The role of emotion and feeling in therapy has not been generally understood. The idea that emotions are important because they are a cause of pathology is true but it is a partial idea: The reason emotions *can be* a cause of pathology is that they energize or activate many other psychological functions (memory, action, perception, cognition, etc.) and lead to the reorganization of these functions. Emotions and feelings can be the source not only of pathology but of growth and creativity, not only defensiveness but the reversal of defensiveness.

The two fundamental reasons fixed images become dysfunctional and frustrating is because: (1) they fail to meet current needs and wants and (2) fixed images tend to block the affective drive (the picture–symbol cognitive system overrides the affective system). In both creative development and therapeutic development there is a strong reliance on subconscious emotions and feelings to break through fixed symbols and pictures.

Historically, insanity and creativity often have been thought to be related. The reason for this basically false historical presumption is that both insanity and creativity are "disorders" of feeling. In one condition, insanity, the feelings serve mainly the negative disintegrative functions. In the other condition, creativity, feelings serve positive disintegration and reintegration. The historically intuitive linking of insanity and creativity is correct at one level but in error overall. So too are the analytic and humanistic theories about "regression in the service of the ego" and the creative use of "primary process" or "right hemisphere" thinking. It is *not* imagery and spatial, nonsequential thinking that is primary, it is feeling. Feeling processes are more basic (both psychologically and physiologically) than cortical hemispheric functioning. That is why feeling–action functions can undercut, redirect, and unfix both pictures and thoughts.

Koestler's Bisociative Theory of Creativity

In 1964 Arthur Koestler published *The Act of Creation,* a book that attempted a general theory of creativity applicable to both the arts and the sciences.[3] In his Foreword to the book, Cyril Burt connects Koestler's theory to the concepts of Galton and James:

> Galton . . . in his later years came to lay almost equal stress on certain supplementary qualities [in addition to inherited general intelligence]. . . . Of these "special aptitudes" the most important was what he called "fluency"—that is "an unusual and spontaneous flow of images and ideas. . . . He added two further characteristics—"receptivity" and "intuition or insight," i.e., what James has called "sagacity." (1964, p. 14)

Koestler identifies one process, bisociation, that he finds common to all kinds of creativity:

> I have coined the term "bisociation" in order to make a distinction between the routine skills of thinking on a simple "plane," as it were, and the creative act, which . . . always operates on more than one plane. The former may be called single-minded, the latter a double-minded, transitory state of unstable equilibrium when the balance of both emotion and thought are disturbed. (Koestler, 1964, pp. 35–36)

Of course this kind of cognitive–affective instability or disturbance also is found during therapeutic change. The ordinary growth or integration process that involves a straight-line progression from Need to Choice to Action to Image requires effective thinking and functioning but not creativity. However, blocked growth and reintegration does require a double-minded, old-new, fixed–unfixed bisociation activity to move beyond the dysfunctional image toward receptivity to new images. "The act of discovery has a disruptive and a constructive aspect. It must disrupt rigid patterns of mental organization to achieve the new synthesis" (Koestler, 1964, p. 104).

The essential connection between creative discoveries and therapeutic changes is found in the way both use emotions to bring about bisociation. Koestler identifies laughing and crying as action emotions. That is, they are emotions that involve immediate involuntary expressions in response to mental and social events. In a chapter on "The Logic of the Moist Eye" he discusses psychology's lack of scholarly attention to the phenomenon of crying, "This indifference towards the manifestation of

---

[3] In 1965 I had the great pleasure of attending Mr. Koestler's "seminar on creativity" at Stanford University, which he gave at the invitation of Dr. Ernest Hilgard. Mr. Koestler was a resident fellow at the Center for Advanced Study in the Behavioral Sciences. I was extremely impressed and stimulated by Koestler's arguments and ideas and immediately applied some of his concepts to my dissertation research project on feelings and remembering. However, it has taken more than 15 years (a long period of incubation!) to appreciate fully and apply Koestler's theory to the problems and phenomena of therapy.

emotions in weeping (which is after all neither an uncommon nor a trivial phenomenon) is itself symptomatic of the contemporary trend in psychology" (1964, p. 271). Koestler identifies weeping as an overflow response for the parasympathetic emotions and laughter as the overflow response for the self-assertive or sympathetic emotions.

He comments specifically on the connections between creativity and psychotherapy:

> Psychotherapy aims at undoing faulty integrations by inducing a temporary regression of the patient to an earlier level, in the hope that he will reintegrate into a more stable pattern. Neurosurgery, shock-therapy, and related methods aim at releasing phylogenetically older centers of the brain from cortical restraints. In a less drastic form, Freudians, Jungians, etc., try to make the patient revert to unconscious and infantile planes of experience. (Koestler, 1964, p. 461)

> Thus psychotherapy may be called an experiment in artificially induced regeneration. (p. 461)

> The fact that art and discovery draw on unconscious sources indicates that one aspect of all creative activity is a regression to ontogenetically or phylogenetically earlier levels, an escape from the restraints of the conscious mind, with the subsequent release of creative potentials. (p. 462)

What is unique about the therapeutic situation, in contrast to ordinary life, is that any complex emotion can be made into an action emotion simply by helping the client express what is usually left unsaid. This is done by helping the person express within different parameters of expression than are typical in ordinary life (it is here that the skillful use of expression dynamics becomes important). In effect, artists, writers, and scientists do the same thing when they are creating: they fill in gaps and express beyond the usually accepted boundaries of expressions in their fields. All creativity works bisociatively at the level of feeling moments.

It is now possible to understand *why* the crucial step in all functional therapies is the facilitation of expression. By identifying feeling moments, using dynamics of expression, and shifting personality dynamisms, the functional therapist can move from the experiential mode to the expressive mode. This allows *any* feeling to become a participatory feeling. This step is crucial because it allows for bisociation. By shifting from the cognitive mode to the feeling–action mode, the client is consciously moving to an underlying level of functioning that can disrupt fixed pictures, thoughts, feelings, and habits.

In creative endeavors in the arts and sciences the creative person uses an external medium of expression (painting, sculpting, mathematical symbols, etc.) to channel the bisociated insights. In therapy, the client talks to the therapist. What both domains have in common is the use of feeling functions as the level at which bisociation takes place to reorder and reorganize old pictures and symbols. To drastically reorganize at any level within the organism there must be a temporary shift to a lower, common level of organization. For both therapy and discovery the medium of growth is in the feeling consciousness that underlies picture and symbol consciousness. Access to feeling consciousness is available simply by filling in feeling gaps, making vague and fleeting feelings into participatory feelings that are just as visible as laughter and crying.

As mentioned earlier, in one way it matters very little to a functional therapist whether a client is working with defensive gaps or emergent gaps. The process of bringing incomplete feelings to complete expression is the same whether the therapist is dealing with defenses that hold back feelings or impulses that promote feelings. In both cases the therapist simply applies the same skills: identifying feeling moments, varying expression dynamics, and shifting levels of the personality dynamisms. These methods all are designed to make partial and fragmentary feelings into complete participatory feelings that will in turn lead to new insights, pictures, choices, and actions, as well as a new openness to neglected needs and wants.

One of the side benefits of the linkage between the process of creativity and the process of therapeutic change is that the many techniques and programs that have been developed to facilitate creativity can be applied directly to the tasks of therapy. (This will be done in Part IV.) A second benefit is that clients can be taught to look upon therapy as an active, positive, creative process rather than a mechanical, medical, passive one. The growth of the self can be seen to resemble the growth of a novel, a song, a poem, or a series of paintings.

IV

Technique
A Functional Manual

13

Designing a Program of Functional Therapy

Considered from a practical down-to-earth stance everything that has preceded this section of the book—all the history, the definitions, the concepts, the arguments, and the critiques—were merely a warm-up for the manual. The practical test of a therapeutic approach is not how well it explains but how well it works. In this manual the basic ideas of functional eclectic therapy will be put to work. Since the functional approach is quite broad and diverse it would be possible to generate many different practical programs. This manual presents only one set of procedures among the many that are potentially available. The closing chapter of this section offers suggestions about how to develop extensions, revisions, and alternatives to this particular program of therapy.

Therapists differ strongly in their willingness to program or structure therapy sessions. Some therapists, such as the operant behavior therapists, believe that the *only* valuable form of therapy is one that can be planned and evaluated in detail, conditioning session by conditioning session. At the other extreme are therapists who believe that the less a therapist plans before a session or across a series of sessions the better. For these experientially oriented therapists everything is directed toward exploring the unique existential moments of the client–therapist interaction, without superimposing a structure of expectations, plans, and exercises. Which is right or best? It depends. In my own therapeutic efforts I have actually used both of these extremes, depending upon the

---

Designing a Program ☐

client, the problem, the goals, and the circumstances and possibilities of the therapy.

Most often, however, the level of planning I have used in therapy might be described as "a flexible outline plan." I have a general plan I use with most clients, a specific overall plan I formulate after meeting a particular client, and the overall plan is revised repeatedly as it is worked out in every session. The point of view espoused here is, "Use a plan as a sail, not as an anchor." The program of therapy described in Part IV is to be used to organize the client's and therapist's activities and provide some direction of movement within a session and across sessions.

Because of the emphasis in functional psychology upon conscious planning, choosing, and acting, it is desirable that *both* the therapist and the client know the overall program that is being used. Both should also know that a particular exercise or theme scheduled for a certain day always can be delayed, skipped, or changed. In other words, keep in mind that this program of functional therapy is always adapted to the client and not vice versa.

The adaptability of the program is actually designed into every session. Almost every session is begun with open-ended questions such as "How's it going?," "How are you doing?," or "What's been happening?" A client who plunges into some important or distressing topic in response to these general questions certainly will lead the therapist to forego or modify any plans that have been set up in advance.

Versions of this manual have been applied in various settings with many different clients. Also, professionals with different kinds of training have made use of the manual. Despite these numerous applications I have never seen a single client or therapist go through the sessions in exactly the same way. Variety persists even though the schematic outline of day-by-day sessions is the same.

The goal for this manual is to find a pathway between the therapy-as-art and therapy-as-engineering approaches. There are just as many pitfalls on the side of undirected therapy as on the side of directed therapy. The middle path is found through sensitivity and understanding. A sensitive, perceptive therapist will be able to apply this manual effectively, departing from its structure on some days and staying close to the planned structure on others. Although the manual is fixed, no responsive therapist will apply the manual in exactly the same way twice.

| | **Preliminary** |

Every session of the manual is intended to be a bit like a topic for improvisation; the lyrics stay the same but the content and style of every improvisation will be different.

To use another metaphor, designing a program of therapy for a particular client can be compared to painting a particular scene. There are certain features that will be roughly the same (preparing the canvas, drawing in the shapes or perhaps sketching a small-scale guide drawing, selecting the medium—oils, acrylics—mixing the paints, etc.) and there are other choices that will be unique to each artistic project (the blending of color and the balancing of shapes are very likely never to have been used before and will never be used again). So, the therapeutic task and the artistic task are similar: how to take care of the technical details in such a way that the creative details are furthered, not blocked. Every successful therapy transaction is in some ways like all others, like some others and like no others.

Structure of the Manual

An outline of the 12-month program is listed below:

Month	Sessions	Themes
1	1–4	Orientation to Therapy—Feeling Moments and Psychological Fitness
2	5–8	The Expression Dynamism
3	9–12	The Activity Dynamism
4	13–16	The Clarity Dynamism
5	17–20	The Feeling Dynamism
6	21–24	The Contact Dynamism
7	25–28	Reorientation—Images and Growth
8	29–32	Relationships
9	33–36	Sex
10	37–40	Play and Recreation
11	41–44	Work
12	45–48	Ending the Therapy

The sessions are organized as though the client was on a one-year schedule of individual weekly sessions (with time out for vacations). In general, any individual session easily can be modified into a group session. (See Session 20a for an example.) Also, if the client is fortunate enough to be going through therapy with a group of clients who are on

---

Designing a Program   ☐

roughly the same schedule, it is extremely valuable to add weekly, bi-weekly, or monthly group sessions that repeat the themes used in individual sessions. Repetitions of session themes in a group setting are very effective both in revealing other facets of the therapy exercises and in testing and aiding each client's integration of what was learned in individual sessions.

In a situation where a client is not going to be able to meet as often as once a week or for as long as a year keep the orientation sessions (1–4) but pick and choose among the other sessions those that seem most relevant to the client's needs and problems. For example, a client who is having trouble with loneliness and shyness should definitely be exposed to the relationship, expression, and contact sessions. Obviously, if a client's life is organized so that certain life areas on the schedule are irrelevant (e.g., if the person is retired), drop the coverage of that area (e.g., work) and substitute double coverage of more relevant life areas (e.g., contact, relationships, play, and recreation and consider adding specific sessions on death and dying, health and sickness, etc.). *Always be flexible* when applying the sessions in this manual; feel free to reorder, repeat, omit, add, and modify sessions that need to be changed for each individual client.

The sessions are ordered so that they begin with an emphasis on dynamisms in the early months and move toward specific life area concerns and problems in the later months. This order stresses styles of functioning before content. Experience has shown that the major content area in the early sessions is really the therapy itself. The person entering therapy is learning how to be an effective client. Once a therapeutic relationship has developed then the examination of life area problems and possibilities can proceed at a more meaningful level.

The general goal of this program of therapy is to help clients feel better and function more effectively. Specific goals include: (1) teaching the psychological fitness approach and exercises that can be used throughout the client's life, (2) helping clients understand and use the integration cycle and the reintegration cycle, (3) achieving an understanding of the positives-to-negatives ratio as it applies to different areas in clients' lives, and (4) helping clients function more effectively from feelings, using expression dynamics and personality dynamisms.

The program is designed with a typical therapeutic setting in mind, in which one client is seeing one therapist for individual sessions in

☐ **Preliminary**

either a private office, a clinic, or a counseling center. (Adaptations of the program to special circumstances and settings and special goals, and the utilization of cotherapists, cogroup leaders, and peer counselors can be made by the therapist who is applying the program. Simply adapt each session exercise to the framework appropriate for the setting and the clients.[1])

Understand that the manual described in the next few chapters was different six months ago and will be modified again six months to a year from now (or maybe next week). The overall structure is likely to stay the same but the particular exercises used in certain sessions will change. There are so many more exercises that can be invented and drawn upon from such a variety of therapies that their number is inexhaustible. Eclectic therapists are constantly adapting techniques to their use.

The basic equipment needed for the sessions in the program includes: (1) a small cassette tape recorder and tapes (including 30″ tape loops), (2) chalkboard and drawing materials, (3) pillows or mattress in the therapy room that can be punched and kicked, (4) a relatively soundproof room for privacy, and (5) a full-length mirror. Also, if at all possible, it is very useful for therapists to have a video cassette recorder (VCR) and camera. The VCR can be used to present movies that elicit feeling and to give videotape feedback about the client's emotional responsiveness and defensiveness. Assignments sometimes are given preceding or following sessions that make use of resources in the community (theatres, gyms, restaurants, discos, bars, etc.).

In functional therapy it is considered very desirable that clients understand as fully as possible just what the therapist is doing and why. For that reason several of the orientation sessions involve going over the structure of the program with the client. It is desirable, because of the premium placed upon awareness and choosing, that clients know where every session fits. In functional therapy the therapist's plans,

---

[1] The program described in this book has been used in private clinics, university counseling centers, hospitals, high school counseling centers, solo office practices, and other settings. The Therapist Training Program of Hart & Associates, 11850 Wilshire Boulevard, Los Angeles, California 90025, (213) 479-3618, under the direction of John Hart, M.S.W. was established to train paraprofessionals and professionals in applying and developing programs of functional eclectic therapy. For information about training programs write to Hart & Associates.

Designing a Program

programs, ideas and methods are open for discussion. In fact, a good part of the therapy consists of teaching clients the theory in ways that can be practically understood and applied.

Therapists vary widely as to how much they use pretesting, post-testing, and within-session evaluations. This program has been applied in settings where no testing was used and in settings where very detailed test batteries were administered (including the MMPI, Shostrom's POI, the Eysenck Personality Inventory, observer reports, and psychophysiological measures of EEG, EMG, and blood pressure).

To do the sessions as described in this manual the only necessary form of testing is found in the sessions in which the client is asked to self-evaluate his or her performance and satisfaction level in a life area or on a personality dynamism. In some sessions clients are asked to keep behavioral records; in others they are asked to keep dream and fantasy diaries; and in others they are asked to write autobiographies. These self-evaluation records can be charted and discussed if the therapist judges that such displays will be helpful.

Therapists also vary as to how much questionnaire information they want to have available before seeing clients. A simple information sheet that is used routinely at the Hart & Associates offices in Los Angeles is presented in Figure 4.

The therapist has this information *before* seeing the client and may spend part of the first session checking and amplifying key points. It is also useful to have the new client sign a consent form. Figure 5 shows a sample form.

Clients who inquire about therapy but who are not yet sure that they want to begin routinely are given two pieces of information: the first is an excellent brochure titled "Clinical Psychologists and Psychological Health Care: Questions and Answers for You and Your Family," which was prepared by the Division of Clinical and Professional Psychology of the California State Psychological Association (1980), and the second a brochure and a few short reprints about functional eclectic therapy. New prospective clients also are told that they can schedule an exploration interview to discuss the therapy program and whether it or some other program is likely to meet their needs. The CSPA brochure covers such questions as: "When should I consult a clinical psychologist?," "What kinds of psychological health care does a clinical psychologist offer to the public?," "How long does psychological treat-

| | Preliminary |

Name: _____ Home phone: _____
Address: _____ Date of birth: _____
       (Street)

_____
       (City, State, Zip)
Referred by: _____

Marital status:
    _____ Never married
    _____ Married, date of current marriage _____
                     Number of previous marriages _____ Self
                                             _____ Current spouse
    _____ Divorced, how long? _____
    _____ Separated, how long? _____
    _____ Widowed, how long? _____
    _____ Living with someone, how long? _____

Education: _____ 0–8 years   _____ Completed college
                     _____ Some high school   _____ Some graduate training
                     _____ Completed high school _____ Advanced degree
                     _____ Some college   in what _____
                     Currently in school _____ Yes _____ No   Where? _____

Persons living with you:
_____ Spouse   Name: _____   Age: _____
                 Occupation: _____ Education: _____
_____ Other   Name: _____   Age: _____
      Adult   Occupation: _____ Relationship: _____
                 _____ Education: _____
                 Name: _____   Age: _____
                 Occupation:_____ Relationship: _____
                 _____ Education: _____
                                              Check if currently
_____ Children Name: _____   Age: _____ living with you_____
                     _____   _____   _____
                     _____   _____   _____
                     _____   _____   _____
                     _____   _____   _____

Employment:
Self: Work full-time _____ Part-time _____ Unemployed _____
      Occupation _____ Employer _____ Work phone _____
Spouse: Work full-time _____ Part-time _____ Unemployed _____
      Occupation _____ Employer _____ Work phone _____

Figure 4. Information sheet—Adult.

(Continued)

Designing a Program

Financial Information:

Yearly salary or earnings (before taxes)	Other income (specify source, e.g., investment, property, unemployment insurance, social security, alimony, or child support)

Self _____

Spouse _____

_____ Source: _____

_____ Source: _____

Do you have insurance that covers psychological services? Yes _____ No _____
If yes, with what company _____

Concerns:

The following is a list of problem areas which may or may not be of concern for you. Please check the ones for which you are seeking assistance:

1.	Employment or finances	_____
2.	Education or vocational choice	_____
3.	Memory, thoughts or concentration	_____
4.	Friendships or social life	_____
5.	Family or marriage	_____
6.	Legal or criminal issues	_____
7.	Sex	_____
8.	Physical conditions (e.g., insomnia, weight control, drugs or alcohol)	_____
9.	Specific habits or behavior patterns (e.g., phobias, assertion problems)	_____
10.	Other (specify) _____	

Please circle the problem area which is of *most* concern to you.

How would you describe your mood, emotional reactions, or feelings at this time? Please check all that apply and circle the most predominant feeling.

1.	Anxiety or nervousness	_____	4. Lack of energy	_____
2.	Depression or sadness	_____	5. Fear	_____
3.	Excitement	_____	6. Overactivity	_____

Are there other people with you today who are also seeking assistance?
If yes, who? _____   Relationship to you _____

_____   _____

_____   _____

Figure 4. *Continued*

Preliminary

Medical Information (to be completed for each person seeking assistance):
Are you or anyone else seeking assistance currently receiving medical care?
Yes _____ No _____
If yes, please describe briefly: _____

Current drugs or medication:

Name of family member	Type of medication	Average dosage	Frequency
_____	_____	_____	_____
_____	_____	_____	_____
_____	_____	_____	_____
_____	_____	_____	_____

If there are other medical or physical problems which you feel might be important in working with you, please explain here:

I have been informed that, in order to assure the high quality of services and training at the clinic, there is always the possibility of observation of therapy sessions by other clinic staff members. It is understood that all information disclosed within these sessions is confidential and may not be revealed to anyone outside the clinic staff without written permission.* Audiotaping or videotaping may be requested for the benefit of the therapy or for the therapist's training.

I understand that, from time to time, the clinic may request completion of questionnaires for research projects conducted within the clinic. A clinic staff member shall always explain these procedures at the time of the request and I shall always have the right to choose not to participate in the research project. As with all clinic information, research data is confidential.

Client Signature(s) _____

Witness _____

Date _____

*This is always true except where disclosure is required by law (for example, when a client waives his or her right to confidentiality in a court of law, in situations of life-threatening suicide, or homicide or child abuse).

Figure 5. Consent form.

Designing a Program

ment usually take?," "What if I need medication?," and "How would I find a clinical psychologist?"

For more information about how to set up services in clinical psychology, counseling, consulting, and school psychology, therapists can consult the APA publication "Speciality Guidelines for the Delivery of Services" (1981).

Guiding Ideas

Keep in mind nine basic guiding ideas from Parts I, II, and III when applying this manual.

1. Different sessions call for the therapist to take on different role models. These range from the most general person-to-person role to specific coach–athlete, doctor–patient, hypnotist–subject, and teacher–student roles that are used for special sessions and objectives. Additionally, the therapist must be willing to innovate and shift to new roles when it is recognized that certain therapist images block rather than facilitate therapeutic progress.

2. Within the functionalist orientation the inclination is to pay attention first to conscious determinants of actions, then subconscious determinants, and finally unconscious determinants. Remember that consciousness is *not* equated with verbal consciousness but includes imagery and feeling awareness.

3. The feeling moment is the critical within-session unit for functional therapists. Therapists work to make clients aware of feeling gaps (experience–expression mismatches) and help clients fully to express feelings that are incompletely expressed. Through complete expression clients are helped to full experiencing and new choices.

4. Dynamics of expression are used both to reveal feeling gaps and to fill the gaps. Partial and distorted expressions are contained within narrow parameters of expression that can be disrupted by varying expression dynamics beyond expected limits.

5. Personality dynamisms (contact, clarity, expressiveness, emotionality, and activity) are used in the same way that expression dynamics are applied in therapy, that is, to work with the *form* of the client's

---

☐   **Preliminary**

response regardless of content. By varying the dynamisms up and down the person can go beyond fixed feelings, images, and actions and be open to new experiences and choices.

6. The functional therapist works with both integration and re-integration, both growth impulses and defensive impulses, as needed. In general, however, the therapist will work with defenses and resistances *only* when growth impulses are blocked by fixed, defensive images.

7. Dreams, fantasies, and memories of waking events are approached similarly, by working from form to content. First the functional meaning of the psychological experience is explored, using expression dynamics and varying relevant personality dynamisms. Then the symbolic meanings are explored, after the client is more or less disengaged from the content and freer to change.

8. The functional therapist is willing to use whatever technique might achieve desirable results. Technical eclecticism is the rule, not the exception.

9. In most sessions the therapist will try to make the theory and technique he or she is using explicit for the client. The modeling effect of the theory and philosophy of the therapy is intentionally used by the therapist. The only exception to this guideline is in the case of placebo techniques in which knowledge of exactly what is being done, and why, might undermine the effectiveness of the technique.

The one common idea that runs through all of these guidelines is an emphasis on the form or process of emotional functioning. This emphasis is found in all functional therapies and functionally influenced therapies from Janet and Burrow to the modern humanistic therapists Rogers, Perls, and Assagioli.

An interesting example of a current functionally derived therapy that clearly has this form versus content emphasis is Neuro Linguistic Programming (NLP). Bandler and Grinder (1975, 1976) developed NLP out of a background in nonverbal communication, psycholinguistics, hypnosis, and imagery. They attempted to study model therapists (Fritz Perls, Virginia Satir, and Milton Erickson) to discover what ways of responding to clients they shared. Over and over again they observed that these therapeutic "wizards" obtained seemingly magical effects by ignoring the content of their client's presentations; instead they worked directly with the form or process:

Designing a Program

> People have always tried to turn body language into a content vocabulary, as if holding your head back *meant* that you were reserved and crossing your legs *meant* that you were closed. But body language doesn't work like words work; it works differently. Eye movements and body movements give you information about *process*. (Bandler & Grinder, 1979, p. 47)

> The kinds of problems that people have, usually have nothing to do with content, they have to do with the *structure*, the *form* of how they organize their experience. Once you begin to understand that therapy becomes a lot easier. You don't have to listen to the content; you only have to find out how the process works, which is really much simpler. (p.47)
> If the outcome we're after is to *teach people how to do what we do*, then we will demand that it be content-free pure process therapy. Then the only things you have available to pay attention to are the pieces of the process. (p. 82)

The theory of consciousness/unconsciousness, which recognizes the possibility of simultaneous dissociated ongoing processes, used by Bandler and Grinder, comes directly from Janet and James. Similarly, Bandler and Grinder's stress on "The meaning of your communication is the response you get" (Bandler & Grinder, 1979, p. 61) comes directly from the James-Pierce theory of pragmatism. Also, the focus in NLP on the use of eye movement cues to signal the form of a person's response relates closely to the early research of Burrow on ditention and cotention. (Bandler and Grinder do not explicitly acknowledge these influences; it is another example of the hidden influence exerted by the functional milieu on clinical theorizing.)

Although NLP is similar, in its emphasis on working with the forms of communications, to the system of functional therapy described in this manual, there are several clear differences. A major one is that functional therapy stresses *expression* while NLP often stops with experiences. There is no formal recognition of expression dynamics or the personality dynamisms in NLP although some case records show clearly that Bandler and Grinder do use these parameters in working with the form of communications. A second difference is that experience–expression mismatches are taken, in functional therapy, as the major source of psychopathology. In NLP the mismatches that most often are pointed up are input mismatches (and consequent storage mismatches). This same emphasis is found in the communication theories of Bateson, Haley, and Watzlawick to which Bandler and Grinder's are closely related (Bateson, 1972; Haley, 1973; Watzlawick, 1978).

Preliminary

One hemisphere is registering the visual input and the tonal input, and the other hemisphere is registering the words and their digital meaning, and they don't fit. They don't fit maximally where the two hemispheres overlap maximally in kinesthetic representation. (Bandler & Grinder, 1979, p. 49)

Within functional theory the maximal mismatching is posited to occur not in the cerebral representations but in the lower level feeling centers and action centers of the brain. Here again is found the important practical and theoretical difference that exists between an emphasis on horizontal versus vertical brain organization. Attention to triunal or vertical organization requires that the therapist be concerned with action and feeling mismatches as primary, while visual-auditory, tactile-visual, and other such mismatches are of secondary concern. Primary mismatches cannot effectively be undone simply by changing representational fits (as in hypnosis) but require that the client change the modes of expression that are attached to the incongruent experiences.

Although therapists must be concerned with the disordering that occurred when clients received mismatched communications in their past, the only disorder that is visible in the present relationship of the client and therapist is the mismatch between what clients show verbally and what they show facially and posturally. This verbal or nonverbal mismatch indicates a disordering of experience and expression that can be brought into awareness.

This short theoretical excursion previews similar commentaries that will be inserted here and there throughout the manual. It is important for manual users to realize that the simple and concrete directions for every one of the 48 sessions are embedded within a theoretical rationale.

Designing a Program

14

Month One
Orientation

Month One is used both as an extended trial period and as an orientation to the therapy. The therapist and the client can take the time to decide if this program of therapy is best fitted for them. The therapist should introduce each new client to the first four sessions by saying something such as: "Let's use the first four sessions to do two things. First, I can learn more about you and your problems and what you want from therapy and, second, you can learn more about the kind of therapy I do here and decide if it's really right for you. Let's consider these first four sessions as an introduction to the therapy and also as a trial period in which we can both make a decision at the end of the fourth session about whether to continue."

If the client understands and agrees to this way of proceeding it is, in effect, an informal contract. This agreement will prepare the client for more formal and specific behavioral contracts that will be used later in the therapy.

The four specific goals of Month One are (1) to teach the client, cognitively and experientially, about the psychological fitness approach and about feeling moments; (2) to introduce the client to some kind of relaxation technique that can be used immediately and in the future; (3) to introduce the client to a method of experiential focusing that will be used repeatedly in future sessions and in outside exercises; and (4) to allow the client time to tell his or her story and give the therapist a chance to hear both *what* and *how* the client tells about himself or herself.

1 | **Month**

To accomplish these goals the therapist can use a great variety of procedures and resources, including assignments, outside reading, and specific within-session techniques. The specific methods used in this version of the manual are, of course, open to modification. Session one is structured as a long two-hour intake interview. The therapist in this session mostly listens to the client's story, asks questions, and takes notes. Therapists who prefer to shift clients immediately into a process mode rather than a content mode may want to move the intake interview to session two or three and begin with a more dynamic therapist–client interaction. Some therapists even may choose to have the intake interview done by another therapist. Whichever order or procedure is chosen for the intake interview, it is designed both to get the client's story and to begin to teach the client about the psychological fitness approach. Many of the questions and ratings that the interviewer uses are couched in the language of fitness.

Session 1—Intake Interview

  I. Introduction
      A. General statement for therapists
          1. The diagnostic intake evaluation is a key part of a suc-
              cessful outpatient program. The interview is the pro-
              spective client's *first* working experience with the style
              and feeling of treatment at the clinic. It may also be that
              person's first experience with "psychotherapy." It is a
              client–professional relationship and should be con-
              ducted in a competent and assured manner.
          2. The client is checking out, evaluating, and testing whether
              the clinic and you as its representative are capable of
              helping him with whatever the problem is and whether
              you are capable of meeting his expectations. He or she
              is diagnosing and evaluating his or her own experience
              of you and using it as an indicator of whether or not to
              enter into treatment. The client will expect:
              (a) Professional expertise and knowledge and de-
                  meanor

Intake Interview   1

        (b) A professional handling of the interview and pro-
cedure

        (c) Feedback about the interview and your impressions

        (d) A professional recommendation for further treat-
ment if indicated

        (e) A warm, intimate human approach

B. General procedures for therapists

    1. Be on time.

    2. Be well-groomed.

    3. Set up the room in advance.

    4. Speak clearly, explain all professional jargon in a way
that your client understands. Be sure to invite and answer questions.

    5. Your main roles are:

        (a) Teacher

        (b) Psychological expert

        (c) Sympathetic listener

II. Beginning the interview

A. Greet the client in the lobby. Be warm, friendly, direct, pleas-
ant, shake hands, and make eye contact.

B. Seat yourselves in the therapy room; let the client know that
this room will be used regularly.

III. Intake: Life satisfaction chart

A. (Warm and Professional Tone): "Research shows that people
having a sense of well-being, a sense of being satisfied with
their inner selves, have a high probability of achieving success in their lifetime. To begin our interview this morning,
I'd like to graph your life satisfaction." (Draw a graph on
the board with five point satisfaction rating scale on the
vertical axis and age on the horizontal axis.) Have your client
draw his life up to the present. Discuss any dips or peaks.
Use this chart to gather information about your client in a
friendly and professional manner. Track any feelings immediately and point out any feeling statements your client
makes. Notice only—do not do therapy. Allow feelings to
occur.

B. "Now, I'd like you to take this other colored pen and draw
your parents' life satisfaction for me." Discuss all dips and

---

1 **Month**

---

peaks here also. Again, watch for feeling moments that can be explored in future sessions.

C. "Now, let's talk about your future. I want you to predict with me your future. Draw a prediction for me: What will your life look like if you continue the way you have been going?" Discuss peaks and dips, watch for feeling, compare to parents' chart.

D. "Now, let's talk about your future from a new perspective. Draw another prediction for your future; one that includes your success here in therapy." Discuss peaks again, discuss dips, compare to parents' previous charting.

E. "Now, I am going to teach you more about success in therapy. These are some of the discoveries we have made about success here at the clinic.
   1. *Success* means *with* people and the environment, not at the expense of other people.
   2. *Success* means *adding* to peoples' lives, not taking from their lives.
   3. *Success* means *unlimited* additions, not just some success for some of the time, but full, continued success.
   4. *Success* is straightforward; there is nothing mystical or lucky about success in therapy. Success is a combination of feeling a need, making choices and plans, trying things out and allowing your personality to change."

IV. Intake: Goal setting
   A. "Now, let me ask you a very important question:
      1. Do you feel ready now to undertake a one-year program of therapy?" Yes or No.
   B. If "no," discuss and either resolve or recommend alternatives to therapy.
   C. If "yes," "Good. Let me ask you some more questions:
      1. "What is a major goal that would give you a greater sense of satisfaction in your life?" Write this on the board.
      2. "When would you like to have this goal completed?" Write this on the board, also.
      3. "What are the benefits of attaining this goal?"
      4. "What are the consequences of *not* attaining this goal?"

Intake Interview

5. "How are you going to try and deny attaining this goal? Be specific." Be careful here; this is a very crucial part of the interview.

6. "Do you have all the skills necessary to attain this goal?" Discuss, and suggest some extra skills.

7. "Do you have people who will support you to attain this goal?" "Who?" List three people—add your name.

8. "Do they have the skills to teach you and support you toward achieving this goal?"

9. "Are you a persistent individual? Tell me a time, an event."

V. Intake: Main problem

A. Everyone has goals. Everyone has problems. No one has goals or problems alone.

B. "What is your main problem?" Listen attentively now, without interference.

C. "We've had a lot of experience helping people here at the clinic with their problems, with all sorts of problems—from clinical depression to schizophrenia to budgeting problems."

D. "Anyone who has a problem *experiences* something about that problem and knows something about that problem. What do you experience with this problem?" Listen attentively.

E. "That is the psychological consequence of your problem. That experience will change as a consequence of your therapy. You will learn more about that experiencing process."

F. "What do you know about that problem?" (Listen attentively. Remember that the client is the expert.)

G. "Education is a major emphasis in our clinical programs."

1. Make psychological fitness translations for them: for example, "Your problem is your awareness of your potential. Your problem is your best behavior given the environment you were in. What you need to do is add to your skills."

2. "Problems can be understood in a new way. Problems are made up of personality dynamisms in a particular life area. (Draw on board a graph with five-point scale on the vertical axis and the five dynamisms on the hor-

1 | **Month**

izontal axis.) Briefly explain each personality dynamism (expression, activity, feeling, clarity, and contact). "What we do here is *build up* and *add* to your personality dynamics so that your problem is *solved dynamically.* We do not focus on what is wrong with you but on what can be changed."

3. "Your problem is actually a symptom. There is a big difference between your *actual* self and your *potential* self." (Refer to the graph and draw in where the client feels he is at present on each of the five dynamisms—his actual self—and where he might be as he gains in skills—his potential self.)

VI. Intake: Explaining psychological fitness

A. "Let me tell you a little about how we move you closer. We have developed a very special program to help individuals maximize themselves called the psychological fitness program."

B. "Our program goals are to help you be successful."

C. "One goal is to teach you how to learn so that you can continue to expand your adult development. Another goal is to help you to compete and succeed in the real world."

D. "To do that we have set up a program that lasts 12 months and consists of a specific schedule of 4 individual sessions per month. In the sessions we discuss your main problems and goals. We apply a psychological fitness model to them. We *strengthen* your personality. You make a special, positive bond with your counselor; he becomes like a personal coach for you as he teaches you new skills and helps you to practice them. Any extra groups or workshops are designed to further enhance your growth by establishing an enriched environment for you to practice your new skills."

E. "Above all the program will be individually designed for you. If you need to, you can bring in your family and friends to your sessions; you may need to add extra sessions at crucial times in your program."

F. "This is only a brief look at the program. I'd like you to read this brochure and feel free to ask me any questions about any part of the program next time."

Intake Interview 1

VII.   Intake awareness of resistances
    A.   "Now, can you tell me how you typically resist changing and learning new skills? How would you try to fail?"
    B.   "Tell me how you think you could offset your resistances? What would you be doing successfully to learn new skills and add to your life?"
    C.   "Tell me what you would say if you were talking to your wife or friend about why you chose to come into this program."
    Statement: "Now, I don't really know everything about you and I don't know how much you really know about the work we do here. I want you to use the first month's sessions to experience the program and decide if it is right for you."

VIII.   Intake—Contracts, finances, and additional tests
    A.   "Here are some additional tests that you should complete at home and bring next time. Our next scheduled interview is _____ . Also in these forms is a contract sheet and an information sheet about billing and insurance. Please look over the contract, sign it if it looks all right, and we can discuss the fee schedule."
    B.   Hand out
        1.   Contract form
        2.   Billing and insurance information sheet
        3.   Psychological fitness survey
        4.   History questionnaire
        5.   Goals sheet

IX.   Intake: Final visit
    A.   Spend five minutes visiting with your client.
    B.   Hand client a card with phone numbers listed and date of next appointment filled out.

Special Intake Options—One, A Mental Status Exam

If at any point in the intake interview the therapist notices that the client seems markedly dysfunctional, or possibly psychotic, a mental status exam can be applied. The purpose of this exam is for the therapist to determine if the client may need a referral to inpatient treatment or

 Month

a psychiatric or neurological workup. A sample MSE is listed in the Appendixes.

Special Intake Options—Two, Anything and Everything Else

By all means *do* interrupt the intake interview if it appears that the client has a pressing need to talk about his or her life and problems right now, right away! Try to make a case handling judgment about whether reassurance, ventilation, relaxation training, or some other intervention is called for in session one. With most clients session one can proceed, with variations, more or less as it is outlined. With a few clients the therapist will need to arrive at a mental status judgment and make a referral. With another small number of clients session one will be a plunge directly into some deeper therapeutic exchange. At this point we must rely on the old saw, "It's a matter of judgment—and the judgment matters."

Additional Forms

The forms that clients are asked to fill out at home are: the life-history questionnaire, the psychological fitness survey, and the goals sheet. Also a short post-session form to be completed by the therapist after Session 1 is included. These forms are reproduced in the Appendixes.

Comments on Session 1

The best way to learn to do the intake interview is to administer it to a colleague or friend and to have them administer it to you. Do *not* try to memorize the exact things to say; use the wordings simply as guidelines. The intake interview is not a standardized test. *Do* take the outline of the interview into the session with you and let the client see that you are following a plan. If the clients ask about the plan show it to them and discuss the idea of programming in therapy. Explain that you will bring a plan to most sessions but that the plan can always be modified or skipped if the client has something that takes precedence.

Another point to consider is one brought out by Bandler and Grinder in NLP (1979). The therapist who wants to achieve cognitive rapport

---

Intake Interview

with clients must notice what mode of information processing (visual, auditory, tactile, etc.) they use and speak to them in a language that matches their own favored mode. If the client repeatedly uses visual modes ("I saw him clearly," "I can't picture it," etc.) and the therapist uses tactile modes ("Get a feel for this," "You'll be in touch with it soon," etc.), they are not going to be close in their communications.

Many clients who enter therapy will have experienced other forms of therapy or have definite expectations from the media about how therapy is to be done. An important function of the intake interview is to provide new ideas and expectations and to offset some old images of "therapy," the "therapist," and the "client" from the very beginning. For that reason there is a definite amount of teaching and modeling programmed into the intake interview.

One indirect but definite client model that is developed in Session 1 is that of the "active client." Clients are very quickly involved in describing themselves, making choices, doing homework, and considering long-term benefits and goals. This emphasis is reinforced by the use of the fitness-exercise model that is explicitly conveyed within the session.

Session 2—Focusing and Feeling Moments

Session 2 is a purposeful change of pace and focus from Session 1. Research by Gendlin (1978), Rogers (1967), Truax and Carkhuff (1967), Kiesler (1973), and Strupp (1973) has shown that whether clients will succeed in experientially oriented therapy can be predicted fairly accurately within the first two or three sessions. The critical variable is the degree to which clients are able to focus on their feelings and communicate how and what they are experiencing. Gendlin devised a program to teach clients who have difficulty with this skill how to do it. The core of Session 2 consists of teaching the client about focusing, what it is and how to do it. The therapist, as a secondary goal, also introduces the client to feeling moments. At some point in the session the therapist will point out an incident in which the client's expressions do not completely match what he or she seems to be experiencing; the therapist will explicitly let the client know, "That's something called a feeling moment—we will be working a lot with those kinds of moments in future sessions." At this early stage the therapist usually will not work

1 | **Month**

to help the client complete the feeling moment. The basic thrust of Session 2 is to get across to the person the idea, "That's something important" and to alert the person to pay attention to such experiences.

I. Major theme: Focusing is paying attention to what you are experiencing and how your inner experience changes. Feeling moments are times when your expressions and your experience do not match.

Major goals: Teach clients the focusing procedure as something to be used inside therapy and as a relaxation procedure. Teach clients to notice experience–expression mismatches as something important in therapy. Increase the feeling contact between client and therapist.

II. Procedure

A. Introduction

1. Begin session by asking, "How are things going?" and "Have you had thoughts about our first meeting?" Visit briefly with client for five or ten minutes. Answer questions.

2. Collect homework and say, "We'll use this material in future sessions; today I want to do something different from our first meeting."

3. Introduce focusing exercise by saying, "An important part of therapy is learning to pay attention and communicate how much you are feeling inside. Today I will show you how to do an exercise called focusing which will be very useful to you both inside and outside therapy."

B. Focusing exercise[1]

1. What I will ask you to do will be silent, just to yourself. Take a moment just to relax (5 seconds).

All right—now, inside you, I would like you to pay attention to a very special part of you . . . pay attention to *that part where* you usually feel sad, glad, or scared (5 seconds). Pay attention to that area in you and see how you are now.

See what comes to you when you ask yourself, "How am I now?" "How do I feel?" "What is the main thing for

---

[1] This exercise is from pages 48–49 of Gendlin's *Focusing* (1978).

Focusing and Feeling Moments 2

me right now?" Sense how you feel. Let the answers come slowly from this sensing. When something comes *do not go inside it*. Stand back, say "Yes, that's there. I can feel that, there." Let there be a little space between you and that. Then ask what else you feel. Wait again, and sense. Usually there are several things.

2. From among what came, select one personal problem to focus on. *Do not go inside it*. Stand back from it. Of course, there are many parts to that one thing you are thinking about—too many to think of each one alone. But, you can *feel* all of these things together. Pay attention there where you usually feel things, and in there you can get a sense of what *all of the problem* feels like. Let yourself feel *all of that* (1 minute).

3. As you pay attention to the whole feeling of it, you may find that one special feeling comes up. Let yourself pay attention to that one feeling (1 minute). Keep following one feeling. Don't let it be *just* words or pictures— wait and let words or pictures come from the feeling (1 minute).

   If this one feeling changes, or moves, let it do that. Whatever it does, follow the feeling and pay attention to it (1 minute).

4. Now, take what is fresh, or new, in the feel of it *now* . . . and go very easy.

   Just as you feel it, try to find some *new* words or pictures to capture what your present feeling is all about. There doesn't have to be anything that you didn't know before. New words are best but old words might fit just as well as long as you now find words or a picture to say what is fresh to you now (1 minute).

   If the words or pictures that you now have make some fresh difference, see what that is. Let the words or pictures change until they feel just right in capturing your feeling (1 minute).

5. Check your words or picture. Ask your body "Is that right?" Wait to sense its response.

1 Month

C. Feeling moment explanations. Review the focusing exercise with the client. Point out that at moments when there was not yet a match between what was felt and what was said about the feeling experience *the discrepancy could still be noticed.* Explain that noticing and reporting discrepancies between feelings and expressions of feelings is a major part of therapy. Explain that it is a way of gaining more awareness, awareness that makes a difference for feeling better, choosing, planning, and acting. *Do not* work through the feeling moments that arise. *Do* use the term *feeling moment.* Teach the client the language of the therapy.

III. Homework and assignments
   A. Explain that the focusing method can be used outside of therapy as a meditation or relaxation technique. "Often when you feel tense or upset it's because you haven't fully focused on feelings that are going on inside of you. You can use the focusing method to take some time out from your regular routines and just pay attention to what's happening inside."
   B. Assign the client to try the focusing method for five minutes a day at least five days between this session and his or her third session next week.
   C. Get across the idea of practice and exercise. "Psychological exercises are just like physical exercises. You can't benefit from them by reading about them or just knowing about them, you have to *do* them. Also, like physical exercises, you get better with practice. After a week of practice you'll be able to do focusing more comfortably and effectively than you can right now. You should be able to notice both an exercise effect and a fitness or improvement effect within a week."
   D. If the client is the kind of person who benefits from reading about psychological procedures give him or her the book *Focusing* or have him or her buy the paperback and read it. (Another alternative is to reproduce a few key chapters and have clients read those.) Bibliotherapy is especially effective with some clients who want to fully understand the theories and methods used by the therapist.

Focusing and Feeling Moments 2

Comments on Session 2

If a client has great difficulty with the focusing exercise the therapist should spend the next session and, perhaps, the next several sessions repeating and extending the exercise. It is crucial not to go on unless the client is able, at some level, to successfully pay attention to shifts in his or her inner experiencing and to begin to express those shifts to the therapist. With a few clients it may be necessary to begin working with defenses and resistances if they have personality images that work against doing the focusing exercise. For example, the image "You tell me, you're the doctor. I don't know what's going on inside myself. That's why I'm here" will put the therapist–client relationship into a framework quite different from the one utilized in this manual. Consult Session 41 for specific instructions on working with resistant images.

The most obvious therapeutic step in working with the above image would be to use it as the subject of focusing. For example:

T: O.K. I'll be the doctor and tell you exactly what to do. Repeat what you just said.
C: *(Client approximately repeats.)*
T: Try to repeat exactly.
C: I can't remember exactly. I'm not a tape recorder.
T: I'll play it back to you. (T. *plays back the taped segment.)*
C: *(Roughly repeats.)*
T: Now just repeat the part "I don't know what's going on inside myself."
C: "I don't know what's going on inside myself."
T: Say it louder *(softer, five times in a row, etc.).*
C: *(Repeats with some shifts in expression dynamics.)*
T: Now I want you to notice something. (T. *replays tape segment.)*—how do you feel hearing yourself here?
C: I feel mixed up and angry.
T: How did you feel when you said "I don't know what's going on inside myself" the last time?
C: Angry, but not so mixed up.
T: What you just went through was a kind of focusing on your own feelings. You noticed something change in yourself. That's really important in therapy.
(T. *and* C. *go on from here.)*

The point to keep in mind is that the client always will offer something that can be worked with. The statement "I don't know what's

 Month

going on inside myself" is partially accurate. What the client *does* know is that he or she doesn't really feel clearly what is going on. That feeling meaning can be used as the basis of therapy just as surely as a detailed and sensitive self-report. The therapist can take the client into an examination of focusing and feeling moments through the front door or the back door. It doesn't matter as long as they successfully get inside.

Session 3—More About Feeling Moments

Session 3 continues, deepens, and extends the therapeutic process begun in session two. Because "feeling moments" are so critical to therapeutic change and can pertain to any part of the integration or reintegration process, this session can be considered a "standard session" that should be used repeatedly any time the therapist decides to focus on a particular feeling–expression mismatch. (Remember that such mismatches can be caused by emergent feelings or by defenses.)

I.   Major theme: Help the client understand that feeling moments are one of the basic special events of therapy. By completing gaps or mismatches the client learns something new; the completion of feeling moments extends awareness.

   Major goals: Teach clients to recognize and explore feeling moments.

II. Procedure
   A.   Introduction
      1.   Begin session by asking about homework, "How did the focusing exercise go?" Help clients to resolve difficulties with the exercise, discuss the book *Focusing* if they read it. Answer questions.
      2.   Introduce the direction of today's session by saying "Today we will extend the focusing exercise by looking closely at those times when there is a gap between what you are feeling and what you are able to express about your feelings. Those times are called feeling moments and they are very important in therapy and in the general process of personality growth."

More About Feeling Moments   3

B. Use the basic rule of psychoanalysis to provide material for the exploration of feeling moments. "What I'd like you to do this session is just try to say everything that you experience. Don't try to make sense of what you feel or think and don't hold anything back no matter how strange or embarassing it might be. If you get stopped I'll try to help you continue." Answer questions about the procedure.[2] (For a few clients this procedure will seem too abstract and too threatening. In those instances switch them to a more concrete descriptive task, e.g., "Tell me what you did yesterday. Try to include everything: who you saw and talked to, what they said and what you said, how you felt and what you thought.")

Another alternative instruction to provide material for feeling moments is this one: "Tell me about what the last session we had together was like for you. Try to include everything: what you felt and noticed and what you remember about what you said and what I said." The content of what the client says is less important than the ways he or she communicates. Pick and choose feeling moments to explore. The explorations can range all the way from simply pointing out to the client a mismatch between what they show and what they seem to be experiencing ("You seem to be feeling a lot more than you can say about that") to detailed work with a series of feeling moments using all the functional tools of expression dynamics and personality dynamisms. In general do not go too deeply too quickly at this stage. Pick those moments that can be resolved to some degree or leave them without getting a com-

---

[2] Freud's statement of the basic rule of free association is, "This involves some psychological preparation of the patient. We must aim at bringing about two changes in him: an increase in the attention he pays to his own psychical perceptions and the elimination of the criticism by which he normally sifts the thoughts that occur to him. . . . It is necessary to insist explicitly on his renouncing all criticism of the thoughts that he perceives. We therefore tell him that the success of psychoanalysis depends on his noticing and reporting whatever comes into his head and not being misled, for instance, into suppressing an idea because it strikes him as unimportant or irrelevant or because it seems to him meaningless" (Freud, 1960, p. 101).

---

1 **Month**

plete feeling–experience match. ("We can explore that feeling and its meanings for you more in other sessions. Let's go on.")

    C.   Explorations. Spend several minutes at the end of the session explaining, again, with examples from the session, what a feeling moment is, why it is important in the process of in-search that characterizes therapy, and how it will be used repeatedly in future sessions. ("No matter what we talk about we will always look at those gaps that tell you there is more going on inside than you can show or be aware of right then.")

III.   Homework and assignments

    A.   Explain that the free association method is just a variation of the focusing procedure and that it can be used outside therapy as a meditation or relaxation technique.

    B.   Introduce the idea of a "Therapy Diary" or "Notebook." "I'd like you to begin to keep a notebook of things you want to remember from the therapy sessions and of experiences that come out of the exercises or your everyday life that you might want to bring up in the future therapy sessions. Get a notebook and start to write in it five or ten minutes a day. Bring the notebook with you next week."

    C.   Assign the client to continue to try the focusing exercise, at least three times in the week, and suggest that he or she pay particular attention to feeling gaps, "when you experience gaps or blocks that doesn't mean something is wrong. It's a good sign. It means you have reached a limit of your aware-ness and are aware of the limit. That awareness of limits is essential. It will allow you to expand your personality. If we couldn't be aware of when we reach our limits change would be impossible."

    D.   For a bibliotherapeutic addition to this homework there are many books to recommend. A sampling of books about the use of diaries, journals, and notebooks in therapy and for self-development includes: Progoff's *At a Journal Workshop* (1975), Rainer's *The New Diary* (1978), and Simons's *Keeping Your Personal Journal* (1978).

        Any one of these or others can be recommended, but do not assign them to clients who might be distracted by the

More About Feeling Moments   3

theories or overloaded by the task of writing about their experiences.

Session 4—Choosing

By now the client has had enough exposure to the ideas and basic techniques of functional therapy (and to the therapist) to make a choice about whether to continue. On the other hand, the therapist will know enough about the client to make a judgment about the suitability of the therapy for the client's personality problems and needs. It is very important to use this pivotal session to make a definite decision to continue or discontinue therapy. If therapy is to be continued then a specific commitment to continue for so many sessions over so many weeks in the form of a therapeutic contract is very useful. By discussing the decision and formulating a mutually agreeable contract the therapist can help the client conceptually understand the steps in the integration process (awareness of needs or wants, choosing, acting, developing new images and changing old images).

I. Major theme: Understanding the process of choosing.
   Major goals: To explicitly choose to continue or discontinue therapy. To introduce the Needs or Wants, Choice, Action, or Image cycle. To formulate a specific therapeutic contract.
II. Procedure
   A. Begin by visiting about the client's previous week, "What's been happening?" "How have things been going?"
   B. Inquire specifically about the Therapy Notebook. Look at the entries. Perhaps have the client read some of them aloud. Discuss the client's feelings about keeping a notebook.
   C. Introduce the concept of the growth cycle. Draw on board. "In functional therapy we think of growth as starting from the person's own awareness of his or her needs and wants, from there a choice can be made, and from the choice new actions can be taken. After enough new choices and actions are taken you actually will acquire a new personality image."

1   **Month**

D. Focus on the choice to continue or discontinue therapy. "To-day we need to make a big choice about whether you will continue in therapy. What are your thoughts and feelings." Listen. Reflect feelings. If the person decides not to continue consider whether a referral is appropriate. Also consider whether to offer to be available at a later date. (A brief sample Case Termination Form is included in the Appendixes.)

E. If the person decides to continue, explore the decision process further. "Let's get specific; what needs or wants do you think might be aided by this therapy? What do you want out of therapy? Write clients therapy goals on the board.

F. Introduce idea of a therapy contract. "Now let's continue to be specific. If we were to write a contract together what would you want to put in it? How long do you want to continue therapy?" Give an overview of the remaining 11 months of the therapy program. Explain the purposes of the program. Arrive at a written one- or two-page contract that you both sign and date specifying: what the client wants to accomplish in therapy; how often you will meet and how long; what the client will do in the form of homework. In putting together a contract review the client's goals sheet. Try to get very specific, for example, "I'd like to date at least once a week," "I want to get a raise within six months." Make it clear that the contract can be changed but that any change should be discussed. Mention that you will take responsibility for bringing up changes you want to make but that the client must take responsibility for explicitly bringing up changes he or she wants.

G. Make a copy of the Therapeutic Contract for the client and keep one for yourself. Instruct the client to put the contract in his or her Therapy Notebook.

III. Homework and assignments

A. Show the client the program that will be begun at the next session. Have the person review the fitness survey he or she completed after session one. Ask the person to focus especially on his or her awareness of Expression, since that will be the topic of the next session.

B. Tell the person to continue the Therapy Notebook and to do focusing exercises as desired.

Choosing 4

Comments on Session 4

The use of contracts is well known and widely practiced in education, business, and therapy. The basic purpose of contracting is to: (a) make goals and practices specific, (b) make the commitment to attaining certain goals and carrying out specific tasks explicit, and (c) as much as possible, formulate goals in a way that can be measured so that success and progress can be evaluated. Within functional therapy the contract also is used to teach the concept of a growth cycle that has important steps and is repeated again and again.

General references that discuss the therapeutic contract include: Menninger's *Theory of Psychoanalytic Technique* (1958), Lettenberg's *Handbook of Behavior Modification and Behavior Therapy* (1976), Korchin's *Modern Clinical Psychology* (1976). Three books that discuss contracting at length are: O'Banion and Whaley's *Behavior Contracting* (1981), Gottman and Leiblum's *How to Do Psychotherapy and How to Evaluate It* (1974), and Okun's *Effective Helping* (1976). Among the functional pioneers whose contributions were discussed in Part II, Thorne made the most detailed use of therapeutic contracts. See his book *Psychological Case Handling* (1968) for more information.

Within the fields of psychotherapy and counseling, contracting is sometimes mistakenly taken to be an exclusive method of behavior therapy, indeed "contracting" and "behavioral contracting" are taken as synonyms. However the idea of making goals specific and measurable and obtaining a commitment is a much older and wider practical idea than the narrower concept of "behavioral contracting" which is tied to the theory of arranging contingencies of reinforcement. For example, the management by objectives approach has been widely used in all areas of management for decades but is not usually tied to reinforcement theories (although behavioral versions of MBO do exist). (See Hicks & Gullett, 1981, for a broad discussion of MBO and for further references.) The centuries-old Oxbridge (Oxford and Cambridge) tutorial system depends essentially upon specific agreements between the tutor and the student about what will be covered, what will be read and discussed, what papers will be turned in and what, if any, exams will be completed. In modern American educational systems curriculum plans and teacher–student contracting are widely used. Many of these educational practices derive from the educational-psychological theories of John Dewey (see Sahakian, 1975).

 ## Month

Within the Dewey–James functional tradition the basic reliance in contracting is upon the *mutual* agreement upon the details of a contract that is constructed by the teacher and student or the therapist and client. The process of formulating the contract is thought to be as important as the activity of carrying out the contract because it furthers awareness and responsibility. From the functional perspective contracts that are arranged solely by the teacher or the therapist and followed by the student or client are not thought to engender growth although they may effectively bring about changes.

Conclusions

After examining four sessions several points made repeatedly in Chapter 13 and elsewhere in this book should be concretely understandable.

1. The sessions in this manual describe a map for a 12-month therapeutic journey. No client or therapist will start or end at the same place and the excursions through each specific session will be different. It would not be possible or desirable to make the session instructions more specific and the branchings more orderly because too much depends upon each therapist's judgment and each client's experience.

2. The technical eclecticism ranges throughout the spectrum of therapies and beyond but is held together by several concepts: the concept of psychological fitness, the concept of feeling moments, the concepts of integration and reintegration processes, and the concepts of expression dynamics and personality dynamisms. In addition to these particular concepts there are the general emphases found within functional therapy on feelings, the expression of feelings, and the range of conscious, subconscious, and unconscious mental processes.

Conclusions   4

15

Months Two through Six
Personality Changes

Once clients are fully oriented to the therapy and have made a commitment to continue, the next five months are designed to help them understand and make simple changes in their personalities. When exploring *how* the client functions, any topic of concern can serve as content. The emphasis is on exploring styles and limits of functioning; this allows clients to bring up anything they want to talk about and allows therapists to get across the idea that problems and symptoms often are the result of the ways that a client responds.

Additionally, the emphasis on personality dynamisms allows functional therapists to elaborate very thoroughly the fitness approach, since any exercise designed to go beyond the client's normal personality limits will provide an exercise effect.

The schedule of sessions for months two through six is:

Month	Sessions	Themes
2	5–8	Expression
3	9–12	Activity
4	13–16	Clarity
5	17–20	Feeling
6	21–24	Contact

Month Two—Expression

The expression dynamism is a good concentration for the second month of therapy because it is easy to understand and the expression

2 **Month**

exercises give quick results. Also, most clients come to therapy with the expectation that they will need to say more and show more about their feelings so these sessions fit their images of therapy.

Session 5—Expression

I. Major themes and goals: To teach the one-up–one-down expression exercise and to help the client understand how the expression dynamism can be shifted *voluntarily*.

II. Procedure

    A. Begin by informally visiting with the client. Ask about the week, "How was your week?" and about that particular day, "How do you feel today?" "What's going on today?"

    B. Follow the specifics of the client's comments. Try to understand clearly the client's everyday life, thoughts, and feelings.

    C. Ask, "What would you like help with today?" Listen and notice feeling or expression mismatches.

    D. Introduce the one-up–one-down exercise: "I want to try a different way of talking about _____." (Pick out a topic where there was a significant mismatch.)

        1. "Tell me again about _____.

        2. "Rate your voice from 1 to 5 (if 1 is no expression, 3 moderate expression, 5 intense expression)." Draw on board.

        3. "Now talk about _____ in a voice that is one step down from your regular voice. Decrease your expression." Help client to do this, and ask "How does that feel?"

        4. Take an awareness break: "I want you to focus on how you felt when you decreased expression." Help client to notice any loss of sensation, movement, general feeling awareness, or shifts in feelings.

        5. Now move one step back up to the client's normal level.

        6. Take another focusing awareness break and talk about how the normal level feels in contrast to the stepped-down level of expression.

        7. Now help the client move one up from the regular level of expression. If your client has a hard time with this, let him or her copy you.

Expression   5

8. Take another awareness break and ask the client about shifts in feeling awareness. Be supportive, explain to client that he or she is going beyond limits and that stretching processes can be felt. Use the analogy of physical fitness exercises. Draw the step-up and step-down levels on board and write in new feeling next to the new levels. Explain, "Notice that when you change the way you express, you change the way you feel and your awareness."

III. Closing
A. Tell client *not* to try to do the exercise outside of therapy but simply to notice how his or her level of expression varies in different situations.
B. Ask him or her to think about what life would be like if the expanded range of expression were to become the normal range.
C. Tell client to record any special observations about expression levels in the Therapy Notebook.

Here is an excerpt from a session in which the preceding exercise was applied.[1] The client is a 34-year-old nurse and mother of two children by a previous marriage. A hardworking, very industrious individual, she was invariably number two wherever she worked. She is a very sweet, nurturing, pollyannaish woman who does her best to take care of the needs of everyone around her and make them happy. Privately, she is very lonely and wants to feel "close to other people," but has no ability to express her own wants and needs. Her relationship pattern is to carry on as long as possible with everything sweet and wonderful, doing everything in the way of pleasing the other and then becoming increasingly bitter and resentful toward herself. She had previously been in therapy. She was a very "good" patient.

In this first session the therapist initially visited with the client concerning the week since her previous interview. She felt that what the therapist had said had made a great deal of difference in her thinking and the session had been on her mind a lot.

---

[1] All session excerpts in this manual were contributed by John Hart, from tape recordings of sessions conducted by him at the Hart & Associates clinic in Los Angeles. Some details about the clients' lives have been changed to protect their identities.

 Month

T: You know, last week you talked a lot about how you work very hard but never seem to get the kind of recognition you deserve. What about that this past week?

C: Oh, well, yes, you know one thing is the head nurse and the chief of the department, Dr. B., they just never notice. Last week I stayed late . . . there was a little emergency with two patients. I took really good care of them, but nobody said anything about it . . .

T: Nobody?

C: No, no one did.

T: O.K. Lets talk about expression. See that picture of Muhammad Ali?

C: Yes.

T: You know he is known the world over for boxing, but he is famous for his personality, especially his expression. He always talks for himself. . . . What I mean by that is that he talks in a very positive way about himself. That is something that I want you to notice and to be aware of during the week. . . . People who talk for themselves and also the people who talk against themselves and other people.

T: Now, who did you tell about all the good work you did?

C: No one.

T: Let's stand up now, you stand up over there across the room and tell me what it is you did.

C: Well, two patients got ill and I took care of them, and I really did a good job of taking care of the emergency.

T: Now, on a scale of one to five with one being low and five high, how do you rate the level of expression that you just had?

C: About two and a half.

T: Right, now let's go down one level. Take away one whole level. Now, at one and a half tell me the same thing.

C: (In a faint, dull voice) "I took care of the emergency and I did a good job."

T: Tell me, what is the difference in how that voice feels?

C: Oh, I feel dull and quiet. It sounds like it doesn't matter what . . . (eyes fill up with tears, starts to cry) I always feel like that . . . it doesn't matter . . . nobody notices."

T: What if you went down even further, to one-half.

C: I would just fade away.

T: Is that a familiar feeling?

C: (Sadly) "Yes!" (Client and therapist talk about this familiar fading away feeling.)

T: Now, what if we went back to what you were saying and this time we went up with your expression . . . one up to a three and a half.

C: Well, I don't know.

T: Just the same words. Come on, you can do it.

Expression 5

C: *(In a little bit louder voice)* I took care of the emergency and . . . *(starts to fade out)*.

T: Come on, you fade out. Come on, you can do it . . . just match my voice, do it this loud: "There were two sick patients and I stayed late and I did a great job." *(Therapist and client are both talking in loud voices.)*

T: Go on, one more time, you say it. I can't hear very well you know! *(laughing)*

C: We . . . Look, I did a real good job and took care of the emergency . . . *(starts to look scared)*.

T: What happened?

C: I got scared by being so loud.

T: What did you think?

C: I thought . . .

T: *(Interrupting)* No, not in that voice. . . . What did you think in your stand-out voice.

C: *(In loud voice)* I don't think that I should be this loud . . . *(laughing)* . . . I think this is dumb . . . *(laughing)*. People will think I am bragging about myself and I think I am a big shot. *(laughing)*

T: Great job . . . O.K. Let's sit down.

T: Now, what did you notice this time when you went up with your expression from normal?

C: Well, I felt excited and nervous and . . . *(eyes fill up with tears)* I felt really alive.

T: Yes, you felt yourself talking. *You* saying something that meant something to *you*.

C: Yes.

T: Now, I want you to be aware of the difference you made in how you felt . . . you made yourself feel different in how important you are in a simple way . . . you used your voice. Now during the week until I see you next I want you to try out something.

C: What is that?

T: Sorry, I couldn't hear you. Did you say something?

C: What's that! *(loudly and laughing)*

T: Right. Now I know you have that voice. It's like a gym here for your voice and your personality. You don't have to shout at the supermarket, but here you can work out . . . just the way you did today, really exercising that expression. Just notice when you stand out or fade out. Don't try to change, just notice.

C: Oh, no.

T: What?

C: Oh, no *(in louder voice)*.

T: Here is something to put on your bathroom door . . . for a week as a reminder.

 Month

c: A poster . . ."Standout or Fadeout". . . I like that.
t: Good . . . O.K., see you next week.

Session 6—Expression

The expression dynamism is so important in functional therapy and the one-up–one down exercise so generally applicable that Session 5 can be repeated anytime it seems to fit what the client is talking about. Usually Session 6 should simply repeat Session 5 with new content. However, the homework assignment is different: "This week I want you to try to change your level of expression. When you notice that you are very low in expression try to move up one step. Do that at least three times during the week. Be sure to record the details of one of those incidents in your Therapy Notebook so we can go over it next week."

Session 7—Expression Styles

I.   Major theme: Introduce the idea of expressive styles, that is, that certain levels of expression are tied to certain situations and experiences.

  Major goals: Help the client understand expression styles and their consequences. Help the client comprehend that styles can be changed.

II. Procedure

  A.   Review the previous week's experiences. Have client read from Therapy Notebook. Discuss the feelings and thoughts that came up when client tried to change expression level upward.

  B.   Introduce the notion of expression styles—persistent ways of expressing in certain situations. Talk about different labels for styles: loud, soft, noisy, bitchy, quiet, professional, fatherly, motherly, nagging, supportive, cruel, shallow, deep, friendly, hostile, etc.

  C.   Ask your client to describe his or her expressive style in a particular situation. If this is too difficult, have client describe style he or she is using right then in the therapy room.

Expression Styles 7

D. Complete the picture of one of your client's expressive styles. Ask questions:
   1. "What does this style give you?" (Getting attention, being noticed, being different, being independent, etc.)
   2. "What are the strengths (benefits) of this style?" (People like me, I'm a leader, I know a lot, etc.)
   3. "What are the weaknesses (shortcomings) of this style?" (I'm negative, I act dumb, I'm lonely, I argue, etc.)
   4. "What does this style take away from you?" (Being smart, being outspoken, etc.)
   5. "What kinds of ways *can't* you be in this style?" (Conversational, witty, etc.)
   6. "What ways do you have trouble being in this style?" (Loud, funny, smart, etc.)

E. Take an awareness break:
   1. Help your client notice any *shifts* or changes going on inside during talk. Help client be positive.

F. Have your client paint a verbal picture of "How I would make myself if I were a magician."
   1. Be specific. Only work with his or her expressive style.
   2. Use some of the words just mentioned as you help create a new style.

G. Now, pick *one style* the client can begin practicing immediately. (Be sure that you *both* agree on the style.)
   1. Make this new *expression* style just one simple shift in style. (Use a slightly louder voice, shorter sentences, direct eye contact, a smile, a slower delivery, etc.) You are working with expression dynamics.
   2. Be sure the new style is achievable—not too outrageous or too threatening for the client.

H. Take an awareness break:
   1. Help your client notice any shifts or changes in sensations, movements, or thoughts. Keep this positive.

I. Working with the resistances.
   1. Help your client to say *all* his or her reasons why he or she cannot do this new expressive style.
   2. Express *in this new style*. (For example, have the client say "I can't be loud" with a loud voice, or "I can't look

---

2 **Month**

---

at you" as he or she looks at you, etc.) You may have client talk louder or fuller, or sweeter or stronger or whatever.

    3.   As your client expresses his or her "reasons" in the new style, help client to see that he or she is using the new style right now!

  J.   Take an awareness break:

    1.   Educate your client to any new sensations, movements, thoughts, feelings, etc.

    2.   Help client notice little changes he or she is making.

    3.   Tell client what you noticed about him or her during the session.

III. Closing

  A.   Ask your client to be more aware of his or her expressive style this week.

  B.   Ask him or her to think about what his life would be like if he or she *expanded* (not changed) his or her expressive style.

Session 8—Expression Limits

This session vividly extends the client's expression level. It is a very effective session to use in groups because the sudden changes in expression are very affecting for onlookers.

I.   Major theme: The strenuous exercise of the personality.
Major goal: To extend markedly the client's concept of how much the expression dynamism can vary.

II. Procedure

  A.   Introduce the white noise procedure. "Today we will use a white noise tape to block the sound of your own voice when you are talking. When you are wearing headphones and the tape is off you will be able to hear me and yourself easily, but when the tape is on you won't be able to hear yourself. When that happens, *keep talking anyway*. I'll nod and motion to you so we can communicate. I'll also record your voice on this other recorder so you can hear how your voice changes."

  B.   Put headphones on client and adjust volume so it just blocks the voice feedback but is not painfully loud. Instruct, "Now

---

Expression Limits

just go ahead and tell me about your day. I'll turn the tape on and off as you talk." Let client talk for a few minutes and then turn on tape for 5 to 10 seconds. Repeat the procedure several times. The main result of blocking auditory feedback is that the client will begin to shout but not be aware of this big change in volume. Also, the increase in voice level is usually accompanied by increases in feeling. Pronounced blocking sometimes occurs because the person can no longer smoothly cover over feeling gaps. Mismatches of feeling and expression become easily visible.

   C.   Take an awareness break. Have client talk about how the white noise effected him or her.

   D.   Repeat B.

   E.   Play back the recording of the client's voice. Have client talk about how he or she sounds. Have client rate expression level with noise off versus noise on.

III. Follow-up

   A.   Explain that the feelings of discomfort that arise when a big change is made in expression are just signals that personality limits are being stretched.

   B.   Also explain that the goal is *not* to talk louder all the time but be *able* to go beyond arbitrary internal limits.

   C.   Discuss how the different personality dynamisms interact and are hard to separate: "When you increase one of them very much you also usually increase the others. Today when you markedly changed your expression level you also very much changed your feeling level."

   D.   Assignment: Mention that, "Next week we will start working on another dynamism, activity. So this week, until our meeting, just notice how much you move around and how you hold your body in different situations." Answer questions, explain that the last four sessions concentrated on verbal expressiveness, the next four will examine "body language."

Month Three—Activity

Each set of exercises for the five personality dynamisms more or less parallel one another. So the first exercise in Session 9, activity, is

 Month

similar to the first exercise in Session 5, expression. This paralleling of sessions helps clients to feel more comfortable in the theory and practices of the therapy.

Session 9—Activity

Simply repeat Session 5, substituting activity for expression as the one-up–one-down exercise focus.

An excerpt from an activity session is given below: When initially seen, Barbara was a large obese woman. She was very depressed. Her affect was blunted and she seemed quite scared. She was married and supported her husband. They had no children and lived in a cluttered and unkempt home. She had no "energy" to clean the house. There were "trails" of boxes of old junk, magazines, and boxes that had never been unpacked in the living room since they had moved in several years earlier. She was aware of the condition of the home, in fact was embarrassed by it and had never had a friend inside of the house. She and her husband rarely if ever had sex during a year. She was a rather unusual client referral for a private clinic. She was however very "desperate" to "change."

T: Hi, Barbara; sit down. How is it going?
C: Oh, I had a really good week. I really liked practicing saying my opinions of what I like and dislike.
T: In what way?
C: Well, I told Bob (her husband) that I liked the TV show we were watching. It was real nice because we had a nice visit about the show. It's funny how I can really like and dislike so many things. I just never noticed.
T: Really?
C: No, I just never really said.
T: I like you saying that.
C: I like you saying that (both laugh).
T: Is there anything today that you especially want to talk about.
C: Mmm. Well, I don't think that people at work like me very much.
T: Oh.
C: Yeah. Nobody really ever says much to me, or talks to me.
T: And you . . .
C: Me?
T: Yeah, who do you talk to so much?

Activity   ⑨

c: Why, no one. No one except Sally.

t: She is your friend.

c: Yes.

t: O.K. Let's talk a little about activity as a dynamic. Remember, it is the way you use your body to move and act and express. It is also the way you put yourself in the foreground or the background. By that I mean your role. Do you make yourself the important or unimportant person in situations . . . the star of your own life or the background . . . the "bit" player.

c: I understand. I am definitely a background. But I don't know how to change it.

t: That is right. You are probably the Zen Master of background.

c: Zen Master *(laughing)*.

t: Sure. You know hundreds of ways to fade out and not be noticed and ignored. Like right now with your hands while you're talking . . . What are your hands doing?

c: They are folded.

t: They always are when you talk. What would happen if you moved and gestured while you talked?

c: I . . . I . . . *(moves her hands a little)*.

t: You know how you were saying "I like that"?

c: Yes.

t: Well, underline and emphasize that by moving your hands.

c: "I like that" *(laughing and gesturing)*.

t: Come over here *(moves over in front of mirror)*. Now walk toward the mirror as if you were walking down the hall at work.

c: *(Walks along in her slow slumped manner, head down, no expression.)*

t: Now take a look at this person. Do they look like someone to say "hi" to?

c: No.

t: Why?

c: They don't look good.

t: Why?

c: They look down.

t: Do you feel down?

c: No, not now.

t: O.K. Now if you were going to rate your activity, like we did with your expression on a scale of one to five with one low and five high, what do you say?

c: Two.

t: Right. Now what if you went one down.
   Right, walk along but slump over even more, head down. What is that like?

c: It is down all right.

t: What if you went down anymore?

 Month

C: I would have to stop moving.

T: That happens sometimes, doesn't it?

C: Yes. That is what I felt like before I came here and it scared me . . . if I couldn't move anymore at all.

T: That is a feeling inside isn't it, of not being able to move?

C: Yeah, yes it is.

T: Now, what if we went one up with that activity and just said "hi."

C: "Hi."

T: Did you see any activity? I heard a noise, and saw your mouth move but, hey, where is the activity, Zen Master?

C: *(Laughing)* Move what?

T: How about your face. What if you just smiled a little bit?

C: "Hi" *(and smiles)*.

T: Great, now "hi," smile, and just a little wave.

C: "Hi" *(and smiles with wave)*.

T: What does that look like?

C: Different.

T: Try again.

C: "Hi" *(and smiles and waves)*. It sounds funny but I feel different.

T: How?

C: Friendly, and that is how I look too. I always think people will think I am not friendly but that other way, that is how I look.

T: And what if someone who looked like this said "hi" to you?

C: Well, I would say "hi" right back . . . they look friendly.

T: Hi.

C: Hi.

T: Hey, where's the wave and smile?

C: *(Laughing)* I forgot.

T: Hi.

C: Hi.

T: O.K. Now, this week you try that out . . . at least three people a day. You say "hi" and do your one-up activity. Got it?

C: O.K. Got it. Bye *(laughs and waves, smiling)*.

(Client called in the middle of the week. She had gotten compliments at work from other employees about her "friendliness.")

Session 10—Activity

Session 10 should be a repeat of Session 9, using new content. Also, the assignment following the session should be: "This coming week I want you to try to change your level of activity. When you notice that

---

Activity   10

you are very low in activity and it doesn't feel good, try to move up one step. Do that at least three times during the week. Be sure to write down what happens later in your Therapy Notebook. Next week we'll talk about what it is like for you to try to make activity changes."

Session 11—Activity Styles

This session, on styles of activity, exactly parallels Session 7 on expression styles. Simply substitute "activity" for expression in the instructions. Also make use of the full-length mirror at some point during the session so that the client actually observes certain styles. The basic additional technique to apply is to ask the client to "freeze" at certain points and then talk about the posture and feelings they have accompanying the body position. This technique is briefly illustrated in the following excerpt:

T: Hi, how are you this week?
C: Good. No, not so good. I was thinking a lot about my activity like we talked about last week.
T: Yes?
C: And I just noticed constantly how I think that people are looking at me and criticizing me when they look at me. I know that sounds kind of crazy, but whenever I see someone looking at me I start thinking of what they are thinking about *me*.
T: For example?
C: Well, like thinking that "look how fat she is" or "her hair isn't right" or something else . . .
T: Like what?
C: Well, "look at her skin."
   (*Client has had a blotched and pimpled complexion throughout her teen and adult years with no treatment success.*)
T: O.K. Freeze!
C: What?
T: Don't move.
C: Why?
T: What are you doing with your hand.
C: (*Embarassed*) Picking at my cheek. I didn't realize.
T: Didn't realize?

 Month

C: Didn't realize I was doing that right now, although I know it's a bad habit I do a lot . . . I hate my complexion.

T: Picking again?

C: No.

T: "I hate my complexion" isn't picking?

C: Well . . .

T: Let's take a look at this as an activity style. Just like with your expressive style or anyone else's. . . . People have different ways they use their bodies and allow themselves to have a certain kind of role. What kind of activity have you had, given what we talked about last week?

C: Well, most of the time . . . I guess all the time I try to be in the background to avoid attention, to take a background role.

T: You guess?

C: I *am* in the background.

T: Can't hear you.

C: *(Loudly)* I am in the background.

T: Now you aren't.

C: Now, see what happens? When I do that . . . It's embarrassing and I don't want to look stupid . . . I look so bad anyway.

T: Oh, picking again?

C: Well, I . . .

T: Picking?

C: But I do hate how my complexion looks. You don't know . . . and I have done everything, doctors, X-rays, and its awful.

T: Picking?

C: *(Silent)*

T: O.K. Come on over here in front of the mirror. I would like you to do what you were describing to me. All of that critical thinking . . . see how you look, but take your fingers like this and just pick at your face. Go ahead.

C: I hate this. I hate my skin, my hair looks stupid. I am fat. My clothes look stupid. I hate . . .

T: Stop. O.K., what does that feel like?

C: It's so tense. I just feel so tense and tight and braced. It felt awful . . . really awful.

T: Do it again.

C: I hate . . . I hate *(continues to pick at her skin and criticize and pick at herself).*

T: Stop . . . *(takes her hand and bends her fingers)* now just softly, very softly touch your cheeks.

C: *(Softly touches her face. Looks in mirror and starts crying softly.)*

T: That's it, Barbara, just softly touch those tears, very softly.

C: *(Now deeply crying)* I have never touched . . . nobody ever touched my face like that.

Activity Styles 11

T: Uh huh, that face doesn't need picking. It needs soft touching. What is that like, Barbara?

C: *(Crying, deep sobs)* I've never felt like this toward myself. I have never felt like . . . caring . . . caring about me. My skin feels so different.

T: Just keep touching . . . right . . . just like that. That's what will change that picking, just that feeling inside of you.

C: My skin is soft. You know I haven't ever noticed. I always think its rough and coarse, but its soft.

T: Uh, huh. And that is how you are . . . you don't need to be picked at and criticized. What would happen to something that soft that got picked?

C: It would hurt . . . crying.

T: Right. This is a special, special session for you. You need to remember this feeling. This is a reference for who you are and how you really feel toward yourself inside.

C: I really feel soft.

T: Really soft and really caring. In the coming week, when you notice that critical picking either physically or emotionally, just touch your face like this. It will stop and change that old feeling. You have a real reference for the inside now. *(Interestingly, Barbara's complexion very dramatically cleared. Although there are certain acute flare-ups, generally her complexion has stayed clear for three years.)*

Session 12—Activity Limits

This session is designed to extend vividly the client's activity levels. If at all possible it will be very valuable to use video feedback so that the clients can see how they look when transcending their ordinary activity limits. Like Session 8 on expression limits it is a very good session to repeat in groups because the intense changes in activity are very affecting.

I. Major theme: The strenuous exercise of the personality.
     Major goal: To extend the client's idea of how much the activity dynamism can vary. To explain the idea of a backup level of responsiveness as desirable for fitness, to provide resistance to stress.

II. Procedure
     A. This session draws upon the bioenergetic therapy stress and release techniques developed by Alexander Lowen (1967). In-

3 **Month**

troduce the procedure this way, "Today we will use some special bioenergetic techniques to help you feel more vividly self-imposed limits of activity and what it is like to go beyond those limits."

B. Ask the client to stand with his or her feet about 30 inches apart, toes turned inward, knees bent as much as possible, back arched, and the hand pushed into the back just above the hips. Once the client has approximated this position, tell him or her to stop talking and just breath deeply for several minutes, all the while noticing tension spots in the body.

C. After a few minutes in this position tell the person to bend over and touch the floor and to notice which muscles relax and which become more tense.

D. Repeat B but this time instruct client to talk about his or her day. Let client talk for several minutes and when a mismatch is noticed have the person repeat the last thing he or she said 10 times.

E. Now tell the client, "I want you to repeat what you said 10 more times but now come out of the fixed position you were in—now let yourself move around and let what you say change a little—start to change a few words."

G. Take an awareness break. Ask client what it felt like to shift from the fixed position to more mobile positions. How were feelings and meanings changed as movement and position changed?

H. If time permits, repeat steps D to G. Also, if video tape is available replay the tape and have client comment on how he or she looked.

III. Follow-up:

A. Explain that feelings and thoughts get connected to postures and movements. "Often the easiest way to change what you experience is to change how you move."

B. Also explain that holding fixed positions or repeating the same old movements sometimes perpetuates undesired images. What is sought is flexibility—so new movements and positions can emerge to match new feelings.

C. For clients who are helped by reading, assign Lowen's *The Betrayal of the Body* (1967).

Activity Limits   12

D. Tell client to try to make some activity changes during the week and to notice the thoughts and feelings that go with the changes. "Next week we'll be working with the clarity dynamism and clarity depends upon noticing what's going on around you and inside."

Month Four—Clarity

The clarity dynamism relates to the awareness of both internal and external happenings and to both cognitive and affective awareness. The content of awareness, *what* the person knows, and the form of awareness, *how* the person knows, are both important. One content that the therapist must very carefully check at this early stage of therapy is the client's clarity about the therapy. Does the client understand what the therapist is doing? Does the client understand what feeling moments are and why they are important? Is the notion of psychological fitness and psychological exercise clear to the client? When the therapist works with personality dynamisms and expression dynamics does the client understand what is going on? During this month it is very helpful if the therapist carefully checks to be sure that clients comprehend the structure and purposes of functional therapy. For most clients the most important content in their lives when they are with the therapist is the therapy itself. This is true even though much of the time is spent talking about happenings outside the therapy context.

The four sessions on clarity in month four roughly parallel the eight sessions on expression and activity that preceded them; this parallel structuring is an aid to clarity about what goes on in functional therapy.

Session 13—Clarity

I. Visiting
   A. Begin by informally visiting with your client.
      1. Ask engaging questions such as: "How do you feel today?" "What was your day like?"

Month

2. Follow up each question with a clear response. Let the client know you are listening.

B. Gain impressions of your client:
   1. Watch for resistances (vagueness, hostility, evasiveness, argumentativeness, etc.).
   2. Watch for feelings and feeling or expression mismatches.

C. Obtain a clear understanding of your client's day, thoughts and feelings. Reflect feelings to test and convey your understanding.

II. Pick a Topic
   A. Either pick a dominant concern that emerges from the initial visit or a repeated feeling mismatch or ask the client, "What would you like to talk about today?"
   B. Be willing to shift or extend topics as you proceed.

III. Procedure
   A. After you have established an area to work with, begin by teaching your client about the third personality dynamism, clarity.
   B. "This month we will be working with the third personality dynamism, *clarity*. Clarity deals with your awareness of what's going on inside you and outside you. Your clarity level tells us how much understanding you have of your inner world and of your outer world. Do you consider yourself a perceptive person? Do you speak in a simple and direct way? Or, do you get confused or muddled or sidetracked or complicated or spaced-out when you speak? Perhaps you get "crystal clear" or overly detailed and precise. Whatever your answers are, these are all aspects of your own clarity. This month you will be learning skills on how to have more clarity in your life. This, in turn, will allow you to have more control over and more satisfaction in your life."
   C. Examples or Illustrations
      1. Spend time giving your client examples of clarity.
         (a) Begin by talking to him in a "vague" and "cloudy" way. Keep your sentences incomplete and confusing. Get "lost" in your own story and "space-out." Let your client know that this is a low level of clarity.

Clarity 13

       (b) Now, show the other extreme. Talk in a simple and direct manner. Address yourself right to him or her. Make simple observations; be specific and detailed. Let client see that this is an exciting and pleasurable way to talk.

IV. Exercise: One-up–one-down

    A. Have your client talk about his or her problem in the usual way of talking.

        1. Have client rate level of clarity from one to five (no clarity to intense clarity).

        2. Now tell your client that this rating is a new step toward more clarity. Tell client that he or she is starting to see just how much clarity he or she has.

        3. Next, tell your client what you noticed about his or her clarity. Was the client simple, direct, easy to hear, etc.? Or was client complex, disorganized, foggy, vague, etc.

    B. Ask your client to continue talking about his problem only this time have him talk as "foggy" and as "vague" as he can. Put at a number "1" on the rating scale.

        1. Take an awareness break. Have client tell you what he or she noticed internally. Any sensations? Any feelings? Any numbness? Any uneasiness, etc.? Any simple shifts? (If the client is unaware of what is experienced, help the client find it or talk about what *may* be happening.) Tell the client that these small awarenesses of his or her "inner world" are steps toward more clarity.

    C. Have client talk some more with usual amount of clarity.

        1. Take an awareness break. Discuss what sensations, feelings, movements, etc., are different at this level. What did he or she notice?

    D. Now, have your client move up one clarity level above his or her "normal" rating. You will have to help the client to increase the clarity level with one simple skill. You might have the client talk in short sentences, or in clear sentences; or have sentences begin with "In my opinion . . . or I see . . ."; or have client talk only about himself or herself; or have client talk in a direct and simple way; or suggest using details and specifics, etc.

Month

1. Help client practice this new skill with you.
2. Take an awareness break. Discuss the difference your client notices in sensations, feelings, thoughts, movements, etc., between this level and his or her "usual" level of clarity.

E.   Tell your client what you notice about him or her. Be specific.

V.   Closing
   A.   Do *not* give any assignments.
   B.   Ask your client to be more aware of his or her clarity range this week.
   C.   Ask your client to think about what life would be like if he or she were to expand the clarity range.

Session 14—Clarity Styles

I.   Visit
   A.   Ask client "How was your week?" "Did your last session help you in any way?" "Did you notice any difference in your clarity range?"
   B.   Respond to each answer with either a clear response or another leading question. Follow through on your questions.
   C.   Do not confront the client's resistances. Identify them and engage them with your questions.
   D.   Gain a clear picture of your client's week.
   E.   Remember that some clients will be uncomfortable and scared. You want to establish a friendly and easy baseline before introducing something new.

II. Problem or Issue Presentation
   A.   If you do not have a clear area to work with, ask your client "What would you like help with?" "What would you like to talk about today?" Allow client to talk about the problem with you.

III. Direction
   A.   Positive Approach Talk
      1.   Ask client if any new and/or different sensations or body feelings were noticed over the week.
      2.   Remind client that any signs of awkwardness, discomfort, uneasiness, foolishness, etc., are all indications of getting more in touch with himself or herself.

Clarity Styles

B. When you have established an area to work with, begin your session by teaching your client about clarity styles.
   1. Talk about different clarity styles: Indirect, confused, dumb, foggy, spaced-out, "nit-wit," "sharp-as-a-tack," "clear as a bell," precise, complicated, crystal clear, etc.
   2. Ask client to tell you about his or her own clarity style. Help the client paint a picture of his or her clarity style for you. Do this for *a particular situation*—if he or she can't have him or her talk about the clarity style being used in the room with you, right now.

IV. Exercise: Clarity Styles
   A. Complete the picture of your client's clarity style.
   B. Ask these questions:
      1. "What does this style give you?" (I get attention, I act smart, people have to help me, people feel sorry for me.)
      2. "What are the *strengths* of this style?" (I can make people wait for me, I'm a know it all, I stay in control.)
      3. "What are the *weaknesses* of this style?" (People don't respect me, I'm slower than others, people get mad at me, I act dumb, etc.)
      4. "What does this style take away from me?" (Being as smart and as quick as I really am, I'm not easygoing, I don't make decisions, etc.)
      5. "What kind of ways *can't* you be in this style?" (Smart, witty, soft, relaxed, talking specifically, etc.)
      6. "What ways do you have trouble being?" (Soft, vulnerable, alert, outspoken, talking personally, etc.)
   C. Take an awareness break.
      1. Help your client notice any shifts or changes going on inside as he or she practices clarity style. Be positive. Don't criticize.
   D. Have your client paint a verbal picture of "How I would make myself if I were a magician."
      1. Be specific. Only work with clarity style.
      2. Use some of the words just mentioned as you help the client create a *new* style.
   E. Now, select one new style the client can begin practicing immediately. (Be sure you both agree on it.)

  Month

      1.   Make sure this new clarity style is just a new, simple skill for your client to learn. (Using details, being specific, using short sentences, using the word "I" in sentences, etc.)

      2.   Be sure the new style is achievable—not too different or too threatening for the client.

F. Take an awareness break.

      1.   Help your client notice any shifts or changes in sensations, feelings, movements, thinking, etc. Be positive and supportive.

G. Work with the resistances.

      1.   Help your client to say all the reasons for not being able to do this new clarity style.

      2.   Have client express to you how difficult this new style is—as he or she does the new style (e.g., have client say "I can't talk simply" as he or she talks simply, or "I can't talk without spacing-out" as he or she talks and does not space-out, etc.

      3.   As your client expresses "reasons" with the new style, help him or her to see that the new style is being used right now.

H. Take an awareness break.

      1.   Educate your client to any new sensations, movements, thoughts, feelings, etc.

      2.   Help client notice little changes as he or she makes them.

I. Tell what you noticed about him or her during the session.

V. Closing

A. Do not give any assignments.

B. Ask your client to be more aware of his or her clarity style this week.

C. Ask client to think about what life would be like if he or she expanded (not changed) clarity styles.

Session 15—More About Clarity Styles

This session expands upon the notion of clarity styles by drawing upon the research and theories of Pratt and Nideffer from sports psychology (1981). Nideffer has been able to identify several consistent

More About Clarity Styles   15

dimensions and styles of attention, each of which has advantages in some situations and disadvantages in others. Nideffer's basic dimensions of attention are internal-external and broad-narrow. When people are under stress they tend to use their favored style (e.g., narrow-internal) even when the situation calls for another style (e.g., broad-external). Everyone is capable of every style but people vary in their flexibility, in their ability to adaptively switch styles. Although the Nideffer methods of "attention control training" were devised to help athletes, they also have been applied in business, educational, and counseling settings (see Pratt & Nideffer, *Taking Care of Business*, 1981).

I. Beginning
   A. Unless the client obviously is disturbed about something skip the visiting, instead plunge right into the directions for this session. (Keep in mind that *any* session can be suspended for a standard expression session if needed.)
II. Directions
   A. Explain that one important part of clarity is to be aware of the *direction* of one's attention, inside/outside, and the focus of attention, broad or narrow. Draw on board.
   B. Further explain that tests of attention styles have been developed and that you will give the client a short test so he or she can get some information about himself or herself.
   C. Administer the short form of the TAIS (Test of Attentional and Interpersonal Style). Score with client and chart scores. (See Appendix E.)
III. Exercise
   A. Now take client's highest score and discuss how this style is effectively used by the client. Get specific instances when this style is advantageous (e.g., broad external focusing is desirable when driving a car).
   B. Now take the opposite of the client's high score and discuss when using the preferred style would be inappropriate (e.g., a broad external focus is a distraction when studying; what is needed is a narrow external focus on the book the student is reading). Get specific examples of times when the client made errors because his or her attentional style did not fit the situation.

Month

C. Repeat A and B.
D. Discuss the styles that seem to be most effective during therapy sessions. Explain that focusing exercises teaches an internal focus of attention.
E. Now teach the Pratt Nideffer "Centering Exercise" as a method of shifting attention under pressure:
   1. "The initial step in gaining control over your attention and interpersonal reactions is to become aware of your current tendencies."
   2. "The second step is called *centering* or gaining control over your relaxation response. The goal is to practice breathing and muscle control so that you can bring your tension under control within one or two deep breaths while your shoulders get very loose (like warm, melted chocolate)."
   3. "The final stage emphasizes practice, especially mental rehearsal. It has been discovered and demonstrated that mental rehearsal is more vivid (more sensorially accurate) after good relaxation or centering. As is the case with physical practice of anything from typing to free-throw shooting to public speaking, *practice makes perfect only if the practice is the right kind of practice*. It is at this stage that stages one and two become relevant for complete realization of the benefits of 3. You need centering (2) in order to do the rehearsal well. You require the results from step 1, assessment of tendencies or awareness, in order to know what to rehearse."

IV. Follow-up
   A. Explain that the centering exercise can be used both as a means of attention control and as a method of stress reduction and relaxation.
   B. Tell the client to try the centering exercise during the coming week. Try the exercise in two ways: in real life situations that are stressful and for five minutes every other day when alone.
   C. Tell client that in the next session he or she will have a chance to try out the centering exercise during the session.
   D. For clients who benefit by reading about techniques recommend Nideffer's book *The Inner Athlete* (1976).

More About Clarity Styles   15

Session 16—Clarity Limits

I. Major themes and goal: The goal of this session is to give the client a powerful experience of his or her clarity limits. Help the client to understand that *everyone* has limits but that personality limits can be changed.

II. Beginning
    A. Review the clarity dynamism with your client.
        1. "This dynamism deals with how you perceive what is going on *inside* you and *outside* you."
        2. "Your *level* of clarity tells you how well you know what's *really* going on."
        3. "Sometimes you think you know what's going on—but you keep it silently inside your head. When you see things and think things and talk to yourself in your head, without saying anything out loud, you do not give yourself the *pleasure* of your own clarity.
        4. "You get pleasure from your own clarity when you say what you see, know, or think out loud."
        5. "In other words, it feels good to say out loud what you know, what you think, what you perceive, what you believe, etc. It *feels good* to bring your inside world into your outside world. We will be working with this today."
    B. Remind your client that something that will feel good later does not always feel pleasurable at first.

III. Procedure
    A. Set out a red light and a green light that can be switched on or off. Show client how you can turn the red light on and off and the green light on and off.
    B. Now give directions: (1) "When the green light is on I want you to talk *nonstop* about anything, don't stop at all, talk fast and pay attention only to what you are saying." (2) "When the red light's on talk very slowly and pay attention to what I'm doing and how I look while you talk. O.K., go ahead (switch on green light).
    C. As the client talks, walk around room, bang on the wall, make noises, make comments.

 Month

     D.   Take an awareness pause. Turn off both lights. Ask client what it felt like to talk with the green light on, and with the red light on.

     E.   Repeat B, C and D. Only this time make more disruptive switching between the green and red lights.

     F.   New directions: "Now I want you to respond to the green light and red light differently. When the green is on keep talking but when the red light comes on stop quickly and completely. Don't talk at all when the red light is on."

     G.   Repeat B and C and toward the end of C turn on *both* the red and green lights.

     H.   Note. This can be a very stressful exercise for some clients, especially if the red or green controls markedly disrupt their normal speech rhythms. After G take a long awareness pause, encourage client to talk about feelings. Ask "did you try centering when you started to get upset?" Discuss.

IV. Close

     A.   Talk about the red lights and green lights that client gives himself or herself, the signals that are given by others. What about mixed signals? Discuss.

     B.   Have client keep a record in his or her Therapy Notebook of times during the week when mixed signals occurred and how they were handled.

     C.   Recommend more practice on the centering exercise.

Comments on Session 16

This session can be disruptive and evoke a lot of feeling. By this point in the therapy most clients should be able to experience this kind of limits testing, but vary the use of the red light/green light exercise according to your judgment of how the client is responding.

Month Five—Feeling

In this month several important techniques are introduced to accompany the focus on the feeling dynamism. The most important addition is the use of dreams and fantasies.

Clarity Limits   16

Session 17—Feeling

I.   Major theme and goal: Help the client notice feelings and feeling-expression mismatches.
II. Begin by visiting in the usual way, "How are things?" "What's been happening?"
III. Focus the session: "Has anything happened the last week that you had a lot of feeling about?" Listen and reflect.
IV. Directions
    A. After you have established some content area to work with, remind the client that today you will be helping him or her to understand the feeling dynamism.
    B. Teach about the functional therapy approach to feelings. Explain, "A complete feeling is composed of a sensation, a thought, and an expression that are all matched. When one part is off or mismatched the feeling doesn't 'feel right' to you. So, if you smile when you feel sad or think to yourself 'I'm happy' when you look and feel sad, something will seem strange to you."
    C. Spend time giving your client examples of matched and mismatched feelings. Role play for the client.
        1. Talk in an unmatched way about a situation in which you are very angry. Be sure to underrate and understate your anger; shrug it off; underexpress the feeling.
        2. Talk in an unmatched way about a very sad situation. This time exaggerate the sadness, shout out the sadness. Make it bigger than life, unreal; overexpress the feeling. Use loud expression and lots of activity.
        3. Now talk with matched feelings and expression about one of the above situations. Disclose to the client how this way of expressing feels different to you.
V.   Exercise: One-up–one-down
    A. Have your client talk about his or her problem in usual way of talking.
        1. Help client to identify a particular feeling (e.g., angry at his boss, lonely for his wife, etc.), or help identify a general feeling underlying what is being said (e.g., general excitement for new changes).

5   **Month**

B. Have client rate level of feeling from 1 to 5 (1 is no feeling, 2 slight feeling, 3 moderate feeling, 4 strong feeling, and 5 intense feeling). Tell your client what *you* noticed about his or her feeling as he or she spoke. (Was client intense, direct, clear, making contact, etc.?)

C. Ask your client to talk once more about the problem only this time have client talk at one level below normal rating. "Do this by focusing on side feelings rather than the main feeling."

    1. Take an awareness break. Have client tell you what he or she noticed. Any sensations? Any feelings? Any rigidity? Any uneasiness, etc.? Any simple shifts etc.? Any thoughts, worries, fears? (If client is unaware of what he or she is experiencing, help him or her find it—or tell what he or she may be experiencing.)

D. Now, have your client talk some more only this time with usual amount of feeling regarding his or her problem.

    1. Take an awareness pause. Discuss what sensations, feelings, movements, etc., are different for him or her. What did the client notice?

E. Now, have client talk and move one feeling level above the "normal." (Simply help your client to express the feeling that matches the situation he is discussing and that matches how he really feels inside. Be sure to include an expression level and an activity level that matches this "one-up feeling level.")

    1. Keep this very simple. (For example, "I feel sad"; "That hurts me"; "I'm angry"; "I want more"; "I want to talk"; etc.)

    2. Take an awareness break. Again, discuss the difference in sensations, feelings, thoughts, movements, etc., between this level and the other levels.

F. Tell your client what you noticed about him or her. Be specific. (If videotape playback is available, use it.)

VI. Closing

A. Instruct client to keep track of dreams and fantasies in the following week. Explain that dreams often show feelings that are being ignored during the day or where there are pronounced mismatches between feelings and expressions.

Feeling 17

B.   If client likes to read therapy related material, assign Chapter
9 from this book. Give client tips for remembering dreams that
are in Chapter 9. (This includes making up a short fantasy in
the morning based on feelings that are present when awakening, if the client cannot remember a dream.)

Session 18—Feeling

Begin Session 18 with the usual visiting time and then go directly
to the exercise used in Session 17, but this time use dream reports for
the content of the exercise. Use the same assignments.

Session 19—Feeling Styles

I.   Procedure
   A.   Begin immediately by asking client to pick out a dream and
tell it to you.
   B.   Talk about different feeling styles: gloomy, cheerful, lively,
pessimistic, optimistic, deep, shallow, negative, moody, happy,
etc.
   C.   Ask client to describe the feeling style of his or her dream.
   D.   Now have client identify a real life situation in which he or
she uses the same feeling style (more or less).
   E.   Ask "What would need to go up or down to change that feeling
style?"
   F.   Ask client to repeat the dream but change expression, activity,
clarity, or feeling and see how the dream feeling style changes.
   G.   If time permits do another dream or fantasy and another par-
allel waking incident.
II. Changing feeling styles
   A.   Complete a picture of your client's feeling style as revealed in
the dreams and waking parallels.
   B.   Ask these questions:

    Month

1. "What does this style give you?" (People notice me, people feel sorry for me, I get lots of attention, etc.).
2. "What are the strengths of this style?" (being strong, talkative, smart, feeling special, sexy, etc.).
3. "What are the weaknesses of this style?" (I feel invisible, I get quiet, people don't like me, I'm all alone, etc.).
4. "What does this style take away from you?" (being strong and powerful, being sexy, feeling special, being witty, etc.).
5. "What kinds of ways can't you be in this style?" (intelligent, loud, excited, soft, tender, etc.).
6. "What ways do you have trouble being?" (powerful, loveable, smart, etc.).

C. Take an awareness break
   1. Help your client notice any shifts or changes going on inside him as he moves. Help him be positive.
D. Have your client paint a verbal picture of "How I would make myself if I were a magician."
   1. Be specific. Only work with feeling style.
   2. Use some of the words he or she has just mentioned as you help the client create a new style.
E. Explain that when changes are made in waking then parallel changes will be made in dreaming.

III. Closing
   A. Ask your client to be more aware of his or her feeling style this week.
   B. Ask client to think about what life would be like if he or she expanded (not changed) his or her feeling styles.
   C. Continue dream notebook.

Session 20—Feeling Limits

Two kinds of feeling limits sessions are included here. One is written up as a Group Session 20A and the other as Individual Session 20B. Both sessions are intended to give clients an intense experience and both can be modified for use as either a group or an individual session.

Feeling Limits   20

Group Session 20A—Feeling Limits

I. Greeting
  A. Welcome everyone to group.
  B. Make some contact with each person.
  C. Be friendly.
II. Visit
  A. Review the dynamism *feeling* with your group.
    1. Encourage group participation.
    2. Ask your group what they noticed about their own feelings this week.
    3. Make *your* feeling level affect the entire room. Point out different feelings you notice among the group members as they talk and/or listen.
    4. Keep this visit pleasurable and educational. Make contact with your group.
    5. Emphasize that the feeling dynamism interrelates clarity, expression, and activity.
III. Problem/Issue Presentation
  A. Do not spend a lot of time with personal problems today.
    1. If someone has an emergency, or badly needs special help—then, be sure to help them. Otherwise, the bulk of the group is to be spent on the exercise.
IV. Direction
  A. "Feelings are your emotions. They are *yours*. We are teaching you the skills you need to get in touch with them, to experience them and to make them work *for* you."
    1. "It is a common behavior for some people to spend more time and energy focusing on outside stimulation instead of inside feelings. We lessen our feeling level and get out of touch with our feelings when we spend more time focusing on the *outside* than on the *inside*."
  B. "Today you are going to be focusing on the feelings inside you. You will be doing this by reaching way down deep inside yourself into some of your most hidden compartments where you store your 'secrets.' Each of you is going to think of some secrets, or secret thoughts you may have about others in the group or about yourself. Then you all will be given a blindfold

⑤ **Month**

to place over your eyes so that the outside stimulation will be reduced. This will help you focus on your inside feelings. Then, each one of you can take a turn using the White Noise Machine which will help you to say your secrets and to experience your feelings."

V.   Exercise: White Noise Secrets—Group
    A.   Have the group form a semi-circle around you.
        1.   Have them write down some secrets or thoughts they have about people in the group, or about themselves.
        2.   Have them rate the level of feeling intensity they get from these secrets, on a scale of 1 to 5. Have each person give you a quick rating out loud.
    B.   Hand each person a blindfold.
        1.   Have them put them on.
        2.   Tell your group to take three slow deep breaths and to focus on the feelings they are having inside.
    C.   Now, instruct your group that you will select one person to work with the White Noise Machine.
        1.   Silently select one person and place the headphones on his ears. The rest of the group need not know who you selected.
        2.   Tell the group to listen to the selected person's secrets and to focus on *their own feelings* as he tells his or her secrets.
        3.   Now, turn up the volume on the White Noise Machine. The client with the earphones must increase his or her expression level.
        4.   After the secrets have been said, turn off the machine and work with the client's feelings. (Keep all blindfolds on.)
        5.   Help the client to identify his or her feelings and to admit them. (He or she may be scared, excited, relieved, proud, or worried.) Help him or her to feel himself or herself and to express.
    D.   Now, select another client to work with the White Noise Machine.
        1.   Silently place the headphones on the person's ears without the other members knowing.
        2.   Instruct him or her to begin saying his or her secrets.

Feeling Limits   20

        3.   Turn up the volume.

        4.   Repeat the exercise.

E.   Take an awareness break.

        1.   Have the group, with blindfolds on, share what they are experiencing inside themselves; what feelings, sensations, movements, thoughts, etc.

        2.   Take awareness breaks throughout the group whenever needed.

F.   After everyone who wants to has had a turn, have everyone take off their blindfolds.

        1.   Ask them how they felt differently, using this new focusing skill. Have them be specific.

        2.   Ask the group: "What would you be like if you were to focus on your feelings this week?"

G.   Have a group discussion on "new secrets."

        1.   Let the group know that it feels good to say the secrets and it feels good (intense feelings) to receive them.

        2.   Keep this positive.

        3.   Tell the group that they will have a chance to tell secrets again—but for now they can interrupt the group at any time to ask for a "secret time" when they can say anything with *goodwill*.

VI. Closing

A.   Do not give any assignments.

B.   Have them look around at one another.

C.   "You are learning how to help each other and be honest with each other."

D.   Talk to them about *knowing the difference*. You do not expect them to "change" until they know the difference inside.

        1.   When they begin to know the difference, then they will begin choosing more fit ways to be from inside. You are going to teach them before the end of their therapy program how to know the difference so that they can continue changing and becoming more psychologically fit on their own.

        2.   Remind them: Don't talk about their therapy outside the sessions.

5 Month

Individual Session 20B—Feeling Limits

This session makes use of Fritz Perls's (Perls, 1969) dream dialogue technique to intensify feelings and to bring out feeling/expression mismatches.

I. Visit
   A. Ask client what was noticed about dreams, fantasies, and feelings during the week.
   B. Ask about dream to waking parallels that were noticed.
II. Procedure
   A. Have client pick out the dream that seems the most feelingful.
   B. Have client retell dream *as though it were being experienced right there.*
   C. Notice feeling moments.
   D. Go back over dream. This time have client move to different chairs or places in the room and speak or show the feelings of the different components of the dream. Have the different dream parts communicate to one another.
   E. Now have the client stand in front of mirror and retell the dream, this time allowing the dream feeling style to change in a way that will accomodate more of the different feelings.
   F. Discuss with the client the feelings that occurred during the procedure. Explain that keeping track of the rapid blending and shifting of feelings is not easy.
III. Closing
   A. Mention that next week the contact dynamism will be talked about; ask client to pay special attention to the people who enter his or her dreams and how they respond to client and how client responds to them.
   B. Some clients may benefit from reading Perls's *Gestalt Therapy Verbatim* (1969).

Month Six—Contact

The four sessions this month provide a sensible transition from the first half to the second half of the therapy program. The interpersonal

Feeling Limits   20

contact dynamism unifies the other intrapersonal dynamisms and relates meaningfully to the functioning of the personality in different life areas.

Session 21—Contact

I. Greeting
    A.   Make physical contact with your client.
    B.   Call your client by his or her first name.
    C.   Be friendly and strong.

II. Visit
    A.   Begin by informally visiting with your client.
        1.   Ask engaging questions such as: "How do you feel to-day?" "What was your day like?"
        2.   Follow up each question with either a clear response or another question.
    B.   Gain impressions of your client.
        1.   Watch for resistances (vagueness, hostility, evasiveness, argumentativeness, etc.)
        2.   Watch for feelings (sadness, excitement, fear, etc.)
    C.   Follow the specifics of your client's comments. Gain a clear picture of his day, thoughts, and feelings.
    D.   Remember that you want to continue strengthening the bond you have with your client. You want him or her to feel *safe* and accepted by you.
    E.   Remember that you are deepening your relationship with your client. You want to establish a safe and secure atmosphere for him or her.

III. Problem or issue presentation
    A.   If you do not have a clear area to work with, ask your client "What would you like help with?" "What would you like to talk about today?"

IV. Direction
    A.   After you have established an area to work with, begin your session by teaching your client about the personality dynamism, *contact*.
    B.   "This month we will be working with the fifth personality dynamism, contact. *Contact deals with how much impact and/or*

ⓖ   **Month**

effect you have on others. At its most basic level, contact means being with people. Contact gives meaning to your life. Most of the problems you have experienced or will experience are because of the *lack* of contact. People are social beings. This means they thrive on contact. Some of the contact skills you have learned result in negative contact—such skills as blaming, worrying, arguing, or being shy, quiet, or alone, etc. The contact these skills give you isn't usually fully satisfying. This month I will be teaching you positive contact skills. These skills will be involved with talking and touching. Physical touching makes it possible to have emotional touching. And it is that kind of contact that enables you to live a pleasurable and satisfying life."

C. Examples/illustrations

1. "Today we will talk about three different contact skills: physical contact, eye contact, and emotional contact."

2. Spend some time giving your client examples of *using* these three skills—and of *not* using these three skills—in a normal conversation. Be an illustration for your client.

(a) Talk to your client without making any physical contact, eye contact, or emotional contact. Exaggerate this so he or she really can begin to sense it. For example, keep your body rigid, look down at the rug, and mumble to him.

(b) Next, make aggressive physical contact (such as a strong handshake). Make intense eye contact (look right into his eyes) and deep emotional contact (say something with your feeling, such as, "I enjoy seeing you today," or "I feel excited right now," or "I'm enjoying myself").

(c) Have a good time doing this.

3. Be sure your client has a good time watching you and that he or she is aware of the "contact contrast" you are illustrating.

D. Positive approach talk

1. Remind your client that he or she will be experiencing discomfort, awkwardness, foolishness, vulnerability, etc.

Contact   21

Tell client these are all signs of changing and a new awareness.

V. Exercise: One-up–one-down
A. Have your client talk about problem/issue with his or her usual amount of contact.
1. Have client give an overall rating for the amount of *physical contact*, *eye contact*, and *emotional contact* made.
2. Be sure he or she is aware of the level of contact made— or not made with each type of contact: (1) no contact, (2) slight contact, (3) moderate contact, (4) strong contact, (5) intense contact.
3. Now, tell your client what *you* noticed about him or her. (Did he or she make any physical contact, look at you, could you feel him?)
B. Now, have your client talk about his or her problem/issue with little or no contact at all. Put client at a number "1" on the rating scale.
1. Take an awareness break. Have client tell you what he or she notices in his body. Any sensations? Extra worries or thoughts? Awkwardness? Numbness?, etc. (If client is unaware of what he or she is experiencing, help find it, or tell what *may* be happening.)
C. Now, have your client talk to you making contact at the regular level.
1. Take an awareness break. Discuss what sensation, feelings, movements, etc., are different. What did he or she notice?
D. Now, have client talk to you at one contact level above the "normal."
1. Simply help your client to exaggerate *one* of the three contact skills. He or she may shake your hand or grab hold of your arm as talking, may look directly into your eyes as talking, or may express with some feeling. Be sure to work with *one* skill only.
2. Take an awareness pause. Again, discuss the difference in the client's sensations, feelings, thoughts, movements, etc., between this level and the other levels.
E. Tell your client what you noticed. Be specific.

 Month

VI. Closing
   A. Ask your client to be more aware of his or her contact level this week.
   B. Ask your client to think about what his or her life would be like if the contact range were expanded.

Session 22—Contact

Repeat Session 21, only this time work with another feature of the client's contact dynamism. Be sure to explain that contact, like the other personality dynamisms, varies from time to time and situation to situation. Make it clear that the goal is not constant high contact but the ability to make contact when that is what your client wants to do. Also explain that the contact dynamism and the other personality dynamisms will be worked with in the coming months when talking about different life areas. Add to the assignment, "Pick out one contact situation you would like to change. Describe the situation in your Therapy Notebook and we will go over it next week."

Session 23—Contact Styles

I. Visit
   A. Ask your client "How was your week?" "Did your last session help you in any way?" "Did you notice any difference in your contact range?"
   B. Respond to each answer with either a clear response or another leading question. Follow through on your questions.
   C. Do not confront the client's resistances. Identify them and engage them with your questions.
   D. Gain a clear picture of your client's week.
II. Content focus
   A. Ask your client to read from his or her Therapy Notebook the contact situation he or she would like to change.
   B. Give these instructions: "Imagine that you are reading a dream. Picture yourself in this dream."
   C. "Rate your contact level in this dream."

Contact Styles

D.   "Describe your contact style in this dream. Were you aloof, involved, touching–feeling, overbearing, etc.? Try to come up with five words to describe your contact style. Now try to come up with five words to describe a positive change in your style."

III.   Exercise: Contact Styles

A.   Complete this picture of your client's contact style.

B.   Ask these questions:

1.   "What does this style give you?" (I take control, I stay safe, people respect me, etc.)

2.   "What are the strengths of this style?" (No one bothers me, I am a leader, I'm the aggressor, I get taken care of, etc.)

3.   "What are the weaknesses of this style?" (I always feel lonely, no one notices me, I act unimportant, I don't trust anyone, etc.)

4.   "What does this style take away from you?" (Being opinionated, being well-liked, being sexual, being warm and tender, etc.)

5.   "What kinds of ways *can't* you be in this style?" (Positive, silly, intelligent, talkative, etc.)

6.   "What ways do you have trouble being?" (Strong, loud, powerful, gentle, caring, etc.)

C.   Take an awareness break.

1.   Help your client notice any shifts or changes going on as he or she talks about contact style.

D.   Have your client paint a verbal picture of "How I would make myself."

1.   Be specific. Work only with contact style.

2.   Use some of the words just mentioned as you help him or her create a new style.

E.   Now, pick one style that the client can begin practicing immediately. (Be sure you *both* agree on it.)

1.   Make sure that this new contact style includes just one simple skill (a friendly greeting, a personal statement, a hug or handshake, a gentleness, etc.).

2.   Be sure the new style is achievable—not too threatening for the client.

 Month

     F.   Take an awareness break.
         1.   Help your client notice any shifts or changes in sensations, movements, thinking, etc. Keep this positive.
     G.   Work with the resistances.
         1.   Help your client to say all the reasons he or she has for not being able to do this new contact style.
         2.   Have the client express the resistance in this new style (for example, say "I can't be friendly" with a friendly tone, or, "I don't like to shake hands" as client shakes your hand, or "I won't talk about myself" as he or she talks about himself or herself, or, "I can't be tender" in a tender tone of voice, etc.).
         3.   As your client expresses these "reasons" with new style, help him or her to see that he or she is doing the new style right now.
     H.   Take an awareness break.
         1.   Help your client notice any shifts or changes in sensations, movements, thoughts, feelings, etc.
         2.   Help client notice little changes being made as he or she makes them.
     I.   Tell client what you noticed about him or her during the session.
VI. Closing
     A.   Ask your client to be more aware of his contact style this week.
     B.   Ask him or her to think about what his or her life would be like if he or she expanded (not changed) contact styles.

Session 24—Contact Limits

This session is designed as a group session but it can be run as an individual session. What is important in this session is that the client get an opportunity to take on the role of a teacher. It is a familiar fact in education that students often learn best when they have the opportunity to teach the subject they are learning; the same is true in therapy.

Contact Limits

I. Greeting
   A.   Welcome everyone to group.
   B.   Make some special contact with each person.
   C.   Be friendly and assertive.
II. Visit
   A.   Be strong and cheerful.
   B.   Encourage group participation. Ask if anyone wants to talk
        about their week.
        1.   Mainly, you are to carry the conversation for this part of
             the group.
        2.   Ask engaging questions to keep the feeling level up.
        3.   Make *your* feeling level affect the entire room by talking
             forcefully.
III. Problem or issue presentation
   A.   Ask if anyone wants to talk about a problem.
        1.   If so, let the person talk freely.
        2.   Encourage group participation.
   B.   As people begin to discuss their problems, point out to the
        group any changes that this person has made over the past
        three months.
        1.   For example, the person may talk slower, or make eye
             contact, or smile, or talk louder, or clearer, etc.
        2.   Let client know that you notice changes.
IV. Direction
   A.   Talk to the group about contact styles.
        1.   Ask them what they know about their own contact styles
             and other group members' styles.
        2.   Point out specific contact styles of people in the group.
        3.   Keep this educational. You are not working with their
             styles, simply pointing them out.
        4.   Be friendly and supportive.
   B.   Ask them what they know about their own contact strengths
        and weaknesses.
        1.   Point out particular strengths and weaknesses you notice
             in certain group members' contact styles.
   C.   Remind them that each time you learn something about some-
        one else, you actually learn something about yourself.

 Month

1. Tell them how teaching and learning are very important to changing and to growing.
2. "It feels good to be a teacher and it feels good to be a learner. The more you teach something, the better you know it."

V. Exercise: Teacher or Learner—Contact Strengths
   A. Pair up your group.
   B. "You are going to teach one of your contact strengths to your partner and your partner in turn is going to teach one to you."
      1. Select the contact strength you want to teach . . . handshake, eye contact, personal statements, etc.
      2. Take time to teach it.
         (a) Explain it.
         (b) Illustrate it.
         (c) Exaggerate it.
         (d) Have your partner model you as you do it.
         (e) Be sure he does it to your satisfaction.
      3. Now, switch. The teacher becomes the learner. Follow the above steps.
   C. Bring the group back together.
      1. Encourage participation.
      2. Ask them what they learned.
      3. Take an awareness break.
         (a) Have the group talk about shifts and changes, feelings, sensations, more or less thoughts, etc.
         (b) Have them all take three deep breaths to help them better notice themselves inside.
   D. Be supportive and positive.
   E. Keep the atmosphere friendly and helpful.
VI. Closing
   A. No assignments.
   B. Congratulate them for completing their sixth month of the program.
   C. Teach them to appreciate themselves for being here and for trying to change no matter what their thoughts may tell them.
   D. Close on a positive note.

Contact Limits   24

16

Months Seven through Twelve
Resistances, Defenses, and Negative Images

The schedule of sessions for the next six months is:

Month	Sessions	Themes
7	25–28	Reorientation: Images and Growth
8	29–32	Relationships
9	33–36	Sex
10	37–40	Play and Recreation
11	41–44	Work
12	45–48	Ending the Therapy

Month Seven—Reorientation: Images and Growth

During this time period, the fitness themes are continued but more attention is directed to specific resistances, defenses, and negative images that may impede the client's growth in different life areas.

Session 25—Review

This session is set up to review the client's ideas about his or her personality functioning. As presented, the session is described as a group exercise but it can be modified to apply to an individual meeting.

⁊ **Month**

I. Greet everyone.
II. Procedure
   A. Have each participant graph his or her profile for their "most satisfying" life activity and "least satisfying" life activity.
   B. At first, do not have clients identify the content of the activity, make it "Activity X" and "Activity Y." Let each person discuss how they function when in "Situation X" and in "Situation Y."
   C. Have other group members guess what situation or activity the person is presenting.
   D. Have each person describe the real content of X and Y, using the dynamism profile of X while discussing X and the profile of Y while discussing Y. Get responses from group members, how are they affected by the X and Y personalities.
III. Follow-up
   A. Leader should explain that everyone has many personalities, a whole alphabet of personalities from A to Z, which are used in different situations.
   B. Leader: "In therapy everyone has a chance to learn about how their personalities function in different situations. Also, everyone can start to change those profiles that are least satisfying."
   C. Assignments
      1. "Notice during the week if there are certain profiles you use over and over in similar situations. Are they satisfying? Are you choosing to use that personality pattern or is it just a habit?"
      2. "Write some of your observations in your Therapy Notebook."

Session 26—Images: Old and New

I. Major theme: The counteraction and disintegration of old images that are nonfunctional; integration and reintegration cycle of therapy.

   Major goals: To effectively educate the client to dysfunctional old-image behavior. To deepen the client's feeling level.

Images: Old and New   26

II. Procedure

A. Draw a chart on board with "Old Images" as left side heading and "New Possible Images" as right side heading. Put life areas (therapy, sex, relationships, work, and play) in middle.

B. Explain, "Today I want you to talk about your old images or ideas in these areas and possible new images. Let's generate some ideas." Then go through the life areas and write "in client's words" some phrases that capture old dysfunctional images, for example, Therapy: "Therapy is for sick people; Relationships: "I'm a loner"; Sex: "I'm not sexy"; Work: "I get by"; Play: "I'm not athletic."

C. Pick one area and talk with client about how that image developed. What did it do for the person in the past? Who did the client learn from? Is the old image satisfying in the present? Why not?

D. Teach the Needs and Wants-Choices-Actions-Image cycle. Draw on board. Answer questions. "When you have new needs or new priorities for your needs and wants then you must develop new images." Teach about what happens when the cycle is reversed, with images dictating actions, choices, and needs.

E. Now go back through the list and help the person generate potential new images, for example, Therapy: "I want more for myself through therapy"; Relationships: "I want to be with people"; Sex: "I'm learning to be sexy"; Work: "I want to have a career"; Play: "I'm learning how to play."

F. Now pick one area and image and work on the defensive side of the image. Get the client to deny systematically all the needs and wants that can not be served by the old image. Pace this expression exercise so that the person begins to feel in a concentrated way the denial process. Spend time developing a feeling reference point for resisting.

G. Teach the person that when an old image blocks the development of new images the way through the old image is to experience intensely its effects.

III. Closing

A. Assign the client to write an autobiography and to bring in a selection of photographs that show different stages of his of her life. The autobiography should cover the four life areas of

7 **Month**

relationships, work, play, and sex, plus school and home life. Make it at least 10 pages long. (Clients who have special difficulties with writing can prepare a tape-recorded autobiography.)

B.   There is a wide range of reading that can be recommended on the use of autobiographies. Some good books to recommend are: Franklin's *The Autobiography and Other Writings* (1961); Mathews and Radar's *Autobiography, Biography and the Novel* (1973); Lillard's *American Life in Autobiography* (1956); Terkel's *American Dreams: Lost and Found* (1981).

Therapists should consult the above, plus these technical references: Allport (1942), Annis (1967), Buhler (1964), Butler (1963), Dollard (1949), Hahn (1963), Lieberman and Falk (1971), Piechowski (1975), Shaffer (1954), Tyler (1953), and White (1959). Also relevant are many of the references discussed in Chapter 10 on "Adult Growth and the Goals of Therapy."

Session 27—The Influence of Old and New Images

This session continues the themes developed in Session 26, this time using the autobiography and the client's photographs as a reference for old and new images.

I.   Beginning
  A.   Visit with client: "How are things?" "What's been happening?" "How have you been feeling?" Give time for client to bring up concerns and problems.
  B.   Ask specifically, "What was it like to write an autobiography?" and "How did it feel to go through the old photographs?" Listen, notice feelings and feeling mismatches.
II.   Procedure
  A.   Ask client to pick out the photographs that "meant something special." Have client describe the people and the setting in the photos. Pin some of the photos up on the wall.
  B.   Position chairs so that you and the client can look at the photos.

The Influence of Old and New Images   27

C.   Ask client to read parts of the autobiography. While the client is reading notice shifts in feeling; also notice if the client changes images.

D.   Go back through the autobiography, this time underline sentences that summarize an old image, for example, "I always felt helpless at home." Ask client if these images affect him or her now.

E.   Draw an image chart on the board. List life areas on one side (work, play, relationships, school, etc.) and My Old Image, My New Image, My Father's Image, My Mother's Image in columns at top. Go through these categories with the client and arrive at descriptions for each person and area. Talk about overlapping images.

F.   Pick out an old dysfunctional image that your client clearly shares with mother or father. Work with activity dynamism. Have client move, talk, and hold the posture of his or her parent in the old image. "How does that feel when you live the old image?"

G.   Ask client what would be the consequences if he or she continues to act out the old image? "What were the consequences for your mother (father)?"

Note: This exercise may be rather painful for some clients. Be careful not to exceed the client's ability to integrate the feelings that come up. Switch to a present-day focus if old feelings become too strong.

III. Closing
A.   Help clients to recognize that they and their parents made the best choices and developed the best images they could. Now your client can make new choices.

B.   Assign to the client a Future Autobiography. Have client chart 1-year, 5-year, and 10-year goals in different life areas (work, marriage, friends, sex, play, and others). Specify the needs and wants he or she feels now and the images he or she needs to develop to fulfill the goals.

C.   Also, tell client to have several (three or four) of the key photographs blown up to poster size and to bring those posters next time.

---

7 Month

Session 28—Goals and Images

This session relates the growth cycle and images to Bradburn's concept of life satisfaction and positive-negative affect balance.

I. Introduction
   A. Begin by putting up the client's poster photographs on the wall. Explain that these posters will be kept in the therapy room so that they can be used in future sessions.
   B. Ask client about feelings concerning the posters.
   C. Introduce the idea that satisfaction in life comes not from avoiding all negatives or stress (which is impossible), but from "making sure that the positives in your life most of the time exceed the negatives."
II. Exercise
   A. Go over the modified *Bradburn Affect Balance Scale* with the client. Have client answer the questions verbally and you fill in the answers on the sheet.

Directions: We are interested in the way people are feeling these days. We have described below some of the ways people feel at different times. We would like you to answer two questions about each of these feelings. First, have you felt that way over the past week? Then, if you have, how often have you felt that way over the past week?
During the past week did you ever feel:

   1. Pleased about having accomplished something.
      (a) Yes   (b) No
   2. Pleased about having accomplished something.
      (a) None   (b) Once   (c) Several times   (d) Often
   3. So restless that you couldn't sit in a chair long.
      (a) Yes   (b) No
   4. So restless that you couldn't sit in a chair.
      (a) None   (b) Once   (c) Several times   (d) Often
   5. That things were going your way.
      (a) Yes   (b) No
   6. That things were going your way.
      (a) None   (b) Once   (c) Several times   (d) Often

Goals and Images 28

7. Bored
   (a) Yes   (b) No
8. Bored
   (a) None   (b) Once   (c) Several times   (d) Often
9. Proud because someone has complimented you on something you had done.
   (a) Yes   (b) No
10. Proud because someone had complimented you on something you had done.
    (a) None   (b) Once   (c) Several times   (d) Often
11. Depressed or very unhappy.
    (a) Yes   (b) No
12. Depressed or very unhappy.
    (a) None   (b) Once   (c) Several times   (d) Often
13. Particularly excited or interested in something.
    (a) Yes   (b) No
14. Particularly excited or interested in something.
    (a) None   (b) Once   (c) Several times   (d) Often
15. Very lonely or remote from other people.
    (a) Yes   (b) No
16. Very lonely or remote from other people.
    (a) None   (b) Once   (c) Several times   (d) Often
17. On top of the world.
    (a) Yes   (b) No
18. On top of the world.
    (a) None   (b) Once   (c) Several times   (d) Often
19. Upset because someone criticized you.
    (a) Yes   (b) No
20. Upset because someone criticized you.
    (a) None   (b) Once   (c) Several times   (d) Often
21. Angry at something that usually wouldn't bother you.
    (a) Yes   (b) No
22. Angry at something that usually wouldn't bother you.
    (a) None   (b) Once   (c) Several times   (d) Often
23. Vaguely uneasy about something without knowing why.
    (a) Yes   (b) No
24. Vaguely uneasy about something without knowing why.
    (a) None   (b) Once   (c) Several times   (d) Often

7 Month

B.   Now total, with the client, the positives and negatives, look at the ratio or balance between positives and negatives.
C.   Have the client look at a photograph that shows his or her father or mother (pick the parent who seemed to have the greatest emotional influence on the client, or do both). "I want you to imagine how your mother (father) would have answered these questions at this time in her (his) life. Just guess at your parent's answers."
D.   Now score the side for the parent. Compare the client's score and his or her parent's score. Talk about similarities and differences.

Note: For some clients this comparison may be full of feelings. The therapist may choose to work with the feelings and feeling moments or not, as seems best.

III.   Closing
A.   Explain that in the coming months you will be helping the client examine his or her life satisfaction at work, in relationships, and so on. Connect the idea of overall life satisfaction as a positive imbalance of positives to negatives with the affect balance in each area of the client's life. Make it clear that changes are required when a negative imbalance exists in a life area.

Commentary on Month Seven

Sessions 25 to 28 mark a turning point in the therapy. There is a shift from intrapersonal to interpersonal emphases, from present-centered concerns to the client's past and future, and from personal awareness to personal changes. These emphases will continue during the next five months. There also is more attention paid in every session to defenses and resistances and to the disintegration cycle (counteraction, catharsis, and proaction). This is necessary because, as soon as practical personality changes are attempted, negative images are most likely to emerge. Of course, for some clients, the therapist will necessarily have been working with negative images right along, from day one of the therapy. But for most clients the focus during the first six months of

Commentary on Month   7

this program can be on growth and fitness and strengths rather than weaknesses. From this point on, however, the therapist must keep in mind that many of the feeling moments that show up will occur because of the conflicts emerging between the client's new awareness of needs and wants in different life areas and old images that are opposed to the fulfillment of those needs and wants.

Month Eight—Relationships

The format of the sessions for the next four months is roughly the same. Each month a different life area is focused upon and the client's life satisfaction in that area is evaluated along with the client's positive and negative images, goals, needs, and wants. The basic working event in every session continues to be feeling-expression mismatches, especially as they relate to the client's typical dynamism profile for this life area. (Is the client typically low in expression, activity, and contact while high in clarity and feeling for relationships? If so, the natural entry for change would be to work on the weak dynamisms.) Keep in mind that the life areas covered for these months (relationships, sex, work, and play) will apply to most clients but not to all. Some clients, for example, should spend several months in a row on the relationships area. The module of sessions on relationships easily can be expanded by consulting the primary source, Trower, Bryant, and Argyle (1978), from which the exercises are drawn. Similarly, the sex, work, and play areas all can be covered more or less extensively, depending on each individual client.

There is ample research to support the proposition that loneliness is a debilitating, serious problem for many people. For a sampling of research surveys on this social problem see: Buss (1980) *Self-Consciousness and Social Anxiety*; Peplau and Perlman (1978) "Current Research on Loneliness"; Trower, Bryant, and Argyle (1978) *Social Skills and Mental Health.* Many of the exercises used in this month's therapy program are drawn from the outstanding social skills training program developed by Trower, Bryant, and Argyle (1978) at the Livermore Hospital in Oxford, England, during the period 1968 to 1976. The Livermore program was applied to both inpatients and outpatients and constitutes a model eclectic approach that deserves to be widely studied and used by therapists. The designers of the Livermore program drew upon a great variety

 Month

of disciplines, including: drama, sociology, communications and linguistics, and social psychiatry, plus social, experimental, and clinical psychology. The techniques and theoretical influences they utilized ranged from psychodrama to transactional analysis, behavioral modeling, Rogerian, Jungian, and Freudian therapy, milieu therapy, and even Dale Carnegie's popularized social skills training program, *How to Win Friends and Influence People*.

The authors describe their program this way,

> The form of social skills training that we recommend is different, in practice, from the procedures developed by some others, but the basic idea is usually the same. That is that patients or others deficient in skills can be taught directly a new and more socially accepted repertoire of skills, which will enable them to influence their environment sufficiently to attain basic personal goals. This *training* approach stands in contrast to other therapies, aimed at eradicating or inhibiting maladaptive behaviour or symptoms, or changing underlying neurotic defences or conflicts. Training does not preclude these other approaches, and our purpose is partly to explore fruitful combinations. (Trower, Bryant, & Argyle, 1978, p. 5)

The Livermore group align their program with other forms of didactic therapy as described by Authier, Gustafson, Guerney, and Kasdorf (1975) in "The Psychological Practitioner as a Teacher: A Theoretics-Historical and Practical Review,"

> The educational model means psychological practitioners seeing their function not in terms of abnormality (or illness)—diagnosis—prescription—therapy—cure; but rather in terms of dissatisfaction (or ambition)—goal setting—skill teaching—satisfaction (or goal achievement). (Authier *et al.*, 1975, p. 31)

This didactic model is, of course, in line with the integration model used in this book, the difference being that in functional therapy the need for an accompanying disintegration model and techniques related to handling reintegration processes is specified. (See also Brown, 1971; Jones, 1968; Nyberg, 1971.)

Session 29—Relationships

I. Visit
    A. Begin by welcoming your client into this new phase of the program. Remind him or her that this second phase will be

Relationships

dealing with life areas, whereas phase one dealt more with personality dynamisms. Now the dynamisms will be applied.

B.   Spend some time informally visiting with your client. Ask: "How do you feel today?" "What was your day like?" Follow each question with either a clear response or another question.

II. Theme

    A.   Remind your client that this month you will be working on his or her relationships—ask which relationship he would like to get help with today.

    B.   After you have established an area/relationship to work with, allow your client a little bit of time to talk with you about it.

III. Direction

    A.   "This month we will be working with the life area of *relationships*. A relationship is primarily two or more individuals *relating*. The emphasis is on the relating (the verb) not on the state of being related, such as your brother, your uncle, your mother, your son, etc. (the noun). You have, so far, learned the key dynamics to understanding and changing your life. This month you will learn specifically how to apply those dynamics to your life of relationships."

        1.   Ask your client to pick his primary relationship. Who is it with?

        2.   Next, you are going to help your client evaluate how well he relates dynamically with that person.

            (a)   Do this by filling out the analysis graph on the board.

            (b)   Instruct him or her to rate (1–5) each of the five dynamisms regarding this particular relationship.

            (c)   Take a look at the form he or she just filled out.

            (d)   Point out places on the form where he or she appears to be "off balance."

    B.   Now, discuss the concept of being *in tune*. "Being in tune simply means that your five dynamisms are all in balance—or are on the same line in the graph. It doesn't matter if all of your dynamisms fall on line five or on line one. What does matter is that you are in tune with yourself. If you rated some of your dynamisms high, and some low, then we have a good indication that you are not functioning at your fullest. What we want to do for you is to give you a "tuning-up" on your

---

8   **Month**

dynamisms so that they are in balance and you then can function at your optimal potential."

    1.   "This means different adjustments for different people. Some people may talk your head off, but make no eye contact or no physical contact at all. Other people may have a true understanding of their relationship, but not be able to feel any love or compassion. Still other people may have deep feelings of love for their partner but never express it. Consider the professional ballplayer who relates beautifully to his fellow teammates, but doesn't feel close to his wife; or the doctor who relates perfectly with his patients, but has no personal friends of his own. Both these people are doing a lot of things right—what is needed are some 'fine tune-ups.' "

    2.   "Today we will make some fine tuning adjustments for you so that your life can be happier."

IV.   Exercise: "Tuning Up"

    A.   Have your client continue talking about his particular relationship.

        1.   Now, ask your client to role-play in that relationship. (Have him talk to his "partner" as if he was in the room. Be sure your client is relating to his or her "partner" in the usual way, with his or her usual amount of expression, activity, clarity, contact, and feeling.)

            If your client does not want to do this, or does not want to talk about a relationship, you can work on his relationship with *you*. Follow this same exercise.

        2.   Have your client tell you which of his dynamisms are high and low. (Then you must make the decision either to raise the low dynamisms up to the high ones or to lower the high ones down to the low ones. Whichever you choose, you want *all* the dynamisms to be on the same level.)

        3.   Now, tune up the dynamisms you are going to work with.

           (a)   Have your client help you with the tuning up according to his prior understanding of the five dynamisms.

           (b)   Allow your client to role-play with you so that he can practice on you and you become the "partner."

Relationships

4. Examples of tuning up:
   (a) Tuning up expression: You may have your client speak louder, or speak fuller, or speak faster, etc., or you may have him speak softer, or slower, or in a different tone, etc.
   (b) Tuning up activity: You may have your client move his or her arms more, or walk around the room, or reach out and touch, etc., *or* use fewer gestures, or slower pacing, or uncross his or her legs, etc.
   (c) Tuning up clarity: You may have your client admit what he or she knows, such as "I love you" or "I want to talk more with you" or "I need you," etc., *or* you may have him or her admit what he or she fears, such as "I feel bad," or "I'm dissatisfied," or "I hurt myself when I don't talk," etc.
   (d) Tuning up contact: You may have your client reach out and grab hold, or shake hands, or look into your eyes, *or* you may have your client make some emotional contact by talking from his or her feelings so that you can feel him or her, etc.
   (e) Tuning up feeling: You may have your client admit and share his feelings by saying, "That hurts me," "I feel sad," "I'm angry," etc., *or* you may have your client express his or her feelings by saying "I want you," "I'm lonely," "I want more," etc.

B. Once you have tuned up your client with his or her assistance, and he or she has all the dynamisms on one level, practice this new way of relating. Help him or her to enjoy it.
C. Conclude the exercise by taking an awareness break. Have your client tell you what he or she notices. Any sensations? Thoughts? Worries? Awkwardness?

V. Closing
A. Ask your client to be more aware of being "in tune" with relationships this week.
B. Close with a feeling of success for phase two of the program and be sure to instill hope for the future. Let the client expect that change is possible.

---

8 Month

Session 30—Relationships and Satisfactions

In this session simply apply the Bradburn Affect Balance Scale used in Session 28 to the life area of relationships. Then give the client a chance to talk about and express feelings about different relationships and how they might be made more satisfying. Use methods from standard Session 2. For homework give the client the Social Situations Questionnaire (which is reproduced in the Appendixes) to complete and bring to the next session. This questionnaire was developed for use in the Livermore Hospital program and will provide a self-assessment of the client's social skills and social deficiencies. The therapist should complete the Social Behaviors Rating Scales for the client before the next session (consult the Appendixes).

Session 31—Relationship Images and Behaviors

This session focuses on helping the client to make specific changes in how he or she relates to other people. The session uses another client or a cotherapist as a target person for the client's efforts to make changes. The particular technique applied is the bug-in-the-ear technique which has been used in training teachers and counselors, (Flanders, 1970) and in the Livermore program (see Trower *et al.*, 1978, p. 79). The method, under the name of "the Cyrano technique" is also under investigation by the social psychologist Stanley Milgram (see Colligan, 1980). If available, it is also very valuable to use videotape recordings and the client can observe how he or she was able to make relationship changes during the session. The bug-in-the-ear method uses an ear microphone inserted in one of the client's ears so that he can be given coaching instructions by the therapist during the role-playing part of the session. The most frequent difficulty that clients have in making changes in their relationship behaviors is that events happen so quickly they cannot think of what to do or say. By giving direct, simple instructions for change the therapist can, in effect, *be* the new model for the client. Milgram has found that the "Cyrano effect" works so effectively in many instances that people who do not know the role players are wearing a bug do not notice anything artificial in their actions.

Relationship Images and Behaviors

I. Introduction

Begin by reviewing the client's social situations questionnaire. Give client plenty of time to talk about situations that provoke anxiety. Then pick out one target situation that can be role played.

B. Explain the bug-in-the-ear procedure: "All you have to do is follow some of the directions I'll give you for talking and moving. You'll be surprised at how easy it is. Let yourself notice what it is like to do and say things that are different for you. You won't be asked to do anything that is embarrassing or painful."

II. Procedure One

A. Introduce the client to the role-playing partner by using the bug-in-the-ear method to guide the meeting. (This procedure works best if the therapist can view the client and the client's partner through a one-way viewing screen, but if that is not available simply use a large room. Arrange the client and partner in one corner of the room and give directions from the far corner, beyond the direct hearing range.)

B. Therapist: "Many of the difficulties that people have in relationships are concerned with starting and maintaining conversations. Some can't start, some people can't think of things to say once started, some feel nobody wants to listen to them. So we will begin by having you meet someone new. You will start, maintain, and end a short conversation. First, I'll explain the steps involved, then I'll demonstrate those steps, and third I'll ask you to try it out and I'll guide you through the earphone. Then we'll talk about your experiences."

C. Then explain the steps:
1. Say hello to the person.
2. Tell the person your name and listen for his or her name.
3. Ask two questions.
4. Answer any questions.
5. Close the conversation.

D. Demonstrate the steps with the role player so the client can look on.

E. Then guide the client through a short five-minute conversation.

 Month

    F.   Discuss the experience with the client. Have the role player give the client feedback. If videotape feedback is available, play back the taped exchange.

III. Procedure Two

    A.   Repeat the above procedure but target another specific social situation. A good second step is to target "Getting Information About the Other's Feelings and Attitudes."

    B.   Therapist: "We often need to know what people feel and believe and we can do this by observing how they respond and by checking our impressions of them."

    C.   "Next I'd like you to role play attending a party in which one of the guests you notice looks depressed. I'll demonstrate."

    D.   Therapist goes through demonstration; client observes.

    E.   "O.K., it's your turn. I'll guide you at times to try out changes."

    F.   Guide the client through a longer role-playing period of 10 to 15 minutes.

    G.   Go back over the situation and give the client feedback; listen to your client's account of how it was for him or her to try out new styles of expression.

IV. Closing

    A.   Tell the client to keep a record of meetings with new people in his or her Therapy Notebook and of meetings with acquaintances or friends in which new things were tried.

    B.   "Be sure to include: number of attempts, number of successes, a description of what happened, and any guidepoints you used in changing your image and actions."

    C.   Among the several very good popular books on social skills learning that can be recommended to clients, two outstanding ones are: Edrita Fried's *Active/Passive: The Crucial Psychological Dimension* (1971) and Philip Zimbardo's *Shyness: What It Is and What to Do About It* (1977).

Session 32—Relationship Images and Behaviors

Session 32 simply repeats the procedures of Session 31, but targets different relationship behaviors. This procedure can be repeated as often as necessary depending upon the client's needs and responsiveness to

---

Relationship Images and Behaviors

the exercise. (The bug-in-the-ear procedure is especially good for use in groups in which clients can take turns role-playing and the group as a whole can give feedback about the practice sessions.)

Month Nine—Sex

The month planned for talking about the client's sex life is not "sex therapy" in the sense of a treatment of sexual dysfunctions. For the small percentage of clients who do have definite sexual problems a special program should be designed along the lines recommended by specialists such as Kaplan (1974) and Masters and Johnson (1966), or the therapist can make a referral to such a program. The focus of month nine is on developing sexual fitness—that is, on optimizing the client's sexual satisfactions through personality exercises and through understanding the way personality dynamisms affect sexuality.

The number one difficulty most clients have with sex revolves around desire. People lose interest and excitement in sex in the same way that zest and fulfillment are lost in work, play, relationships, and other life areas. This loss occurs when old images of sexuality do not give way to new images that allow for fuller and more subtle expressions of feeling. Understood in this way sexual difficulties can be approached as problems of intimacy and feeling-fulness, not as special symptoms.

In a survey conducted by Pietropinto and Simenauer for their book *Husbands and Wives* (1979) only 11% of the couples said they were significantly unhappy in their sex life; nearly 40% rated it "very good," 40% "satisfactory-to-good," and 11% called their sex lives "variable."

In 1977, an extensive and sophisticated survey study of 1,990 American men (ages 18 to 49) was conducted by Louis Harris (1977) that was commissioned by *Playboy* magazine. The survey found some important trends in the American males' attitudes toward sexuality that were at odds with the "playboy image." For example: Married men expressed greater sexual satisfaction with their lives than single men; three out of four respondents said they considered sexual fidelity for both males and females to be "very important" for success in a marriage; asked their reasons for marrying 74% specified "having another person to share one's life." These statistics suggest that intimacy comes first and if a

   Month

couple's life together is close and exciting and satisfying their sexual life also will be.

In a survey of 500 psychiatrists in their thinking and observations about the most common cause of lack of interest in sex for their clients 45% picked preoccupation and fatigue, 36% lack of love or attraction in the relationship, and 15% mentioned inadequate parental love (cited in *Sexuality Today*, 1979).

The sessions that follow are designed with the preceding statistics and observations in mind. Clients are taught that sexuality is a part of their lives that requires the same kind of psychological fitness efforts as other parts.

Session 33—Sex

I.   Greeting
   A.   Greet your client by his or her first name. Shake hands.
   B.   Be friendly and enjoy yourself.
II. Visit
   A.   Ask your client "How was your week?" "Did your last session help you in any way?" "Did you notice any difference in your relationships?"
   B.   Respond to each answer with either a clear response or another leading question. Follow through on your questions.
   C.   Do not confront the client's resistances. Identify them and engage them with your questions.
   D.   Gain a clear picture of your client's week.
   E.   Allow your client the pleasurable experience of talking to you.
III. Problem or issue presentation
   A.   Today you will be working on your client's *sexual fitness.*
   B.   "I am going to ask you some feelingful and pertinent questions regarding your sex life. Allow yourself to feel awkward and vulnerable as you answer them. Let yourself have the experience of talking to me and the experience of being talked back to by me."
IV. Exercise: "Sexual fitness checklist"
   A.   Take out your psychological fitness checklist. Turn to the sexual fitness checklist.

Sex 33

       1.   Read the first question on the checklist; after your client answers it, follow it up with the corresponding questions from today's program.

B.   Spend approximately five minutes on each question.

C.   Make contact with your client as you relate to him or her.

D.   Encourage your client to talk to you and to open up to you when answering questions. Be sure to help your client feel safe and accepted by you.

E.   Begin by reading the first question of the sexual fitness checklist and then follow up by reading the corresponding questions listed below:

       1.   What do you enjoy sexually? Do you enjoy oral sex? Anal sex? Various positions? Kissing? Holding? Talking? Touching? Foreplay?, etc. What could you do to enjoy more? Do you enjoy giving? Getting? Asking? Being asked?

          (a)   Discuss these choices with your client.

          (b)   Help your client feel. Make contact.

          (c)   Take an awareness break. Help your client notice any shifts or changes going on inside. Support his or her vulnerability.

       2.   How often do you have sex? What do you do in order to have sex as often as you want? What do you do in order to have *less* sex than you want? Take an awareness break. Help your client notice and share any feelings, thoughts, or sensations he or she is experiencing.

       3.   Do you have any secret thoughts you've never been able to say? What limits do you use to keep yourself from saying your secret thoughts? What beliefs do you have about those limits? Would you like to make yourself more vulnerable by saying more secret thoughts?

       4.   Take an awareness break. Educate your client to what he or she is experiencing inside himself or herself. This is an important part of the session, teaching that *new* talking brings *new* feelings.

       5.   What feelings do you experience during sex? What feelings do you censor during sex? What are your reasons for censoring your feelings? Would you like to express

 Month

more during sex? Take an awareness break. Help your client experience his or her own awkwardness and discomfort. Make contact with the client.

6. What is the quality of your sex life? What is a typical sexual experience like for you? How long does it last? How would you change it? Take an awareness break. What thoughts, feelings, sensations, worries, and fears is your client experiencing? Help him to *enjoy* it.

7. How often would you like to have sex? Do you think sex should be on a regular basis? Do you believe you have sex too often? What are those beliefs? Do you believe you don't have sex often enough? What are those beliefs? Take an awareness break. Help your client to talk about his or her choices. Help your client see that there is always a choice.

8. Tell me all the beliefs you have about sex. Heterosexuality? Oral sex? Anal sex? Homosexuality? etc. Tell me the beliefs you have about *you* sexually. Encourage your client to speak freely. Support and encourage the client. Help him or her maintain a vulnerability. Congratulate your client.

9. What *were* your beliefs about sex? Heterosexuality? Oral sex? Anal sex? Homosexuality? etc. What *were* your beliefs about yourself sexually. Support and encourage your client. Help him or her to be vulnerable.

10. Express how you feel about sex. Satisfied? Dissatisfied? Be specific. Help your client to express fully his or her thoughts and feelings about being satisfied and/or dissatisfied with sex. Help him or her to raise his or her own feeling level with full expression.

11. What specific sex skills do you know? What general skills do you have to make and keep a satisfying sex life? What new skills are you learning that will help you enjoy a satisfying sex life? Finish with one more awareness break. Help your client to notice and share all that he or she is experiencing inside—feelings, fears, thoughts, worries, sensations, etc.

Sex 33

12. Additional questions: Are you meeting your *own* sexual needs? Which ones? How are you meeting them? Are you getting what you want sexually? What *do* you want? What are you getting?

V. Closing

A. Ask your client to be more aware of his or her sexual fitness this week.

B. Ask him or her to think about what life would be like if sexual needs and wants were satisfied more fully.

C. Close with a feeling of hope for the present and for the future.

D. For some clients, assign *The Joy of Sex* (Comfort, 1972) or a similar sex manual to give more information about sex; another valuable book is *A New Look at Love* (Walster, E. & Walster, G.W., 1978).

Session 34—More Sex

For most clients, the questions and feelings raised by the previous session will provide ample material for a follow-up session. Simply do a standard session, with a focus on feeling moments and new sexual images.

The session reproduced below shows how the functional approach can be applied to work with couples. (It is, of course, often desirable when doing these sessions on sex to bring in the client's spouse or steady sexual partner.) The couple in this session are instructive for clinicians because, as often happens, they had many sexual complaints and worries, but their real problems were general relationship difficulties, not specific sexual dysfunctions.

Session Sample

Jeff and Peggy are being seen conjointly at the request of Peggy. She and her husband are "bored with each other." They increasingly blame each other for the lack of feeling and excitement. They wonder whether they really still love each other. They frequently flare up and fight over incidental matters. Their agenda for this session was to "get some things off their chests and try to clear the air."

  Month

T: Hi, Peggy.

P: Hi. This is my husband, Jeff.

T: Hello, Jeff. It's good to have you here. Why don't you two sit down right over here.

T: I know the two of you have felt some tension and you have said that you have felt like you have trouble communicating.

J: Yeah. It's like we are trying to talk to each other, but all we have are little nags or fights or something. She's always telling me she wants me to talk to her but . . . I don't know . . .

T: You don't know what's missing even though you're trying.

J: Right. I mean I still want to try. We wouldn't come here today if we didn't, but it's like we lost something.

P: Well, I don't feel anything missing, except that he doesn't talk to me.

J: That's ridiculous. What is the use of talking to you when all that happens is that I am wrong about something?

T: O.K. Now, is this the kind of talking that is typical?

J: Yes.

P: Uh huh, this is what happens.

T: And this is how it feels between you a lot, too? So let's try this. We can get back to what's wrong, but let's see if there is anything right. Move your chairs closer . . . right, very close so that your knees are touching. Haven't been this close for a while, huh? *(Both laugh.)* Now take a look at your partner. Right, look right at them. That's a little hard to do, huh? Maybe that's as far as we will get today . . . *(Both laugh again, shyly and uncomfortably.)*

T: Right, now just while you are looking, just listen to my voice. You both have been through a lot together. You have known each other for nearly nine years. That is a long time. That face is very familiar to you and very special . . . more than any other. For the next 60 seconds or so I would like you just to think of some things that you appreciate about the person sitting across from you . . . things that you really know about them, things they do or the way they are that you appreciate. Just think about it, and keep looking for the next minute. *(Silence.)*

T: O.K., Jeff, I would like you to start. Just say some of those things that you thought of about Peggy, and I would like you to say it just like this: "I appreciate   ," and you fill in the blank. Got it?

J: Uh, O.K. Peggy, I appreciate, uh I appreciate that you really have encouraged me all the time I've been on the job. Even when I wanted to quit you really told me I could do it. I really appreciate that. And I appreciate how you look and how well dressed you are and I appreciate the way you take care of the house and the kids.

More Sex 34

T: Great. That's just right. Now, what happened, Jeff, what impact did those words have?

J: She's crying.

T: Right, but does she look sad?

J: No. She looks happy.

T: Right. Whose words made her happy?

J: I did.

T: O.K. Peggy, what was it like to hear those words?

P: I . . . it was wonderful!

J: But she knows I think that about . . .

T: That's true, Jeff, but to hear the words makes a difference. O.K., Peggy, you say some things to Jeff the same way.

P: I appreciate that you are a kind man. I appreciate the way you treat me and include me when we are with your friends. I appreciate the way you treat the kids. I appreciate how hard you work. I really appreciate . . . *(crying)* . . . how you have been my friend all these years.

J: *(Visibly moved)* I appreciate you too, Peggy.

T: Just keep looking at each other . . . just hold on to the feeling each of you have right now. It isn't missing or gone. It's right there. Its just important to talk and affect each other like you have to remember that feeling.

T: Now, I want you to say some even deeper kind of appreciation. You know, people who are close to each other appreciate even each other's weaknesses . . . the little struggles our partner has. You know, like their shyness or their fear to speak in front of a group or give a speech or something about their body. Those aren't usually things you appreciate out loud but let's do that today. Just take another 60 seconds to think about it. *(Silence.)*

T: O.K. Jeff, you start again and just use that same kind of voice.

J: I appreciate . . . well, I appreciate the trouble you have with your weight . . . and how you really try with your diets and your exercise and that you worry about how people think you look. *(Takes a deep breath.)*

T: O.K. Peggy, what was that like?

P: Oh, I thought he was going to say something that would really hurt my feelings. I appreciate that, Jeff. I really do. I have always thought you think I am crazy or something, or you wished you had someone else that looks better. It makes me feel so different that you . . . *(starts to cry)* . . . really appreciate what it is for me.

T: O.K. Peggy, your turn.

P: Jeff, I appreciate the way you feel when you take people out from the office to entertain. I've known since we were in school how shy you are socially and how you hate it, and I appreciate you when you go out like that and

 Month

we are there and you are making conversation to make the business. I really appreciate that.
J: Thanks.
P: Jeff, and I appreciate your way with your Mom and her drinking. I appreciate how tough that has been for you all your life.
T: Those are wonderful words, Peggy. You can see that you affected him and moved him with what you said. For the two of you this is a good start. What I would like is for you to start off and do this appreciation exercise every day until we meet next week. Don't change anything else. Just do this for five minutes each day. All right? Any questions?

Comments

Although the therapist never talked about sex with these clients, their sex life improved very much. They were able to carry over the feeling and excitement of talking together and sharing feelings into their sexual life.

Session 35—Sexual Images

I.   Goals: to have the client reevaluate old images of sexuality and consider new images.
II. Instructions
  A.   "Today we will look specifically at your images of yourself as a man (woman)."
  B.   "I want you to complete these ten sentences:

     "Sexually I am . . ."
     "I like sex when . . ."
     "I don't like sex when . . ."
     "I fantasize about sex being . . ."
     "I most like sex when . . ."
     "For me sex is . . ."
     "I feel sexiest when . . ."
     "The worst sex is when . . ."
     "My sexual goal is . . ."

Sexual Images   35

    C.   "Good, now I'd like you to make a sexual map of yourself. Draw on this big sheet of paper with different colored inks your different sexual personalities. Draw in the lines between them what they think of one another."

Note: This kind of internal sociogram is often useful in defining images and can be used for other life areas.

    D.   Take an awareness time period. Explore with your client any feelings that have emerged. If necessary, work with defenses.
    E.   Next, tell your client to consider these questions:

"Who taught my old sexual images to me?"
"What do I like about my old images?"
"What do I dislike?"
"How might I like to change?"
"What new images are possible?"

III. Follow-up
    A.   Suggest to your client that he or she try out some new features of a new sexual image this week. Pick something simple and nonthreatening.
    B.   Instruct client to write up one sexual experience in his or her Therapy Notebook just as though recording a dream. Bring it to the next session.

Session 36—Images and Feelings

Do a standard functional therapy session following up on the homework. Allow client to talk fully about the recorded sexual experience and explore feeling moments. Also, at some point show client how certain of his or her sexual images go with certain levels of expression, feeling, clarity, activity, or contact.

Month Ten—Play and Recreation

This month follows the same general format as the preceding ones: the client self-evaluates his or her fitness in the life area, new goals are

 Month

considered along with old and new images, the client's play profile is evaluated in terms of the personality dynamisms. Additionally, this is a good time to take up the whole question of what part rest, relaxation, and recreation can and should have in the client's life. Session 38 reviews relaxation techniques to make sure that the client has some method that he or she can rely upon.

Session 37—Play and Recreation

I. Visit.
II. Introduce theme by going over the client's psychological fitness survey for the play area. Talk about each question and answer with the client. Look for feeling moments and work with them.
III. Use the board to go over your client's dynamism profile for play. Talk about the low and high personality dynamisms. How much satisfaction does the client get from this life area? What styles or images does he or she use?
IV. Closing
  A. Tell client to try out some new kind of play activity and write about it in the Therapy Notebook.
  B. For next time have client bring in the sports pages and the leisure and entertainment section of the Sunday newspaper.

Session 38—Goals in Play

Play and recreation can include everything from ballet to bowling, from watching a boxing match to going out to dinner to acting in a play. In his book *The Three Boxes of Life (and How to Get Out of Them)* Richard Bolles (1981) argues that people are less willing in modern times to put off play and recreation until retirement. The modern trend is to mix work, play, and social relationships and to search for a career that allows a satisfying combination of all three life areas. This session is intended to explore how successfully clients integrate play and recreation into their weekly activities.

Goals in Play 38

I.   Begin by talking with the client about how it was for him or her
     to try a new recreational activity. Listen. Respond with questions
     and comments. Get a clear understanding of the client's experience.
II. Next, go through the newspaper with a pair of scissors. Clip out
     the stories and pictures relating to "things I like" and "things I
     don't like."
     A.   See if persistent images or roles emerge. For example, is the
          client always competitive and aggressive? Never? Does the
          satisfaction come from doing the activity or after the outcome?
     B.   Have the client construct his or her play and recreation weekly
          schedule for you. Ask "Is this the ideal schedule for you? What
          would you like to change? How would you need to be different
          to change your weekly schedule?"
     C.   If client has extremely negative images—"I can't play," "I'm
          not athletic," etc.—talk about how these images were devel-
          oped. How would the client need to change to develop new
          images?
III. Closing
     A.   Tell client to go through the telephone company's yellow pages
          and pick some new sports or recreational activity to try.
     B.   If client does not regularly schedule "play breaks" during the
          week have client use his or her "play schedule" that week.

Session 39—Relaxation

No client should complete therapy without acquiring at least one
technique of relaxation and a sense of how and when to use the technique. The relaxation techniques can range from napping to autohyp-
nosis, from hot baths to tank flotation, from mantra meditation to EMG
or EEG biofeedback training. What technique is used doesn't matter as
long as the client can use the procedure successfully to get a 15 to 30
minute time-out period from the regular routines of the day.

When the author was a college student he taught for two summers
at a swimming camp. The method used at that camp to teach beginners
how to swim was: *one* use a shallow pool where the swimmer could
stand up and *two*, teach a variety of swim techniques because each
swimmer would find some styles easier than others. (Some people who

  Month

could not swim at all on their stomachs would do very well immediately with the backstroke or sidestroke. Eclectic swimming!) Therapists should be sure to expose clients to a variety of relaxation techniques because it is not possible to predict in advance which ones will work for which client. (By *work* is meant not only that the client feels benefited by the technique but is willing to use the technique.)

I.   Visit with client about her or his experiences from the previous week.

II. Introduce theme

    A. "Everyone needs to be able to be fully active when they want to be and to be inactive and relaxed when they want to take some time out from the pressures of the day."

    B. "Do you use any regular method of relaxation?" Spend time talking about the widest possible range of relaxation techniques. Find out what works (if anything) and what does not work for your clients?

    C. Remind the client that some of the techniques the client has already learned, for example, free association, focusing, and centering, can be used as relaxation methods.

    D. Ask client "do you have an interest in learning a few new methods?" Mention a variety of techniques—visualization, mantra meditation, autohypnosis, autogenic training, progressive relaxation, breath counting, etc. Be prepared to teach the client several of these techniques. Pick at least two and teach the client the steps of the method.

III. Closing

    A. Tell client to schedule at least one 15-minute relaxation period every day. Try out the two techniques on alternate days.

    B. For client who benefits by reading, recommend one or more of the many popular books available on relaxation methods. A few suggested readings might draw from: M. Davis, Eshelman, and McKay's (1980) *The Relaxation and Stress Reduction Workbook* (this book covers almost all the techniques mentioned in II.D), Benson's *The Relaxation Response* (1975), Woolfork and Richardson's *Stress, Sanity and Survival* (1978), Page's *How to Lick Executive Stress* (1961), Ubell's *How to Save Your Life* (1976), Pelletier's *Mind as Healer, Mind as Slayer* (1977), Schutz's

---

Relaxation

Joy: Expanding Human Awareness (1967), Lilly's *The Deep Self* (1977), Clynes's *Sentics* (1978), and the classics by Jacobsen (1962) *You Must Relax* and Selye (1974) *Stress Without Distress.* These books represent a very wide range of viewpoints so the therapist should be prepared to relate the practices and ideas conveyed in them to the general themes of psychological fitness, particularly the fitness emphasis on taking responsibility for one's own positive level of health by developing a stress resistant personality and life style.

Month Eleven—Work

By and large, counselors are better trained to help clients with work problems than are many psychotherapists. Counselors learn about vocational and career guidance and about career and retirement planning; they are familiar with the career crises that often accompany adult stages of development. Psychotherapists may explore the psychodynamics of a client's work but do not talk about the practical details of how the client works, how satisfied or dissatisfied the client is at work, and what the client's short-term and long-term work goals are. From the functional viewpoint, both the inner dynamics and the specific work details are important to consider.

For younger clients who are still in school, this month's sessions can be refocused to apply to school work and career planning. For clients who are having special difficulties with this life area it would be useful to spend more time and take the client through a complete career planning interview such as those described in Bolles (1980) and Weiler (1977).

Session 41—Work

I. Introduction
    A. Introduce the topic for the month by asking client to take the work fitness section of the Psychological Fitness Inventory. Go over the client's answers in detail. Get specific.

Month

    B.   Ask client to come up with several trait labels that describe his or her work personality, for example, "successful," "hard-working," "lazy," "focused," etc.

II. Procedure
    A.   Ask client to diagram his or her typical dynamism profile at work. Discuss highs and lows.
    B.   Role play with client. Be a fellow worker or boss. Have client do one-up–one-down exercise.
    C.   Take time for focusing. What does the client experience when going up? going down?
    D.   Ask client "What would be the consequences for you if you constantly elevated your 'at work' personality profile?"
    E.   If appropriate, work with defenses and resistances that show up. Help client to feel the consequences and understand the long-term effects of the resistant activity.

III. Closing
    A.   Ask client to write about one incident at work in Therapy Notebook and bring next time.
    B.   Have client think of work slogans that capture his or her positive images about work, such as "Plan ahead," "When the going gets tough, the tough get going," or "If you think education is expensive, try ignorance."

Session Sample

The following session illustrates how a therapist can work with a general personality characteristic (in this case, passivity) that detrimentally affects several areas of a client's life (work, sex, and friendships for this client). This particular client was so extremely unassertive that he had allowed a friend to stay with him for a week, and nine months later the friend and the friend's girl friend still were living in his front room. What the therapist does in this session might be labeled assertion training but, in functional therapy, it fits within the general process of counteractively working with a negative image.

Bob is a young man in his early twenties. He works at a steady paying but monotonous job. Friendly, engaging, and easy to get along

Work   41

with, he has many friends at the beach and at the bars he hangs out in during his time off from work. He has been unable to form a solid relationship with a woman. He has been increasingly bored with his job and sees his life as going nowhere. He is drinking more and more. His parents are very disappointed and frustrated that he has not formed the career, home, and life-style appropriate to the upper middle-class expectations he was raised in. Depressed, bored, and unhappy, he entered therapy in order to "find some kind of direction."

T: Hi, Bob.
C: Hi.
T: You sound tired.
C: Yeah. I'm working the night shift now, 11 to 7. I am kind of spaced out today.
T: Spaced out?
C: Yeah . . . you know, not really here. I always feel like this when I change shifts.
T: How did you do with your homework?
C: Oh, great *(smile)*.
T: Oh.
C: Yeah, really great . . . I mean I called up the guy and he says he'll call me back this week. He really wanted to have me, I think. I think I can get the job.
T: That is terrific. You did a great job.
C: Yeah, I think so too. I am even going to call him up this week. I'm not waiting, like you said . . .
T: What is it?
C: Uh, oh yeah, well . . . I . . . you know my roommate Gary?
T: Yes.
C: Well, he has a girl friend and he . . . well, they sleep in my living room and they are there a lot of the time.
T: How do you mean?
C: It was just temporary at first. He needed a place to stay until he could find something. You know, maybe a week or a month, but now he's been there about eight months.
T: Not so temporary.
C: No, not so temporary *(laughs)*.
T: O.K. Let's look at this on the graph and start you learning how to use this on your own. If you were going to score yourself on the expression, activity, feeling, clarity, and contact scales how would you look?

 Month

C: (*Marks in the graph as he sees himself functioning in the situation.*) It's an expression problem.

T: How?

C: Well, I am clear about what I want . . . and I am sure that I am uncomfortable. I am not talking to him and not making any contact.

T: Right. What are you doing?

C: Well, I am being friendly on the outside . . . (*laughs*) and that's usual, but I am really tense and uptight inside.

T: All right, let's just be as friendly as possible . . . just the absolute best friendly guy ever. Get a big smile on your face . . . force it as big as possible. Now, just be as friendly as you can for two minutes, O.K.? Now give me that cushion behind you . . . gee thanks, and the one next to you . . . thanks, and that one and that one. (*Therapist keeps taking cushions until client is sitting on bare couch very uncomfortably.*) "Thanks, Bob."

C: Hey.

T: Hey.

C: I don't have anything to sit on.

T: Thanks for the cushions . . . you know you are sure a good guy.

C: (*Silent.*)

T: Keep smiling, Bob. You don't look friendly that way. Force it.

C: (*Smiling, but straining and upset.*)

T: Right, just keep that smile on no matter what, Bob. Bob?

C: Yeah?

T: Hold this cushion for me will you . . . and this one, and this one (*piles cushions up.*) Thanks.

C: Hey! Hey, these are heavy.

T: Right, but you know, just keep smiling.

C: Hey . . . Hey, I don't like this.

T: What? I can't hear you.

C: I don't like this (*very loudly*)!

T: So?

C: I don't like it and I am dumping them.

T: But what about me, Bob?

C: (*Still holding the cushions.*)

T: Thanks, Bob. I knew I could count on you.

C: Goddamn it, shit! (*Drops cushions.*) (*Very angry . . . sucks in a deep breath near crying.*) I hate that!

T: (*Steps in close.*) What, Bob? Tell me again.

C: I hate that (*crying and angry*)! I hate this shit of being the nice guy. Goddamn it!

T: You don't sound friendly.

Work

c: No, I don't feel friendly, I'm pissed *(shouting)*! I don't want this friendly shit.

t: No, you don't want it, do you? No, because what happens?

c: I don't get anything . . . I get tense. I want that guy out . . . out of my house. I can't believe it . . . I want to live in my own house.

t: What kind of feeling do you have?

c: Angry.

t: And?

c: And loud.

t: And?

c: Strong . . . *(starts laughing and crying)* I am strong.

t: Right. O.K., now let's sit down over here for a minute. For the next week, for 5 minutes during the morning and again in the afternoon and in the evening . . . 15 minutes altogether . . . be the big smiling friendly guy. Really force it the way you did in here today. Notice the feeling and what you have to do and tell yourself. Then contrast that by saying things you like and dislike. You understand . . . it's like one of your old expression sessions.

c: Right.

t: O.K. I will see you next in three days, on Thursday. I liked seeing that strength today.

c: Me, too.

t: Bye, Bob.

Session 42—Work

For Session 42 do a standard therapy session focusing on feeling moments; use the work incident from the client's notebook as content. If time permits, go over several incidents. See if client can come up with new slogans to describe his or her new work style.

Session 43—Work Images

In this session do another standard session but focus on new and old work images. Help the client understand how choosing or not choosing has consequences.

     Month

Session 44—Work Goals

This session is set up as a group therapy session because it is often useful for a client to hear other people talk about their careers and career goals in order to put his or her own goals, problems, and feelings in perspective.

I.   Major theme: Work is a necessary and vital part of being an adult.
     Major goals: To educate clients about how to function in work.
II. Procedure
     A. Discussion
         1. "We will not be doing career advising today. We will be teaching you a new way to look at your career."
         2. "We are not telling you all to go out and get better jobs with more money. As you have already learned, we don't deal with generalities but with each individual. Each individual must decide what he wants to do for his career. What is most important is that people in this therapy begin to choose careers that fit into their lives rather than lives that fit into their careers."
     B. Exercise
         1. Pair up clients.
         2. "Discuss your work life—past, present, and future." Therapist will interfere and keep discussion realistic.
             (a) Help each patient to uncover his or her beliefs and attitudes about working and/or having a career.
             (b) Help each client uncover his or her secret "schemes" regarding that career. Stress that skills and action are the basic keys to a satisfying career.
         3. Hand out work schedule sheets. "Describe your work week on this schedule sheet."
             (a) "Discuss your weekly schedule with your partner. Does it fit your old or your new images?"
             (b) "Talk about how you would need to revise your weekly schedule to accomplish the goals and desires that go with new images."

Work Goals 44

    4.   "Write down your one-year, five-year, and ten-year career goals." (Pause.) "Now let's talk about them here." Have each client talk about his or her goals and get feedback from the other group members.

III.   Homework

    A.   "Revise your weekly schedule and your career goals based on what you've learned today. Remember that paper plans are always open to changes."

    B.   "Make a list of all the jobs you might want in your future and relate this list to your short- and long-term goals."

    C.   For clients who need special help in the time management assign a book on the subject, such as Lakein's *How to Get Control of Your Time and Your Life* (1973).

Month Twelve—Ending the Therapy

The termination of the therapy relationship may come before the 12th month or later, but whenever it occurs, it is desirable to spend several weeks before the last session making plans with the client and giving time for a review of the therapy experience. Some clients may decide to taper off their meetings with the therapist rather than stopping completely. Others may want to know that they can call on the therapist for emergency or follow-up sessions in the future. All of these possibilities should be considered and an informal, verbal agreement reached as to when and how the therapy will end. (A reminder: The therapist should be sure to fill out a termination report following the last session, mentioning the informal agreement.)

Session 45—Reviewing the Therapy Experience

I.   Goals: to give the client time to reflect on his or her therapy experiences and to talk about personality changes.

II.   Instructions

    A.   Bring a polaroid camera to the session. (The camera is a useful therapeutic tool, it often can be introduced in month one and

Month

then the client and therapist can look at before and after photographs.)

B. Tell the client: "Let's talk today about what therapy has been like for you and how you've changed since we started together."

C. Take several photos of the client. Have the client take several photos of you. Pin the photos on the wall. Explain: "I'd like you to talk about 'Me Then' and 'Me Now.' What is different about you since you started therapy?"

D. Encourage client to talk about memories, thoughts, and feelings.

E. Make a list on the board (if this is not disruptive) under the columns "Me Then" and "Me Now."

F. Encourage client to talk about you. "Look at my photograph. How did you see me at first? and now?" Listen, respond.

G. Put photographs of you and the client close together. "We have a relationship, we're now part of each other's memory album."

III. Assignments

A. Tell client to continue to think about how he or she has changed. Write insights and feelings in Therapy Notebook.

B. Suggest to client that he or she begin thinking about what it will be like not coming for therapy regularly. "We'll talk about that the next time."

Session 46—Reviewing and Previewing

I. Goals: To continue the self-examination begun in the previous session and to talk specifically about leave-taking.

II. Visit with client about his or her previous week. Notice feelings and feeling moments.

III. Procedure

A. Put up photos on wall again. Ask: "Did you have any more thoughts or feelings about how you've changed?" "Did you have any more thoughts and feeling about our therapy relationship?"

Reviewing and Previewing

   C. Get specific about changes. Have client read excerpts from Therapy Notebook corresponding to the first month's sessions. Then read from recent entries. Ask: "Do you sound different?" "How?" Listen and reflect feelings. Give client your responses to the excerpts.
   D. More specifics. "If you charted a time log for your typical day in month one and your typical day now, how would they differ?" Help client generate the two time logs. Talk about the two schedules. "What is significantly different?"
   E. More specifics: Have client compare the dynamism profile he or she first charted with one done for "me now." What is different?"
   F. Lastly, ask "What thoughts and feelings have you had about ending the therapy?" Listen. Respond.
IV. Ending: Suggest that the client go back through the Therapy Notebook and pick out experiences and happenings that now seem especially important.

Session 47—Goals and Philosophy

   I. Major objective: Help client plan aloud about the future.
  II. Procedure
   A. Explain: "As we get ready to end the regular weekly therapy I'd like to hear what some of your goals are for the future. We've talked about a lot of your life and I know you've made changes, but I'm sure you have important goals we haven't talked about or maybe we did but now you are more definite about some things."
   B. Instruct client to list at least two short-range and two long-range goals (within one to three years and within five to ten years).
   C. Next, go through each goal with client covering: (1) an *inventory* of skills or personal chracteristics needed for attaining the goal, (2) the *actions* the person needs to take to reach the goal, and (3) *time lines* for the goals and the actions.
   D. Work with feeling–expression mismatches. Help person talk feelingfully and insightfully about these goals.

 Month

     E.   If client has omitted some goals in a life area you know they need to change or develop, ask "What about _____, what are your goals for that?" Work with these additional goals as in C and D.

III.   Ending: Tell client, "Next week will be our last regular meeting. Think about whether you have anything special to bring up then."

Session 48—Saying Goodbye

This session should be a standard functional therapy session focusing on the feelings that are involved in saying good-bye. Do not let the client get into fixed negative images of leave-taking. As much as possible, celebrate the successful completion of the therapy program. For most clients, convey the message, "You are moving on but I'm still available."

Afterword to the Manual

This manual section of the book includes many "how tos" of therapy with very few descriptions of the activity itself. It is like a book about how to scuba dive, without underwater photographs. Unfortunately, there are just not enough pages available to provide the long and detailed case studies and session transcripts, with commentaries, that would show the many wonders of the deep.

I hope that what is not deep will not appear shallow. The manual simply provides the methods and the structure for a therapeutic exploration that can be as full and human, as creative and lively, and as diverse, involving, and profound as each therapist and client can be.

Saying Goodbye   48

17

Extending the Manual
Creative Programming

There are several ways this manual can be effectively extended. First, simply by applying the manual as is to different clients, every therapist will develop a diversity of variations by responding to the experiences and problems different clients bring to the session exercises.

Second, by taking an open-minded eclectic attitude toward what he or she reads every therapist can find or adapt new techniques and new exercises. One interesting training exercise used with graduate students, postgraduate professionals, and paraprofessionals is this: Assign the students to consult four sources (the daily newspaper, a research journal, a clinical journal, and a book of history). The students try to develop a new exercise method from each source. Many trainee therapists are accustomed to believing that techniques are derived from theories or that they emerge, magically, from flashes of clinical intuition by brilliant therapists. It is a welcome relief for most of them to recognize that a wealth of potential therapeutic methods surround them at all times. All that is required is that they read and observe creatively, without setting up artificial boundaries about what is and is not relevant for therapeutic applications.

A third device is to apply one of the many manuals available for the training of counselors and psychotherapists (such as Egan's *Exercises in Helping Skills*, 1975) to clients. The training exercises in books such as Egan's are designed to teach therapists skills of listening and responding but can be applied equally well to clients.

	Concluding

A fourth device is to transcribe therapy sessions, one's own or sessions of another therapist who uses the manual, then do a written or oral commentary on the transcription and notice junctures where the techniques could be varied. An example of this procedure follows.

Transcription and Commentary

The following session would fit into the manual in Month 4 on Clarity. The commentary accompanying the transcription was added by the author to point out what the therapist and client were doing and what other possibilities might be considered. Readers going through this transcription can add their own commentaries. It will become evident that many branchings or possible directions of therapeutic work are present even in this very short therapeutic interaction.

T: Hi, Bob.
C: Hi.
T: How are you today?
C: Oh, O.K., I guess.
T: You guess?
C: Oh, yeah, well they are, or everything is going along at work pretty good, but I am worried about Carole *(his girl friend)*.

(**Commentary.** *The client introduces a topic of concern almost immediately. The therapist will follow up by getting more information.*)

T: How do you mean?
C: She, well I am not sure about this, but she seems kind of spaced out. You know, like she is there but not really there, but it might just be me too. I don't know.

(**Commentary.** *Notice that the client introduces not only content but shows in the style of his responses how the problem is bothering him. In other words, he performs the problem, in miniature, right there. In the next sentence the therapist introduces the focus point for the session and relates it to what the client has said.*)

T: You know today we will start a new part of your therapy, that is called clarity.
C: Sounds like a good idea *(laughing)*.
T: *(Both laughing)* Yes, it seems right on time, doesn't it? You remember that clarity is about knowing and sensing. Knowing and sensing the world around you and also the thoughts and feelings that occur inside you. Clarity is very

---

Extending Program □

important; it's not just about knowing things intellectually, it's also about being functional about what you know. If you knew everything there was to know and were not saying anything about it, then it's not functional. A functional clarity works for you. What do you think your "old" clarity style is, Bob?

C: Oh, humm, I don't know.

(**Commentary.** *Notice how quickly the therapist zero's in on the client's clarity style. It would have been possible to let the client go on, but then he might have become lost in the content. Here the therapist immediately makes the client aware of something he was not fully aware of before. This is counteraction; the therapist is making the client aware of a defense and soon will elaborate the counteractive work to help the client not only to notice the defense more clearly but also to feel it more intensely, recognize some of the consequences of this defensive style, and, finally, help the client start to change. He will very quickly move the client from counteracting the defensive image "I don't know" (which is a false image since, obviously, the client does know more than he says and acts upon) to proacting, that is, acting differently with the therapist. If the client were more resistant, the therapist might need to spend more time on helping the client recognize the defensive image as an image. For example, the therapist could tape record the client saying "I don't know" and play it back to him repeatedly. The therapist might even put the "I don't know" expression on a 30" tape loop and assign the client to listen to the tape loop at home for 15 minutes every day until he returned for another session. How long to stay with the counteraction phase is a decision that must be based upon the therapist's judgment of how able the client is to move outside the defensive image as opposed to staying inside the image.*)

T: Right.
C: What?
T: I said "right." Your old style is "I don't know."
C: I say that a lot.
T: Because?

(**Commentary.** *Notice that the therapist here asks the client to think about the reasons behind his own clarity style. In working with other dynamisms the therapist might have focused on the feelings connected with the image or on the expression, activity, or contact levels. Here, he very appropriately asks the client to make a cognitive response. This request, in itself, already moves the client away from the low level of clarity he was showing.*)

C: Well, because I am not sure.
T: So in your old clarity style you have to be *sure* before you can say anything. Let's write down some of the things that work as . . . or used to work

Concluding

as . . . advantages in this old "I don't know style." If you have to be sure before you say anything what will happen?

C: I won't make any mistakes or be wrong.

T: Right.

C: That way I won't get in any trouble.

T: Right. So it really works in some ways to "not know."

(**Commentary.** *The therapist helps the client acknowledge that at some times in his past this defensive image was functional. If the client were more attached to this image it might be desirable to explore some of the old feelings connected to it abreactively by soliciting specific childhood memories connected to the "I don't know" style of responding. In this instance, it did not seem necessary and the therapist made the judgment that it would be more valuable to help the client make specific changes in the present with his girl friend and at work, rather than to focus on the source of the defensive image in the past. Several months later, because this defensive image was a central one for this client, the therapist did extensively explore the historical source of the style and helped the client to release feelings that had been repressed in the past.*)

C: Well, it used to, but not now so much, I guess.

T: You guess?

C: (*Laughs*) Oh, I did it again!

T: Can you think of ways it does not work for you, ways it works against you to "not know"?

C: Yes. A lot of times I let things go and don't say anything to people when I really do know the answer. Or at work, at meetings I will have something to say about something, but I won't be sure and then later someone else will say it and get all the credit.

T: Those are good observations. That is good clarity.

(**Commentary.** *The therapist points out, correctly, that the client can function in a "I do know" mode contrary to the defensive image. The therapist could continue in this direction but, instead, chooses to help the client feel and recognize the old clarity style more intensely.*)

T: If you were going to rate that "old style" of clarity on a scale of one to five, how would you rate it, Bob?

C: About one.

T: O.K. Now let's see how that works. Just respond with that old style.

C: All right.

T: I am going to ask you questions. How are you?

C: I don't know.

Extending Program

T: How is Carole?
C: I don't know.
T: Do you like your job?
C: I am not sure.
T: What are you wearing?
C: I am not sure . . . I feel stupid.
T: What?
C: I feel stupid.
T: Are you stupid?
C: I don't know. I mean I always feel stupid.
T: It feels stupid inside you?
C: Yes.

> (**Commentary.** *Here the therapist has helped the client identify the feeling that often is tagged to this clarity style, "feeling stupid." At times the feeling may precede the style; at others the style elicits the feeling. But the result is the same, the client ends up not responding as effectively as he might and feels stupid. The therapist and client have here targeted the mediating feeling that will serve to alert the client in the future to when he is or is not functioning from within the old image. Notice that in the next exchange the therapist helps the client verbalize clearly the feeling of stupidity and thereby uses the feeling produced by the old image to go beyond the image. This is the paradox of working with defensive images. Once they are expressed, the conscious expression of the image becomes the way out of the image boundaries.*)*

T: Then just say this: "I feel stupid, I am sure about it."
C: I feel stupid. I am sure about it.
T: That is saying what you sense. You couldn't be smarter about what you know. Were you smart about that?
C: Yes, I was sure about that.
T: Do you think that something is bothering Carole? Do you sense something inside you that you are sure about?
C: Yes . . . Yes, yes! I am sure that there is something that is bothering her. I like that. I am sure about it.
T: Good. O.K., let's sit down over here again. You know that a functional clarity doesn't demand that you be right, Bob. You can be right from the inside just when you feel like there is something to say. I want you to start trying an exercise for clarity. It's called "I see and I sense." For example, (*pointing to client*) I see that you have a blue shirt. I see that you are looking at me. I see that you are smiling. I see that you are starting to blush. See how that works? I am just saying things that I see. It is a strong tool to do that. Just to see that saying things you observe is very strong. It affects people.
C: I could really feel that.

| | **Concluding** |

T: The other part, "I sense," is just what you sense or feel inside. I sense you like this. I sense you are excited about trying this out. You know what I mean . . . one is things you see outside, the other is what you sense inside. Both are very important in relationships. Even if you are wrong, at least you start something. You start a conversation.

(**Commentary.** *The therapist creates a special exercise designed simply to switch the client from an "I'm not sure" mode of functioning to an "I'm sure of what I see and sense" mode. He makes sure that the client comprehends intellectually and emotionally what he can do to offset the old image and gives him an assignment to try out the new style. It is important to give assignments and exercises that are sufficiently difficult to let the client experience an exercise affect when doing them, but not so difficult that the client is unable to experience success.*)

C: I like that. I can just start to say things.
T: Right. For your homework I would like you to practice saying at least three things that you see about people each day and three that you sense. O.K.?
C: O.K. I'll mark them in the journal to keep track.
T: Great. See you next week.

Even in this short edited transcription, many of the basics of functional therapy are visible: the therapist is working with both the past and the present defensive images and with emergent images; with both conscious and subconscious processes; and with feelings, thoughts, and expressions. The feeling moment is very quickly targeted, within the first 15 seconds of their meeting, when the therapist questions the client's expression "I guess."

Considering Theories as Instructional Sets

The problem with transcriptions such as these, especially when a commentary is added, is that they may make the therapeutic interaction seem much more plotted and planned than it actually is. The therapist in this example did *not* think to himself at each critical moment, "This is a feeling moment," "this is his old image," "now I will get him to recognize the defense," and so on. No, the therapist simply worked within the framework of functional theory and responded naturally and easily. A good theory of practice acts like an instructional set: the therapist is set to respond in certain ways but not in other ways and does

---

Extending Program

not need to reflect distractingly and deliberate before each response. If a person is given the set "tell me synonyms," he or she does not need to repeat "synonym," "synonym," "synonym" before every response. Similarly, a functional therapist uses the theory and the manual to set up his or her responses and is free, within this theoretical action set, to respond very quickly and completely.

Therapists whose theory of practice is not well specified are like subjects in an experiment who are given unspecified instruction sets: they must *decide* how to respond each time rather than simply responding. Therapists whose theory of practice is too narrow will respond quickly but the response often will not fit. They are like subjects who are told "say synonyms when you see a green light accompanying a word" but do not know what to do when a red light flashes.

One of the most important research and theoretical developments in the history of psychology was formulated in the late 1800s and early 1900s by Oswald Kulpe and his coworkers at the University of Würzburg. The Würzburg school conducted the first, and what are still the most detailed, experiments on the influence of instructional sets on mental contents and response tendencies. They established clearly that thoughts and responses could occur *without* the presence of sensory images. These experiments marked the first major shift from content psychology to functional psychology. Both the early gestalt theorists and the early functional theorists were strongly influenced by Kulpe, Mayer, Orth, Watt, Ach, Messer, Buhler, and the other Würzburg experimenters.

Unfortunately, not only have the Würzburg experiments not been revived and continued by modern cognitive psychologists but the possibility that theories of instructional sets could be used as paradigms for a theory of practice has never been appreciated. Any theory of therapy can be viewed as elaborate sets of instructions or "determining tendencies" that set up in the therapist an inclination to make one response rather than another and to notice one kind of happening rather than another. From this perspective, a theory is effective when it teaches therapists to notice and respond quickly to some events and to disregard others—and when those therapeutic responses bring about desirable changes in clients' personality functioning.

Exactly how general sets operate; how conscious and subconcious sets influence perceptions, thoughts, and actions; and how different levels of instructional sets can be established and altered are questions

Concluding

still very much open to investigation. What is exciting, here, is that advances in the functional study of consciousness and actions should relate directly to applications in therapy.[1]

Life and therapy are so complicated and rich and changeable that no theory of practice ever will be able to guarantee that the therapist can avoid making therapeutic responses that are too narrow or too slow or simply unhelpful, but the best therapeutic theories are at least self-correcting. By examining critical incidents where the theory and the manual did not provide adequate guidance, therapists should be able to expand and revise both their thinking and their practices. Practice does not make perfect; good therapeutic practice makes realists out of idealists.

---

[1] Consult Sahakian's (1975) *History and Systems of Psychology* (Chap. 6) for a thorough discussion of the Würzberg school. Also consult Humphrey (1951). A modern bio-humanistic theory that attempts to apply the idea of awareness of self-instructions to the modification of personality and consciousness is Lilly's *Programming and Meta-programming in the Human Bio-computer* (1968). Lilly states his approach in these terms: "This human computer has the properties of modern artificial computers of large size, plus additional ones not yet achieved in the nonbiological machines. This human computer has stored program properties and stored meta-program properties as well. Among other known properties are self-programming and self-metaprogramming" (Lilly, p. 3).

An approach that is related to Lilly's but draws more upon educational and training procedures, is Koberg & Bugnall's *The Universal Traveler, A Soft-systems Guide to: Creativity, Problem-solving and the Process of Reaching Goals* (1976). From counseling see Hutchins (1982) and Stum (1982).

From the behavioristic side, Meichenbaum's studies of "self-instructional training" also relate closely to the Würzberg tradition. However, Meichenbaum does not specifically discuss or credit the Würzberg school.

Sports psychologists are extremely interested in the study of instructional sets as are coaches and sports instructors. One approach to golf instruction that resembles Lilly's programming and meta-programming formulations is that of Kelley. In his book *The Golfing Machine* (1979) Kelley emphasizes, "It will be realized that *conscious* hand manipulation is indispensable in the learning process. . . . The Computer . . . is a built-in analyzer that everyone seems to have, though few are aware of it and even fewer use it and almost none of those use it consciously. It is a true computer. Information is fed into it which it will correlate and then adjust the mechanism to produce the intended result under the conditions at hand. . . . So every Stroke Component must also be correctly programmed. If the computer programming is neglected or erroneous—intentionally or unintentionally—it will make incorrect adjustments to mysteriously plague one's game" (Kelley, pp. ix, 226–227).

Extending Program

At any point in a therapy session where a therapist does not "know what to do" it means either: 1) that the theory does not provide therapeutic instruction for the phenomenon at hand or 2) that the therapist does not fully understand those instructions. In either case the theory, considered as a set of instructions, must be revised.

Notice that this approach to therapy research differs from the dominant approach which is to evaluate whether what therapists do has a positive effect on their clients. Such outcome research certainly has a place in the field but it gives very little information about the direct connections between what the therapist believes and what he or she does.

Philosophy and Therapy

It is hoped that the excerpts from actual sessions that were interspersed here and there throughout the manual showed that the instructions for each session were merely guidelines. It would be misleading if the format of a therapy manual (repetitive instructions, exercises, charts, and assignments) conveyed the impression that going for therapy is much like taking one's car in for a tune-up. (Although the metaphor of a personality tune-up is used explicitly in Session 29, therapy is much more complicated and involved than mechanical repair work.) Sometimes it helps the client to progress if the therapist talks *as though* therapy were nothing more than tuning up or exercising or planning or gaining new insights or releasing feelings, but the wise therapist knows that he or she is simplifying to achieve a short-term benefit.

At its largest, therapy is practical philosophy, an exploration of the nature of reality. (And even this metaphor can be turned back upon, viewed from a distance, examined, and criticized.) Awareness is not a stream, a flow, a process; nor is living a game, a biological survival test, an opportunity for self-development—these are all images and concepts *about* awareness and living.

Looking on therapy as practical philosophy and the process of therapy as acquiring a more functional sense of reality provides therapists with a very wide perspective for extending this manual (but it is only one among many possible and useful perspectives).

Every age has its favored metaphors. In Freud's time, biological and

Concluding

mechanical metaphors dominated thinking about therapy (hence the emphasis on adaptability and hydraulics of consciousness). In modern times the dominant metaphors came from information processing (hence the emphasis today on cognitive programming). The advantages of this modern emphasis are that it forces the therapist–programmer to give very precise, sequential instructions and to evaluate the effects of the instructions. The disadvantages are that the most effective kind of human programming may be meta-programming. Computers do not seem to have either ideas or ideas about ideas, but human beings have thoughts, feelings, images, and actions plus thoughts about thoughts, feelings about feelings, images about images, actions about actions, thoughts about feelings, and so on.

Eavesdrop on this scene for a moment: A young man and woman have just made love; for the young woman it is the first time since her husband was killed a year previously. The couple lounge in bed, talking idly and then the woman says, "I feel funny, it's like I'm outside myself." Man: "What's wrong?" Woman: "I don't know."

Her sense of reality has shifted slightly. She has simply experienced a closeness and fullness of feeling that she had shut herself off from. To bring the new feelings into self-awareness she must feel that she has been "outside herself." What does this common expression mean? How can people be "outside" or "out of touch" with themselves? These common expressions convey the realization that one's sense of reality is changing.

In his book *Man's Search for Meaning* (1962) Frankl approvingly quotes the German philosopher Nietzsche: "He who has a why to live can bear with almost any how (p. 164)." Therapy is an opportunity to construct a personal philosophy. The therapist is the companion in the dialogue; the client is the practical philosopher who seeks to formulate "whys" and "hows"—along with a number of "why nots" and "so whats."

Personality and the Sense of Reality

The point of intersection where philosophy and psychology must definitely cross is in each individual's sense of reality. A person's sense of reality is closely tied to his or her personality; this means that the continued development of one's sense of reality (the ability to know

---

Extending Program □

what is real and what is unreal and to use that knowledge) is linked to the development of personality. Without continued personal development, a person's sense of reality will be faulty and incomplete.

Every individual's sense of reality must begin with an accurate sensing of what he or she needs and wants and of the choices, actions, and images that fulfill those needs and wants. This sensing of needs and wants is closely connected with the ability to perceive feelings. The trying out of different expressions of feeling is a kind of fundamental reality testing; until a match is found between the experience and the expression of the experience the person will sense something lacking. The ability to check matches and mismatches of feelings/expressions is a fundamental means of forming personal reality.

This feeling-based sense of reality is intimately connected to the search for quality because it is the ground of self-directed awareness. The psychologist John Shotter, in *Images of Man in Psychological Research* (1975), states the argument this way:

> So it must not just simply be by the mere possession, but by the *quality* of the consciousness that he possesses that man distinguishes himself from all else that there is. And to the extent that he can modify or transform the quality of his own consciousness he can modify or transform himself (Shotter, p. 14). . . . Psychology is a *moral science of action* rather than a *natural science of behavior*. (Shotter, p. 23)

In his book *A Guide for the Perplexed* (1977) the philosopher-economist E. F. Schumacher states the same argument from a philosophical perspective:

> Man has powers of life like the plant, powers of consciousness like the animal, and evidently something more: the mysterious power "z." What is it? . . . This power z has undoubtedly a great deal to do with the fact that man is not only able to think but is also *able to be aware of his thinking*. Consciousness and intelligence, as it were recoil upon themselves. . . . This power z, consciousness recoiling upon itself, opens up unlimited possibilities of purposeful learning, investigating, exploring, and of formulating and accumulating knowledge. . . . As it is necessary to have word labels I shall call it *self-awareness*. (Schumacher, p. 17)

Schumacher goes on to identify four fields of knowledge that every human being must develop qualitatively. They are organized around four questions: What do I feel like? What do you feel like? What do I look like? What do you look like? This search for knowledge about the inner world of one's self and of others, and about how one appears in the outer world and what one actually observes in the outer world can

Concluding

never end. To stop refining one's self awareness and one's answers to any of these four questions is to lose one's sense of reality.[2]

There's an old story about a drunk found looking for his keys under a streetlight rather than in the darkness where he dropped them, who explained, "There's more light over here." Psychology is a sober subject and has managed to reverse the drunk's logic: The keys were dropped in the light and searched for in the darkness. In psychology's efforts to rid itself of ties with philosophy and religion, traditional concerns with self-awareness and morality often have been abandoned. Functional eclectic therapy aligns itself with these concerns and carries on the psychological-philosophical tradition of James and Dewey. Therapy is the search for self-awareness and right action.

Conclusion

Coming to the end of a long book is something similar to reaching the end of a long trip. No matter how fascinating the journey, the traveler is ready to stop lugging around the mental baggage and stay in one familiar place. This book has taken the reader to many times and places; many dialects of thought have been heard; and many people have been introduced. Some ideas and methods will have been new and strange, others, old and familiar. Whatever memorabilia the reader retains from this intellectual journey eventually will fade away and what will remain of value will be what each therapist decides to try out for himself or herself.

Therapists often are the most enthusiastic of empiricists. Jung's image of the alchemy of self-exploration fits many therapists very well— they search for golden transmutations amid every life experience. In the words of Bandler and Grinder, this book provides for *one* "structure of magic" (1975, 1976). It is desirable for therapy to have a definite structure; otherwise the therapist and the client become lost in their own illusions. But it is essential that the therapist and client both know that the struc-

---

[2]Many other modern philosophers recognize the centrality of feeling awareness and personal development (see, for example, Arendt, 1958; Boulding, 1956; Dubos, 1974; Langer, 1967, 1972; and Polanyi, 1958, 1966). To trace this theme in counseling consult Whiteley (1980) and Zytowski and Rosen (1982).

Extending Program

ture is not the magic, without that insight human growth and self-insights become trivial events, like rabbits popping out of hats. The underlying structure of functional therapy is based on working with feeling moments, using expression dynamics, and varying personality dynamisms within the overall perspective of integration and reintegration processes.

What is interesting about magic is that, to the onlookers, the feats seem extraordinary, astonishing, and inexplicable but to the magicians they are predictable outcomes of hours of careful practice. Therapy is not as predictable as magic but the functional manual and the theory do provide a structure for practice and repetition. The therapist and the client should have a relationship like that of magicians and their assistants, both are in on the act, both know more than the audience. The magic of functional therapy is the same as the magic of all therapies—awareness, human contact, and genuine personality change.

| | **Concluding** |

Appendixes

A

Mental Status Examination

I. Procedure
   A. Begin with, "What is your present address?" "What is your phone number?" "Do you remember your home address where you grew up as a child?"
   B. Continue with, "Very good, now what I would like to do is ask you to remember three things that I will be asking you about at the end of the interview. One is the color green; two, apples; and three, Detroit, Michigan." (You are checking out recall and recent and remote memory functioning.)
   C. "Now, I'd like to ask you to count backward from 100 by 7s. Right, subtract 7 from 100 and then just keep on doing that." (Note the time it takes, mistakes, frustration, and way of handling the problem. This measures concentration and attention span as well as simple arithmetic ability.)
   D. "Okay, very good. Now, I would like to ask you some questions about simple sayings or parables that are common."
      1. "What do you think that people mean when they say 'Still waters run deep?' or 'People who live in glass houses shouldn't throw stones,' or 'A rolling stone gathers no moss'?" (What you are noting here is abstracting ability. People who have thought disorders or certain kinds of schizophrenic thinking styles often have difficulty here. They think concretely, which means that they interpret "Still waters run deep" as meaning something about water. Or they may have bizarre or unusual associations here such as, "There are bloody sharks in deep waters."
   E. "Now, I'd like to ask you how things are alike. For example, How are an orange and an apple alike; what about a hammer and a ladder; what about a tree and a fly?" (Again, you are checking out a thinking skill. Notice unusual or bizarre associations.)
   F. "Okay, very good. Now, let me ask you this: If you were walking down the street and saw a stamped, addressed envelope on the sidewalk, what would you do with it? If you were sitting in a movie theater and were the first person to notice smoke and fire, what would you do?" (Here you are looking for judgment, for appropriate responses to these situations.)
   G. "Now, I would like to ask you some general information questions: Who is the president of the United States? How many states are there in the union? Where is the state capitol? Name the last four presidents. How many days are there in a year? What is the boiling point of water? What is the freezing point?" (Here

you are getting a brief idea of general intelligence and whether or not recall and mental functioning approximates education and expected ability.)

H. "Okay, now I would like you to remember the three things that I asked you at the beginning of our interview. What color? What kind of fruit? What city? Okay,

1. "Have you felt different or unusual lately?
2. "Have you had any strange, unusual, or out of the ordinary experiences?
3. "Have you noticed any changes in your sensory experiences? The way you hear things, the way things sound or taste or smell?
4. "Have you noticed anything unusual out of the corner of your eye?
5. "Have you had any experiences like seeing visions or shapes at night when you are in bed?
6. "Do you ever hear voices or sounds when no one is there? Is this frightening to you? Does it occur very often?"

(Here you are checking for auditory, the most common type of hallucinations, visual hallucinations, and other types of sensory disturbances. Note also delusions and fixed false beliefs. Check religiosity. Take these questions and answers seriously if someone is having these kinds of experiences. It is likely to be frightening them.)

I. What you are doing is establishing how your client's internal world is functioning. Ask these questions:

1. "Have you noticed any recent changes in the way that you usually think? Has it speeded up or slowed down?
2. "Do you have thoughts or worries that you can't seem to not think of even when you do not want to?
3. "Do you feel that your thinking is getting out of control?"

(If your client answers yes to these kinds of questions, explore them more specifically to determine the pattern and content of the person's thinking.)

II. *Note:* Be concerned, interested, and accepting of the person's thinking and thought process. If it appears disturbed in the areas that you have covered, then note that and comment upon it. Identify it as an indication that something is happening and that changes are a way of surviving and dealing with what is happening in the best way possible. *Do not put out clinical kinds of diagnosis* to the client. Let clients know that you know that they are doing their best to function well as human beings.

History Questionnaire

Purpose: This questionnaire is designed to gather background information. By completing these questions as fully and as accurately as you can, you will facilitate your own therapy program.

Confidentiality: We understand that some of this information is of a personal nature. *All case records, including this questionnaire,* are strictly confidential. No outsider is permitted to see your case records without your written permission.

PLEASE TRY TO ANSWER AS FULLY AS YOU CAN. IF YOU NEED MORE SPACE FOR ANY ITEM, PLEASE CONTINUE ON THE BACK OF THE PAGE.

Date _____

1. **General**
   Name _____
   Address _____
   Telephone Numbers *(Day/evenings)* _____
   Age _____ Occupation _____ By whom were you referred?

   _____

   With whom do you live? *(List people)* _____
   Do you live in a house, hotel room, apartment, etc.? _____
   Marital Status *(Circle one):* Single Engaged Married Remarried
                                 Separated Divorced Widowed

2. **Clinical**
   A. State in your own words the nature of your chief problem and its duration.

   B. Give a brief account of the history and development of your problem (from onset to present).

   C. On the scale below please estimate the current severity of your problem.*(Make one check only)*

No longer a problem	Mildly Upsetting	Moderately Severe	Very Severe	Extremely Severe	Totally Incapacitating

337

D. Whom have you previously consulted about your present problem?

E. Have you ever had any other form of therapeutic treatment?

3. **Personal Data**
    Date of Birth _____ Place of Birth _____
    A. *Underline* any of the following that applied during your childhood: nightmares; thumb sucking; fears; bed wetting; nail-biting; happy childhood; sleep-walking; stammering; unhappy childhood; others _____
        Health during childhood? _____
        List major illnesses _____
        What is your height? _____ Weight? _____
        Health during adolescence? _____
        Any surgical operations? (Please list them and give age at time) _____

        Any accidents? _____

    B. List your main fears:
        1. _____
        2. _____
        3. _____
        4. _____
        5. _____
    C. *Underline* any of the following that you feel apply to you in your present condition: headaches; dizziness; fainting spells; palpitations; stomach trouble; no appetite; bowel disturbances; fatigue; insomnia; nightmares; take sedatives; alcoholism; feel tense; feel panicky; tremors; depressed; suicidal ideas; take drugs; unable to relax; sexual problems; unable to have a good time; don't like weekends and vacations; over-ambitious; shy with people; can't make friends; feel lonely; can't make decisions; can't keep a job; inferiority feelings; home conditions bad; financial problems; memory problems; concentration difficulties.
        Others _____
    D. *Underline* any of the following words which you feel apply to you: worthless, useless, a "nobody," "life is empty," inadequate, stupid, incompetent, naive, "can't do anything right," guilty, evil, morally wrong, horrible thoughts, hostile, full of hate, anxious, agitated, cowardly, unassertive, panicky, ugly, deformed, unattractive, repulsive, depressed, lonely, unloved, misunderstood, bored, restless, confused, unconfident, in conflict, full of regrets.
    E. Any athletic participation? _____
    F. Present interests, hobbies, activities: _____
    G. How do you occupy your free time? _____
    H. What is the last school grade that you completed? _____
    I. Scholastic abilities, strengths, and weaknesses: _____
    J. Do you make friends easily? _____ Do you keep them? ___
    K. Are you *currently* taking any drugs or medication? _____
        If yes, what are they? _____
    L. When was your last physical examination by a doctor? _____
        What state of health were you in then? _____
        What state of health are you in now? _____

4. **Occupational Data**
   A. What sort of work are you doing now? _____
   B. Kinds of jobs held in the past? _____
   C. Does your present work satisfy you? (If not, in what ways are you dissatisfied?)

   Approximately how much do you earn? _____
   About how much does it cost you to live? _____

   Ambitions
   D. Past _____
   E. Present _____

5. **Sex Information**
   A. Parental attitudes to sex (e.g., was there sex instruction or discussion in the home?)

   B. When and how did you get your first knowledge about sex? _____
   C. When did you first become aware of your own sexual impulses? _____
   D. Did you ever experience any anxieties or guilt feelings arising out of sex or masturbation? If "Yes" please explain.

   E. Is your present sex life satisfactory?

   F. Is your sexual orientation heterosexual, homosexual, bisexual, or asexual?_____

6. **Marital History (Answer where applicable)**
   A. How long did you know your spouse before engagement? _____
   Husband's or Wife's present age _____ Occupation of husband or wife __
   Describe the personality of your husband or wife in your own words.

   B. In what areas are you compatible? _____
   C. In what areas are you incompatible? _____
   D. How many children do you have? _____
   E. Do any of your children have special problems? _____
   F. Give details of any previous marriage and its termination. _____

7. **Family Data**
   A. *Father*
   Living or deceased? _____ If deceased, your age at time of his death __
   If alive, father's present age _____
   Occupation _____ Health _____
   B. *Mother*
   Living or deceased? _____ If deceased, your age at time of her death __
   If alive, mother's present age _____
   Occupation _____ Health _____
   C. *Siblings*
   Number of brothers and sisters _____
   Quality of relationship with brothers and sisters _____

In past _____
In present _____

D. Give a description of your father's personality and his attitudes toward you (past and present).

E. Briefly describe your attitude toward your father (past and present).

F. Give a description of your mother's personality and her attitude toward you (past and present).

G. Briefly describe your attitude toward your mother (past and present).

H. How were you disciplined by your parents as a child?

I. Give an impression of your home atmosphere (i.e., the home in which you grew up. Mention compatibility or otherwise between parents and between parents and children.)

Were you able to confide in your parents? _____
If you have a stepparent, give your age when parent remarried _____
Give an outline of your religious training _____
If you were not brought up by your parents, who did bring you up and between what years? _____
Has anyone (parents, relatives, friends) ever interfered in your marriage, occupation, etc.? _____

J. Who are the most important people in your life? _____
Does *any* member of your family suffer from alcoholism, epilepsy, or anything that can be considered a "mental disorder"? _____
Are there any other members of the family about whom information regarding illness, etc., is relevant? _____

K. Recount any fearful or distressing experiences not previously mentioned.

L. List the benefits you hope to derive from therapy _____
M. List any situations that make you feel calm or relaxed _____
_____
_____

N. Have you ever lost control (e.g., temper or crying or agression)? If so, please describe
_____

C

Psychological Fitness Survey

Name _____

Code No. _____ Date _____

A. WORK FITNESS

		YES	NO
1.	In general, do you enjoy working?		
2.	Are you financially successful according to your own standards in your work?		
3.	Are you successfully pursuing your chosen career?		
4.	Are your work skills improving?		
5.	Do you work well alone?		
6.	Do you work well with others?		
7.	Do you have a positive opinion of the way you work?		
8.	Do you have a positive opinion of your potential to work?		
9.	Have your attitudes about work improved when you compare yourself now with earlier times in your life?		
10.	Do you have the skills you need to work as successfully as you want to work?		
	TOTALS		

Additional comments about this life area:

B. PLAY FITNESS

		YES	NO
1.	Do you enjoy playing sports?		
2.	Do you enjoy playing household games (cards, box games, etc.)?		
3.	Do you enjoy participating in competitive play?		
4.	Do you enjoy participating in noncompetitive play?		
5.	Do you play well with others?		
6.	Do you play three times or more a week?		
7.	Do you have a positive opinion of yourself as a "player"?		

8. Do you have the skills you need to play as well as you want to play? ___|___
9. Do you play as much as you want?   ___|___
10. Has your *satisfaction* with your play increased when you compare your-
    self now with earlier times in your life?   ___|___
                                                   TOTALS   ___|___

Additional comments about this life area:

C. RELATIONSHIP FITNESS

                                                                      YES | NO
1. Do you enjoy friendships?   ___|___
2. Do you trust and depend on your friends when you need someone to
    lean on?   ___|___
3. Do your friends trust and depend on you when they need someone to
    lean on?   ___|___
4. Do you see friends regularly (at least three times a week)?   ___|___
5. Do you have close friends of both sexes?   ___|___
6. Do you have long-term friendships of three years or more?   ___|___
7. Do you have a positive opinion of your ability to make and keep friends?___|___
8. Do other people have a positive opinion of your ability to make and
    keep friends?   ___|___
9. Are you satisfied with your friendships?   ___|___
10. Do you have the skills you need to make and keep as many friends as
    you want?   ___|___
                                                   TOTALS   ___|___

Additional comments about this life area:

D. SEXUAL FITNESS

                                                                      YES | NO
1. Do you enjoy sex?   ___|___
2. Do you have sex as often as you want?   ___|___
3. Do you usually express your secret thoughts during sex?   ___|___
4. Do you usually express your intimate feelings during sex?   ___|___
5. Do you have the sexual skills to do what you want to do during sex? ___|___
6. Do you have sex regularly?
    How often? _____   ___|___
7. Do you have a positive opinion of your sexual life?   ___|___
8. Do other people have a positive opinion of your sexual life?   ___|___
9. Have your attitudes about sex improved when you compare yourself
    now with earlier times in your life?   ___|___
10. Are you satisfied with all aspects of your sex life?   ___|___
                                                   TOTALS   ___|___

Additional comments about this life area:

E.   EMOTIONAL FITNESS

	YES	NO
1. Can you express anger easily?		
2. Can you express sadness easily?		
3. Can you express happiness easily?		
4. Can you express fear easily?		
5. Do you express your emotions to others easily and freely?		
6. Do you use your emotions to help you to make your decisions?		
7. Do you have a positive opinion of your potential to be emotional?		
8. Do you have a positive opinion of the way you are using your present emotional skills?		
9. Are those around you as emotional as you want?		
10. Do you have the skills you need to be as emotional as you want to be?		
TOTALS		

Additional comments about this life area:

F.   INTELLECTUAL FITNESS

	YES	NO
1. Do you *enjoy* thinking and solving problems?		
2. Are your intellectual skills improving?		
3. Do you share your ideas and thoughts with others?		
4. Do you learn easily?		
5. Do you have the skills you need in order to be as intellectual as you want to be?		
6. Do you think creatively?		
7. Do you have a positive opinion of the way you use your present intellectual skills?		
8. Do other people have a positive opinion of your intellectual abilities?		
9. Do you have a positive opinion of your potential to be intellectual?		
10. Are you satisfied with your intellectual abilities?		
TOTALS		

Additional comments about this life area:

G.   PHYSICAL FITNESS

	YES	NO
1. Is your physical fitness improving?		
2. Are you a good weight for your age and health?		
3. Do you have a physical vitality, an energetic, healthy presence?		
4. Are you physically flexible and supple?		
5. Do you have a positive opinion of your potential to be physically fit?		
6. Do others have a good opinion of your physical fitness?		
7. Are you well coordinated?		
8. Are you satisfied with the way you are using your present fitness skills?		

9. Have your physical fitness attitudes improved when you compare your-
    self now to earlier times?
10. Do you have the skills you need to be as fit as you want to be?

                                                            TOTALS

Additional comments about this life area:

H.   SLEEP AND DREAM FITNESS

		YES	NO
1.	Do you use your dreams to help yourself understand and change your life?		
2.	Do you have the skills you need to understand and use your dreams?		
3.	Are you satisfied with your dream life?		
4.	Generally, do you feel good in your dreams?		
5.	Do you remember your dreams three times a week?		
6.	Do you discuss your dreams with friends and acquaintances at least once a week?		
7.	Do you feel rested and alert upon waking?		
8.	Do you sleep soundly?		
9.	Do you fall asleep easily and naturally without drugs or alcohol?		
10.	Are you satisfied with your sleep fitness?		
	TOTALS		

Additional comments about this life area:

GOALS SHEET

Name _____ Date _____

Instructions: List the major goals that you hope to achieve by the end of the program, for each life area. Be as specific and realistic as possible. This form will have future therapeutic use, so please complete it with as much detail as possible. To help you fill out this form, briefly complete this sentence for each life area: "By the end of this program, I want to _____."

                                                            Office
                                                            Use
                                                            Only

Work or Career

Play

Relationships with Friends

Relationships with Lovers

Sex

Emotional

Intellectual

Physical Fitness

Sleep and Dreams

D

Case Termination Form

Client(s) _____

Counselor _____

Termination date _____

Total number of sessions _____

Reason for termination *(check one)*

_____ Treatment conducted to conclusion

_____ Client dropped out of counseling *(specify reasons):*

_____ Counselor terminated treatment *(specify reasons):*

_____ Mutual agreement to terminate prior to conclusion *(specify reasons):*

List pinpointed problems worked on:

1.
2.
3.
4.

For each pinpointed problem, rate the estimated success of your intervention. *(Check appropriate category for each problem):*

		Problem			
Rating	1	2	3	4
Worse than before				
Same				
Some improvement				
Reasonable improvement				
Significant improvement				

Additional comments:

Was a referral recommended? *(Specify)* _____

The Test of Attentional and Interpersonal Style (TAIS)

The TAIS is a nonthreatening, 144-item, paper and pencil test which is easily administered in 25–30 minutes to people over 15 years old. The test can be immediately hand-scored and interpreted by computer (by return mail). There currently are available computerized interpretations for business executives and sales personnel, athletes, teachers/counselors, and health service personnel. Another one is directed to the professional working with a client. By cooperating with trainers and decision makers, it is possible to tailor an interpretation to any group and performance situation. *TAIS feedback should always be mediated by a person trained to interpret the results for the situation in which the results will be used.*

Following is a short version of the TAIS. It contains the lead items for the six attentional dimensions (i.e., two questions per scale instead of six to eleven). It does not contain the interpersonal questions. As such, there is little cause for worry that an individual will be upset by the results.

Answer the following questions as they pertain to you across situations.

ATTENTIONAL STYLE

1. I am good at quickly analyzing a complex situation such as how a play is developing in football or which of four or five kids started a fight.

   Never ( ) Rarely ( ) Sometimes ( ) Frequently ( ) All the time ( )

2. In a room filled with children or on a playing field I know what everyone is doing.

   Never ( ) Rarely ( ) Sometimes ( ) Frequently ( ) All the time ( )

   BET Total

3. When people talk to me, I find myself distracted by the sights and sounds around me.

   Never ( ) Rarely ( ) Sometimes ( ) Frequently ( ) All the time ( )

4. I get confused trying to watch activities such as a football game or circus where many things are happening at the same time.

   Never ( ) Rarely ( ) Sometimes ( ) Frequently ( ) All the time ( )
                                                                    OET Total

5. All I need is a little information, and I can come up with a large number of ideas.

   Never ( ) Rarely ( ) Sometimes ( ) Frequently ( ) All the time ( )

6. It is easy for me to bring together ideas from a number of different areas.

   Never ( ) Rarely ( ) Sometimes ( ) Frequently ( ) All the time ( )
                                                                    BIT Total

7. When people talk to me, I find my self distracted by my own thoughts and ideas.

   Never ( ) Rarely ( ) Sometimes ( ) Frequently ( ) All the time ( )

8. I have so many things going on in my mind that I become confused and forgetful.

   Never ( ) Rarely ( ) Sometimes ( ) Frequently ( ) All the time ( )
                                                                    OIT Total

9. It is easy for me to keep thoughts from interfering with something I am watching or listening to.

   Never ( ) Rarely ( ) Sometimes ( ) Frequently ( ) All the time ( )

10. It is easy for me to keep sights and sounds from interfering with my thoughts.

    Never ( ) Rarely ( ) Sometimes ( ) Frequently ( ) All the time ( )
                                                                    NAR Total

11. I have difficulty clearing my mind of a single thought or idea.

    Never ( ) Rarely ( ) Sometimes ( ) Frequently ( ) All the time ( )

12. In games, I make mistakes because I am watching what one person does and forget about the others.

    Never ( ) Rarely ( ) Sometimes ( ) Frequently ( ) All the time ( )
                                                                    RED Total

Score each of the subscales (NAR, RED, BET, etc.) by assigning a value of: 0 for *Never;* 1 for *Rarely;* 2 for *Sometimes;* 3 for *Frequently;* 4 for *All the time.* Total the score for the two items in each scale.

Graph the total for each of the six attentional scales on Figure 1. Connect with a straight line the following pairs: BET and OET; BIT and OIT; NAR and RED. For an understanding of what the scores mean, refer to Table 1.

RESULTS OF THE TAIS

1. Identify the relative strengths and weaknesses in an individual's ability to concentrate under normal and pressure conditions. Those conditions each person will find most uncomfortable and those individuals likely to lose attention control under pressure are specified. By comparing how an individual scores on one TAIS scale with how she or he scores on another (within-person comparison), the test can be used for counseling people with dramatically different performance capabilities, helping each overcome, or compensate for, attentional and interpersonal weaknesses while maximizing strengths.

2. Feed information back to the layperson in his/her language which sensitizes that person to the mental demands of the various performance situations relevant to that individual. Such guidance replaces inexact directives like "concentrate" and "relax" with details about what one is doing correctly and incorrectly. This leads to awareness of specific changes needed to improve performance.

3. Support the underlying theory in providing an easily understood foundation for integrating physical and mental performance across job, school, athletic, home, and interpersonal situations.

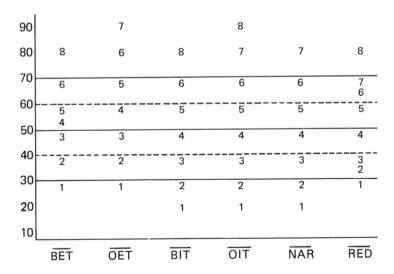

Figure 1. Attentional profile.

Table 1. The Test of Attentional and Interpersonal Style (TAIS) Scale

	Attentional variables
BET	*(Broad External attentional focus):* High scores on this scale are obtained by individuals who describe themselves as being able to integrate effectively many external stimuli at one time. They know what is going on around them at all times, can spot the open teammate in sports, have what police call a "street sense."
OET	*(Overloaded by External stimuli):* The higher the score, the more individuals make mistakes because they become confused and overloaded with external stimuli, i.e., distracted.
BIT	*(Broad Internal attention focus):* High scores indicate individuals who see themselves as able to integrate effectively ideas and information from several different areas. Accordingly, they are analytical and philosophical, good at planning ahead and anticipating consequences. They tend to be creative and ideational.
OIT	*(Overloaded by Internal stimuli):* The higher the score the more mistakes individuals make because they confuse or distract themselves by thinking about too many things at once, becoming lost in thought, daydreaming.
NAR	*(Narrow attentional focus):* The higher the score, the more effective individuals see themselves with respect to being able to narrow their attention when they need to (e.g., to study or watch a ball). They sustain concentration on one person, item, or thought. Typically they are good at finishing tasks before starting others.
RED	*(Reduced attentional focus):* A high score on this scale indicates that the individual makes mistakes because he or she narrows his or her attention too much, such as on irrelevant fears (of failure) or distracting noises.

The TAIS provides insight into the interactions between the individual(s) tested, other people, and situations. This means it is quite useful in examining communication problems and team building. It helps people "own" their contributions to difficulties in which they find themselves. This is especially true when they can see them as an interaction and not just their fault alone.

The TAIS has been used extensively in the United States, Canada, Europe, Russia, Australia, and South America. It has been found effective in counseling, training, and matching people to tasks, and team building with business executives and sales personnel; professional athletes and musicians; students exploring careers; undergraduate, graduate, and seminary students; police; health service personnel and patients; married couples, psychiatric patients; and juvenile offenders. The TAIS measures general characteristics of each individual (traits), yet is able to specify situational factors influencing the moment (state).

Social Situations Questionnaire and Social Behaviors Ratings

ASSESSMENT MEASURES

Relationships

Name:
Date:
Relationships

Mixing with others	Childhood	Adolescence	Since adolescence
1. Had many friends and mixed easily	————	————	————
2. Mixed only with close friend or group of friends	————	————	————
3. No close friends; very few friends, never quite accepted by friends	————	————	————
4. Quiet; aloof; preferred to be by self	————	————	————
5. Antisocial	————	————	————
Interest in opposite sex*			
1. Shows healthy interest in opposite sex with regular "dating" or marriage		————	————
2. Some interest; circle of friends included opposite sex; some attempts at "dating"		————	————

* Scale can be modified for homosexual clients.

Adapted with modifications from *Social Skills and Mental Health* by Peter Trower, Bridget Bryant, and Michael Argyle. Copyright 1978 by the University of Pittsburgh Press. Originally published by Methuen & Company, Ltd., London, England. Reprinted by permission of A. D. Peters & Company, Ltd.

3. Little interest in opposite sex;   _____   _____
   unsuccessful encounters with them;
   preferred to be with own sex
4. Little interest in opposite or same sex;   _____   _____
   preferred to be by self
5. Definitely avoided by opposite sex   _____   _____

SOCIAL SITUATIONS QUESTIONNAIRE

This questionnaire is concerned with how people get on in social situations, that is, situations involving being with other people, talking to them, etc.

PART 1: HOW DIFFICULT?

The first part deals with how much difficulty, if any, *you* have in these situations. Having difficulty means that the situation makes you feel *anxious* or *uncomfortable*, either because you do not know what to do, or because you feel frightened, embarrassed, or self-conscious.

1. Across the top of Part 1 you will see five different choices of difficulty, each with a number underneath (e.g., "no difficulty" = 0).
2. Down the left hand side of the page are listed 30 situations you might encounter which some people have said they find difficult. If some of these situations are ones in which you have never found yourself, please imagine how you would feel if you did.
3. Down the right hand side of the page are two columns which refer to two different times. They are headed (a) the present time; (b) this time a year ago.

For each situation, and for each time, select the choice of difficulty which most closely fits how you feel, and write the number of your choice in the appropriate column. Examples:

	Present time	Year ago
A. Going to a public meeting	3	1
B. Going to the cinema	0	0

Example A means that someone had great difficulty (3) at the present time, and slight difficulty (1) a year ago.

Example B means that someone had no difficulty (0) at either of these times.

Please note: Choice "avoidance if possible" should only be used if you find the situation so difficult that you would avoid it whenever you could. It should *not* be used for situations you avoid because they are not to your taste—for example, not going to concerts because you dislike music.

PART 2: HOW OFTEN?

The second Part deals with how often you have found yourself in each of the 22 situations listed on the left hand side of the page. The procedure is exactly the same as that for Part 1.

1. Across the top of Part 2 are seven different "how often" choices, each with a number underneath (e.g., "at least once a week" = 2).

2. Down the right hand side of the page are two columns referring to two three-month periods: (a) the last three months and (b) the same three months a year ago.

For each situation, and for each three-month period, select a "how often" choice and write the number in the appropriate column.

Please note: Choice "never" (7) means that you have never in your life been in that particular situation. It should therefore be used in both columns.

PART 1

Date: Sex: Name:

No difficulty 0	Slight difficulty 1	Moderate difficulty 2	Great difficulty 3 At the present time	Avoidance if possible 4 This time a year ago

1. Walking down the street	_____	_____
2. Going into shops	_____	_____
3. Going on public transport	_____	_____
4. Going into bars	_____	_____
5. Going to parties	_____	_____
6. Mixing with people at work	_____	_____
7. Making friends of your own age	_____	_____
8. Going out with someone you are sexually attracted to	_____	_____
9. Being with a group of the same sex and roughly the same age as you	_____	_____
10. Being with a group containing both men and women of roughly the same age as you	_____	_____
11. Being with a group of the opposite sex of roughly the same age as you	_____	_____
12. Entertaining people in your home, apartment, etc.	_____	_____
13. Going into restaurants or coffee shops	_____	_____
14. Going to dances, dance halls, or discotheques	_____	_____
15. Being with older people	_____	_____

16. Being with younger people   _____   _____

17. Going into a room full of people   _____   _____

18. Meeting strangers   _____   _____

19. Being with people you do not know   _____   _____
    very well
20. Being with friends   _____   _____

21. Approaching others—making the   _____   _____
    first move in starting up a
    friendship
22. Making ordinary decisions affecting   _____   _____
    others (e.g., what to do together in
    the evening)
23. Being with only one other person   _____   _____
    rather than a group
24. Getting to know people in depth   _____   _____

25. Taking the initiative in keeping a   _____   _____
    conversation going
26. Looking at people directly in the   _____   _____
    eyes
27. Disagreeing with what other people   _____   _____
    are saying and putting forward
    your own views
28. People standing or sitting very   _____   _____
    close to you
29. Talking about yourself and your   _____   _____
    feelings in a conversation
30. People looking at you   _____   _____

PART 2

Every day or almost every day 1	At least once a week 2	At least once a fortnight 3	At least once a month 4	Once or twice in three months 5	Not at all in three months 6	Never 7

	Last three months	Three-month period a year ago
	_____	_____
1. Walking down the street	_____	_____
2. Going to the shops	_____	_____

3. Going on public transport   _____   _____

4. Going into bars   _____   _____

5. Going to parties   _____   _____

6. Mixing with people at work   _____   _____

7. Making friends of your own age   _____   _____

8. Going out with someone you are
    sexually attracted to   _____   _____

9. Being with a group of the same sex and
    roughly the same age as you   _____   _____

10. Being with a group containing both
    men and women of roughly the same
    age as you   _____   _____

11. Being with a group of the opposite sex
    of roughly the same age as you   _____   _____

12. Entertaining people in your home,
    apartment, etc.   _____   _____

13. Going to restaurants or coffee shops   _____   _____

14. Going to dances, dance halls, or
    discotheques   _____   _____

15. Being with older people   _____   _____

16. Being with younger people   _____   _____

17. Going into a room full of people   _____   _____

18. Meeting strangers   _____   _____

19. Being with people you do not know
    very well   _____   _____

20. Being with friends   _____   _____

21. Approaching others—making the first
    move in starting up a friendship   _____   _____

22. Making ordinary decisions affecting
    others (e.g., what to do together in the
    evening)   _____   _____

Comments. If you wish to add any comments about your ratings of difficulty or frequency, please do so below.

SOCIAL SITUATIONS INTERVIEW

The therapist can use the following questions to probe into the nature of the social difficulties reported in the Social Situations Questionnaire. The therapist should take each situation in turn which is rated 2, 3, or 4 (moderate, or great difficulty, or avoidance).

What was the situation?
When and where did it happen?
Who was involved?
What led up to this?
What did you want to do in this situation?
What actually happened?
What did you feel?
What did you think of the others?

SOCIAL INTERACTION TEST

Patients are told that it is essential for training purposes that we observe their actual performance in a situation they might encounter in everyday life. The situation we have chosen resembles a casual three-person encounter between strangers, such as might occur at a social club. The patients are told that the two strangers they will meet are just ordinary people (in our case a woman secretary and a male student), who are in no way connected with their treatment and who think that this encounter is part of a social psychology experiment. We stress that this is not an interview and they should not talk about their problems as they would to the doctor. They are assured that the filming (if any) and the whole procedure are entirely confidential.

The test takes place in a room set up as a lounge, preferably equipped with video apparatus. The patient and confederates are introduced and shown to their seats, with the following instructions: "As you all know, this is part of an experiment on communication, so I wonder if you (patient) would start the ball rolling by talking about yourself, what you do, where you come from, and so on, and then keep the conversation going for four minutes (indicate the clock), and then would you (woman confederate) do the same for the next four minutes? It is not meant to be a speech—the idea is simply to give one person the responsibility for keeping the conversation going, and then another person—so you can talk or ask questions or carry on any kind of conversation you want. Finally, would you (male confederate) chip in whenever you feel like it?"

Unknown to the patient, some of the confederates' behavior is prepared. The woman adopts a warm and friendly style. She uses full listener responses while the patient talks, with helpful nondirective questions where necessary, but interrupts this with at least one period of nonresponse. She also interrupts her own period of talking with a similar period of nonresponse. The nonresponse periods should last about 15 seconds. The male confederate adopts a cold and dominant style. After 8 minutes he takes over control of the conversation by asking the patient questions about his work, interests, but withholds any positive feedback and discloses little information about himself. The confederates should not be therapists and should preferably come from a similar social class to the patient's. They should have no other involvement with the patient, either prior to or following the test.

RATING SCALE

The scale is in two parts. The first part deals with specific elements—verbal and nonverbal behavior and physical appearance—and the second with psychological impressions, such as warmth and dominance, which are formed from these elements.

The rater proceeds by first concentrating on the patient's *actual behavior*, scoring the elements as he goes along, in the way described in the scale.

After completing the elements section, the rater then concentrates on the *general impression* the patient gives, and notes down his impressions on thirteen seven-point, bipolar adjective scales.

Finally, the rater draws together the two aspects of the rating scale by writing behavioral descriptions for some of the general impressions he considers most faulty. Two examples of this are given in the companion rating guide.

Raters should watch the film of the interaction test through once, and then work systematically through the scale while watching further replays. If no video is available, ratings can be made immediately after the interaction, with the aid of a tape recording.

The raters should include the two confederates from the interaction test, and at least one of the therapists. All raters should familiarize themselves with the scale and the definitions of the elements, through the companion rating guide, and rate some sample films before rating the patient. There will usually be reasonable agreement on the elements and adjectives which most characterize the deficits.

In making their judgments, raters should bear the following points in mind:

1. The appropriateness of the behavior should be thought of in the context of the situation being observed. Thus, for example, intimate behavior which might be acceptable at a party would not be appropriate in the interaction test.

2. Raters should also be cautious about making generalizations from behavior in the observed situation to others. Recent evidence suggests that patients' behavior is more dependent on specific situations than previously realized.

3. The ratings should be thought of in relation to normal social behavior and not psychiatric disorders. Thus, for example, while gaze avoidance might be appropriate to a depressed state in a clinical interview, it would be inappropriate in normal social interaction.

4. Related to the above, the therapist should supplement his observations from the interaction test with observations made in other settings (interviews, reports by others), and adjust his ratings where necessary. Some parts of the scale cannot in any case be rated from the interaction test, and information must be obtained elsewhere.

VOICE QUALITY

1.	*Volume*	
	0	Normal volume.
	1(a)	Quiet but can be heard without difficulty.
	(b)	Rather loud but not unpleasant.
	2(a)	Too quiet and difficult to hear.
	(b)	Too loud and rather unpleasant.
	3(a)	Abnormally quiet and often inaudible.
	(b)	Abnormally loud and unpleasant.
	4(a)	Inaudible.
	(b)	Extremely loud (shouting).

2.   *Tone*
    0   Normal voice quality.
    1   Fair voice quality—not unpleasant or boring.
    2   Unmodulated and poor voice quality (dull, flat, thin, etc.). Rather unpleasant and boring.
    3   Abnormally unmodulated and expressionless. Unpleasant and boring.
    4   Extremely flat, expressionless and poor quality. Very unpleasant and boring.

3.   *Pitch*
    0   Normal pitch.
    1   Moderately high or low or monotonous but not unpleasant.
    2   Too high or low or monotonous and rather unpleasant.
    3   Abnormally high, low, or monotonous and unpleasant.
    4   Extremely high, low, or monotonous and unpleasant.

4.   *Clarity*
    0   Normal clarity.
    1(a)   Tends to mumble, slur, or drawl words but not unclear.
    (b)   Tends to clip, over-articulate words but not unpleasant.
    2(a)   Too much mumbling, slurring, and drawling. Difficult to understand.
    (b)   Too much clipping, over-articulation. Rather unpleasant.
    3(a)   Abnormally unclear enunciation. Often impossible to understand.
    (b)   Abnormally precise and over-articulated. Unpleasant.
    4(a)   Extremely unclear. Impossible to understand.
    (b)   Extremely over-articulated. Very unpleasant.

5.   *Pace*
    0   Normal Pace.
    1(a)   Slow but not difficult to follow.
    (b)   Fast but not difficult to follow.
    2(a)   Too slow and difficult to follow.
    (b)   Too fast and difficult to follow.
    3(a)   Abnormally slow and often impossible to follow.
    (b)   Abnormally fast and often impossible to follow.
    4(a)   Extremely slow, impossible to follow.
    (b)   Extremely fast, impossible to follow.

6. *Speech disturbances*
   0   None.
   1(a)   Occasional stuttering, repetitions, omissions, etc., but no negative impression.
    (b)   Occasional use of pause fillers but no negative impression.
   2(a)   Too much stuttering, repetition, omission, etc. Negative impression.
    (b)   Too many pause fillers. Negative impression.
   3(a)   Abnormal stuttering, repetition, omission, etc. Embarrassing.
    (b)   Abnormally frequent pause fillers. Unpleasant.
   4(a)   Extreme stuttering, repetition, omission etc. Extremely embarrassing.
    (b)   Extremely frequent pause fillers. Very unpleasant.

NONVERBAL

7. *Proximity*
   0   Normal casual/personal range.
   1(a)   Rather distant but no negative impression.
    (b)   Rather too close but no negative impression.
   2(a)   Too distant. Negative impression.
    (b)   Too close. Negative impression.
   3(a)   Abnormally distant for casual/personal interaction. Unrewarding.
    (b)   Abnormally close for casual/personal interaction. Unpleasant.
   4(a)   Outside range for social interaction.
    (b)   Extremely close and intimate. Very unpleasant.

8. *Orientation*
   0   Normal orientation for casual/personal interaction.
   1   Turned slightly away but no negative impression.
   2   Turned too far away. Negative impression.
   3   Abnormal orientation—90 degree angle.
   4   Turned completely away—more than 90 degree angle. Very unpleasant.

9. *Appearance*
   0   Normal appearance.
   1   Unusual appearance but no negative impression.
   2   Appearance unusual, unattractive, unacceptable. Negative impression.

3   Appearance abnormally unusual, unattractive, unacceptable. Unpleasant.

4   Appearance extremely unusual, unattractive, unacceptable. Very unpleasant.

10.   *Face*

0   Normal range of emotional expressions.

1(a)   Face tends to be inexpressive but not unpleasant.

(b)   Some mildly negative expressions but not unpleasant.

2(a)   Face often blank, expressions weak or limited in range. Rather unpleasant.

(b)   Frequent mildly negative expressions. Rather unpleasant.

3(a)   Face abnormally blank and range limited. Unpleasant.

(b)   Some abnormally strong negative expressions. Unpleasant.

4(a)   Totally blank face. Very unpleasant.

(b)   Frequent strongly negative expressions. Very unpleasant.

11.   *Gaze*

0   Normal gaze frequency and pattern.

1(a)   Tends to avoid looking, but no negative impression.

(b)   Tends to look too much, but no negative impression.

2(a)   Looks too little. Negative impression.

(b)   Looks too much. Negative impressions.

3(a)   Abnormally infrequent looking. Unrewarding.

(b)   Abnormally frequent looking. Unpleasant.

4(a)   Completely avoids looking. Very unrewarding.

(b)   Stares continually. Very unpleasant.

12.   *Posture tonus*

0   Normal relaxed tonus.

1(a)   Rather stiff and immobile but no negative impression.

(b)   Relaxed and rather slouched but no negative impression.

2(a)   Too stiff, immobile, symmetrical. Negative immpression.

(b)   Too relaxed, slouched. Negative impression.

3(a)   Abnormally stiff, immobile, symmetrical. Unpleasant.

(b)   Abnormally slouched. Unpleasant.

	4(a)	Extremely rigid, immobile, symmetrical. Very unpleasant.
	(b)	Extremely slouched. Very unpleasant.

13. *Posture position*

0	Normal open style.
1	Slightly reclined or closed but no negative impression.
2	Too reclined or closed. Negative impression.
3	Abnormally reclined or closed. Unpleasant.
4	Extremely reclined, tightly closed. Very unpleasant.

14. *Gesture*

0	Normal amount and variety of gesture.
1	Limited use of gesture but no negative impression.
2	Use of gesture too limited in frequency and range. Negative impression.
3	Abnormally limited use of gesture in frequency and range. Unrewarding.
4	Never gestures. Very unrewarding.

15. *Autistic gesture*

0	Unnoticeable amount of autistic gesture.
1	Noticeable level of autistic gesture but no negative impression.
2	Too many autistic gestures. Negative impression.
3	Abnormal amount of autistic gesture. Embarrassing, stressful.
4	Extremely frequent autistic gestures. Extremely embarrassing, stressful.

CONVERSATION

16. *Length*—Note: Rate actual speech, excluding pauses

0	Normal speech length.
1(a)	Speech brief but no unfavorable impression.
(b)	Speaks at length but no unfavorable impressions.
2(a)	Speaks too briefly. Negative impression.
(b)	Speaks too long. Negative impression.
3(a)	Abnormally brief speech. Unpleasant impression.
(b)	Abnormally lengthy speech. Unpleasant impression.
4(a)	Speech monosyllabic. Extremely unpleasant.
(b)	Speaks at great length. Extremely unpleasant.

17.   *Generality*
    0   Normal mixture of general and specific content.
    1(a)   Content mainly general but no unfavorable impression.
    (b)   Content mainly detailed and specialized but no unfavorable impression.
    2(a)   Content too general and uninformative. Negative impression.
    (b)   Content too detailed and specialized. Negative impression.
    3(a)   Content abnormally generalized. Irritating impression.
    (b)   Content abnormally detailed and specialized. Irritating impression.
    4(a)   Content at extremely general level. No information. Very irritating.
    (b)   Content at extremely detailed and specialized level. Extremely irritating.

18.   *Formality*
    0   Normal level of informal talk.
    1(a)   Content rather formal but not uninteresting.
    (b)   Content rather personal but no negative impression.
    2(a)   Content too formal and uninteresting.
    (b)   Content too intimate, etc. Negative impression.
    3(a)   Content abnormally formal and boring.
    (b)   Content abnormally intimate, etc. Embarrassing, annoying, etc.
    4(a)   Content extremely formal and boring.
    (b)   Content extremely intimate, etc. Extremely embarrassing, annoying.

19.   *Variety*
    0   Normal variety of topic.
    1   Variety of content lacking but not uninteresting.
    2   Too little variety of content. Uninteresting.
    3   Abnormally unvaried topic content. Boring.
    4   Content all of one kind. Very boring.

20.   *Humor*
    0   Normal level of humor.
    1   Little humor but no negative impression.
    2   Content too serious—hardly any humor. Negative impression.
    3   Content abnormally serious—no humor. Unrewarding.

| | 4 | Content extremely serious and humorless. Very unrewarding. |

21. *Nonverbal "grammar"*

0	Normal nonverbal accompaniments of speech.
1	Tends to underuse nonverbal accompaniments of speech but no negative impression.
2	Underuses nonverbal accompaniments of speech. Somewhat confusing, boring.
3	Abnormal underuse of nonverbal accompaniments of speech. Confusing, boring.
4	Hardly uses any nonverbal accompaniments of speech. Incomprehensible, boring.

22. *Feedback*

0	Normal listener feedback.
1(a)	Feedback infrequent or some elements omitted but not unpleasant.
(b)	Feedback mildly critical or inaccurate but not unpleasant.
2(a)	Feedback too infrequent, unvaried. Rather unpleasant.
(b)	Feedback too critical or inaccurate. Rather unpleasant.
3(a)	Feedback abnormally infrequent, unvaried. Unpleasant.
(b)	Feedback abnormally critical, inaccurate. Unpleasant.
4(a)	No feedback. Very unpleasant.
(b)	Very critical or inaccurate feedback. Very unpleasant.

23. *Meshing*

0	Normal meshing.
1(a)	Responses delayed but no negative impression.
(b)	Interrupts occasionally but no negative impression.
2(a)	Responses too delayed. Negative impression.
(b)	Rather too many interruptions, negative impression.
3(a)	Responses abnormally delayed. unpleasant.
(b)	Abnormally frequent or long interruptions. Annoying.
4(a)	Responses extremely delayed. Very unpleasant.

(b)   Interruptions extremely frequent or long.
             Very annoying.

24.   *Turn taking*
       0   Normal turn taking.
       1(a)   Tends to offer or take up floor infrequently,
                   but no negative impression.
       (b)   Offers or takes up floor frequently but no
                   negative impression.
       2(a)   Offers or spontaneously takes up floor too
                   infrequently. Negative impression.
       (b)   Offers or takes up floor too frequently.
                   Negative impression.
       3(a)   Abnormally infrequent offering or
                   spontaneous taking up floor. Unrewarding.
       (b)   Abnormally frequent offering or taking up
                   floor. Irritating.
       4(a)   Never offers or spontaneously takes up floor.
                   Very unrewarding.
       (b)   Continually offers or takes up floor. Very
                   irritating.

25.   *Questions*
       0   Normal use of varied questions.
       1(a)   Few or unvaried questions but no negative
                   impression.
       (b)   Frequent use of questions but no negative
                   impression.
       2(a)   Questions too few and unvaried. Negative
                   impression.
       (b)   Questions too frequent. Negative impression.
       3(a)   Abnormally infrequent or unvaried questions.
                   Unrewarding.
       (b)   Abnormally frequent questions. Unpleasant.
       4(a)   Never asks questions. Very unrewarding.
       (b)   Continually asks questions. Very unpleasant.

26.   *Supportive routines*
       0   Normal use of main routines.
       1   Low use of routines but no negative
                   impression.
       2   Important routines performed too
                   infrequently and inadequately. Negative
                   impression.
       3   Important routines omitted. Unpleasant.
       4   Essential routines omitted. Very unpleasant.

27.   *Assertive routines*
       0   Normal use of main assertive routines.
       1(a)   Low use of assertive routines but no negative
                   impression.

	(b)	High use of assertive routines but no negative impression.
	2(a)	Assertive routines performed too infrequently or inadequately. Negative impression.
	(b)	Assertive routines performed too frequently. Negative impression.
	3(a)	Important assertive routines omitted. Abnormally submissive impression.
	(b)	Abnormally frequent use of assertive routines. Unpleasant.
	4(a)	Essential assertive routines omitted. Extremely submissive impression.
	(b)	Continuous use of assertive routines. Very unpleasant.

28. *Behavior in public*

0	Normal prescribed behavior.
1	Some minor transgression of publicly prescribed behavior but no negative impression.
2	Frequent minor transgression of public behavior.
3	Some major transgressions of public behavior. Unpleasant.
4	Frequent major transgressions of public behavior. Very unpleasant.

29. *Situation-specific routines*

0	Normal prescribed behavior.
1	Some minor transgressions of situation rules but no negative impression.
2	Frequent minor transgression of situation rules. Negative impression.
3	Some major transgression of situation rules. Unpleasant.
4	Frequent major transgressions of situation rules.

GENERAL IMPRESSIONS

Warm/like	—	—	—	—	—	—	—	Cold/dislike
Superior/dominant	—	—	—	—	—	—	—	Inferior/submissive
Socially anxious	—	—	—	—	—	—	—	Relaxed
Happy	—	—	—	—	—	—	—	Sad
Rewarding	—	—	—	—	—	—	—	Unrewarding
Controlling	—	—	—	—	—	—	—	Uncontrolling
Feminine	—	—	—	—	—	—	—	Masculine
Attractive	—	—	—	—	—	—	—	Unattractive
Poised	—	—	—	—	—	—	—	Awkward
Passive	—	—	—	—	—	—	—	Active
Difficult	—	—	—	—	—	—	—	Easy

Emotional   — — — — — — —   Unemotional
Socially skilled — — — — — — —   Socially unskilled

Behavioral description (1):

Behavioral description (2):

Therapist Notes

Intake Session

Session 1
  A. Present Life Situation:
    1. Work:

    2. Play:

    3. Sex:

    4. Relationships:

  B. Analysis of personality dynamisms:
    1. Activity:

    2. Expression:

    3. Feeling:

    4. Clarity:

    5. Contact:

    C.   Comments about dynamics of expression which can be explored in future sessions:

    D.   General comments and notes for future directions of the therapy:

References

Allen, G. W. *William James: A biography.* New York: Viking Press, 1967.

Allport, G. W. The use of personal documents in psychological science. *Social Science Research Council Bulletin* (Vol. 49). New York: Social Science Research Council, 1942.

Allport, G. W. *The nature of personality: Selected papers.* Cambridge, Mass.: Addison-Wesley, 1950.

Allport, G. W. *Pattern and growth in personality.* New York: Holt, Rinehart & Winston, 1961. (Originally published as *Personality: A psychological interpretation,* 1937.)

Allport, G. W. Introduction to *William James: Psychology, the briefer course.* New York: Holt, 1961.

Allport, G. W. *Letters from Jenny.* New York: Harcourt, Brace & World, 1965.

Allport, G. W., & Vernon, P. E. *Studies in expressive movement.* New York: Hafner, 1967. (Originally published 1933.)

Anderson, P., & Fisch, M. H. *Philosophy in America.* New York: Appleton-Century, 1939.

Angell, J. R. The province of functional psychology. *Psychological Review,* 1896, *3*(4), 357–370.

Annis, A. The autobiography: Its uses and value in professional psychology. *Journal of Counseling Psychology,* 1967, *14,* 9–17.

Anonymous. *Clinical psychologists and psychological health care: Questions and answers for you and your family.* Division of Clinical and Professional Psychology, California State Psychological Association: 1980.

Appelbaum, S. A. The idealization of insight. *International Journal of Psychoanalytic Psychotherapy,* 1975, *4,* 272–302.

Appelbaum, S. A. *Out in inner space: A psychoanalyst explores the new therapies.* New York: Doubleday, 1979.

Arendt, H. *The human condition.* Chicago: University of Chicago Press, 1958.

Assagioli, R. *Synthesis in psychotherapy.* Paper presented at the Sixth International Congress of Psychotherapy, London, August 1964.

Assagioli, R. *Psychosynthesis: A manual of principles and techniques.* New York: Hobbs, Dorman, 1965.

Authier, J., Gustafson, K., Guerney, B., & Kasdorf, J. A. The psychological practitioner as a teacher: A theoretical-historical and practical review. *The Counseling Psychologist,* 1975, *5,* 31–49.

Bakan, D. *Sigmund Freud and the Jewish mystical tradition.* Princeton, N.J.: Van Nostrand, 1958.

Bandler, R., & Grinder, J. *The structure of magic* (Vol. 1). Palo Alto: Science & Behavior Books, 1975.

Bandler, R., & Grinder, J. *Frogs into princes: Neuro linguistic programming.* Moab, Utah: Real People Press, 1979.

Bargar, J. Ernest Hilgard: Sprouting a new role as historian. *APA Monitor,* August/September 1981, pp. 14–15.

Baruk, H. Modern neuropsychiatry and Freudian psychoanalysis. In H. Riese (Ed.), *Historical explorations in medicine and psychiatry.* New York: Springer, 1978. (a)

Baruk, H. *Patients are people like us.* New York: Morrow, 1978. (b)

Bateson, G. *Steps to an ecology of mind.* New York: Chandler, 1972.

Benson, H. *The relaxation response.* New York: Morrow, 1975.

Bergin, A. E., & Strupp, H. H. *Changing frontiers in the science of psychotherapy.* Chicago: Aldine-Atherton, 1972.

Berkman, L. F. Social networks, host resistance, and mortality. Doctoral dissertation, School of Public Health, University of California at Berkeley, 1977.

Beutler, L. E. *Eclectic psychotherapy: A systematic approach.* New York: Pergamon Press, 1983.

Birk, L., & Brinkley-Birk, A. W. Psychoanalysis and behavior therapy. *American Journal of Psychiatry,* 1974, *131,* 499–510.

Bolles, R. N. *What color is your parachute?* Berkeley, Calif.: Ten Speed Press, 1980.

Bolles, R. N. *The three boxes of life and how to get out of them.* Berkeley, Calif.: Ten Speed Press, 1981.

Boulding, K. E. *The image.* Ann Arbor: University of Michigan Press, 1956.

Bower, G. Mood and memory. *American Psychologist,* 1981, *36,* 129–145.

Bowerman, W., & Harris, W. E. *Jogging.* New York: Grosset & Dunlap, 1967.

Boylston, W. H., & Tuma, S. M. Training of mental health professionals through the use of the "bug-in-the-ear." *American Journal of Psychiatry,* 1972, *129,* 124–127.

Bradburn, N. M. *Reports on happiness: A pilot study of behavior related to mental health.* Chicago: Aldine, 1965.

Bradburn, N. M. *The structure of psychological well-being.* Chicago: Aldine, 1969.

Brady, J. P. Psychotherapy by combined behavioral and dynamic approach. *Comprehensive Psychiatry,* 1968, *9,* 536–543.

Breger, L., & McGaugh, J. Critique and reformulation of "learning theory": Approaches to psychotherapy and neurosis. *Psychological Bulletin,* 1965, *63,* 338–358.

Breuer, J., & Freud, S. *Studies on hysteria.* New York: Basic Books, 1957.

Brewer, W. F. There is no convincing evidence for operant or classical conditioning in adult humans. In W. B. Weimer & D. S. Palermo (Eds.), *Cognition and symbolic processes.* Hillsdale, N.J.: Erlbaum, 1974.

Brown, G. I. *Human teaching for human learning.* New York: Viking Press, 1971.

Buhler, C. The human course of life in its goal aspects. *Journal of Humanistic Psychology,* 1964, *4,* 1–18.

Burrow, T. Character and the neuroses. *The Psychoanalytic Review,* 1914, *1,* 121–128.

Burrow, T. The genesis and meaning of "homosexuality" and its relation to the problem of introverted mental states. *The Psychoanalytic Review,* 1917, *4,* 272–284.

Burrow, T. The origin of the incest-awe. *The Psychoanalytic Review,* 1918, *5,* 243–254.

Burrow, T. *The neurosis of man.* New York: Harcourt, Brace, 1949.

Burrow, T. *Science and man's behavior.* New York: Philosophical Library, 1953.

Burrow, T. *A search for man's sanity: The selected letters.* New York: Oxford University Press, 1958.

Burton, A. (Ed.). *What makes behavior change possible?* New York: Brunner/Mazel, 1976.

Buss, A. H. *Self-consciousness and social anxiety.* San Francisco: Freeman, 1980.

Butler, R. The life review: An interpretation of reminiscence in the aged. *Psychiatry*, 1963, *26*, 65–76.

Cairns, R. B. Developmental theory before Piaget: The remarkable contributions of James Mark Baldwin. *Journal of Contemporary Psychology*, 1980, *25*, 438–439.

California Department of Mental Health. *In pursuit of wellness*. San Francisco, Calif.: Office of Prevention, 1979.

Campbell, A. *The sense of well-being in America*. New York: McGraw-Hill, 1981.

Cantril, H. *The pattern of human concerns*. New Brunswick, N.J.: Rutgers University Press, 1965.

Cantril, H., & Roll, C. W. *Hopes and fears of the American people*. New York: Universe Books, 1971.

Carlson, E. T. The history of multiple personality in the United States: I. The beginnings. *American Journal of Psychiatry*, 1981, *138*, 666–668.

Cattell, R. B. *Personality and mood by questionnaire*. San Francisco: Jossey-Bass, 1973.

Cavanagh, M·E. *The counseling experience: A theoretical and practical approach*. Monterey, Calif.: Brooks/Cole, 1982.

Circincione, D., Hart, J. L., Karle, W., & Switzer, A. The functional approach to using dreams in marital and family therapy. *Journal of Marital and Family Therapy*, 1980, *6*, 147–151.

Clynes, M. *Sentics: The touch of the emotions*. New York: Anchor Press, 1978.

Colligan, D. Milgram and his cyranoid. *Omni*, March 1980, pp. 108–115.

Comfort, A. *The joy of sex*. New York: Crown, 1972.

Corriere, R., & Hart, J. *The dream makers*. New York: Funk & Wagnalls, 1977. (French edition: *Les maîtres rêveurs*. Montreal, Scriptomedia, 1977.)

Corriere, R., & Hart, J. T. *Psychological fitness*. New York: Harcourt, Brace, Jovanovich, 1979.

Corriere, R., Hart, J., Karle, W., Binder, J., Gold, S., & Woldenberg, L. Toward a new theory of dreaming. *Journal of Clinical Psychology*, 1977, *33*, 807–819.

Corriere, R., Hart, J. Karle, W., Switzer, A., & Woldenberg, L. Application of the process scoring system to waking, dream and therapy reports. *Journal of Clinical Psychology*, 1978, *34*, 700–706.

Cousins, N. *Anatomy of an illness as perceived by the patient*. New York: Norton, 1979.

Dabrowski, K. *Positive disintegration*. Boston: Little, Brown, 1964.

Dabrowski, K. *Personality-shaping through positive disintegration*. Boston: Little, Brown, 1967.

Dabrowski, K., & Piechowski, M. M. *Theory of levels of emotional development* (2 vols.). New York: Dabor Science, 1977.

Darwin, C. *On the origin of species by means of natural selection*. London: Murray, 1859.

Darwin, C. *The descent of man*. New York: Appleton, 1871.

Darwin, C. *The expression of the emotions in man and animals*. Chicago: University of Chicago Press, 1965. (Originally published, 1872.)

Darwin, C. *The illustrated origin of the species* (Abridged by R. E. Leakey). New York: Hill & Wang, 1979.

Davidson, H. A. The image of the psychiatrist. *American Journal of Psychiatry*, 1964, *121*, 329–334.

Davis, L. E., & Cherns, A. B. *The quality of working life*. New York: Free Press, 1975.

Davis, M., Eshelman, E. R., & McKay, M. *The relaxation and stress reduction workbook*. Richmond, Calif.: New Harbinger, 1980.

DeBartolo, D. *The MAD guide to self improvement*. New York: Warner, 1979.

Dewald, P. A. Toward a general concept of the therapeutic process. *International Journal of Psychoanalytic Psychotherapy*, 1976, *5*, 283–299.

Dewey, J. The reflex arc concept in psychology. *Psychological Review*, 1896, *3*, 357–370.

Dollard, J. *Criteria for a life history.* New York: Peter Smith, 1949.

Drucker, P. *People and performance.* New York: Harper & Row, 1977.

Dubos, R. *Beast or angel?: Choices that make us human.* New York: Scribner's, 1974.

Egan, G. *Exercises in helping skills.* Monterey, Calif.: Brooks/Cole, 1975. (a)

Egan, G. *The skilled helper.* Monterey, Calif.: Brooks/Cole, 1975. (b)

Ekman, P. Universals and cultural differences in facial expression of emotion. In J. K. Cole (Ed.), *Nebraska Symposium on Motivation.* Lincoln: University of Nebraska Press, 1971.

Ekman, P. (Ed.). *Darwin and facial expression.* New York: Academic Press, 1973.

Ekman, P., & Friesen, W. V. *Unmasking the face.* Englewood Cliffs, N.J.: Prentice Hall, 1975.

Ekman, P., Friesen, W. V., & Ellsworth, P. *Emotion in the human face.* New York: Pergamon Press, 1972.

Ellenberger, H. F. *The discovery of the unconscious.* New York: Basic Books, 1970.

Erikson, J. *Activity, recovery, growth.* New York: Norton, 1976.

Evans, R. I. *Carl Rogers: The man and his ideas.* New York: Dutton, 1975.

Ey, H. Pierre Janet: The man and his work. In B. Wolman (Ed.), *Historical roots of contemporary psychology.* New York: Harper & Row, 1968.

Eysenck, H. J. The effects of psychotherapy: An evaluation. *Journal of Consulting Psychology,* 1952, *16,* 319–324.

Fadiman, J., & Frager, R. *Personality and growth.* New York: Harper & Row, 1976.

Feather, B. W., & Rhoads, J. M. Psychodynamic behavior therapy: Theory and rationale. *Archives of General Psychiatry,* 1972, *26,* 496–502.

Ferster, C. B. The difference between behavioral and conventional psychology. *The Journal of Nervous and Mental Disease,* 1974, *159,* 153–157.

Fey, W. F. Doctrine and experience: Their influence upon the psychotherapist. *Journal of Consulting Psychology,* 1958, *22,* 403–409.

Fiedler, F. A. A comparison of therapeutic relationships in psychoanalytic, nondirective, and Adlerian therapy. *Journal of Consulting Psychology,* 1950, *14,* 436–445.

Fish, J. M. *Placebo therapy.* San Francisco: Jossey-Bass, 1973.

Fisher, S., & Greenberg, R. P. *The scientific credibility of Freud's theories and therapy.* New York: Basic Books, 1977.

Flanagan, J. C. A research approach to improving our quality of life. *American Psychologist,* 1978, *33,* 138–147.

Flanders, N. A. *Analysing teaching behavior.* Reading, Mass.: Addison-Wesley, 1970.

Foster, G. The psychotherapy of William James. *Psychoanalytic Review,* 1943, *32,* 300–318.

Foulkes, D. *Children's dreams: Longitudinal studies.* New York: Wiley, 1981.

Foulkes, D., & Griffin, M. L. An experimental study of "creative dreaming." *Sleep Research* (BIS/BRI), 1976, *5,* 129. (Abstract)

Foulkes, D., Larson, J. D., Swanson, E. M., & Rardin, M. Two studies of childhood dreaming. *American Journal of Orthopsychiatry,* 1969, *39,* 627–643.

Fournies, F. *Coaching for improved work performance.* New York: Van Nostrand Reinhold, 1978.

Fozard, J. J., & Popkin, S. J. Optimizing adult development—ends and means of an applied psychology of aging. *American Psychologist,* 1978, *33,* 975–988.

Frank, J. *Persuasion and healing* (Rev. ed.). New York: Schocken Books, 1974.

Frankl, V. *Man's search for meaning.* New York: Pocket Books, 1963.

Franklin, B. *The autobiography and other writings.* New York: New American Library, 1961.

Freidman, M., & Rosenman, R. *Type A behavior and your heart.* New York: Fawcett, 1974.

Freud, S. *A general introduction to psychoanalysis.* New York: Permabook, 1953.

Freud, S. *The interpretation of dreams*. New York: Basic Books, 1960.

Freud, S. *New introductory lectures in psychoanalysis*. (J. Strachey, trans.) New York: Norton, 1965. (Originally published, 1933.)

Fried, E. *Active/passive: The crucial psychological dimension*. New York: Harper, 1971.

Galton, F. *Memories of my life*. London: Methuen, 1908.

Garfield, S. L. *Psychotherapy: An eclectic approach*. New York: Wiley, 1980.

Garfield, S. L., & Kurtz, R. Clinical psychologists in the 1970s. *American Psychologist*, 1976, *31*, 1–9.

Gendlin, E. *Focusing*. New York: Everest House, 1978.

Gendlin, E. Personal communication, October 27, 1979.

Goldfried, M. R. Some views on effective principles of psychotherapy. *Cognitive Therapy and Research*, 1980, *4*, 271–306.

Goldfried, M. R., & Davison, G. *Clinical behavior therapy*. New York: Holt, Rinehart & Winston, 1976.

Goldschmid, M. L., Stein, D. D., Weissman, H. N., & Sorrells, J. A. A survey of the training and practices of clinical psychologists. *The Clinical Psychologist*, 1969, *22*, 89–107.

Goleman, D. 1,528 little geniuses and how they grew. *Psychology Today*, 1980, *13*, 28–53.

Gooch, S. *Total man*. New York: Holt, Rinehart & Winston, 1972.

Gooch, S. *Personality and evolution*. London: Wildwood House, 1973.

Gottman, J. M., & Leiblum, S. *How to do psychotherapy and how to evaluate it*. New York: Holt, Rinehart & Winston, 1974.

Gould, R. *Transformations: Growth and change in adult life*. New York: Simon & Schuster, 1978.

Grinder, J., & Bandler, R. *The structure of magic* (Vol. 2). Palo Alto, Calif.: Science & Behavior Books, 1976.

Guenther, R. Employers try in-house fitness centers. *Wall Street Journal*, November 10, 1981.

Hahn, M. E. *Psychoevaluation*. New York: McGraw-Hill, 1963.

Haley, J. *Strategies of psychotherapy*. New York: Grune & Stratton, 1963.

Haley, J. *Uncommon therapy*. New York: Norton, 1973.

Hall, C., & Lindzey, G. *Theories of personality* (3rd ed.). New York: Wiley, 1978.

Hall, G. S. *Adolescence*. New York: Appleton, 1904.

Hall, G. S. *Senescence: The last half of life*. New York: Arno Press, 1972. (Originally published, 1922.)

Hall, G. S. *Life and confessions of a psychologist*. New York: Arno Press, 1977. (Originally published, 1923.)

Harlow, H. Manipulation drive. *Journal of Experimental Psychology*, 1950, *40*, 228–234.

Harlow, H. *Learning to love*. New York: Ballantine, 1971.

Harris, L. *The Playboy report on American men*. New York: Playboy, 1977.

Harris, L. *The Perrier survey of fitness in America*. New York: Harris, 1979.

Hart, J. T. Memory and the feeling-of-knowing experience. *Journal of Educational Psychology*, 1965, *56*, 208–216.

Hart, J. T. Memory and the memory-monitoring process. *Journal of Verbal Learning and Behavior*, 1967, *6*, 685–691.

Hart, J. T. Beyond psychotherapy—the applied psychology of the future. In J. T. Hart & T. M. Tomlinson (Eds.), *New directions in client-centered therapy*. Boston: Houghton Mifflin, 1970. (a)

Hart, J. T. Looking back and ahead: A conversation with Carl Rogers. In J. T. Hart & T. M. Tomlinson (Eds.), *New directions in client-centered therapy*. Boston: Houghton Mifflin, 1970. (b)

Hart, J. T. The significance of William James' ideas for modern psychotherapy. *Journal of Contemporary Psychotherapy*, 1981, *12*, 88–102.

Hart, J. T., & Binder, J. *Making dreams work for you*. Abstract of family therapy workshop, Experience the Experts in Family Therapy, Forest Hospital, Chicago, October 24, 1976.

Hart, J. T., & Cousins, N. Personal communication, University of California, Los Angeles, October 3, 1980.

Hart, J. T., & Tomlinson, T. (Eds.). *New directions in client-centered therapy*. Boston: Houghton Mifflin, 1970.

Hart, J. T., Corriere, R., & Binder, J. *Going sane*. New York: Aronson, 1975. (Delta Paperback, 1976.)

Hart, J. T., Corriere, R., Karle, W., & Woldenberg, L. *Dreaming and waking: The functional approach to using dreams*. Los Angeles: The Center Foundation Press, 1980. (Reprinted by Peace Press, 1981.)

Hart, J. T., Corriere, R., & Karle, W. Functional psychotherapy. In R. Corsini (Ed.), *Handbook of innovative therapies*. New York: Wiley Interscience, 1981.

Hartshorn, K., Corriere, R., Karle, W., Switzer, A., Hart, J., Gold, S., & Binder, J. A re-application of the process scoring system for dreams. *Journal of Clinical Psychology*, 1977, *33*, 844–848.

Heath, D. *Explorations of maturity*. New York: Appleton-Century-Crofts, 1965.

Herink, R. (Ed.). *The psychotherapy handbook: The A to Z guide to more than 250 different therapies in use today*. New York: New American Library, 1980.

Hersey, P., & Blanchard, K. H. *Management of organizational behavior* (3rd ed.). Englewood Cliffs, N.J.: Prentice Hall, 1977.

Herzberg, F., Mauser, B., & Snyderman, B. B. *The motivation to work*. New York: Wiley, 1959.

Hicks, H. G., & Gullett, C. R. *Management*. New York: McGraw-Hill, 1981.

High, R. P., & Woodward, W. R. William James and Gordon Allport: Parallels in their maturing conceptions of self and personality. In R. W. Rieber & K. Salzinger (Eds.), *Psychology: Theoretical-historical perspectives*. New York: Academic Press, 1980.

Hilgard, E. R. *Divided consciousness: Multiple controls in human thought and action*. New York: Wiley, 1977.

Holmes, T. H., & Rahe, R. H. The social readjustment rating scale. *Journal of Psychosomatic Research*, 1967, *11*, 213–218.

Holt, J. *Never too late: My musical life story*. New York: Delta, 1978.

Houston, J. P., Bee, H., Hatfield, E., & Rimm, D. C. *Invitation to psychology*. New York: Academic Press, 1979.

Hudson, L. *The cult of the fact*. New York: Harper, 1972.

Humphrey, C. *Thinking*. London: Methuen, 1951.

Hutchins, D. E. Ranking major counseling strategies with the TFA/Matrix system. *Personnel and Guidance Journal*, 1982, *60*, 427–431.

Jacobs, A., & Wolpin, M. A second look at systematic desensitization. In *Psychology of private events* (Report). New York: Academic Press, 1971.

Jacobson, E. *You must relax*. New York: McGraw-Hill, 1962.

Jacobson, E. *Progressive relaxation*. Chicago: University of Chicago Press, 1974.

Jahoda, M. *Current concepts of positive mental health*. New York: Basic Books, 1958.

James, W. What is an emotion? *Mind*, 1884, *9*, 188–205.

James, W. *Psychology: Briefer course*. New York: Holt, 1892.

James, W. What is an emotion? *Mind*, 1894, *9*, 188–205.

James, W. Philosophical conceptions and practical results. *The University Chronicle*, University of California, 1898, *1*, 289–309. (Reprinted in P. R. Anderson & M. H. Fisch (Eds.), *Philosophy in America*, New York: Appleton-Century, 1939.)

James, W. *The principles of psychology* (2 vols.). New York: Dover, 1950. (Originally published, 1890.)

James, W. The energies of men. In W. James, *Essays on faith and morals*. New York: World, 1962. (Originally published, 1907.)

James. W. The religion of healthy-mindedness. In N. Kiell (Ed.), *Psychological studies of famous Americans*. New York: Twayne, 1964.

Janet, P. *Principles of psychotherapy*. New York: Macmillan, 1924.

Janet, P. *The major symptoms of hysteria*. New York: Macmillan, 1929.

Janet, P. Autobiography. In C. Murchison (Ed.), *A history of psychology in autobiography* (Vol. 1). Worcester, Mass.: Clark University Press, 1930.

Jastrow, J. *Keeping mentally fit*. New York: Greenberg, 1928.

Jenkins, C. D. Behavioral risk factors in coronary artery disease. *Annual Review of Medicine,* 1978, *29,* 543–562.

Jenkins, C. D., Rosenman, R. H., & Friedman, M. Development of an objective psychological test for the determination of the coronary-prone behavior pattern in employed men. *Journal of Chronic Disease,* 1967, *20,* 371–379.

Jenkins, C. D., Rosenman, R. H., & Zyzanski, S. J. Prediction of clinical coronary heart disease by a test for the coronary-prone behavior pattern. *The New England Journal of Medicine,* 1974, *290,* 1271–1275.

Jones, E. *The life and work of Sigmund Freud* (Vol. 2). New York: Basic Books, 1955.

Jones, R. M. *Fantasy and feeling in education*. New York: Harper Colophon, 1968.

Jourard, S. M. *Healthy personality: An approach from the viewpoint of humanistic psychology*. New York: Macmillan, 1974.

Jung, C. G. *Memories, dreams, reflections*. New York: Vintage, 1961.

Jung, C. G. Psychological factors in human behaviour. In *Collected works* (Vol. 8). Princeton, N.J.: Princeton University Press, 1969.

Jung, C. G. *The archetypes of the collective unconscious*. Bollingen Series XX. Princeton, N.J.: Princeton University Press, 1974.

Kane, J. Fulfillment—it requires balanced satisfaction. *Psychology Today,* 1977, *11,* 33.

Kaplan, H. S. *The new sex therapy*. New York: Brunner/Mazel, 1974.

Karasu, T. B. Toward unification of psychotherapies: A complementary model. *American Journal of Psychotherapy,* 1979, *23,* 555–563.

Kardiner, A. *My analysis with Freud*. New York: Norton, 1977.

Karle, W., Hopper, M., Corriere, R., & Hart, J. The alteration of sleep patterns in psychotherapy. In M. H. Chase, M. Mitler, & P. L. Walter (Eds.), *Sleep Research,* 1977, *6,* 150.

Karle, W., Hart, J., Corriere, R., Gold, S., & Maple, C. Preliminary study of psychological changes in Feeling Therapy. *Psychological Reports,* 1978, *43,* 1327–1334.

Karle, W., Corriere, R., Hart, J., & Woldenberg, L. The functional analysis of dreams: A new theory of dreaming. *Archives of the Behavioral Sciences,* 1980, *55,* 1–78. (Also published in *The Journal of Clinical Psychology Monograph Supplement,* 1980, *36,* 5–78.)

Karle, W., Hopper, M., Corriere, R., Hart, J., & Switzer, A. Two preliminary studies on sleep and psychotherapy. *Physiology and Behavior,* 1980, *19,* 419–423.

Keleman, S. *Sexuality, self and survival*. San Francisco: Lodestar Press, 1971.

Kelley, H. *The golfing machine*. Seattle, Wash.: Star System Press, 1979.

Kelly, E. L. Clinical psychology—1960. Report of survey findings. *Newsletter, Division of Clinical Psychology,* 1961, *14*(1), 1–11.

Kelly, E. L., Goldberg, L. R., Fiske, D. W., & Kokowski, J. M. Twenty-five years later: A follow-up study of the graduate students in clinical psychology assessed in the V.A. selection research project. *American Psychologist,* 1978, *33,* 746–755.

Kiesler, D. J. *The process of psychotherapy*. Chicago: Aldine, 1973.

Kirsch, I., Wolpin, M., & Knutson, J. L. Comparison of in vivo methods for rapid reduction of "stage-fright" in the college classroom. *Behavior Therapy*, 1975, *6*, 165–171.

Knowles, M. *The adult learner: A neglected species* (2nd ed.). Houston: Gulf, 1978.

Koberg, D., & Bagnall, J. *The universal traveler, a soft-systems guide to: Creativity, problem-solving, and the process of reaching goals*. Los Altos, Calif.: Kaufman, 1976.

Koestler, A. *The act of creation*. New York: Macmillan, 1964.

Koestler, A. *Janus*. New York: Vintage Books, 1979.

Kohl, H. *Half the house*. New York: Bantam, 1976.

Kohut, H. *The restoration of the self*. New York: International Universities Press, 1977.

Kohut, H. *The search for the self* (Vols. 1 & 2). New York: International Universities Press, 1978.

Korchin, S. *Modern clinical psychology*. New York: Basic Books, 1976.

Kroner, I. N., & Brown, W. H. The mechanical third ear. *Journal of Consulting Psychology*, 1952, *16*, 81–84.

Kuhn, T. *The essential tension*. Chicago: University of Chicago Press, 1977.

Laing, R. D. *The politics of experience*. New York: Ballantine, 1967.

Laing, R. D. *Self and others*. New York: Pantheon, 1969.

Lakein, A. *How to get control of your time and your life*. New York: Signet, 1973.

Langer, S. K. *Mind: An essay on human feeling* (2 vols.). Baltimore: Johns Hopkins Press, 1967-1972.

Larson, D. Therapeutic schools, styles, and schoolism: A national survey. *Journal of Humanistic Psychology*, 1980, *20*(3), 1–20.

Lawrence, D. H. *Psychoanalysis and the unconscious and Fantasia of the unconscious*. New York: Viking Press, 1960. (Originally published, 1921.)

Lazarus, A. A. *Multi-modal behavior therapy*. New York: Springer, 1976.

Lazarus, A. A. Has behavior therapy outlived its usefulness? *American Psychologist*, 1977, *32*, 550–554.

Lecky, P. *Self-consistency: A theory of personality*. New York: Island Press, 1945. (Revised 1951.)

LeClair, R. C. (Ed.). *The letters of William James and Theodore Flournoy*. Madison, Wisc.: University of Wisconsin Press, 1966.

Lettenberg, H. (Ed.). *Handbook of behavior modification and behavior therapy*. Englewood Cliffs, N.J.: Prentice-Hall, 1976.

Levinson, D. J. *The seasons of a man's life*. New York: Ballantine, 1978.

Lewis, W. C. *Why people change*. New York: Holt, Rinehart & Winston, 1972.

Lewis, W. C., Wolman, R. N., & King, M. The development of the language of emotions. *American Journal of Psychiatry*, 1971, *127*, 1491–1497.

Lieberman, M., & Falk, J. M. The remembered past as a source of data for research on the life cycle. *Human Development*, 1971, *14*, 132–141.

Lillard, R. G. *American life in autobiography*. Stanford, Calif.: Stanford University Press, 1956.

Lilly, J. C. *Programming and metaprogramming in the human biocomputer: Theory and experiments*. Baltimore, Md.: Communications Research Institute, 1968.

Lilly, J. C. *The deep self*. New York: Simon & Schuster, 1977.

London, P. *The modes and morals of psychotherapy*. New York: Holt, Rinehart & Winston, 1964.

London, P. The end of ideology in behavior modification. *American Psychologist*, 1972, *27*, 913–920.

Lovin, B. C., & Casstevens, E. R. *Coaching, learning, and action*. New York: American Management Association, 1971.

Lowen, A. *Physical dynamics of character structure.* New York: Grune & Stratton, 1958.

Lowen, A. *The betrayal of the body.* New York: Macmillan, 1967.

Lowenthal Fiske, M. Changing hierarchies of commitment in adulthood. In N. J. Smelser & E. Eriksen, *Themes of work and love in adulthood.* Cambridge: Harvard University Press, 1980.

Lowenthal Fiske, M., Thurnher, M., & Chiriboya, D. *Four stages of life: A comparative study of women and men facing transitions.* San Francisco: Jossey-Bass, 1976.

Luce, G. *Your second life.* New York: Delacorte Press, 1979.

Luft, J. *Of human interaction.* Palo Alto, Calif.: Mayfield, 1969.

Luft, J. *Group processes.* Palo Alto, Calif.: Mayfield, 1970.

Luthe, W. (Ed.). *Autogenic therapy* (6 vols.). New York: Grune & Stratton, 1969.

Luthe, W. *The creativity mobilization technique.* New York: Grune & Stratton, 1976.

Lynch, J. J. *The broken heart.* New York. Basic Books, 1977.

Mackinnon, D. W., & Dukes, W. F. Repression. In L. Postman (Ed.), *Psychology in the making.* New York: Knopf, 1964.

MacLean, P. *A triune concept of the brain and behaviour.* Toronto: University of Toronto Press, 1973.

MacLean, P. The evolution of three mentalities. In S. L. Washburn & E. R. McCown (Eds.), *Human evolution: Biosocial perspectives.* Menlo Park, Calif.: Benjamin/Cummings, 1978.

Madison, P. *Freud's concept of repression and defense.* Minneapolis: University of Minnesota Press, 1961.

Mahl, G. F. Disturbances and silences in the patient's speech in psychotherapy. *Journal of Abnormal and Social Psychology,* 1956, *53,* 1–15.

Mahl, G. F. Sensory factors in the control of expressive behavior: An experimental study of the function of auditory self-stimulation and visual feedback in the dynamics of vocal and gestural behavior in the interview situation. *Acta Psychologica,* 1961, *19,* 497–498.

Mahl, G. F. People talking when they can't hear their own voices. In A. Siegman & B. Pope (Eds.), *Studies in dyadic interaction.* New York: Pergamon Press, 1972.

Mailer, N. *The executioner's song.* New York: Warner, 1979.

Marmor, J. Dynamic psychotherapy and behavior therapy: Are they irreconcilable? *Archives of General Psychiatry.* 1971, *24,* 22–28.

Marston, A. R. Behavior ecology emerges from behavior modification. *Behavior Modification,* 1979, *3,* 147–160.

Marston, A. R., Hart, J., Hileman, C., & Faunce, W. Toward the laboratory study of sadness and crying: A more realistic analogue of psychotherapy. In *American Journal of Psychology,* 1983, in press.

Martin, D. G. *Learning-based client-centered therapy.* Monterey, Calif.: Brooks/Cole, 1972.

Maslow, A. H. *Motivation and personality.* New York: Harper, 1954.

Maslow, A. H. *The psychology of science: A reconnaissance.* Harper & Row, 1966.

Maslow, A. H. *The farther reaches of human nature.* New York: Viking Press, 1971.

Masters, W., & Johnson, V. *Human sexual response.* Boston: Little, Brown, 1966.

Mathews, W., & Rader, R. *Autobiography, biography, and the novel.* Los Angeles: University of California at Los Angeles Press, 1973.

Mayo, E. *The psychology of Pierre Janet.* Westport, Conn.: Greenwood Press, 1972. (Originally published, 1952.)

McKeachie, W. Psychology in America's bicentennial year. *American Psychologist,* December 1976, pp. 819–833.

McNair, D. M., & Lorr, M. An analysis of professed psychotherapeutic techniques. *Journal of Consulting Psychology,* 1964, *28,* 265–271.

Mead, G. In C. W. Morris (Ed.), *Mind, self, and society.* Chicago: University of Chicago Press, 1934.

Meehan, M. C. Psychiatrists portrayed in fiction. *Journal of the American Medical Association,* 1964, *188,* 255–258.

Meichenbaum, D. *Cognitive-behavior modification: An integrative approach.* New York: Plenum Press, 1977.

Menninger, K. *Theory of psychoanalytic technique.* New York: Basic Books, 1958.

Miller, G. A. *Psychology: The science of mental life.* New York: Harper & Row, 1962.

Minkoff, N. Illnesses and deaths linked to recession. *Los Angeles Times,* December 13, 1980.

Montague, A. *Growing young.* New York: McGraw-Hill, 1981.

Montague, A., & Matson, F. *The human connection.* New York: McGraw-Hill, 1979.

Monte, C. F. *Beneath the mask: An introduction to theories of personality.* New York: Holt, Rinehart & Winston, 1980.

Mowrer, O. H. *The crisis in psychiatry and religion.* Princeton, N.J.: Van Nostrand, 1961.

Munsterberg, H. *The film—a psychological study.* New York: Dover, 1970. (Originally published, 1916.)

Murray, H. A. *Explorations in personality.* New York: Oxford University Press, 1938.

Murray, H. A. *Assessment of men.* New York: Rinehart, 1948.

Murray, H. A. *Endeavors in psychology.* New York: Harper & Row, 1981.

Nideffer, R. M. *The inner athlete.* New York: Crowell, 1976.

Nideffer, R. M. *The ethics and practice of applied sports psychology.* Ann Arbor, Mich.: Mouvement Publications, 1981.

Nideffer, R. M., & Sharpe, R. C. *A.C.T.: Attention control training.* New York: Wyden, 1978.

Norbeck, C. (Ed.). *The complete book of American surveys.* New York: New American Library, 1980.

Nyberg, D. *Tough and tender learning.* Palo Alto, Calif.: National Press Books, 1971.

O'Banion, D., & Whaley, D. L. *Behavior contracting.* New York: Springer, 1981.

Oberndorf, C. P. *History of psychoanalysis in America.* New York: Grune & Stratton, 1953.

O'Donnell, J. M. The crisis of experimentalism in the 1920's: E. G. Boring and his uses of history. *American Psychologist,* 1979, *34,* 289–295.

Okun, B. F. *Effective helping: Interviewing and counseling techniques.* Belmont, Calif.: Wadsworth, 1976.

Ornstein, R. *The psychology of consciousness.* New York: Penguin Books, 1975.

Page, R. C. *How to lick executive stress.* New York: Cornerstone Library, 1961.

Palmer, S. *A primer of eclectic psychotherapy.* San Francisco: Brooks-Cole, 1979.

Pelletier, K. R. *Mind as healer, mind as slayer.* New York: Delta, 1977.

Peplau, L. A., & Perlman, D. Current research on loneliness: A survey. Mimeographed paper, University of California at Los Angeles, 1978.

Perls, F. S. Theory and technique of personality integration. *American Journal of Psychotherapy,* 1948, *2,* 565–586.

Perls, F. S. *Ego, hunger and aggression.* New York: Random House, 1969. (a)

Perls, F. S. *Gestalt therapy verbatim.* Lafayette, Calif.: Real People Press, 1969. (b)

Perls, F. S. Hefferline, R., & Goodman, P. *Gestalt therapy: Excitement and growth in the human personality.* New York: Julian Press, 1951.

Pervin, L. A. *Current controversies and issues in personality.* New York: Wiley, 1978.

Piechowski, M. A theoretical and empirical approach to the study of development. *Genetic Psychology Monographs,* 1975, *92,* 231–297.

Pietropinto, A., & Simenauer, J. *Husbands and wives.* New York: Times Books, 1979.

Plimpton, G. Ernest Hemingway. In G. Plimpton (Ed.), *Writers at work* (2nd series). New York: Penguin Books, 1963.

Polanyi, M. *Personal knowledge.* Chicago: University of Chicago Press, 1958.

Polanyi, M. *The tacit dimension.* Garden City, N.Y.: Doubleday, 1966.

Pratt, R. W., & Nideffer, R. M. *Taking care of business: A manual to guide the refinement of attention control training.* San Diego, Calif.: Enhanced Performance Associates, 1981.

Pribram, K. The neuropsychology of Sigmond Freud. In A. J. Bachrach (Ed.), *Experimental foundations of clinical psychology.* New York: Basic Books, 1962.

Prince, M. *The dissociation of personality.* New York: Meridian Books, 1957. (Originally published, 1905.)

Privette, G. Transcendent functioning: Full use of potentialities. In H. Otto & J. Mann (Eds.), *Ways of growth.* New York: Grossman Press, 1968.

Privette, G. Dynamics of peak performance. *Journal of Humanistic Psychology,* 1981, *21,* 57–67. (a)

Privette, G. The phenomenology of peak performance in sports. *International Journal of Sport Psychology,* 1981, *12,* 51–58. (b)

Prochaska, J. O. & Norcross, J. C. Contemporary psychotherapists: A national survey of characteristics, practices, orientations, and attitudes. *Psychotherapy,* 1983, *20,* 161–173.

Progoff, I. *At a journal workshop.* New York: Dialogue House Library, 1975.

Psychiatrists current thinking on sexual inadequacy. *Sexuality Today,* February 12, 1979, p. 1.

Pudovkin, V. I. *Film technique and film acting.* New York: Grove Press, 1970.

Raimy, V. C. (Ed.). *Training in clinical psychology.* Englewood Cliffs, N.J.: Prentice Hall, 1950.

Raimy, V. C. *Misunderstandings of the self.* San Francisco: Jossey-Bass, 1975.

Rainer, T. *The new diary.* Los Angeles: J. P. Tarcher, 1978.

Rank, O. *Will therapy and truth and reality* (Jessie Taft, trans.). New York: Knopf, 1945.

Reich, W. *Character analysis* (3rd ed.) (T. P. Wolfe, trans.). New York: Noonday Press, 1949. (Originally published in German in 1933.)

Reich, W. *Selected writings.* New York: Farrar, Straus & Cudahy, 1960.

Reich, W. The function of the orgasm. New York: Noonday Press, 1961. (Originally published in 1942.)

Reinhold, M. Darwinian evolution of certain aspects of mind. In H. Reise (Ed.), *Historical explorations in medicine and psychiatry.* New York: Springer, 1978.

Reisman, J. M. *A history of clinical psychology.* New York: Irvington, 1976.

Report of the Research Task Force of the National Institute of Mental Health. *Research in the service of mental health.* DHEW Publication No. (ADM) 75–236. Rockville, Md.: 1975.

Rice, D. G., Gurman, A. S., & Razins, A. M. Therapist sex, "style," and theoretical orientation. *Journal of Nervous and Mental Disease,* 1974, *159,* 413–421.

Robinson, V. (Ed.). *Jessie Taft: A professional biography.* Philadelphia: University of Pennsylvania Press, 1962.

Rogers, C. R. *On becoming a person.* Boston: Houghton Mifflin, 1961.

Rogers, C. R. (Ed.). *The therapeutic relationship and its impact: A study of psychotherapy with schizophrenics.* Madison, Wisc.: University of Wisconsin Press, 1967.

Rosenblatt, D. Dreams in the dream factory. *Film Society,* 1963, 33–34.

Rosenzweig, S. William James and the stream of thought. In B. Wolman (Ed.), *Historical roots of contemporary thought.* New York: Harper & Row, 1968.

Ross, B. William James: A prime mover of the psychoanalytic movement in America. In G. E. Gifford (Ed.), *Psychoanalysis, psychotherapy, and the New England medical scene. 1894–1944.* New York: Science History, 1978.

Ross, D. G. *Stanley Hall*. Chicago: University of Chicago Press, 1972.

Ross, D. American psychology and psychoanalysis: William James and G. Stanley Hall. In J. M. Quen & E. T. Carlson (Eds.), *American psychoanalysis: Origins and development*. New York: Brunner/Mazel, 1975.

Rychlak, J. *A philosophy of science for personality theory*. Boston: Houghton Mifflin, 1968.

Rychlak, J. *The psychology of rigorous humanism*. New York: Wiley, 1977.

Rychlak, J. The stream of consciousness: Implications for a humanistic psychological theory. In K. S. Pope & J. L. Singer (Eds.), *The stream of consciousness*. New York: Plenum Press, 1978.

Sagan, C. *The dragons of Eden*. New York: Ballantine, 1977.

Sahakian, W. S. *History and systems of psychology*. New York: Wiley, 1975.

Schachter, S. The interaction of cognitive and physiological determinants of emotional state. In C. D. Spielberger (Ed.), *Anxiety and behavior*. New York: Academic Press, 1966.

Schellenberg, J. A. *Masters of social psychology*. New York: Oxford University Press, 1978.

Schultz, D. P. *A history of modern psychology*. New York: Academic Press, 1960.

Schumacher, E. F. *A guide for the perplexed*. New York: Harper & Row, 1977.

Schutz, W. C. *Joy: Expanding human awareness*. New York: Grove Press, 1967.

Schwartz, G. E., Fain, P. L., Salt, P., Mandel, M. R., & Klerman, G. L. Facial muscle patterning to affective imagery in depressed and nondepressed subjects. *Science*, 1976, *192*, 489–491.

Schwartz, T. *The responsive chord*. New York: Anchor Press, 1974.

Schwitzgebel, R. K., & Taylor, R. Impression formation under conditions of spontaneous and shadowed speech. *Journal of Social Psychology*, 1980, *110*, 253–263.

Scott, R., Karle, W., Switzer, A., Hart, J., Corriere, R., & Woldenberg, L. Psychophysiological correlates of the spontaneous K-complex. *Perceptual and Motor Skills*, 1978, *46*, 271–87.

Sears, R. R. Sources of life satisfactions of the Terman gifted men. *American Psychologist*, 1977, *32*, 119–128.

Sears, R. R., & Feldman, S. (Eds.). *The seven ages of man*. Los Altos, Calif.: Kaufman, 1973.

Segraves, R. T., & Smith, R. C. Concurrent psychotherapy and behavior therapy. *Archives of General Psychiatry*, 1976, *33*, 256–263.

Selye, H. *Stress without distress*. New York: Signet, 1974.

Shaffer, E. E. The autobiography in secondary school counseling. *Personnel and Guidance Journal*, 1954, *32*, 395–398.

Shaver, P., & Freedman, J. Your pursuit of happiness. *Psychology Today*, 1976, *10*, 28.

Sheehy, G. *Passages: Predictable crises of adult life*. New York: Bantam, 1976.

Sheehy, G. *Pathfinders*. New York: Morrow, 1981.

Shotter, J. *Images of man in psychological research*. London: Methuen, 1975.

Silverman, L. H. Some psychoanalytic considerations of non-psychoanalytic therapies: On the possibility of integrating treatment approaches and related issues. *Psychotherapy: Theory, Research and Practice*, 1974, *11*, 298–305.

Simons, G. F. *Keeping your personal journal*. New York: Paulist Press, 1978.

Skinner, B. F. *Beyond freedom and dignity*. New York: Bantam, 1971.

Slusher, H. *Man, sport and existence*. Philadelphia: Lee & Febiger, 1967.

Smalley, R. E., & Bloom, T. Social casework: The functional approach. In J. B. Turner (Ed.), *Encyclopedia of social work* (Vol. 2). Washington, D.C.: National Association of Social Workers, 1977.

Solow, H. Reflections of psychotherapy and the psychotherapist in the cinematic eye. Unpublished doctoral dissertation, California School of Professional Psychology at San Diego, 1978.

Speciality guidelines for the delivery of services. Washington, D.C.: American Psychological Association, 1981.

Spoerl, H. D. Abnormal and social psychology in the life and work of William James. *Journal of Abnormal and Social Psychology,* 1942, *37,* 3–19.

Strange, J. A search for sources of the stream of consciousness. In K. S. Pope & J. L. Singer (Eds.), *The stream of consciousness.* New York: Plenum Press, 1978.

Strupp, H. *Psychotherapy: Clinical, research, and theoretical issues.* New York: Jason Aronson, 1973.

Stum, D. L. DIRECT—a consultation skills training model. *Personnel and Guidance Journal,* 1982, *60,* 296–302.

Stumphauzer, J. S. A low cost "bug-in-the-ear" sound system for modification of therapist and parent behavior. *Behavior Therapy,* 1970, *2,* 249–250.

Suinn, R. (Ed.). *Psychology in sports.* Minneapolis, Minn.: Burgess, 1980.

Sulloway, F. J. *Freud, biologist of the mind.* New York: Basic Books, 1979.

Sundland, D. M. Orientations of psychotherapists. In A. S. Gurman & A. M. Razin (Eds.), *The therapist's contribution to effective psychotherapy: An empirical assessment.* London: Pergamon, 1976.

Sundland, D. M., & Barker, E. M. The orientation of psychotherapists. *Journal of Consulting Psychology,* 1962, *26,* 201–212.

Surgeon General's Report. *The health consequences of smoking.* Washington, D.C.: U.S. Government Printing Office, 1982.

Swan, G. E. On the structure of eclecticism: Cluster analysis of eclectic behavior therapists. *Professional Psychology,* 1979, *10,* 732–734.

Swan, G. E., & MacDonald, M. L. Behavior therapy in practice: A national survey of behavior therapists. *Behavior Therapy,* 1978, *9,* 799–807.

Syz, H. A summary note on the work of Trigant Burrow. *International Journal of Social Psychiatry,* 1961, *3*(4), 283–291.

Syz, H. Reflections on group- or phylo-analysis. *Acta Psychotherapy, Supplement,* 1963, *11,* 37–88.

Syz, H. Value problems in psychotherapy against the background of Trigant Burrow's group analysis. In H. Riese (Ed.), *Historical explorations in medicine and psychiatry.* New York: Springer, 1978.

Taft, J. *Social aspects of mental hygiene.* New Haven: Yale University Press, 1925.

Taft, J. *Otto Rank.* New York: Julian Press, 1958.

Taft, J. *The dynamics of therapy in a controlled relationship.* New York: Dover, 1962. (Originally published, 1933.)

Taft, J. (Ed.). *Couseling and protective service as family case work: A functional approach.* Philadelphia, Pa.: Pennsylvania School of Social Work, 1946.

Taylor, E. William James on psychotherapy, psychical research, and religious experience. Paper presented at the William James Symposium, American Psychological Association, New York, September 1, 1979.

Taylor, E. Impact of the Jamesian unconscious on American social movements. Paper presented at the William James Symposium, American Psychological Association Convention, Montreal, Canada, September 1980. (a)

Taylor, E., William James and C. G. Jung. *Spring, an Annual of Archetypal Psychology,* 1980, 1157–168. (b)

Taylor, E. Personal communication, January 2, 1981.

Taylor, R. In search of health. Paper presented to California State Department of Mental Health, March 20, 1979.

Terkel, S. *American dreams: Lost and found.* New York: Ballantine, 1981.

Thorne, F. C. *Principles of personality counseling: An eclectic viewpoint.* Brandon, Vt.: Journal of Clinical Psychology Press, 1950.

Thorne, F. C. *Principles of psychological examining.* Brandon, Vt.: Journal of Clinical Psychology Press, 1955.

Thorne, F. C. *Personality: A clinical eclectic viewpoint.* Brandon, Vt.: Journal of Clinical Psychology Press, 1961.

Thorne, F. C. Tutorial counseling: How to be psychologically healthy. *Clinical Psychology Monograph,* 1965, *20,* 1–157.

Thorne, F. C. *Integrative psychology.* Brandon, Vt.: Clinical Psychology, 1967.

Thorne, F. C. *Psychological case handling.* (Vol. 1): *An eclectic system of counseling and psychotherapy.* Brandon, Vt.: Clinical Psychology, 1968.

Thorne, F. C. Toward better self-understanding. In T. S. Krawiec (Ed.), *The psychologists* (Vol. 1). New York: Oxford, 1972.

Thorne, F. C. Unfrocking phoniness and pretensions. *Journal of Clinical Psychology,* 1979, *35,* 921.

Toffler, A. *The third wave.* New York: Morrow, 1980.

Tough, A. *The adult's learning projects.* Toronto: Ontario Institute for Studies in Education, 1971.

Trower, P., Bryant, B., & Argyle, M. *Social skills and mental health.* Pittsburgh, Pa.: University of Pittsburgh Press, 1978.

Truax, C. B., & Carkhuff, R. R. *Toward effective counseling and psychotherapy.* Chicago: Aldine, 1967.

Tyler, L. *The work of the counselor.* New York: Appleton-Century-Crofts, 1953.

Ubell, E. *How to save your life.* New York: Penguin Books, 1976.

Vaillant, G. *Adaptation to life.* Boston: Little, Brown, 1977.

Van de Castle, R. L. His, hers and the children's dreams. *Psychology Today,* 1970, *4,* 37–39.

Veroff, J., Douvan, E., & Kulka, R. A. *The inner American: A self-portrait from 1957 to 1976.* New York: Basic Books, 1981.

Veroff, J., Kulka, R. A., & Douvan, E. *Mental health in America: Patterns of help-seeking from 1957 to 1976.* New York: Basic Books, 1981.

Wachtel, P. L. *Psychoanalysis and behavior therapy.* New York: Basic Books, 1977.

Wallach, M. S., & Strupp, H. H. Dimensions of psychotherapists' activity. *Journal of Consulting Psychology,* 1964, *28,* 120–125.

Walster, E., & Walster, G. W. *A new look at love.* Reading, Mass.: Addison-Wesley, 1978.

Watson, R. I. The experimental tradition and clinical psychology. In J. Brozek and R. B. Evans (Eds.), *R. I. Watson's selected papers on the history of psychology.* Hanover, N.H.: University Press of New England, 1977.

Watzlawick, P. *The language of change.* New York: Basic Books, 1978.

Weiler, N. W. *Reality and career planning: A guide for personal growth.* Reading, Mass.: Addison-Wesley, 1977.

Weiss, P. *Sport: A philosophic inquiry.* Carbondale, Ill.: Southern Illinois University Press, 1969.

Weissman, H. N., Goldschmid, M. L., & Stern, D. D. Psychotherapeutic orientation and training: Their relation to the practices of clinical psychologists. *Journal of Consulting and Clinical Psychology,* 1971, *37,* 31–37.

White, T. Motivation reconsidered. *Psychological Review,* 1959, *66,* 297–333.

Whiteley, J. M. *The history of counseling psychology.* Monterey, Calif.: Brooks/Cole, 1980.

Whyte, L. L. *The unconscious before Freud.* New York: Basic Books, 1960.

Winget, C., & Kramer, M. *Dimensions of dreams.* Gainesville: University of Florida Press, 1979.

Winick, C. The psychiatrist in fiction. *The Journal of Nervous and Mental Disorders,* 1963, *136,* 43–57.

Wolfenstein, M., & Leites, N. *Movies: A psychological study.* New York: Arno Press, 1970. (Originally published by Free Press, 1950.)

Wolman, B. J. (Ed.). *Historical roots of contemporary psychology.* New York: Harper & Row, 1968.

Wolpe, J. *The practice of behavior therapy.* New York: Pergamon Press, 1969.

Wolpin, M. Desensitization by novice undergraduates: Some data at variance with Wolpe's reciprocal inhibition model. Paper delivered to Los Angeles Behavior Modification Group, January 12, 1969. (a) (Abstract)

Wolpin, M. Guided imagining to reduce avoidance behavior. *Psychotherapy,* 1969, *6,* 122–124. (b)

Wolpin, M., & Kirsch, I. Visual imagery, various muscle states and desensitization procedures. *Perceptual and Motor Skills,* 1974, *39,* 1143–1149.

Wolpin, M., & Raines, J. Visual imagery, expected roles and extinction as possible factors in reducing fear and avoidance behavior. *Behavior Research and Therapy,* 1966, *4,* 25–37.

Wondersman, A., Poppen, P. J., & Ricks, D. F. (Eds.). *Humanism and behaviorism: Dialogue and growth.* Elmsford, N.Y.: Pergamon Press, 1976.

Wood, J. *How do you feel? A guide to your emotions.* Englewood Cliffs, N.J.: Prentice Hall, 1974.

Woolfolk, R. L., & Richardson, F. C. *Stress, sanity, and survival.* New York: Simon & Schuster, 1978.

Zaleznik, A., Christensen, C. R., & Roethlisberger, F. J. *The motivation, productivity, and satisfaction of workers.* Boston: Harvard Business School, 1958.

Zimbardo, P. *Shyness: What it is and what to do about it.* Reading, Mass.: Addison-Wesley, 1977.

Zytowski, D. G., & Rosen, D. A. The grand tour: 30 years of counseling psychology in the *Annual Review of Psychology. The Counseling Psychologist,* 1982, *10,* 69–81.

Index